Gail Geff

Gail Geff

~WORLD~
RELIGIONS

Liberated Soul
From Jainism page 45

~WORLD~
RELIGIONS

JOHN BOWKER

Contributing Consultants: David Bowker • Dr. Heather Elgood
Dr. Paul Dundas • Dr. Ian Harris • Dr. Eleanor Nesbitt • Dr. Stewart McFarlane • Clark Chilson
Lavinia Cohn Sherbok • Dr. Margaret Bowker • Dr. David Thomas • Dr. Paul Heelas

Christus Victor
From Christianity page 144

Detail of
Jagannatha Temple
From Hinduism
page 19

Project Editor Antonia Cunningham
US Editor Mary Sutherland
Art Editor Heather McCarry
Editor Will Hodgkinson
Designer Joanne Mitchell
Managing Editor Gwen Edmonds
Managing Art Editor Tracy Timson
Senior Managing Editor Sean Moore
Production Controller Sarah Coltman
Picture Researcher Julia Harris-Voss
Teaching Consultant David Bowker

Kuba Mask from Zaire
From Native Religions page 186

A DK PUBLISHING BOOK
First American Edition, 1997
2 4 6 8 10 9 7 5 3 1

Published in the United States by
DK Publishing, Inc.
95 Madison Avenue
New York, New York 10016
Visit us on the World Wide Web at http://www.dk.com

Copyright © 1997
Dorling Kindersley Limited, London
Text Copyright © 1997 John Bowker

Bowker, John Westerdale.
World Religions / by John Bowker. — 1st American ed.
    p. cm.
Includes index
ISBN 0-7894-1439-2
1. Religions—Handbooks, manuals, etc. 2. Religion— handbooks,
manuals, etc. I. Title.
BL82.B68 1996   96–38277
200—dc20   CIP

Color reproduction by GRB Editrice s.r.l.
Printed in Italy by A. Mondadori, Verona

CONTENTS

WHAT IS RELIGION?
Author's Preface 6

ॐ
HINDUISM
Consultant: Dr. Heather Elgood

JAINISM
Consultant: Dr. Paul Dundas

Model Temple
From Buddhism pages 60-61

BUDDHISM
Consultant: Dr. Ian Harris

Guru Nanak
From Sikhism page 78

SIKHISM
Consultant: Dr. Eleanor Nesbitt

Three Chinese Star Gods
From Chinese Religions
page 94

**Palm Sheaf,
Myrtle, Willow,
and Etrog**
From Judaism
page 129

Detail from
The Lotus Sutra
From Japanese Religions
pages 110–11

Detail from
Muhammad's Ascent
From Islam page 164

WHAT IS RELIGION?

AUTHOR'S PREFACE

WHAT DOES IT MEAN TO BE RELIGIOUS? It means almost everything because religions deal with the whole of human life – and death. For thousands of years people have searched for the meaning and truth of their own nature and of the universe and of religions, which deal with the whole of human life and death, are the result. Even the natural sciences were originally religious; only in the last 300 years have religion and science come apart as ways of exploration. We look at religions now as communities of people who share practices and beliefs (often in God or gods), who gather in special buildings for worship or meditation, and who live in special ways in the world. We know that more than three-quarters of the world's population consider that they belong to a religion, however little or much they do about it.

Vairocana

Amitabha

So what does it mean to be religious? It means so many things to so many different people that they often contradict each other. It can mean believing that God is the source and the goal of life, or that this is at best a juvenile distraction; loving one's neighbor as oneself, or excommunicating him or her to a fate far worse than death; it can mean consulting witches for wisdom, or burning them alive; having a soul, or not having a soul; obeying the command to be fruitful, or taking a lifelong vow to be celibate; withdrawing into silence, or speaking in tongues; it can require shaving one's head, or never cutting one's hair; going to mosque on Friday, synagogue on Saturday, or church on Sunday; it can mean praying, meditating, levitating, worshiping, entering into trance and ecstasy; building St. Paul's Cathedral, the Golden Temple, and the Great Pyramid; crossing oceans and continents to go on pilgrimages to holy places; to convert others; to fight crusades, holy wars, or *jihads*; it has also meant the inspired

creation of music, art, icons, symbols, poetry at the very farthest stretch of human imagination, and yet it can also reveal itself as trivial sentiment.

RELIGIONS AND NATURAL SELECTION
So what is religion? The Latin word *religio* means something done with over-anxious or scrupulous attention to detail, and from that use it was applied to what we call religion, because of the way in which people performed sacrifices in those early days (see pp.14–15). The word may come from a verb, *religare*, meaning to bind things closely together, which tells us something very important about religions. Religions bind people together in common practices and beliefs; they draw them together in a common goal of life. This goal may be "life" in the most literal sense, since religions are the earliest protective systems we know about that enable people have children and to raise them to adulthood. The importance of this is obvious: natural selection and evolution means that wherever the processes of birth and bringing up

Monk's Headdress
This headdress, worn by a monk or lama, shows the five Buddhas most important in Tibet. They are Amitabha, Vairocana, Akshobhya, Ratnasambhava, and Amoghasiddhi. They control the different regions of paradise where Buddhists may be reborn. Beings in paradise have not yet achieved enlightenment; they are still subject to rebirth and therefore, to suffering, which is caused by desire. Buddhists believe that only through the elimination of desire can enlightenment be found.

children (that is, passing on genes and looking after children) are best protected, there human communities survive and flourish. All of us are built by genes and proteins, which are protected in two ways. The first is our skin, the second is the culture in which we live. Early worship of gods and goddesses was very important, for it provided a shared culture where symbols and stories, community approval and disapproval, were held in common. Culture and cult both come from the same Latin word *cultus*, worship of the gods (see pp.14–15) or of a supreme being. Worship and belief in a higher power form the foundation of culture, although as people learned more of the One with whom they had to deal, the ideas, pictures, and beliefs have changed greatly. Culture is protective; religions, with their various patterns of belief and practice, are the earliest cultural systems that we know about for the protection of gene replication and the nurture of children.

RELIGIONS, SEX, AND FOOD
The question of survival is the reason many religions are so preoccupied with sex and food. The rules say what you can and cannot eat; who you can and cannot marry; what kinds of sexual behavior may

A Jain Tirthankara
This statuette depicts one of the 24 tirthankaras, the leaders of the Jain religion who, by their example, showed the path to spiritual liberation. Jainism was founded by the 24th tirthankara, Mahavira, in India in the 6th century BCE.

Akshobhya

Ratnasambhava

Amoghasiddhi

Religious Organisations

All this explains why humans need protection, and why they need to make sure that wisdom inherited or acquired in one generation is passed on to the next. Religions are organized systems for protecting information and for passing it on from one generation to another. The ways in which religions may be organized vary greatly. Some are strongly organized, with hierarchies of authority and control (like Roman Catholicism), others are loosely organized, with virtually no structure at all (like Hinduism; but among Hindus there are very strong sub-systems, based, for example, on teachers, gurus, or temples, or holy places). Organization evokes religious specialists – priests, witches, shamans, gurus, imams, rabbis, bhikkus, nuns, monks, popes – the list is almost endless.

Religions and Exploration

Religion often serves to bind people together, but it does much more than that. Once effective protective systems were established, they

be allowed; and they control the status and activities of women very carefully. This made sense when so little was known about reproduction and when life was hazardous, especially for infants and children. The fact that much of this has come into question, now that contraception enables couples to have sex without conceiving a child, does not affect the fact that for thousands of years religions have been the best systems that humans could devise to ensure survival. And they have worked: here we are; and without good protection in the past, we might now be dinosaurs or dodos - extinct.

enabled people to make explorations of themselves and of the world around them. The most important of these explorations were of the human body, finding out what it can experience and what it can become. Some of these explorations concentrated on going inward and on finding truth within the body in enlightenment, peace, emptiness, the Buddha-nature (see pp.64–65). The exploration of what the philosopher Thoreau called "the private sea," the streams and oceans of your inner nature, has led to such religions as Jainism and Buddhism. But other explorations have concentrated on the outer world, the world of relationships, and have found truth and value in the ways we are related to each other and to a higher power. This has produced religions like Judaism, Christianity, and Islam, in which this higher power is recognized as God and as the supreme source of all life and all creation, who continues in being whether this or any other universe happens to exist or not.

These explorations have produced the practices that are characteristic of religions, such things as worship, prayer, meditation, yoga, and zazen. These practices, seriously undertaken, can lead

A Japanese Teahouse
The Japanese tea ceremony incorporates principles fundamental to Zen Buddhism. The "tea way" is born of the belief that enlightenment is a gradual process that comes from highest fulfillment in every gesture; it is the performance of an action that contains its own value, rather than the goal of the performance.

A Greek Orthodox Icon
Icons are a tradition central to the Orthodox Christian church. They are pictures of Christian people or events. But rather than acting as a photograph, they are intended to bring into being the reality of that which they illustrate, as windows into God. This icon depicts the Resurrection of Christ.

people into experiences so real to them that all else in life fades away in comparison. All of these are related to beliefs that, in turn, create pictures of what human life is and what the world or the universe is like. These "worlds" are vivid with gods and spirits, full of power and presence, both for good and ill. Their reality is at least in their effect. To inquire further is a major part of the philosophy of religion.

WORLD PICTURES

These world pictures are called cosmologies and include cosmogonies, that is, accounts of how the world began. Often these have been evaluated as quasi-scientific accounts and have then been measured for worth against current cosmological theories in the natural sciences. In fact, a religion may have many cosmogonies, often contradictory to each other, each of which serves a different purpose. There are at least five creation stories in Jewish scripture (not just in Genesis), and many more than that among Hindus. The point is that religions devise and elaborate cosmogonies and cosmologies, not in order to anticipate the brief episode of 20th-century

science but in order to display the universe as an arena of opportunity, the opportunity to live in the ways and for the purposes that a religion suggests or demands. The cosmos is the bearer of meaning, and this demands particular ways of acting and living.

MATTERS OF LIFE AND DEATH

The world pictures also include accounts of time, human nature, destiny, and of ways in which the living can continue to care for the dead. Originally, there was no belief that there would be a worthwhile life after death. At the most, people believed that a vague shadow would continue, kept "alive" in the memory of others and in descendants. This means that the great religious traditions, both Eastern and Western, are founded on a this-life experience of what the body is capable of experiencing and being. The belief that there will be some kind of continuity through death (variously described in different religions) was developed by our ancestors through their discoveries in the long process of religious exploration. What there is about us that might survive is also very differently described. But what all religions have in common is that they protect the information that enables people to set out for goals of value and worth, in this life (proximate goals) and beyond death (ultimate goals).

All this information has to be organized, protected, and shared. Much religious information is never put into words; it is conveyed in signs and symbols (Hindus can put the whole of the universe into a diagram the size of a place mat, and Christians can put God into a piece of bread as small as a coin), in art and decoration, in gestures, often in silence. Even the most fundamental of human necessities, breathing,

Ganesh, Remover of Obstacles
Ganesh is one of the most popular Hindu deities. He is said to have an elephant head because his father, the god Shiva, did not recognize him while Ganesh was guarding his mother. Shiva cut off his son's head, and upon realizing his error, replaced the head with that of an elephant. Ganesh is revered as the Remover of Obstacles.

A Menorah
The menorah, a seven-branched candlestick, is an ancient symbol of Judaism and also the emblem of the modern state of Israel. It was originally in the great Temple in Jerusalem. This eight-branched menorah, the Chanukiah, is used for the festival of Chanukah (see p.128). Each branch is for a day of the festival. The central branch, the sanush, holds the candle used to light the other eight.

becomes in many religions, such as Buddhism, a way of entering into truth.

RELIGION AS STORY

A great deal of information, however, is put into words, and storytelling is of paramount importance in all religions. In fact, religions themselves have been regarded as great stories that people learn and translate into the biography of their own lives. There is much in religions, in addition to stories, that helps them to do this: liturgy, festivals, and pilgrimage are obvious ways in which the tenets of a religion are translated into a person's life. In addition to stories passed on by word of mouth, religions also produce texts. Of these, some are regarded as revelations, coming from that which people have understood to be God. In this way text becomes authority: the Bible says . . . but so also does Tanach (Jewish scripture), the Qur'an (Muslim scripture), Shruti (Hindu scripture), the Angas (Jain scripture), the Guru Granth Sahib (Sikh scripture), and so on. The fact that they do not all say the same thing, and may indeed contradict each other, reinforces the radical division between religions (see pp.188–89).

RELIGIOUS BELIEF AND BEHAVIOR

Religions, therefore, bind people together and supply the means through which their lives can be lived with truth and purpose. Religions are extended families. They extend the family to the tribe or kinship group, and many of them then extend the tribe even farther, making one family of all the people of the earth, as Christians might say, or making them a single community or *umma* as Muslims would say. By creating codes of behavior (as ethics or as law), and by establishing a shared picture of reality, religions enable people to live with confidence. Faith is the belief that what is affirmed in religions is trustworthy; confidence is the reinforcing of faith by sharing it with others. This means, for example, that people can distinguish friends from enemies and can recognize whether someone is approaching them with hostile intent or not. The religious codes of recognition and of expected behavior (even beyond the scope of ethics) not only bring order into society, often organizing hierarchies, but also give to all members, including the poorest and least privileged, the opportunity of religious success, however that is described. Religion thus creates light in darkness and contests evil and death: religion is aspiration, vision, and hope for that which transcends the present moment it raises us up from guilt and failure, from what Freud called "the abject points of our departure." As it does so, its claims are often – though not always – confirmed in our experience of life on the way.

Guru Gobind Singh
The Sikh religion had ten Gurus, or religious leaders, before the last one, Guru Gobind Singh, handed over authority to the community and to a sacred book.

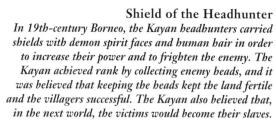

Shield of the Headhunter
In 19th-century Borneo, the Kayan headhunters carried shields with demon spirit faces and human hair in order to increase their power and to frighten the enemy. The Kayan achieved rank by collecting enemy heads, and it was believed that keeping the heads kept the land fertile and the villagers successful. The Kayan also believed that, in the next world, the victims would become their slaves.

MYTH AND RITUAL

The supreme intellectual instruments of all this religious creativity are myth and ritual. The word "myth" has been debased in recent years so that it is now, in popular usage, another word for something false or invented. Yet myth is, in fact, one of the greatest of human achievements. Myths are narrations, usually stories, which point to truths of a kind that cannot be told in other ways - for example, in the categories of natural science. That is why myth was seized upon in the 19th century by those like Richard Wagner, who accepted that science has a true story to tell, but a limited one: it cannot tell us anything about the truths of human love and suffering. Myth places individual biographies and local events into a much larger context and story, thereby giving them both meaning and significance. Myth may provide us with explanations of ritual, but rituals may also be independent of myth. Rituals are actions repeated in regular and predictable ways, which create order in the otherwise random process of time. They may therefore be entirely secular (as, for example, at the opening of an Olympic Games or on New Year's Eve), but they are extensive in religions. Some are rites of passage (marking the movement of individuals or groups through significant moments of life and death), others give protection in dangerous worlds; some initiate, others terminate membership in a religious group; some seek to effect change, others to express meaning. Ritual is the enacted language through which human hopes and fears are articulated and dealt with, and life is constantly renewed.

THE ACHIEVEMENTS OF RELIGION

From this account, it can be seen that religions are among the greatest of all human achievements - and of such a kind that it was only within

religions that people discovered that religion is much more than a *human* achievement. They found that they were met halfway, so to speak, by grace and by God, taking them farther than anything they could possibly have achieved on their own. This is why religions are so important; they are the context and the consequence of literally the most mind-blowing of human discoveries about their own nature and destiny. Religions are the resource and inspiration for virtually all the most enduring art, architecture, music, drama, dance, and poetry. But in addition, they point to the greatest truth of all: that which endures when all else passes away.

THE DANGER OF RELIGION

Religions, therefore, have achieved a great deal. That is why they are so dangerous. People will die (and kill) for their religion. That is why religions are involved in most of the bloody and intransigent disputes around us, for example, in Northern Ireland, Bosnia, Cyprus, the Middle East, Kashmir, the Sudan, and Sri Lanka. Religions, as we have seen, are systems that establish boundaries so that information can be protected. The boundaries may be literal (a holy land) or they may be metaphorical (beliefs and

Lao-Tzu, Father of Taoism
This 16th-century painting by the artist Qian-Gu depicts the Chinese sage and philosopher Lao-Tzu, who is regarded as the inspiration for Taoim, one of the three main religions of China. Taoism is based on texts such as the Tao Te Ching (The Way of Power), and stresses the importance of a simple, detached life and a unity with nature. Lao-Tzu lived in the 6th century BCE.

nonviolence) justify war in some circumstances. They protect so much that is so important that people would die rather than lose such inherited treasure. This is the paradox of religions: religions can be such bad news because they are such good news.

THE FUTURE OF RELIGIONS

Another reaction may be change and renewal in the face of challenge. All religions have changed through time, some more reluctantly than others. Religion will not disappear. We are all basically religious; we are prepared from birth for religion, just as we are prepared for many other basic behaviors. We are prepared for using language, for eating and drinking, for sexual development and behaviors. We are prepared also for those behaviors that we call religious. What is not predetermined is what we do with our "preparedness" – biology does not dictate what language we will speak, let alone what we will say. So also with religion: biology does not determine what we will do with our religious possibilities. We can decide to abstain from religion, just as we can decide to abstain from sex or (for short intervals) from food. But perhaps to abstain altogether from something so basic as religion is to make oneself less than fully human.

The issue is much more how to recognize the wicked and destructive evils of religion (of which there are many), and turn instead to that kind of religion that raises up the wrecked and desolate from their despair and commits itself to the renewal of the earth.

FROM PAST TO PRESENT

In doing this, there is much to be learned from the past. Religions have always been in the process of change and transformation. Some, like Zoroastrianism (see p.13), have an immensely long history in which the basic texts remain the inspiration and control of life, but they are applied in new ways. Others, like the religions of Rome

or Greece (see pp.14–15), seem to have disappeared long ago. But ancient religions are rarely dead religions. Much from Greece and Rome continued in Christianity, and in the Renaissance they gave form and inspiration to art and music and literature in the West. The only dead religions are those that cannot leave the past and find new life in the present. At the end, and in the End, the questions of truth are paramount: religions make claims about what this human life is worth and what it may become. They offer choices that have to be made about the opportunity of life. Which of them, if any, are true? And in what ways?

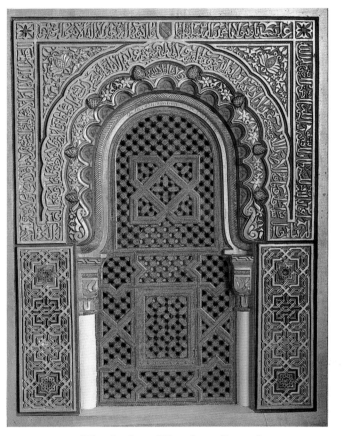

The Arch at Alhambra, Granada
The Islamic faith, which was founded by in Saudi Arabia by Muhammad in 570 CE, spread through Arabia, Asia, and southern Europe within three centuries. Islamic architecture is characterized by a highly ornamental style, a product of the ban on figurative art in Islam. The arch at the Alhambra in Granada, Spain, is an example of this, with its Arabic inscriptions praising Allah.

practices that confer and maintain identity); wherever there are boundaries, there will inevitably be border incidents when the boundary comes under threat. The threat may be a literal attack on a religious community, as was the case extensively in Communist countries, or it may be a threat to the continuing practice of a religion, as, for example, in what is known as secularization. One reaction may be a turn to fundamentalism (the insistence that there are non-negotiable fundamentals of a religious tradition), another may be war. All religions (including those, like Jainism, most committed to *ahimsa* or

NOTE FOR READERS

The dates in this book are followed by the letters CE or BCE, which mean "Common Era" and "Before Common Era." These terms are synonymous with AD *Anno Domini* (in the year of our Lord) and BC, which means "Before Christ."

In the section on Christianity, all biblical quotations are taken from the New Jerusalem Bible, unless otherwise stated. The biblical quotations in the Judaism section come from the Revised Standard Version Bible.

All Chinese words in the text are transliterated accorded to the Wade-Giles system. Pin Yin equivalents are in the index. However, Pin Yin romanized spelling has been used for Chinese place names on the maps on page 192. For some well-known places the traditional spelling has been added in brackets.

ANCIENT RELIGIONS

HOLDING HANDS ACROSS THE CENTURIES

THERE HAVE BEEN no human communities in the past, and few in the present, without religion because religion seems to be an intrinsic part of human life. Even though many people would deny that they are religious, it is clear that we are prepared for religion in the same way as we are physically prepared for breathing, speaking a language, being musical, eating, and so on. There are many different religions, ancient and modern, because the ways in which we are all prepared for life do not tell us exactly what to do with that "preparedness." All people need to eat, but there are many varieties of food from which to choose. There are many varieties of religion, but all societies have had a religion at their heart.

When following a religion, the time, the family, and the country into which we are born becomes important. The culture, the country, and the moment in history when we are born are the reasons why we put our brain and body preparation into practice in so many different ways: we speak different languages, engage in different sexual behaviors, eat different foods, live in different places, and so we follow different religions. Even if we live in the same country as our ancestors, we now differ from them, even though they were speaking something like the same language and valuing the same customs. There is always a process of building and correction going on, in which we learn from the wisdom of the past, while at the same time recognizing and correcting what we believe to have been wrong. This does not mean that there is inevitable progress; the way we use our religious "preparedness" may be full of error and wickedness. But it does mean that the past is not dead. The people of the past were very different in culture, but they built their cultures and societies in much the same way as we build ours. That is why we can hold hands across the centuries with those who lived before us, and take delight in their explorations into life. In these ancient religions, there is much that is clearly mistaken from our point of view. But there is much more that lives on as poetry, wisdom, and imagination, which we can translate into the new language of our own lives.

Christian Influence
This 10th-century Scandinavian emblem depicts the cross of Christ as well as the hammer of Thor.

Greek Gods and Goddesses
This detail from a vase depicts Greek gods. Greek religion was characterized by a pantheon of gods and goddesses.

ANCIENT RELIGION TIMELINE

There are many more ancient religions than those shown here. Some, such as Egyptian religion, seem far in the past. Others, such as Zoroastrianism, are ancient but have a direct line into the present (Parsis). The Greek, Roman, and Norse religions have lent themselves to a new religion, Christianity, and others, the Celtic, for example, are revived in a new form, which is why a "final" date cannot be given for them.

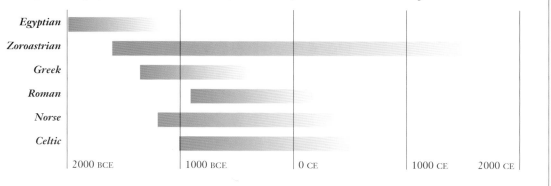

	Egyptian	Zoroastrian	Greek	Roman	Norse	Celtic
2000 BCE	1000 BCE	0 CE	1000 CE	2000 CE		

EGYPTIAN RELIGION

ANCIENT EGYPT IS AN EXAMPLE of how the religion of an area can maintain common features over a long period, even while it absorbs changes and draws in local beliefs and customs. In Egyptian religion, beliefs and practices changed whenever circumstances demanded it. Egypt is an oasis 600 miles (965 km) long, made fertile by the Nile River. An early hymn says: "Hail to you, O Nile, rushing from the earth and giving life to Egypt." The land was divided into Upper Egypt (the south, isolated by desert and the Nile's cataracts), and Lower Egypt (the Nile Delta, open to the Mediterranean world through trade and conquest). This vast area needed strong central rule and shared beliefs to hold it together, and the Pharaohs and religion provided this.

The Egyptian kingdom of the Pharaohs, which was eventually divided into 31 dynasties, lasted from about 3100 to 323 BCE. The Pharaohs became God-kings, using the diversity of beliefs and deities to support their power. The sun god Re (or Ra) of Heliopolis was linked with the Pharaohs, who were called the "Sons of Re." Each morning Re travels across the sky, overcoming chaos and evil. Even during the night he holds evil at bay, until he is reborn in the morning. In the cult of Re, the rulers were made a part of his victories. The gods of other major centers, such as Thebes and Memphis, were then made his allies: when a dynasty from Thebes became Pharaohs, they brought their god with them, and this produced Amon-Re. This happened with other deities: the Pharaohs won respect from the many different tribes by linking the local gods to themselves. Eventually, the priests tried to bring order into the vast accumulation of deities by creating families of gods, for example, the Ennead, with nine levels of supreme deities. Most daring of all, Amenophis IV (1379–62 BCE) declared that Aten, the sun opening its arms to give life to the world, was the only god; the others were his servants. This monotheism did not last, and Egypt reverted to adapting gods, cults, and beliefs to serve the needs of the day.

Osiris, God of the Underworld
Osiris was originally a fertility god who embodied vegetation, but came to be god of the underworld after being murdered by his brother. It was in this role that Osiris achieved popularity, for he gave Egyptians hope of being ruled justly after death.

The Symbol of Life
The ankh was a symbol carried only by kings, queens, and gods. It indicates that the wearer has the power to give and take life.

LIFE AND DEATH
As God-kings, the Pharaohs could not be destroyed, even by death. The claim that the Pharaohs were immortal was strongly reinforced when Egyptians discovered how to mummify dead bodies. Their immortal life was expressed in the huge pyramids of the early dynasties. Later the cult of the dead and the belief in immortality spread, and by the time of the 18th dynasty (1567–1320 BCE), those who could observe and pay for the suitable funeral arrangements could be sure of immortality. Manuals were produced to give guidance, called Coffin Texts because they were often placed in coffins. The most famous is the Book of Coming Forth by Day, often called the Egyptian Book of the Dead.

ISIS AND OSIRIS
Egyptians took out insurance by developing magical techniques to help them through death, and they also developed the worship of gods and goddesses who might help them. Among the most famous were Isis and Osiris. Osiris began as a local fertility god in Lower Egypt. Since he could bring life from dead ground, he was portrayed as dead himself, and from this he was regarded as the ruler of the dead. When the Pharaohs wished to emphasize their power over death, they made Osiris equal with Re, and as a way of controlling people's behavior, they made him the judge of the dead. Osiris was said to have civilized the people of Egypt, making them give up cannibalism. The cult of Isis, originally independent in the Northern Delta, was later combined with that of Osiris, producing a myth and a cult of a dying and rising god: when Osiris was drowned by his evil brother Set, Isis recovered the body, conceived a son from it, and by embalming it, restored Osiris to immortal life. Other stories were added, all to the same effect of life rising from death.

Wadjeti eye

Scarab beetle

Bastet, Cat-headed Goddess
Bastet, the patron deity of the region of Bubastis, was the daughter of the sun god and represented the power of the sun to ripen the crops. In her capacity as a goddess of pleasure, she came to be one of the most popular Egyptian deities, and great festivals were celebrated at her temple in Bubastis. To please the goddess, her worshipers made statues of her in great numbers, and cats were venerated as animals sacred to Bastet.

Horus was often worshiped as the "divine infant"

Isis and Horus
Isis, the wife (and sister) of Osiris, conceived Horus after her husband had been murdered by his brother. She raised Horus in seclusion to protect him from danger, and he grew to become the national god of Egypt and ancestor of the Pharaohs, who called themselves "the living Horus."

ZOROASTRIANISM

ZOROASTRIANS FOLLOW THE TEACHINGS of the prophet Zarathustra (known in the West as Zoroaster). Some of them, after persecution by the Muslims, migrated in the 10th century to India, and became known as Parsis – the people from Pars or Persia. Zarathustra's dates are uncertain, but probably he flourished in what is now northeast Iran about 1200 BCE. His teaching is mainly preserved in 17 hymns, known as *Gathas*, which are in the Yasna, part of the sacred Avesta scripture. He was a practicing priest, and the language of his hymns is difficult, so interpretations of his teaching (which has links with the Hindu *Rig Veda*; see pp.30–31) differ greatly. He believed that God, Ahura Mazda, had taught him personally through a series of visions that called him to mission.

The Coming of Age Ceremony
Young Zoroastrians are initiated into their faith in the Navjote ceremony, at which they symbolically take on the responsibility to uphold the ideals of Zoroastrianism. They are given a sacred thread and a sacred vest. The 72 strands of the thread symbolize a universal fellowship.

The resulting stress on personal responsibility remains paramount for Zoroastrians. There are two opposing forces: Ahura Mazda, creator of life and goodness (aided by *ahuras*—good spirits or angels), and the evil and destructive Angra Mainyu (aided by demonic spirits known as *daevas*). A person's fate depends on the choice made between them. After death, the soul is led by *daena* (conscience portrayed as a maiden) to the Chinvat Bridge, the Bridge of Judgment. Those whose good deeds predominate are led to paradise; those whose evil deeds predominate fall off into the House of the Lie, a place of torment. Dead bodies are regarded as the place where Angra Mainyu is powerfully present, so they cannot be buried in earth or at sea, nor can they be burned, because they are good creations. They are therefore exposed for vultures to devour on a specially constructed tower, a *daxma*, often known as "The Tower of Silence."

The Guardian Spirit
This image is a **fravashi** *or guardian spirit. It represents the essence of god within people, as well as the "spiritual self" or Ahura Mazda.*

The teaching of Zarathustra is essentially optimistic, since it is not difficult to choose what is good; and Zarathustra is said to be the only baby that laughed at his birth instead of crying.

By the 7th century BCE, his teaching had spread across the Iranian plateau. When Cyrus the Great established the Persian Empire in the 6th century, Zoroastrianism became the official state religion and was thus practiced from Greece to Egypt to north India. Zoroastrians are tolerant of other religions because judgment rests on works, not on beliefs. As a result, the teaching was influential on other religions, not least on Judaism, when the Jews were in exile in Babylon at the time when Cyrus was coming to power, and on Christianity: angels, the end of the world, a final judgment, the resurrection, and heaven and hell received form and substance from the Zoroastrian beliefs.

In the 3rd century CE, the Sassanians from the southwest overthrew the Parthian northerners and established a splendid dynasty: they relied on the priests to endorse their coup and their subsequent empire, so that religion and the state are spoken of as "twins, born from one womb, never to be divided." The dominance of the priests produced a new interpretation, Zurvan, which was claimed as orthodox, so that dissent was not only heresy but treason – though in fact it denied traditional teaching on free will and questioned the essential goodness of the world.

Zoroastrian imperial history ended with the Muslim conquests in the 7th century CE. Increasing oppression led Zoroastrians to retreat from the cities and eventually to take refuge in India. Persecution of Zoroastrians in Iran increased under the Qajar dynasty (1796–1925), but a remnant of the faithful continued. When Reza Shah Pahlavi displaced the last of the Qajars in 1925, there was a respite, as they were seen as the ancient nobility of Iran. The overthrow of the Shah led many to join the dispersion overseas. Parsis in India are a major part of Indian life, where some have developed new interpretations, linked to theosophy or to modernizing simplifications of old ritual.

Fruits, wine, milk, and water represent plants, humans, cattle, and oceans

Burning sandalwood represents God, the source of light and life

A Ceremony of Thanksgiving
A Jashan is a ceremony of thanksgiving that ensures the well-being of the spiritual and physical worlds. The seven bounteous immortals – sky, water, earth, plants, cattle, humans, and fire – are symbolically represented by the implements used.

Tray of sandalwood and incense

Flower-buds represent the bounteous immortals

Metal implements represent sky

Flat spoon used by the assistant priest to offer sandalwood and incense to the fire

GREEK RELIGION

IN ITS SIMPLEST FORM, Greek religion meant the worship of the 12 Olympian deities, whose king, Zeus, resided among the peaks of Mount Olympus. Each deity had several different attributes. Thus Apollo was the god of light and music; Athena was the goddess of wisdom and war, and also patroness of Athens. The reality of Greek religion is, however, more complicated, since many thousands of local deities also existed, many of whom became identified with the Olympians. This was made possible by what is known as syncretism or the fusion of cults. The Greeks had no word for "religion" nor any vocational priesthood. Nevertheless, Greek religion was pervasive, playing a part in almost every activity of the *polis* or city-state. Thus no distinction was seen between the sacred and the secular.

A principal form of worship was sacrifice, in which some gift, often the haunch of a selected animal, was offered to the god at the altar, which was placed outside the temple. The purpose of sacrifice was to ask the deity to grant some favor or, more often, because Greek gods were naturally jealous and angry, to refrain from doing harm. Sacrifice would work only if the ritual was performed with rigorous precision. This involved careful choice of the victim and of the method of sacrifice, as well as the use of all the cult names of the god. Sacrifice was an important preliminary rite at the major oracles, sacred places where a god would respond to questions asked by the worshiper.

FESTIVALS

The ceremonial aspect of Greek religion was nowhere more apparent than in the festivals, and the Greek year was full of them. The most important were the four pan-Hellenic (national) festivals, which attracted large numbers from a wide area. In Athens, festivals were unique in their lavishness. No fewer than 120 days of the year were devoted to festivals, and through these, and also through many fine temples built on the prominent ridge of the Acropolis ("high part of the city"), the city-state and the gods became indissolubly united.

PRIVATE RELIGION

There was also a more secretive side to religion, which showed itself in mystery cults that required special initiation ceremonies. One was at Eleusis near Athens, in which Demeter, the Earth Mother, and other divine beings were worshiped. The nature of the Eleusinian mysteries is unclear, but a central thread seems to be the story of the abduction of Demeter's daughter, Persephone, by Hades, the god of the underworld. She remained with Hades for four months, spending the rest of the year with Demeter, and her return to the upper world symbolizes the return of spring, as the joyful Demeter gives life to plants. The devotees of the mysteries had assurance of a satisfying after-life, significant because for most Greeks there was little prospect of this. Once souls had been ferried across the river Styx, they would enter the twilight of a shadowy underworld, ruled by Hades. Another mystery cult was that of Dionysus, the Wine God. This cult offered to the female participants a release from tension, and they would be uplifted by ecstatic moods. It was even said that in their frenzy they tore living animals to pieces. The darker side of Greek religion is reflected in beliefs in witchcraft and curses. Many curse tablets, known as *katadesmoi*, have been discovered, each bearing a name and the hope that some disaster might befall the named person. There was also a belief in ghosts. Unburied souls were said to wander the earth in a kind of limbo, and according to Plato, people who were rich on earth might not die properly because of their attachment to their riches.

Persephone and Hades
Persephone, the wife of Hades, is the daughter of Zeus and Demeter. She was abducted by Hades, ruler of the underworld. Hades is also Pluto, god of wealth.

Zeus, King of the Gods
Zeus is the sky god and the guardian of all mortals. He is also the protector of laws and morals, punishing the wicked but assisting those in need.

Consulting the Oracle
In moments of crisis Greeks would consult an oracle, the most famous of which was Apollo's at Delphi. It gained such a reputation that people would come from all over the Greek world to consult it. Here, a king consults the Pythia, the priestess acting as a medium for Apollo.

The gods take up battle against the giants

A Dionysian orgy, with wine, music, and dance

Clash of Gods and Giants
The top frieze of this vase shows Athena, goddess of war as well as patroness of arts and learning, overpowering the giant Enceladus, in a battle between gods and giants, which the gods won. The lower frieze shows a Dionysian orgy.

ROMAN RELIGION

THE ROMANS, like the Greeks, had no word for "religion." The nearest equivalent is *cultus deorum*, worshiping the gods. The word "religion" has more the sense of scruple and strict observance. The central feature of Roman religion was the performance of cult acts—making rituals, festivals, and sacrifices important. Their purpose was to preserve the favor of the gods; providing that was achieved, no personal feelings were necessarily involved, even though the spectacles themselves might be impressive or moving. The Greek pantheon was largely adapted by the Romans. Jupiter is the Indo-European Dyaus and Greek Zeus; Venus, a garden spirit, was identified with Aphrodite, Greek goddess of love. Native deities remained important: the woodland spirit Faunus became identified with Pan, Greek god of the countryside, but remained recognizably Italian.

The Sun God Apollo
This 16th-century fresco depicts the sun god Apollo driving his chariot across the skies. The worship of Apollo, originally a Greek god, became important in the time of Emperor Augustus (27 BCE–14 CE), since he was a god associated with youth, and Augustus wished to show that he was giving Rome a new start.

Roman religion was closely associated with public life. The gods were not remote but were deeply concerned with Rome's affairs and changing fortunes, so that religion and politics overlapped. Priests were a subgroup of the political elite, whose function was to offer advice on religious matters and to perform rituals and sacrifices. It was not, however, the priests who provided the link between the human and the divine, but members of the senate or council: it was they who controlled people's behavior in relation to the gods, handling any religious issues that might arise.

Religious ritual preceded such activities at assembly meetings in order to determine whether the gods approved of their being held, while augurs had the task of interpreting the omens.

The link between religion and public life is seen clearly in the reign of Emperor Augustus (27 BCE–14 CE), who used religion to strengthen his regime. He claimed to be giving Rome a new start after a period of tremendous political upheaval. Appropriately,

therefore, he founded a temple of Apollo on the Palatine Hill, because Apollo was the god of peace and civilization, both apt for the new age. From his time on, much religious worship was focused on the emperors themselves. Traditionally, famous Romans had believed themselves to be personally associated with some god, for it was assumed that nothing great could be achieved without divine aid. In the Roman Empire, however, rituals and public celebrations declared the emperor to *be* a god. All coins carried a picture of the emperor's head and his name, while the reverse showed symbols illustrating his power and success. Such practices became an important force for religious (and political) unity throughout the empire, although an immense diversity of local religious practices remained.

The Lares and the Snake
This Pompeiian shrine portrays the more private side of Roman religion. The figures are Lares, household spirits that would protect the home and its inhabitants. They would be invoked on all aspects of family life. The snake is a symbol of death.

household shrine, or *lararium*. Penates were guardian spirits of the family larder, worshiped in conjunction with Vesta, goddess of the private and public hearth. In the public arena, Vesta's holy hearth was tended by vestal virgins, who had to remain strictly chaste during their period of office.

There were also various mystery cults (so called because of their secret rites and initiations). One was that of Bacchus (equivalent to the Greek Dionysus), who attracted orgiastic worship. Others include that of Isis and Osiris from Egypt (see pp.12–13), and of Mithras, a Persian deity of light and truth who became especially popular with soldiers and traders. He is commonly shown slaying a bull, representing his functions as "savior from death," and "warrior." These mystery cults coexisted with state religion, and yet Christianity, since it spread like a mystery religion into the Roman Empire, suffered bouts of persecution. A possible reason is that Christians were defiant in refusing to worship any god but their own. This threatened the *pax deorum* (favor of the gods), and it may be no accident that some persecutions coincided with disasters for which Christians could be blamed.

HOUSEHOLD RELIGION

Equally important was the more private side of religion, as seen in the worship of the Lares and the Penates. Lares seem to have been spirits of the farmland, associated with ancestors buried there, often having a

Mithras Slays the Bull
Mystery cults were an important part of Roman religion. Mithras was a Persian savior god, and to be initiated into his mystery cult one had to take part in rites such as being drenched with the blood of a sacrificial bull. Here, the bull that Mithras slays is a symbol of life.

NORSE RELIGIONS

NORSE OR SCANDINAVIAN RELIGION is often thought of as the religion of the Vikings, who flourished in the 9th and 10th centuries CE and left traces of their activities across much of northern Europe, as well as Iceland and Greenland. But its origins lie farther back, in the Scandinavian Bronze Age (c.1600–450 BCE), when the first recognizable figures of gods and goddesses can be discerned. Later, from the 3rd to the 6th centuries, Celtic and Germanic peoples moved west and north across Europe, bringing new religious cults. During this period, there flourished in northern Europe the cult of Wodan or Odin, who became the chief of the pantheon worshiped by the Vikings.

Religion helped the Vikings make sense of an inhospitable and harsh world, where winters were long and threatening. The Vikings were often believed to be harsh themselves: their religion provided means by which warlike actions and brutality could be justified. It also provided a framework of proper conduct toward friends and strangers alike, and the advice of Odin, the All-Father, on such matters was regarded as sacred.

Scandinavian mythology saw the universe as being divided into nine worlds. Asgard was the realm of the gods and goddesses, known as the Aesir, and Midgard was the home of humans. Stretching through these nine worlds and linking earth and heaven was a World Tree, Yggdrasil, which was commonly represented as a gigantic ash tree. Midgard was created around it, and its roots stretched into spirit worlds, which humans rarely penetrated. At its foot sat the Norns, the Three Fates of Destiny, often regarded as more powerful than the gods and goddesses, for they spun the threads of life and were arbiters of the destiny of every human being. The Tree itself was linked with human fate, since it was viewed as the source of unborn souls.

Important also was the constant struggle against the savage forces of darkness and chaos that constantly threatened Midgard. Jotunheim was the home of the frost giants, whose intention was to pelt the world with snow and ice. One of the Aesir gods, Thor the great thunderer and god of fertility, often ventured into this realm to destroy the giants with his hammer, Mjollnir. A common practice was to paint Thor's hammer on barn doors to ward off evil spirits, and as Vikings journeyed to new lands and took in new influences, they wore the hammer as Christians wore the cross, thus learning practices from their Christian neighbors.

THE AFTERLIFE

The Vikings held a variety of beliefs about the afterlife. Those who died from sickness or old age went to the kingdom of Hel, a witch who was the offspring of Loki, the trickster god. This was a shadowy domain where the walls were a mass of writhing serpents; the knife in the banqueting hall was called Hunger and the plate Starvation. The honor in which a person was held represented a kind of immortality, since famous deeds would be remembered by succeeding generations or immortalized in the songs of the bards. Warriors who died in battle would be rescued by Valkyries, the maidens of Odin, who took them to the hall of Valhalla to feast and engage in mock battles.

RAGNAROK

A remarkable feature of Viking religion is Ragnarok, the final battle in which it was foretold that the gods and forces of evil would destroy each other. Out of the destruction a new world would rise, together with two humans, Lif and Lifthrasir. They would not worship the old Aesir gods, but God Almighty, who dwells in Gimlé, the paradise above all else. This probably represents a blending of Viking mythology with Christianity as it spread across northern lands. This fusion can be seen in architecture; for example, the Viking-Christian cross at Gosforth, Cumbria, which shows both pagan and Christian influences.

A Viking Picture Stone
This picture stone from Gotland contains within it several stories. At the top, Odin's eight-legged horse Sleipnir carries the god across the sky. The small boat below the Viking ship full of warriors may contain the god Thor fishing with the giant Hymir. Thor was said to have caught the world-serpent of Nordic myth, but Hymir was so terrified that he cut the line.

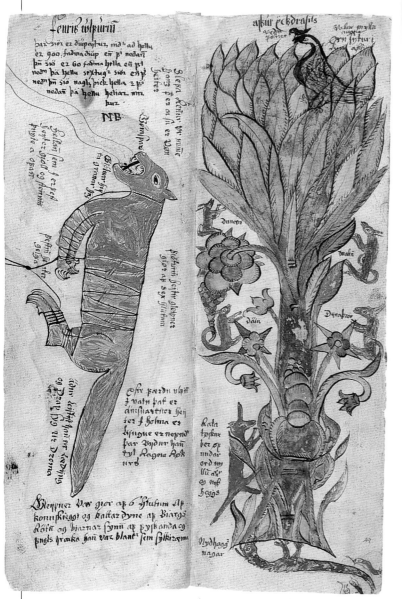

Yggdrasil, the World Tree
Yggdrasil links the nine Norse worlds. Here, the dragon Nidhogg gnaws at its roots, while Ratatosk the squirrel carries abuse from Nidhogg to the noble eagle at the top, who keeps watch over all nine worlds. Four deer eat the tree's leaves, demonstrating the constant process of death and renewal in the world, while Fenrir, the wolf, and a symbol of evil, lurks on the left.

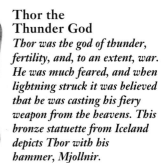

Thor the Thunder God
Thor was the god of thunder, fertility, and, to an extent, war. He was much feared, and when lightning struck it was believed that he was casting his fiery weapon from the heavens. This bronze statuette from Iceland depicts Thor with his hammer, Mjollnir.

CELTIC RELIGIONS

DETAILS OF CELTIC RELIGION are unclear. Much has been lost, and little was written down until about the 7th century CE. The Celts spread over much of Europe from 3000 BCE onward, eventually being absorbed into the Roman world. Only on the edges of the Roman Empire, in Ireland, Scotland, Wales, and Cornwall, did they persist, influencing a form of Christianity that was distinct from that of Rome or Greece. The religion of the tribes was quite localized. Each clan had its own pantheon of deities, with only a few gods worshiped over wide areas. Deities from other cultures, such as Rome, were also appropriated. Central to belief were the warrior-heroes with supernatural powers, the sacredness of the earth, and the dominance of the Earth Mother, the goddess of fertility and protection, and the bringer of life.

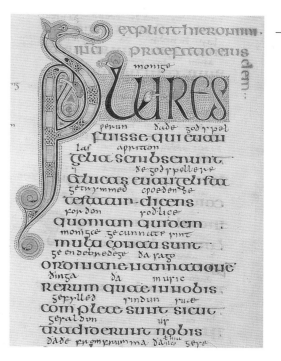

The Illuminated Bible
This page from the Lindisfarne Gospels, which shows the preface to the text of St. Jerome, is the earliest surviving translation into Anglo-Saxon of the four Gospels and shows Celtic manuscript illumination. The Celts had no written history until the Christian period; the Druids orally passed down the Celtic history and learning.

Celtic religion mingled historical with mythological events, so the gods of the Irish aristocracy were largely based on the early invaders of Ireland, the *Tuatha Dé Danaan*. They had defeated the demon Fomorians before being dispossessed by the Sons of Mil, the last invaders of Ireland. The *Tuatha* then retired to the *sidhs*, halfway states between this world and the Otherworld of the gods, where deities resided.

GODS AND GODDESSES

Among the *Tuatha* was Dagda, the "father of all," an ugly, potbellied dwarf, who had a club that could kill nine men at once as well as revive them. As nourisher of all, he had a cauldron that could never be emptied. Lugus or Lugh was "the many-skilled," the ideal warrior, harper, smith, poet, and sorcerer, the

Solid gold

only deity to appear throughout the Celtic world. Gobniu was a smith and brewer of beer. In Britain, the Children of Don filled a role similar to that of the *Tuatha*. Their successors, the Children of Llyr, included Bran. He was a giant who walked across the Irish Sea to fight the Irish king; ultimately, he sacrificed himself for his people. King Arthur may have been a historical figure following Roman rule in England, but he has also been interpreted as a god, Artor the Plowman. The goddesses were of even greater importance as the source of life and fertility, especially the triad, Danu, Macha, and Brigit – the bestower of learning, culture, and skill who survives in Christianity as St. Brigid. The gods of the Celts lived in the Otherworld, which consisted of the *sidh*, the natural mounds and tumuli, the *Tir forthuinn*, "the land under the waves," *Tir na nOc*, "the land of youth," and *Mag Mel*, "the field of happiness." The Otherworld was usually seen as a land of contentment, where all are immortal and any wound inflicted in battle would be cured the next day. At the New Year, Samhain, gods could visit the earth: elements of Samhain passed into Halloween. Celtic heroes possessed superhuman powers while remaining human. One of the most famous was Cu hulainn, whom Christians later interpreted as Christ contesting evil.

WORSHIP

Worship was often in the open, with a cult involving the human head (captives were often decapitated) and human sacrifice. Lakes, hills, groves, and islands were cult sites and retained their association with the sacred long after the Celts

A Golden Boat
This model boat from Co. Derry, Ireland, represents the sacred number seven: the seven oars on each side of the boat symbolize the seven openings of the body. It is also a reminder of the story of the sea god Manannán Mac Lir, who carried the Celtic heroes to the Otherworld beneath the sea.

The High Cross of Co. Meath
The cross was a widespread religious symbol before Christian times, and the typical Celtic cross had ornamental and symbolic decoration on the shaft and the base. Christianity spread through Britain and Ireland in the 4th and 5th centuries, and ancient Celtic styles were reborn in Christian art.

disappeared. Druids were the ritual and cult experts, performing rituals and acting as judges and teachers. Mistletoe is thought to have been a part of Druid rites.

CELTIC CHRISTIANITY

When Patrick and others took Christianity to Ireland, and when missionaries from there, such as Columba, Aidan, and Brendan, returned to the mainland, a form of Christianity different from that of the Roman Empire was established. Celtic Christians preserved ancient forms of art that decorated crosses and, later, manuscripts with twining plants and animals rather than with the human form. Soul-friendship (*anamchairdeas*) and austere penitence were emphasized. Prayer related to all aspects of life, from lighting the fire in the morning to putting it out at night. Monasteries, like Iona and Lindisfarne, were the center of Christian life. After the Romans left England, paganism returned. Gregory the Great (d. 604) sent Augustine (d. 604/5) to convert the Anglo-Saxons, and this style of Christianity from the south met the Celtic Christianity of the north. Each of them had different practices (for example, the date of Easter), and at the Synod of Whitby (663/4 CE) an attempt was made to resolve the differences. The Anglo-Saxon Church, in its manuscript decoration and its missionary practice, bore many marks of its Celtic origin. Today, Celtic Christianity, in its style of prayer and reverence for the created order, is enjoying a revival.

Vishnu Temple
This detail of the Vishnu temple at Tamil Nadu (see pp.32–33) shows the central chamber where the worshiper sees and is in the real presence of the god.

HINDUISM
THE ETERNAL TRUTH

HINDUISM IS THE NAME GIVEN in the 19th century to describe a broad range of religions in India. It comes from the Persian word *hindu*, in Sanskrit *sindhu*, which means "river" and refers to the people of the Indus valley; it therefore means Indian. About 80 per cent of India's one billion people consider themselves Hindus, and there are about 30 million more dispersed throughout the world. There are many common threads running through the religion, but no one expression of "Hinduism" is likely to exhibit them all, and there are many ways of being Hindu: village religion, for example, is very different from philosophical religion.

Historically, Hinduism is seen as unfolding in stages, but this is misleading, because some of the earliest forms persist to the present, relatively unaffected by later innovations. The roots spring from the traditions of the peoples of the Indus valley (2500 BCE – 1500 BCE), in the more developed Dravidian culture (which persists among the Tamils in southern India), and from the Vedic religion of the Aryans. The Aryans invaded northwest India from about 1500 BCE on and brought a religion based on oral texts known as *Vedas*, which are, for Hindus, eternal truth.

The *Vedas* consist of four collections of texts, and with the later *Samhitas*, *Brahmanas*, *Upanishads*, and a few *Sutras*, are known as *Shruti*, which means "that which is heard." They are considered eternal truth and were transmitted orally until the beginning of the present age—the age of degeneration— when they had to be written down. This age is called the *Kali Yuga* and is part of the Hindu cycle of time (see pp.40–41). Other texts, known as known as *Shmriti*, or "that which has been remembered," reinforce *Shruti* and include the great epics such as the *Ramayana* and the *Mahabharata* (see pp.30–31), which contains the epic poem the *Bhagavad Gita*. Vedic religion is characterized by an elaborate world of elemental gods and goddesses such as Indra and Rudra, and led to the later trinity, or *trimurti*, of the gods Brahma, Vishnu, and Shiva (see pp.20–21). They are approached through rituals and sacrifices. The *Rig Veda* text consists mainly of hymns and prayers addressed to them.

DEVELOPMENTS IN INDIAN RELIGION
In the early period, religion became dominated by the Brahmins, or priests, as society was dvided into four roles (*varna*), the others being *kshatriyas* (warriors), *vaishyas* (traders and farmers), and *shudras* (menials and servants). Scholars disagree whether the more elaborate caste system (*Jati*) developed from this or was a parallel elaboration of rules governing marriage. The caste system still dominates Indian society, even though the government has tried to improve the often desperate condition of the outcastes and untouchables, who perform the foulest, most polluting tasks. These divisions in Indian society are made bearable by the belief that within the human is an eternal soul, or *atman*, that is reborn millions of times and in many forms, from the heavens to the hells, according to the moral law, or *karma*, that prevails in the universe. *Karma* is not itself reward or punishment; it is a law as impersonal and as certain as gravity. But release, or *moksha*, from rebirth is possible, and Hinduism is a coalition of ways in which it might be reached.

Sacred OM
OM, or AUM, is the most sacred sound for Hindus and is the seed of all mantras, or prayers. In Sanskrit, it is the sound used in mystical contemplation.

Jagannatha Temple at Orissa
This painting of the temple dedicated to Krishna as the Lord Jagannath dates from the late 19th or early 20th century. It would have been purchased by a pilgrim as a memento of pilgrimage. The Jagannatha was originally an image that came from the jungle tribes of Orissa.

The major paths to *moksha* are known as *margas*: *jnana-marga*, the way of knowledge or insight; *karma-marga*, the way of action or appropriate works; and *bhakti-marga*, the way of devotion to God. There are many practical applications of the *margas*, such as yoga, or the way of individual holiness. Organized traditions of teaching and practice gradually developed and are known as *sampradaya*; some are well known in the West, such as the *sampradaya* derived from Caitanya (1485–1534), a descendant of which is the International Society of Krishna Consciousness.

Most of the ways of progressing toward *moksha*, or release, share a belief in *maya* and *dharma*. *Maya* is the power of Brahman or God to make things manifest. When people impose wrong views on appearance, the world becomes illusory and ensnaring. Therefore, the basic ill that must be dealt with is ignorance, or *avidya*. *Dharma* means many things, but "appropriateness" is perhaps the best translation: Hinduism is really a map of *dharma*, of appropriate behavior, and thus of a path to a good rebirth and to *moksha*. The usual Hindu name for "Hinduism" is *Sanatana Dharma*, or Everlasting Dharma.

For virtually all Hindus there are four *purushartha*, or desirable goals of life: *dharma*; *artha*, the pursuit of legitimate worldly success; *kama*, the pursuit of legitimate pleasure; and *moksha*. A Hindu would normally expect to pass through four *ashramas*, or stages of life: those of student, *brahmacarya*; householder, *grihastha*; one who withdraws for reflection, *vanaprastha*; and world-renouncer, *samnyasin*. So basic are these social structures that another Indian name for Hinduism is *varnashramadharma*. Even so, some forms of Hinduism maintain that *moksha* will never be attained until you have shown that you are detached from *all* feeling tying you to the world, including the repulsive and polluting. Therefore, some sects or cults, such as "left-handed" Tantra (see pp.24–25 and p.37) require living in cremation grounds or partaking of the five polluting *pancamakra*: wine, meat, fish, parched grain, and sexual intercourse with a menstruating woman.

Hindus are helped in their quest for *dharma*. As well as gurus and philosophy, there is also help from God. Philosophical Hindus came to understand Brahman as the source and pervader of all appearance who is present in humans as *atman*, or the soul. The *Advaita* philosophy, being nondualist, believes that the appearance of diversity in the world is an illusion, and that in essence all reality—the earth, sun, moon, sky, birds, and animals—is one. Therefore *Advaita* understands *moksha* as the realization that the individual and Brahman has always been one, *tat tvam asi*, "That thou Art." But most Hindus believe that Brahman has the character of God, or uses God to create and sustain the universe, so that *moksha* is union with God for ever. God as Lord is known as Bhagavan and Ishvara, but Hindus may have their own personal devotion to a cult or a specific deity, as well as a sense that God becomes manifest in many ways. In particular, he or she (the feminine aspect of divinity is extremely important) may take form as *avatara*, which means "descent." The most important *avatars* are those of Vishnu— above all as Krishna. Among the many personal devotions to God or Goddess, those of Vaishnavas, who are devoted to Vishnu, Shaivas, devotees of Shiva, and Shaktas, who worship Shakti (see pp.24–25), are the most widespread.

THE IMPORTANCE OF WORSHIP

Worship, both *darshan*, viewing the image, and *puja*, ritual, is of paramount importance in the home and in the temple. The temple is built to house the image of God and to bring his presence into it through ritual (see pp.32–33). The temple is built in accordance with the structure of the universe, leading up to the highest point above the image, the pivot of the world. This "entering" into the sacred power of the universe is also achieved though different kinds of cosmic diagrams called *yantras* and mandalas (see pp.40–41), and is summed up in *mantras*, sacred chants that turn random sound into power and order.

The Ten Avatars of Vishnu
Nine of the ten avatars of Vishnu (see pp.26–27) have already come to earth at difficult times in its history and rescued it from evil or brought people a greater understanding of the ways in which they should be living their lives. Krishna, shown in the center, is one of the most important. His counsel to the charioteer Arjuna, in the Bhagavad Gita, sums up the Hindu ideal of the duty of the individual, and his relationship with both God and society.

ORIGINS OF HINDUISM

ON ITS OWN ACCOUNT, "Hinduism" has no origin: it is the eternal way that follows the basic rules and demands of cosmic order as it passes through unending cycles. So Hindus call their own faith and practice *sanatana dharma*, the everlasting *dharma* (see p.19) Historically, it is seen as passing through successive stages (see p.18), the pre-Vedic, the Vedic, the Puranic, the Upanishadic, the medieval, and the modern. But this is misleading because practices and beliefs from all periods still persist, and elements of other religions in India, such as Tamil beliefs from the south, have been absorbed. Pre-Vedic religion is mostly known from the Indus valley civilization where symbols of fertility and the Earth Mother have been found. Natural symbols, such as water, lotuses, and animals were important; trees and pillars were seen as the center of the earth's strength. In Vedic religion, the Divine was manifest and approachable in many aspects of life, to be worshiped as gods and goddesses.

Indra, God of Storms
Indra is the Vedic god of storms. Once the king of all the gods, he became less important in the post-Vedic period. Legend tells of his anger when his followers gave up his cult and began to worship Krishna instead (see pp.26-27). When he sent a storm to punish them, they prayed to Krishna, who lifted a mountain to protect them from the storm's force.

THE VEDIC RELIGION

Vedic religion was based on sacrifice, reenacting that of Purusha, the perfect man, which brought the world into being. Sacrifices, which maintain the order of the cosmos, were performed by trained functionaries, or Brahmins, who drank Soma, the "medicine of immortality" during the rituals. Agni (Fire), still important in home rituals today, carried the offerings to heaven. The sacred chants laid the basis of *mantras* (see p.32), also a way of linking heaven and earth.

Agni, God of Fire
Agni, the Vedic god of fire who presides over the earth, has made the transition into the Hindu pantheon of gods, without losing his importance. With Vayu and Surya, who presided over the air and sky, he is one of the supreme gods in the Rig Veda. The link between heaven and earth, he is associated with Vedic sacrifice, taking offerings to the other world in the fire. His vehicle is the ram.

THE TRINITY
This 12th-century carving from Warangal in India shows the three principle Hindu gods: Brahma, who creates the universe at the beginning of each cycle of time; Vishnu, who preserves it; and Shiva, who destroys it.

BRAHMA THE CREATOR ●
Brahma is not worshiped in the same way as other gods, because he has done his task and will not come into his own again until the next creation of the world. In his eight hands he holds the four *Vedas*, a scepter, spoon, string of beads, bowl of holy water, which is a symbol of fertility, and a lotus flower, a symbol of creation.

Nandi the Bull
Nandi the Bull is the vehicle of the god Shiva. In paintings he is white as snow. The bull is said to embody sexual energy. Riding on its back, Shiva is in control of these impulses. Nandi is also a remnant of the associations of a much earlier deity with the prolific depiction of the bull and buffalo image.

● **SWAN**
Brahma's vehicle is a swan or goose, the symbol of knowledge. Brahma is the source of all knowledge. His consort, Saraswati, is the goddess of knowledge.

● **FOUR HEADS OF BRAHMA**
Brahma originally had five heads, which he acquired when he fell in love with his consort Saraswati. Saraswati was shy and moved to escape his gaze. So Brahma created five heads so that he could see her wherever she moved – left, right, backward, forward, and above him. Brahma's fifth head was destroyed by Shiva because Brahma offended him.

Shiva, Lord of Time
Shiva (see pp.22-23) holds a skull that, like the circle of skulls on which he appears to be sitting, represents samsara, the cycle of life, death, and rebirth. Samsara is a central belief in Hinduism (see p.18). Shiva himself also represents this complete cycle because he is Mahakala the Lord of Time, destroying and creating all things. He is carrying a string of beads, a symbol of his teaching.

Shiva holds up one of his hands in a gesture of blessing

RUDRAKSHA BEADS
Shiva wears sacred Rudraksha beads, perhaps a reference to his earlier name Rudra.

Vishnu's crown, symbol of royalty

Vishnu, God of Many Forms
Vishnu appears to be a prime example of how older gods and cults have been absorbed into Hinduism. Thought to be linked with an earlier sun god, Vishnu's ten incarnations or avatars (see pp.26-27) may also be examples of older deities that have been amalgamated. Krishna, the eighth incarnation of Vishnu, is particularly associated with altruistic love and may be partly derived from the ancient cult of a young erotic hero, whose sexual characteristics have become eroded over time.

THREE QUALITIES OF NATURE
Shiva's trident is said by some scholars to represent the threefold qualities of nature: creation, preservation, and destruction, although strictly speaking, preservation is usually attributed to Vishnu.

POT OF FOLIAGE
Foliage is a symbol of the growth, abundance, and fertility associated with water.

LOTUS OF CREATION
The lotus is associated with water, fertility, and the creation myth in which Brahma comes forth from the lotus growing in the navel of the sleeping god Vishnu.

THE FIRST SOUND OF CREATION
The conch represents "Om," the first sound of creation and also the beginning of matter, since sound and matter are considered to be synonymous. Worshipers intone "Om" as a means of trying to attain oneness with a deity.

VISHNU'S WEAPON
Vishnu's discus is thought to symbolize the sun.

GARUDA THE EAGLE
Garuda, the giant eagle or kite, is Vishnu's vehicle. He is often shown as a winged human-shaped figure with a beaklike nose. Garuda carries Vishnu to Vaikuntha (Heaven), where he lives.

SHIVA THE DESTROYER
Shiva, originally known as Rudra, was a minor deity, addressed only three times in the *Rig Veda* (see pp.30-31). He gained importance after absorbing some of the characteristics of an earlier fertility god and became Shiva, part of the trinity, or *trimurti*, with Vishnu and Brahma.

VISHNU'S MACE
Vishnu's weapon, the mace, represents the elemental force from which all physical and mental powers derive.

VISHNU THE PRESERVER
Vishnu, like Shiva, was originally a minor deity, with only five out of 1,028 hymns in the *Rig Veda* addressed to him. He seems to have been derived from a solar deity.

Garuda, Bird of the Skies
Garuda, like Vishnu's discus, has associations with the sun. He derives from a mythical horse called Tarksya, which also had links with the sun. A further connection is the relationship between the falcon's path and the passage of the sun across the sky.

❝*Only the unlearned deem myself (Vishnu) and Shiva to be distinct; he, I, and Brahma are one, assuming different names for the creation, preservation and destruction of the universe. We, as the triune Self, pervade all creatures; the wise therefore regard all others as themselves.* **❞**
VISHNU EXPLAINS THE NATURE OF THE TRINITY

SHIVA THE DESTROYER

SHIVA IS THE THIRD IN THE HINDU TRINITY, or *trimurti*, along with Vishnu and Brahma. He is everything, and therefore appears in many different forms. In the *Shiva Purana* text, he has over 1,000 names, such as Maheshvara, the Lord of Knowledge, and Mahakala, the Lord of Time. He is creator, destroyer, and preserver, and is often depicted with three faces: two opposites, such as male and female, great yogi and diligent householder, or Bhairava the destroyer and the giver of rest; and the third, serene and peaceful, reconciling them. His city is Varanasi (see pp.34–35), and anyone who dies there will go straight through death to Shiva, even if they are burdened by bad *karma* (see p.19). Shiva is often worshiped through the *linga*, male energy surrounded by the *yoni*, the female source of life. According to the *Shiva Purana*, "it is not the *linga* that is worshiped, but the one whose symbol it is."

Symbol of Destruction
Fire is associated with the god Shiva, who is often depicted holding a flame in one of his four hands, emphasizing his destructive nature.

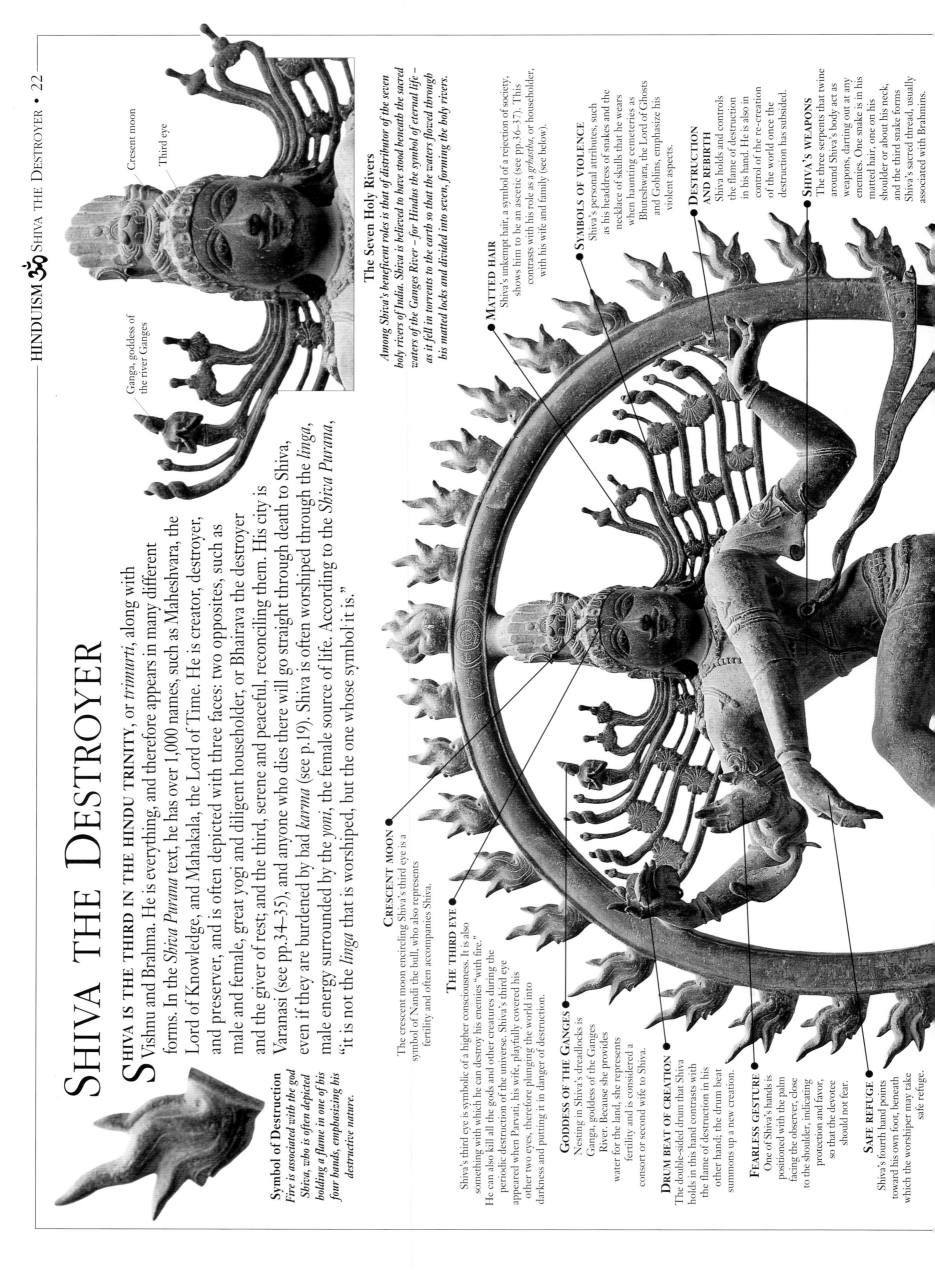

Cresent moon

Third eye

Ganga, goddess of the river Ganges

The Seven Holy Rivers
Among Shiva's beneficent roles is that of distributor of the seven holy rivers of India. Shiva is believed to have stood beneath the sacred waters of the Ganges River – for Hindus the symbol of eternal life – as it fell in torrents to the earth so that the waters flowed through his matted locks and divided into seven, forming the holy rivers.

MATTED HAIR
Shiva's unkempt hair, a symbol of a rejection of society, shows him to be an ascetic (see pp.36–37). This contrasts with his role as a *grhastha*, or householder, with his wife and family (see below).

SYMBOLS OF VIOLENCE
Shiva's personal attributes, such as his headdress of snakes and the necklace of skulls that he wears when haunting cemeteries as Bhuteshvara, the Lord of Ghosts and Goblins, emphasize his violent aspects.

DESTRUCTION AND REBIRTH
Shiva holds and controls the flame of destruction in his hand. He is also in control of the re-creation of the world once the destruction has subsided.

SHIVA'S WEAPONS
The three serpents that twine around Shiva's neck act as weapons, darting out at any enemies. One snake is in his matted hair, one on his shoulder or about his neck, and the third snake forms Shiva's sacred thread, usually associated with Brahmins.

CRESCENT MOON
The crescent moon encircling Shiva's third eye is a symbol of Nandi the bull, who also accompanies Shiva.

THE THIRD EYE
Shiva's third eye is symbolic of a higher consciousness. It is also something with which he can destroy his enemies "with fire." He can also kill all the gods and other creatures during the periodic destruction of the universe. Shiva's third eye appeared when Parvati, his wife, playfully covered his other two eyes, therefore plunging the world into darkness and putting it in danger of destruction.

GODDESS OF THE GANGES
Nesting in Shiva's dreadlocks is Ganga, goddess of the Ganges River. Because she provides water for the land, she represents fertility and is considered a consort or second wife to Shiva.

DRUM BEAT OF CREATION
The double-sided drum that Shiva holds in this hand contrasts with the flame of destruction in his other hand; the drum beat summons up a new creation.

FEARLESS GESTURE
One of Shiva's hands is positioned with the palm facing the observer, close to the shoulder, indicating protection and favor, so that the devotee should not fear.

SAFE REFUGE
Shiva's fourth hand points toward his own foot, beneath which the worshiper may take safe refuge.

BHAIRAVA'S CHARACTER
In the role of Bhairava, Shiva's violent nature is intensified, for he is then said to take pleasure in destruction for its own sake.

CIRCLE OF FIRE
Shiva is the original Lord of the Dance, Nataraja, surrounded by a ring of flames as he dances and reconciles the opposing forces of darkness and light. He is the deity in which all opposites meet and become resolved in a fundamental unity.

THE CULT OF SHIVA

Shaivism, or Saivism, is one of the most popular Hindu cults. It embraces many theologies and practices, although all agree on three principles: *pati*, or God; *pasu*, or individual soul; and *pasa*, or bonds that confine the soul to earthly existence. The aim of Shaivites is to rid their souls of bondage and achieve *shivatta*, the "nature of Shiva." They achieve this through ascetic practices and penances, with an emphasis on yoga and renunciation. Many Shaivites become wandering sadhus, or holy men (see pp.36–37). Shaivites mark their foreheads with three horizontal marks representing the three aspects of Shiva.

LIBERATION
Shiva's raised left foot indicates liberation.

DANCE OF DEATH
This 11th-century statuette shows Shiva dancing the Tandava dance, which symbolizes both his glory and the eternal movement of the universe as he annihilates the world at the end of an age. The dance represents the destruction of Maya, the illusory world (see p.19). Shiva is watched by anyone fortunate enough to see him, and the gods assemble to watch the spectacle. Even demons are brought under his spiritual power when they watch his dancing.

DEMON SLAYER
Shiva is often depicted dancing above the body of the demon, Apasmara, whom he has killed; in this role he is called Natesa. Apasmara, the dwarf demon, represents the ignorance of the teaching that all opposites (for example, good and evil) are false.

> 66 *Because You love the Burning-ground, I have made a Burning-ground of my heart — That You, Dark One, hunter of the Burning-ground, May dance Your eternal dance.* 99
>
> BENGALI HYMN

SHIVA'S CONSORTS: DURGA, KALI, AND PARVATI

Shiva's many consorts express the different elements of his character, the multiple facets of nature, and, by association, womanhood. The female consorts of the gods derive from the ancient cult of the Mother Goddess (see pp.24–25), which was absorbed into Hinduism by marriage with Shiva, Vishnu, and Brahma. A symbolic marriage is sometimes celebrated in temples where the original goddess shrine has been usurped by a later deity.

Kali
Kali (see pp.24–25) is one of Shiva's most terrifying consorts. Although she is depicted in a wild, violent, and sometimes hideous form, she is often the subject of intense devotion.

Parvati
Parvati, daughter of the sacred mountain, the Himalaya, is the most modest, conservative, and benign of Shiva's consorts. Renowned for her gentleness, she showed uncharacteristic determination in seducing and marrying Shiva, who initially spurned her for her dark color. To win him she engaged herself in ascetic practices to make her body glow. She is often shown with Shiva and her sons Ganesh and Kartikeya (see pp.28–29).

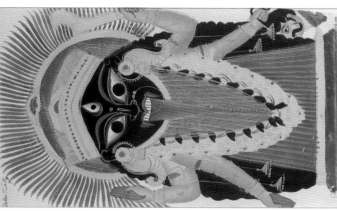

Durga
Durga is a powerful goddess created from the combined forces of the anger of several gods. She holds the javelin of Agni, the trident of Shiva, and the discus of Vishnu (see pp.26–27). She rides a lion or a tiger and is often shown triumphing over a buffalo demon that is threatening the stability of the world.

THE MOTHER GODDESS

THE MOTHER GODDESS (MAHADEVI) is manifested either as a consort of the principal male Hindu deities, or in a generic form that encompasses thousands of local goddesses or *devis*. These can be benign and fruitful, such as Lakshmi or Parvati, or powerful and destructive, such as Kali or Durga (see p.23). Throughout India there are shrines to a huge number of goddesses. Many have a tribal origin, are based on the ancient idea of an earth or mother goddess associated with agriculture and fertility, and may need to be appeased with sacrificial blood offerings. The worship of the Goddess as female energy, or *shakti*, is particularly important in the ancient texts that are collectively known as the Tantras. In some Tantric traditions *shakti* is viewed as a purely abstract creative power of the male god Shiva; in others Shakti is personified in various gentle or ferocious divine forms.

Third eye, symbol of the higher consciousness and enlightenment associated with Shiva

Half a human skull filled with blood, the sustenance of Kali and the required offering of her devotees

Kali's Maidens
On either side of Kali are two young girls, separations from herself, with the third eye and the crescent moon associated with Shiva on their foreheads.

SHAKTI AND THE CULT OF TANTRA
The importance of Shakti is emphasized in Tantra (see p.37). In Tantric belief the energy of Shakti is contrasted with Shiva: the passive, masculine consciousness that is powerless without the female energy; and the intercourse of the two gives rise to all creation. Tantric practitioners endeavor to experience the power of the Goddess, or Shakti, through a combination of unorthodox ritual action and the recitation of texts. Tantric rites include caste-free sexual intercourse in order to harness sexual energy for a spiritual end, the offering of sexual substances to the goddess, and the drinking of alcohol in spiritually polluted places, such as cremation grounds.

TANTRIC KALI
This 19th-century painting shows Kali as the goddess Chinnamasta. This form, astride Shiva in the cremation grounds, is a Tantric image. Here, she is also worshiped by Vishnu on the left, and Brahma on the right. Kali is the female, active energy (shakti) of these gods who, without her, particularly in Tantric beliefs, are considered passive and without force.

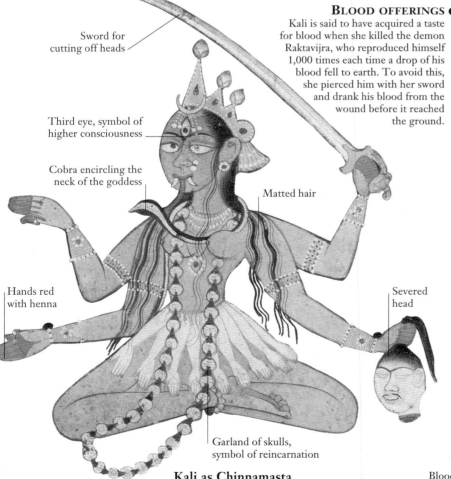

Sword for cutting off heads

Third eye, symbol of higher consciousness

Cobra encircling the neck of the goddess

Matted hair

Hands red with henna

Severed head

Garland of skulls, symbol of reincarnation

BLOOD OFFERINGS
Kali is said to have acquired a taste for blood when she killed the demon Raktavijra, who reproduced himself 1,000 times each time a drop of his blood fell to earth. To avoid this, she pierced him with her sword and drank his blood from the wound before it reached the ground.

Kali as Chinnamasta
The most powerful consorts of Shiva are Durga, the fearless killer of the Buffalo Demon; Chamunda, a skeletal hag with sagging breasts; and Kali, perhaps the most terrifying of all the manifestations of the Goddess. As Chinnamasta, Kali holds a sword, has a withered tongue that drips with the blood of victims, a skirt of severed arms, and a necklace of skulls. Chinnamasta is one of the ten Mahavidyas; the goddess manifestations of Kali that are central to Tantric Hinduism.

LIFE-BLOOD
Blood is the life-energy of the universe. In some images of Chinnamasta, her head has been cut off and blood from the wound feeds her own head and the two maidens on each side.

CREMATION PYRE
The cremation fire allows the spirit of the dead to move on freely to a new birth (see p.18) Fire is an important symbol in Hinduism, particularly in Tantric beliefs where it is regarded as a means to meditation and initiation into a stage of wisdom.

PARVATI AND SHIVA
Parvati, another aspect of the Mother Goddess, lies with Shiva, corpselike under Kali. Parvati's role is to attract Shiva into the domestic world, while Kali's role is to force him into action, annihilating evil and ignorance and initiating new birth.

SHAMANISTIC POSSESSION

Shamanistic spirit possession is a component of the ritual worship of the Mother Goddess, particularly prevalent in village and tribal India. Questions are sometimes addressed to the Goddess who is believed to possess the person while he or she is in a state of trance. Here the shaman is photographed in a trance state; he has matted hair and the goddess Kali's characteristic lolling tongue. This possession by the goddess is a manifestation of the mobility and the transitory nature of the possession of images by the gods.

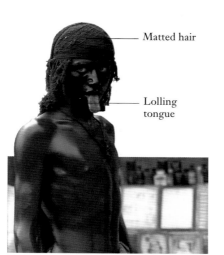

Matted hair

Lolling tongue

A shaman possessed by Kali

KALI, DESTROYER OF EVIL
Kali is the terrifying form of the Mother Goddess. She destroys evil and at the same time is responsible for creating life.

BRAHMA WORSHIPS THE GODDESS
Brahma with his four heads (see p.20) is shown worshiping the Goddess. The male and female deities contrast in the active forcefulness of the female and the remote transcendence of the male.

CREMATION GROUND
To orthodox Hindus the cremation ground is a place of pollution. However, in Tantric circles it has become part of the Kali legend, as she is both creator and destroyer, overcoming time, and must be worshiped in both her aspects. For some, the cremation ground is considered a place of meditation.

GIRDLES AND GARLANDS
Kali wears a girdle of arms around her waist, possibly those of the evil demons she has destroyed. The garland of skulls and the snake around her neck represent her regenerative aspects, namely reincarnation and cosmic and sexual energy.

KALI'S TONGUE
Kali's tongue dripping with blood represents *Rajas*, the material force in the universe that gives rise not only to effort as well as passion and suffering. It may also relate to Kali as the name of one of the seven tongues of Agni, the god of fire (see p.20), which are known as the seven red sisters.

SCAVENGING ANIMALS
A jackal or hyena feeds off the dead in the cremation ground, having dragged the body from its funeral pyre.

Lakshmi, Benign Form of the Mother Goddess
Lakshmi is one of the most approachable and benign forms of the Mother Goddess. Although she is Vishnu's consort (see pp.26–27), she also has her own cult. The earliest image that may be identified with her is on a stone railing from the Buddhist stupa of Bharhut dating from the 2nd century BCE. It depicts a cross-legged female sitting on a lotus flanked by two elephants.

Sarasvati's hands are positioned to play the *vina*, a stringed instrument that symbolizes the musical side of her personality

Sarasvati, Consort of Brahma
Sarasvati, consort of the god Brahma (see pp.20–21), is honored by Hindus, Jains, and Buddhists. Referred to in the Vedas, she was once worshiped as a river, now almost dried up, on whose banks Vedic sacrifices were once practiced. The lotus on which she sits is a reminder of this association with the river, which emphasizes her role as a fertile, life-giving mother. Increasingly, she is associated with the spoken word and is known as the goddess of speech and learning. She now represents poetry, music, and all intellectual pursuits.

THE INCARNATIONS OF VISHNU

Vishnu's preserving, restoring, and protecting powers have been manifested in the world in a series of ten earthly incarnations, known as *avatars*. The *avatars* arrive either to prevent a great evil or to effect good upon the earth. Nine are said to have descended already: three in nonhuman form, one in hybrid form, and five in human form. The most important are Rama, fearless upholder of the law of *dharma* (see p.18), and Krishna, youthful hero of the *Bhagavata Purana* (see p.31). Vishnu's final *avatar* is expected to arrive at a time when the earth is at the end of its present cycle, with the purpose of destroying the world and subsequently recreating it.

Kurma the turtle helped create the world by supporting it on his back.

Vamana the dwarf subdued king Bali, a powerful demon.

Matsya the fish saved humanity and the sacred Veda texts from flood.

Narasimha, half-man, half-lion, destroyed a tyrant demon king.

Krishna told the epic poem Bhagavad Gita to the warrior Arjuna.

Varaha the boar raised the earth out of water with his tusks.

Rama rescued his wife Sita and killed the demon Ravana.

Kalki the horse, yet to come to earth.

Parashurama the brahmin destroyed the warrior caste (see p.18).

Buddha, the enlightened one.

VISHNU THE PRESERVER

VISHNU, KNOWN AS THE "PERVADER" or perhaps "the One who takes many forms," was not prominent in the *Vedas* (see pp.18–19) but became a major deity and a member of the Hindu Trinity, or *trimurti* (see pp.20–21). He preserves the universe (when he sleeps, creation is withdrawn to a seed from which it will rise again when he wakes). Vaishnavites, one of the largest Hindu groups, are the devotees of Vishnu as Ishvara, the Supreme Being, worshiped in the forms of his manifestations or incarnations. Because of his pervasive presence, images as the focus of worship are of great importance, as are temple architecture and carving (see pp.32–33). Among the great Vaishnavites are Caitanya (founder of a tradition, *sampradaya*, which includes the *Hare Krishna* movement), Ramanuja, a thinker who placed God at the center of philosophy, and *bhakti* (devoted love) poets like Mirabai and Surdas: "Surdas says: Without devotion to God, you will make yourself into a stale crumb to be eaten by the tiger of Time." The *Vishnu Purana* is one of the 18 Great Puranas (see p.30); it describes Vishnu's relation to the universe and his activity within it.

Garuda, the Eagle Mount of Vishnu

Garuda is the kite that Vishnu and his consort Lakshmi ride. He is a symbol of the sky and the sun, and the snake in its claws symbolizes water. The animals, which are at constant war with each other, are symbols of opposite forces that are harmonized in Vishnu.

VISHNU AS THE UNIVERSE

This 19th-century painting shows Vishnu as the Universe, with all of its forces manifested within him. His left eye is dark, symbolic of the night, and his right eye is light, symbolic of the day. The sun emerges from his mouth, his gown is made of flames, a rainbow appears at his waist, and his hair is made of clouds. Like his avatar Krishna, Vishnu is blue, the color of infinity.

DISCUS
The discus is a symbol of the mind and the sun, which is a symbol of universal domination.

LAKSHMI
Lakshmi is the consort of Vishnu. In another form she is Bhu, the earth or mother goddess.

SURYA THE SUN GOD
Surya is a planetary deity. He is in a chariot with Arjuna, a hero of the epic *Mahabharata*.

ISHANA AND KUBERA
Ishana is one of the *vasus*, a group of eight gods of the elements and the directions of space. He is *vasu* of the north-east. Below him is Kubera, *vasu* of the north. He is worshiped as a symbol of abundance and prosperity.

BRAHMA THE CREATOR
Brahma, the creator of the universe, is at the top of the cosmos.

THE BREATH OF LIFE
From Vishnu's nose comes the breath of life, control of which leads to enlightenment.

CONCH SHELL
The conch shell symbolizes "Om" – the primordial vibration from which creation emerged. It is blown at temples as an indication of the presence of Vishnu.

INDRA
Indra is chief of the *vasus* and king of the east. He is associated with rain and thunder, and wields the *vajra*, a weapon symbolizing the thunderbolt.

Agni, god of fire
Agni is the mediator between the gods and humans and heaven and earth, and the *vasu* of the southeast. Agni can be described as the fire god or fire itself.

Yama, lord of the dead
Yama was the first person in the world to die. He rules over the dead, imparts justice according to a person's deeds, and decides the level at which they will be reincarnated. Yama is *vasu* of the south.

Nirriti
Nirriti is the *vasu* of the southwest. He has destructive powers and is depicted here riding a horse.

Water lotus
The lotus is a symbol of universal purity, as well as fertility. Vishnu's consort Lakshmi is often depicted seated on a lotus.

Vishnu as Viswarupa
In his form as Viswarupa, Vishnu embodies the pantheon of Hindu gods, as well as the cosmos and all of the forces within it.

Vasuki, king of the snakes
The cobra Vasuki is the ruler of the nether regions. He is known by many names, including Nagaraja, and is often shown supporting the world on his head.

The Goddess Lakshmi, Consort of Vishnu
Lakshmi (see pp.24–25) is the goddess of fortune. She is also Vishnu's partner and has appeared with each of his incarnations. When Vishnu came to earth as Vamana the dwarf, Lakshmi appeared as a lotus; when Vishnu was Rama, she came as Sita, and when he appeared as Krishna, she came as Radha. She was born when the gods and the demons brought forth creation by churning the cosmic sea of milk with the sacred mountain Mandara, which was set on the back of Kurma, the tortoise incarnation of Vishnu. The churning created Lakshmi, along with a heavenly nectar that made the gods immortal. When worshiped on her own she is Lokamata, Mother of the World.

Royal headdress

Sesha the snake
Vishnu reclines on the thousand-headed snake Sesha. It is also known as Ananta or Anand Nag, symbol of the infinite.

Snakes of the underworld
Snakes are symbols of the ocean, from which creation emerged and to which it will return. They dwell under the sea.

Vayu, god of the wind
Vayu is the god of the wind as well as the wind itself. Vayu is the *vasu* of the northwest.

Varuna, god of the waters
Varuna, *vasu* of the western quarter, is seated on a *makara*, an imaginary aquatic creature.

Four arms
Vishnu's four arms are a symbol of the four principal directions of space: north, south, east, and west.

Standing Vishnu
This form of Vishnu expresses the axis of the universe, from the heavens at the top to the underworld at the bottom.

Lower regions
The seven lower regions, known collectively as Patala, make up the lower end of the cosmos. The worst is Tala, where those guilty of murder are reincarnated. Snakes live in all the nether regions.

Golden mace
The mace is a symbol of primeval knowledge and the power of the mind, namely control, authority, and the maintenance of order.

OTHER GODS

AS WELL AS THE PRINCIPAL DEITIES of Shiva, Vishnu, Brahma, and the Goddess, there are numerous other deities that retain important positions in the Hindu pantheon. These include the elemental Vedic gods such as Surya the sun god, Agni the fire god, Indra the god of war, Vayu the wind god, and Varuna, guardian of the cosmic order. Many pre-Vedic local cult deities are also still worshiped, and the divine is acknowledged in all living things. Certain animals, reptiles, and even trees are venerated and receive a special place in the divine hierarchy, such as Naga the snake deity, and *yakshas* and *yakshinas*, who are nature spirits. Two of the incarnations of the god Vishnu, Narasimha the lion and Varaha the boar, probably started out as local cults of the animals. Three of the most important gods are Hanuman, the Monkey God, and the two sons of Shiva and Parvati: the elephant-headed Ganesh and the youthful Kartikeyya.

HANUMAN, BRAVE AND LOYAL SUPPORTER OF RAMA

Hanuman the Monkey God is given his chief role in the sacred text, the *Ramayana* (see pp.30–31), where he is acknowledged to have greatly assisted Rama in his victory over the demon Ravana, king of the island of Sri Lanka. He is also worshiped as a symbol of heroism and strength in his own right, and was originally held with special reverence in Sri Lanka, although he is now popular throughout India. Statues of Hanuman are often found at the entrances to temples, since he can fiercely defend them against enemies.

Kartikeyya, the Boy God
Kartikeyya has many names, such as Skanda, Kumara, and Subrahmanya suggesting that he is probably an amalgam of different cults. Many stories exist concerning his origin: both Shiva and Agni are said to be his father, while Ganga, Parvati, and the six stars of the Pleiades have been described as his mother. He was created to defeat the powers of evil, represented by the demon Takara. He is frequently depicted with a peacock, the national bird of India, and a spear, symbolic of his warrior status.

FIVE-HEADED SNAKE
On top of the wheel surrounding Hanuman is a five-headed snake. Snake deities – *nagarajas* – are worshiped in their own right, and play an important part in Vaishnavite Hinduism (see p.26).

NECKLACE
The jeweled necklace that Hanuman wears is south-Indian in style, this is the area of India where Hanuman is most revered.

DAGGER
Hanuman carries the dagger that he used to help Rama defeat the demon Ravana.

FLAMING WHEEL
Hanuman is depicted within a flaming wheel, a symbol usually associated with Vishnu.

KRISHNA OR BALARAMA
The dancing figure is either Krishna or his brother Balarama, emphasizing the fact that the context of the scene is Vaishnavite, the tradition of Hinduism that focuses on the deity Vishnu (see pp.26–27).

MAGIC PLANT
Hanuman is depicted holding the magic plant that will cure Lakshmana, Rama's half-brother, who was wounded on the field of battle while fighting the demon Ravana.

CONCH SHELL
The conch shell is one of the symbols of Vishnu. Hanuman is connected with Vishnu through his association with Rama, one of Vishnu's *avatars*.

WOODEN SHOES
Hanuman wears the wooden shoes of the ascetic (see pp.36–37). This is a refererence to the fact that he remained a celibate for his entire life.

HANUMAN THE MONKEY GOD
This 18th-century bronze from southern India shows Hanuman the Monkey God in a flaming wheel of fire. This may relate to the story in the Ramayana in which Indrajit, Ravana's son, captured Hanuman and set fire to his tail. But Agni parted the fire and made it burn around the tail without touching it.

GANESH, REMOVER OF OBSTACLES

Ganesh is one of the most popular deities in the Hindu pantheon, although it is likely that he was originally a tribal totem that was later absorbed into Hindu practice. According to legend, Ganesh has an elephant head because his father Shiva did not recognize his son and beheaded him while Ganesh was protecting his mother, Parvati. Upon realizing his error, Shiva promised to replace his head with that of the first creature he saw, which was an elephant. Ganesh is revered as the Remover of Obstacles, the Lord of Beginnings, and the Lord of Learning.

> *"In Heaven Ganesh will establish the predominance of gods, on earth that of people, in the nether world that of serpents and anti-gods."*
> FROM A HYMN IN *Sri Bhagavat Tathva*,
> AN ANCIENT SCRIPTURE

THE TREE OF THE YAKSHAS
Behind Ganesh a tree is depicted, a reference to his probable origin as a *yaksha*, the early Indian local nature spirits associated with trees. Shiva, Ganesh's father, managed to tame the *yaksha*s.

FLYING APSARA
Apsaras are celestial nymphs, said to reside in Indra's Heaven. They appear as willing consorts of men and gods and are sometimes seen as those sent to test the fortitude and motivation of spiritual aspirants.

TRIDENT
Ganesh carries a trident, a reminder that he is usually described as the son of Shiva.

MACE
Ganesh carries the mace that is usually associated with Vishnu (see pp.26–27). This may indicate an attempt to incorporate affiliation with the cult of Vishnu.

WATER BOWL
In his trunk Ganesh carries a water bowl, from which he drinks.

SWEETMEATS
Ganesh is almost always depicted holding sweetmeats, usually in the type of bowl known as *laddus*. His appetite for these sweets is legendary, and offerings of them are often left at his shrine.

GESTURE OF FEARLESSNESS
One of Ganesh's hands makes the gesture of fearlessness known as *abhayamudra*.

VYALA THE LION-BEAST
Vyala the lion-beast is a symbol of untamed instincts, which Ganesh succeeds in taming.

GANESH'S RAT VEHICLE
Ganesh's inappropriately sized vehicle is the rat. Since rats are seen as being capable of gnawing their way through most things, the rat symbolizes Ganesh's ability to destroy every obstacle.

GANESH
Statues of Ganesh can be found in most Indian towns. His image is placed where new houses are to be built; he is honored at the start of a journey or business venture, and poets traditionally invoke him at the start of a book. Hindus believe Ganesh was the first scribe and that the epic poem the Mahabharata was dictated to him (see p.30).

ROYAL HEADDRESS
Ganesh wears the headdress of royalty and is often considered the first among gods. One legend states that when Parvati saw her son's elephant head, she burst into tears. To pacify her, the god Brahma told her that among the worship of the gods, Ganesh should forever bear the first preference.

ELEPHANT GOAD
A frequent attribute of Ganesh is the elephant goad, or *ankusha*, a sharp stick that he uses to move elephants.

ELEPHANT HEAD
Various legends explain why Ganesh has an elephant head, the most common being the story of Shiva cutting off his human head. Another legend tells how the god Shani looked at Parvati's child and burned his head to ashes. Parvati then found the head of an elephant to replace it.

GANESH'S CONSORT
Like most of the male Hindu gods, Ganesh has a female consort. She is known either as Siddhi (Success) or Riddhi (Prosperity) and carries a lotus.

BROKEN TUSK
Ganesh carries in his hand his own broken tusk. As the Lord of Learning, Ganesh allegedly broke off his own tusk in order to write down the epic *Mahabharata*.

COBRA
Ganesh's characteristic pot belly is bound around with a cobra acting as the devout Hindu's sacred thread. The cobra is an animal usually associated with Shiva, a reminder that Ganesh is his son.

ROYAL POSTURE
Ganesh's posture, with one leg raised, is a royal one, known as *lalitasana*.

DWARF, OR GANA
Ganesh's name means literally "Lord of the *Gana*." Ganesh was entrusted by Shiva with the leadership of the *ganas*, Shiva's dwarfish, rowdy retinue, in compensation for the loss of his human head.

SACRED WRITINGS

THE FOUR VEDAS, the earliest-known Sanskrit literature from the Brahmanic period, are sacrificial hymns compiled from an earlier oral tradition. The *Rig Veda*, the earliest book, probably dates from *c.*1200 BCE; the fourth, the *Atharva Veda*, dates from *c.*900 BCE and consists chiefly of formulas and spells; the *Brahmanas*, associated with the *Vedas*, are ritual instructions. From 700 to 300 BCE, an era of religious speculation gave rise to philosophical works. These include the *Aranyakas*, or "Forest Books" (arising from reflection on the meaning of ritual), and later, the *Upanishads*. The *Puranas*, stories of the creation and lives of the gods, also appeared. Devotional cults arose, receiving inspiration from and inspiring the great epic literature, such as the *Mahabharata* (*c.*500 BCE), an account of the wars of the house of Bharata. This includes a section called the *Bhagavad Gita*, "the Song of the Lord," which is famous for the dialogue between Krishna, an *avatar* of Vishnu (see pp.26–27), and his charioteer, Arjuna. It is revered by nearly all Hindus and is the heart of the Hindu faith. The *Ramayana*, another great epic, was written between 200 BCE and 200 CE.

THE RAMAYANA

The *Ramayana* consists of 24,000 couplets and tells the tale of Prince Rama; of his enforced abdication as the royal heir; his exile in the forest with his wife Sita and brother Lakshmana; and of Sita's abduction by and rescue from the evil demon Ravana. It has been suggested that Ravana symbolizes ambition and lustful greed, which resulted in upsetting the cosmic order and the sanctity of women and the family.

Sita Imprisoned in Ravana's Castle
Sita, the epitome of chastity, loyalty, and wifely devotion, shared Rama's exile in the forest without complaint before she was abducted by Ravana.

THE DEFEAT OF RAVANA
This illustration shows the battle in the Ramayana between Prince Rama and the demon Ravana. The epic was written in Sanskrit by the poet Valmiki and inspired later versions. The story of Sita's abduction may symbolize the tensions between the Indo-Aryan races, represented by Rama, who entered India around 1500 BCE, and the indigenous Dravidian population, represented by Ravana, who had lived there since 10,000 BCE (see p.18).

RAVANA THE DEMON
Ravana, king of the *rakshasas*, or demons, and ruler of Lanka, fights Rama, who eventually kills him with a sacred arrow. The battle is the culmination of a conflict between the gods and the demons, in which Ravana abducted Rama's wife Sita. He did this to avenge his sister Surpa-nakha who fell in love with Rama, was rejected, and, in attacking Sita out of jealousy, was wounded by his half-brother Lakshmana.

Krishna, the Romantic Hero
The tales of Krishna's life were first compiled in the Bhagavata Purana, *tales very popular in royal circles in India. Legend tells how Krishna was taken to the forests to live with the cow herders to escape the evil designs on his life by his wicked uncle. While he was there his divine powers became evident. He grew up adored by all the village women and the gopis, or cow girls. He is often depicted surrounded by dancing gopis, playing the flute. His favorite gopi was Radha, shown here on Krishna's right.*

66 *Thus ends Ramayana, revered by Brahma and made by Valmiki. He that has no sons shall attain a son by reading even a single verse of Rama's song. All sin is washed away from those who read or hear it read. He who recites Ramayana should have rich gifts of cows and gold. Long shall he live who reads Ramayana, and shall be honored, with his sons and grandsons, in this world and in Heaven.* 99
FROM THE RAMAYANA

ARMS AND HEADS
Ravana has 10 heads and 20 arms. Each time a head is sliced off, another one replaces it. In his 20 hands he wields a variety of weapons.

THE GOLD CITY OF LANKA

Lanka, traditionally believed to be the island of Sri Lanka, was Ravana's home. Sita was brought here and threatened with torture and death if she did not consent to marry Ravana. She was discovered by Hanuman, who set the city alight and battled with the demons before escaping to bring Rama to Sita's aid.

DEMON HORDES

Lanka is defended by Ravana's army of *rakshasas*. They can fly faster than the wind and are hideously ugly, although they can change their appearance. *Rakshasa* literally means "harmer" or "destroyer."

HANUMAN

Hanuman, the Monkey God and general of the monkey army, is selfless and loyal, the Hindu ideal of a perfect servant. He may already have been ancient when the *Ramayana* was conceived — a leftover from an early cult of nature worship. He is capable of changing shape and is said to be the son of Vayu, the god of the wind.

PRINCE RAMA

Rama, Prince of Ayodhya, is the epitome of all that is noble, charming, and talented. With his three brothers, of whom he is the eldest and most noble, he is an incarnation of the god Vishnu, as shown by his blue skin (see pp.26–27). He was born at the request of the gods who were being oppressed by the demon Ravana. Years before, the god Brahma had promised Ravana immunity from attack by all gods and creatures, with the exception of men. So Rama was born to bring Ravana's tyranny to an end.

LAKSHMANA

Lakshmana, Rama's half-brother, is his devoted follower who shared in his exile. Sita was kidnapped while in his care. Tricked into believing Rama was in danger, she forced Lakshmana to leave her, whereupon Ravana whisked her away.

The Monkey Army
The monkeys are ruled by their king Sugriva. Sugriva, "strong, humble, brave, expert, and graceful, good at shifting shapes, and well acquainted with the haunts of every rakshasa (demon)," aided Rama after Rama helped him regain his throne from his evil brother.

Krishna Waiting for Radha
Krishna waits for Radha, his married lover, in the forest. The story of their passion is told in the poem, the Gita Govinda. A tribal origin for Krishna is suggested by his dark skin, his bamboo flute, and the implication of greater sexual freedom, all characteristics of the appearance and behavior of tribal society in India.

RAMA'S BOW

Rama's bow was originally given to the gods by Shiva, who then gave it to an ancestor of Sita's father. Until Rama tried, no one had ever managed to bend it. Rama did so with ease, and as a result won Sita's hand in marriage.

HINDU WORSHIP

HINDU WORSHIP OR PUJA involves images (*murtis*), prayers (*mantras*), and diagrams of the universe (*yantras* – see pp.40–41). The simplest *yantra* is a circle within a square, within a rectangle, with four gates to represent the four directions of the universe. Hindu temples are based on this design, although still open to endless additions and variations in decoration. Central to worship is the icon, or sacred image, which together with the temple is believed to both house and represent the deity. The icon can be worshiped at home or in the temple. Most people worship individually, not in a communal service. Sunrise and sunset are popular times, or when the priest conducts the ritual sustenance of the image and the temple. Worship involves *mantras*, vibrating sounds that summon the deity, and *prasad*, the offering of gifts, a symbol of the earlier practice of sacrifice. While many prayers and offerings are made for the fulfillment of wishes, the ultimate objective is the offering of the self to become at one with the deity. Central to this worship is *darshan*, seeing and being in the presence of the central icon.

Brahmin Priests

The Brahmin priest, who looks after the temple, is vital to temple activity as he acts as an intermediary between the devotee and the god. He alone can enter the inner sanctuary and make the offerings for the worshiper. At the beginning of a puja, or worship, the Brahmin invokes the presence of the deity in the temple by chanting, thereby making sacred vibrations of sound. Although some shrines in rural areas do not have Brahmin priests, a shrine cannot really be considered orthodox unless there is a Brahmin to officiate.

VISHNU TEMPLE

This painting, dating from c.1820, shows the plan of the Vishnu Ranganatha temple at Shrirangam in Tamil Nadu, south India. Such paintings would have been sold to pilgrims as souvenirs.

Vaulted pyramidal roof

Southern Temples

Southern temples are famous for their large gateways and barrel-vaulted pyramidal roofs, which surmount the sacred chamber and temple hall, or garbhagriha and mandapa. The northern style of temple has a more gently curved tower, or shikara.

EXTERIOR SHRINES
Secondary shrines housing other deities often exist on the site of the temple, either within or outside the main temple.

TEMPLE AMALAK
The *amalak* architectural form is derived from the gourdlike myrobalan fruit. It is always found on the upper part of the tower in the temple.

« *At the heart of this phenomenal world, within all its changing forms, dwells the unchanging Lord.* »
FROM THE ISHA UPANISHAD

CLEANSING WATER
Tanks are placed near the temple gates so that devotees can wash and purify themselves before entering the temple complex.

SACRED POOL
Water is very important in making a temple pleasing to the deity. If the deity does not like the temple, he or she will not reside there.

BUDDHA SHRINE
The Buddha is considered the ninth *avatar* of Vishnu and is therefore near the Vishnu shrine.

ENTERING THE TEMPLE
Before entering a temple, worshipers remove their shoes as a sign of respect.

SHRINE TO THE AVATARS
The *avatars* of Vishnu are close to the gateway, perhaps to show they are in the world that they came to save.

CENTRAL TOWER
The tower, or *shikara*, that surmounts the central shrine is the link or cosmic axis between heaven and earth. It can be likened to the foramen, part of the human skull, which is ritually opened at death to allow the soul to rise, or to the smoke hole in the Vedic sacrificial hut. It also recalls Mount Meru, the mythical mountain home of the gods.

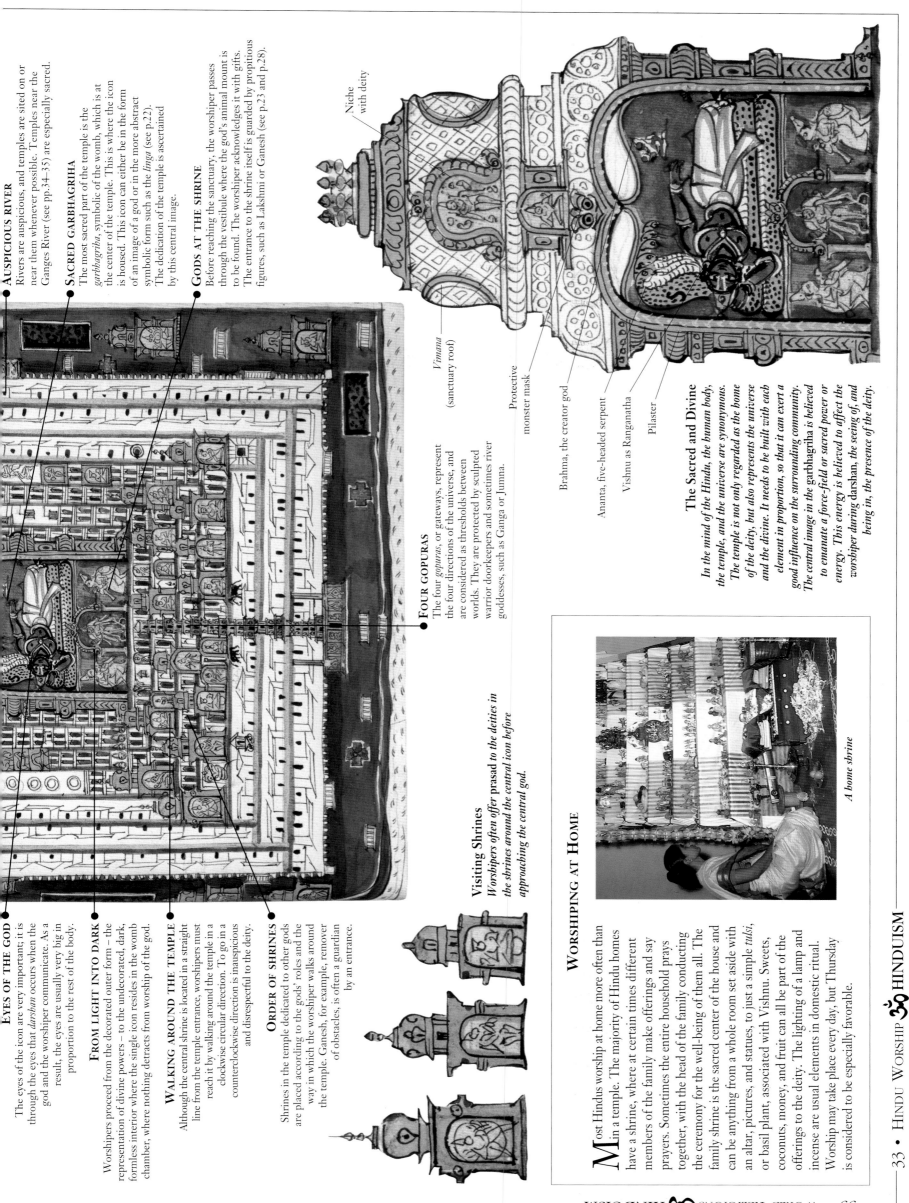

AUSPICIOUS RIVER

Rivers are auspicious, and temples are sited on or near them whenever possible. Temples near the Ganges River (see pp.34–35) are especially sacred.

SACRED GARBHAGRIHA

The most sacred part of the temple is the *garbhagriha*, symbolic of the womb, which is at the center of the temple. This is where the icon is housed. This icon can either be in the form of an image of a god or in the more abstract symbolic form such as the *linga* (see p.22). The dedication of the temple is ascertained by this central image.

GODS AT THE SHRINE

Before reaching the sanctuary, the worshiper passes through the vestibule where the god's animal mount is to be found. The worshiper acknowledges it with gifts. The entrance to the shrine itself is guarded by propitious figures, such as Lakshmi or Ganesh (see p.23 and p.28).

Niche with deity

Vimana (sanctuary roof)

Protective monster mask

Brahma, the creator god

Ananta, five-headed serpent

Vishnu as Ranganatha

Pilaster

The Sacred and Divine

In the mind of the Hindu, the human body, the temple, and the universe are synonymous. The temple is not only regarded as the home of the deity, but also represents the universe and the divine. It needs to be built with each element in proportion, so that it can exert a good influence on the surrounding community. The central image in the garbhagriha is believed to emanate a force-field or sacred power or energy. This energy is believed to affect the worshiper during darshan, the seeing of, and being in, the presence of the deity.

EYES OF THE GOD

The eyes of the icon are very important; it is through the eyes that *darshan* occurs when the god and the worshiper communicate. As a result, the eyes are usually very big in proportion to the rest of the body.

FROM LIGHT INTO DARK

Worshipers proceed from the decorated outer form – the representation of divine powers – to the undecorated, dark, formless interior where the single icon resides in the womb chamber, where nothing detracts from worship of the god.

WALKING AROUND THE TEMPLE

Although the central shrine is located in a straight line from the temple entrance, worshipers must reach it by walking around the temple in a clockwise circular direction. To go in a counterclockwise direction is inauspicious and disrespectful to the deity.

ORDER OF SHRINES

Shrines in the temple dedicated to other gods are placed according to the gods' roles and the way in which the worshiper walks around the temple. Ganesh, for example, remover of obstacles, is often a guardian by an entrance.

FOUR GOPURAS

The four *gopuras*, or gateways, represent the four directions of the universe, and are considered as thresholds between worlds. They are protected by sculpted warrior doorkeepers and sometimes river goddesses, such as Ganga or Jumna.

Visiting Shrines

Worshipers often offer prasad to the deities in the shrines around the central icon before approaching the central god.

WORSHIPING AT HOME

Most Hindus worship at home more often than in a temple. The majority of Hindu homes have a shrine, where at certain times different members of the family make offerings and say prayers. Sometimes the entire household prays together, with the head of the family conducting the ceremony for the well-being of them all. The family shrine is the sacred center of the house and can be anything from a whole room set aside with an altar, pictures, and statues, to just a simple *tulsi*, or basil plant, associated with Vishnu. Sweets, coconuts, money, and fruit can all be part of the offerings to the deity. The lighting of a lamp and incense are usual elements in domestic ritual. Worship may take place every day, but Thursday is considered to be especially favorable.

A home shrine

PILGRIMAGES

PEOPLE GO ON PILGRIMAGES throughout India to see and to be seen by the deity. Some deities are believed to live in specific sacred places. Popular pilgrimage places are *tirthas*, or fords, safe crossing places across rivers. Many important pilgrimage sites, such as Varanasi, also called Benares, are on the banks of the great rivers. The ford was believed in a literal and metaphorical sense to represent the crossing from one world to another, or from *samsara* to *moksha* (see p.36). The pilgrimage, an ancient practice referred to in the *Mahabharata* (see p.30), is still popular today. As well as rivers, the Himalayas and certain temples are also places of pilgrimage. Many sacred sites are associated with legend, others are said to be places where the gods materialized in the world. Famous sites include Kurukshetra, the site of the great war in the *Mahabharata*, Ayodhya, the ancient capital of Lord Rama, or Mathura, the birthplace of Krishna in central northern India.

Temple of Durga
Durga is the fierce consort of Shiva, also known as Kali (see pp.24–25). She is probably the most important Hindu goddess.

MAP OF VARANASI
This map shows the sacred sites of the city. The roundels around the edge show deities, stories from legend, and other famous pilgrimage sites relating to Shiva. Maps such as this one are readily available to pilgrims.

Pilgrim Making Offerings
Pilgrims make offerings to shrines along the banks of the Ganges River. Every morning they offer water from the river as a salutation to the rising sun.

SATI
Sati, wife of Shiva in his form as Virabhadra, died from shame at her father's treatment of her husband. Desolated, Shiva carried Sati's body throughout India. To cure Shiva's obsession, Vishnu cut her up and scattered her pieces. The places where they fell became sacred sites. The ancient ritual suicide of a wife on her husband's funeral pyre, a means of acquiring merit and purification, bears the name Sati or Suttee, after the goddess who is regarded as the ideal wife.

TEMPLE OF ANNAPURNA
Annapurna is an aspect of the goddess Parvati (see p.23), and symbolizes plenty and abundance. Recognized by the holding of a ladle, her symbols are the overflowing pot of rice and the brimming vessel of milk. Her shrine in Varanasi is the most famous and is where the annual festival of Annakuta, the "mountain of food," takes place in the autumn. Devotees fill the temple with food that is given away to the needy as *prasad*, or "holy food."

PASUPATINATH
Pasupatinath is a sacred temple and site in Nepal. It is like a small Benares, with Shiva temples and a sacred river.

CHANDRA THE MOON
When the gods created the earth by churning up the ocean like butter, the moon was one of the things that came forth. Shiva adorned his head with it.

Bowl

Ganga rides a *makara*, a legendary sea monster

Lotus flower

Ganga, the River Goddess
The Ganges River is the holiest river for Hindus and is especially purifying at Varanasi. Worshiped as the goddess Ganga, the river originally flowed only in the heavens. The sage Bhagiratha, whose excellent karma allowed him to ask a favor of the gods, asked for the Ganges to flow to earth. Shiva broke Ganga's fall to earth by catching her in his matted hair. Shiva's wife Parvati is popularly thought to be jealous of Ganga, who is also Shiva's consort.

TEMPLE AT KEDARNATH
Kedarnath in the Himalayas has been described since the 13th century as one of the most important pilgrimage sites dedicated to Shiva.

TEMPLE OF BISWANATH
The famous temple of Biswanath is dedicated to Shiva's *linga* (see p.22) of fiery light.

ASHES ON THE RIVER
To die in Varanasi and to be cremated there, with ashes scattered on the Ganges, leads to Shiva and is the best death for a Hindu.

VARANASI, CITY OF LIGHT

In the British period, the city of Varanasi was known as Benares. Its other name is Kashi, the City of Light. Varanasi is the most important and sacred pilgrimage center in India. Said to be the home of the Lord Shiva (see pp.22–23), it was here, according to legend, that Shiva's fiery *linga* of light or *axis mundi* broke through the earth to reach the heavens. The entire city, with a radius of 10 miles, is said to be a *linga*, the embodiment of Shiva. Varanasi is such a sacred site that many people come and live there until the day they die.

The Sacred Ganges River at Varanasi

Shrines to Shiva
These shrines are dedicated to Shiva in his form as Nagnath, Lord of the Nagas, the snakes or water spirits.

TEMPLE OF LORD VISVANATH
This is the most sacred temple in Kashi, with the sacred fiery column of light, Shiva's *linga*, in the central shrine. Shiva's vehicle, Nandi the bull, lies outside guarding the temple.

SHIVA'S FAMILY
Shiva is in his role as family man with his wife Parvati and Ganesh, their son.

SADASIVA
Sadasiva is a manifestation of Shiva.

DURGA
Durga, Shiva's wife, in righteous anger and violence subdues the buffalo demon, who is threatening the stability of the world.

"The Ganges, Shiva, and Kashi: where this Trinity is watchful, no wonder here is found the grace that leads one to eternal bliss."
KASHI KANDA

BHAIRAVA
Bhairava sprang from Shiva's third eye when Shiva became angry with the god Brahma (see pp.20-21). When Bhairava cut off one of Brahma's heads, it stuck to his hand until he reached Varanasi where all sins are washed away. Shown as a young ascetic, he is accompanied by a dog, an inauspicious animal.

PILGRIMAGE ROUTES
There are two pilgrim routes around the city. The 50-mile (80.5-km) route encircling Varanasi is more meritorious than the shorter route.

MAURYAN COLUMNS AT SARNATH
These columns, with their endorsed lion capitals, were erected in the 3rd century BCE to publicize the edicts of the Buddhist emperor Ashoka. The Buddha is the 9th incarnation of the god Vishnu (see pp.26–27).

LAKSHMI
Lakshmi, consort of the god Vishnu, is the goddess of fortune, and the embodiment of grace and charm. She has no temple exclusively set apart for herself, but is worshiped, along with Ganesh, in many homes and businesses.

The Temple of Ramesvara
The Ramesvaram, Shiva Lord of Rama, Temple is in south India. It marks the place where Rama (see pp.30–31) worshiped Shiva before crossing from India to Sri Lanka in search of his wife Sita.

FUNERAL ON THE GANGES
On the steps down to the river along the banks of the Ganges, River a corpse is about to be placed on the sacred fire. A body must be burned before sunset on the day a person dies. After death, the skull is broken to release the spirit. The eldest son lights the funeral pyre and says the Sanskrit ritual prayers.

SHRINE TO GANESH
Ganesh, son of Shiva, is invoked for good fortune, particularly in business.

ROUTES TO MOKSHA

MOKSHA MEANS "RELEASE" OR "LIBERATION." It is the fourth and ultimate goal, or *artha* (see pp.18–19), of Hindu life, the release from the round of rebirth, or *samsara*, in lower worlds. Because *moksha* is attained when one has overcome ignorance, there is more than one way toward the goal. The three main ways are collectively known as *marga*, the Way. They are *jnana*, the way of knowledge or insight, *bhakti*, the way of devotion, and *karma*, the way of action. Because one may be reborn millions of times, there is no pressure to attempt all these ways in a single lifetime. The important truth is to take up, in any lifetime, whatever seems appropriate for it – this is known as *dharma* (see p.18). In some forms of Tantra (see below), it may be necessary to do things that are against ordinary *dharma*, in order to acquire power to pass beyond all aspects of life on earth. This means that *moksha* is not really a "goal" at all because it can only be attained when all desire and attachment, including the desire for *moksha*, has been abandoned. One who attains *moksha* while in life is known as *jivan-mukta*, or free soul. There is no single savior or redeemer; there are many sects, guides, gurus, and gods who will assist those who seek their help. A prayer from the *Upanishads* sums up the quest: "From the unreal, lead me to the real; from darkness, lead me to light; from death, lead me to immortality."

The Mark of Shiva

Shaivite ascetics are recognizable by the red sectarian mark traced in ash across their forehead. This refers to Shiva's third eye of enlightenment (see p.22) and also signifies the rejection of society and the world. Ascetics sometimes cover their bodies with ash, following Shiva, who is often shown as an ascetic covered in ashes from the cremation ground where he sits concentrating on the transitory nature of existence.

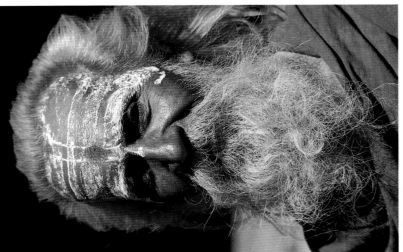

> *"Those who worship the infinite, the transcendent unmanifested, who have all the powers of their soul in harmony, who find joy in the good of all beings – they reach in truth my very self."*
> KRISHNA, FROM THE BHAGAVAD GITA

THE LIFE OF A SADHU

A Hindu holy man, or sadhu, depends on the laity for sustenance. He carries a brass begging bowl for receiving gifts of food or money, and is sometimes approached by the laity for religious guidance or to seek the *darshan* (the connection with God – see pp.32–33) of a sadhu. A sadhu should live outside, away from society. He should wear few clothes and undergo ritual penances, such as fasting or yogic exercises. These penances are supposed to engender *tapas*, or heat, to transform the inner state of the sadhu so he can achieve *moksha*.

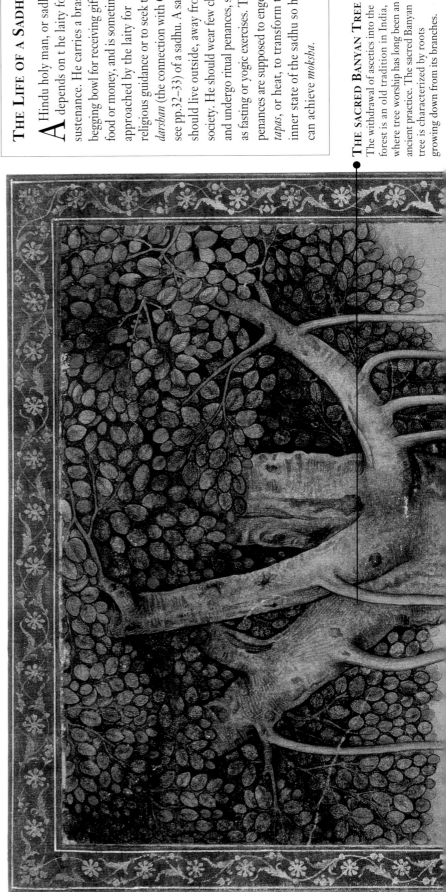

• THE SACRED BANYAN TREE
The withdrawal of ascetics into the forest is an old tradition in India, where tree worship has long been an ancient practice. The sacred Banyan tree is characterized by roots growing down from its branches.

Roles in Life

The family unit is very important within India, and in Hinduism the role of householder, or grihastha, is one of the stages of life through which every Hindu should ideally pass in order to escape eventually from samsara, or reincarnation.

The role of student, or brahmacarya, would, circumstances permitting, precede that of householder. This is one reason why education is regarded as very important, since it plays a role in the development of future spiritual enlightenment.

SADHUS UNDER A TREE

This painting by Inayat dates from 1630 and shows several wandering ascetics, called sadhus, under a sacred Banyan tree. Sadhus are an important part of Hindu life. For the sadhus themselves, it is one of the stages of life required if they are ever to reach moksha. For the rest of the community they are a source of inspiration and teaching.

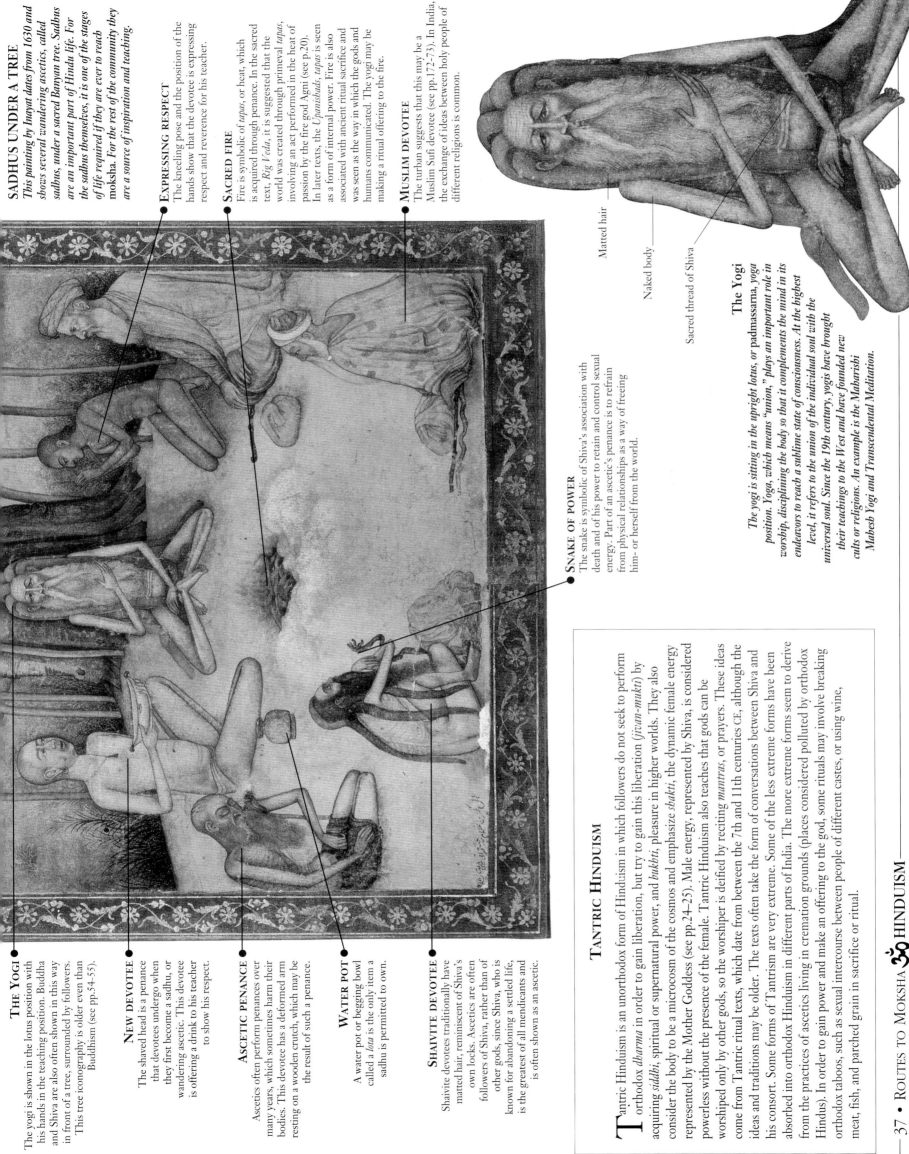

EXPRESSING RESPECT

The kneeling pose and the position of the hands show that the devotee is expressing respect and reverence for his teacher.

SACRED FIRE

Fire is symbolic of *tapas*, or heat, which is acquired through penance. In the sacred text, *Rig Veda*, it is suggested that the world was created through primeval *tapas*, involving an act performed in the heat of passion by the fire god Agni (see p.20). In later texts, the *Upanishads*, *tapas* is seen as a form of internal power. Fire is also associated with ancient ritual sacrifice and was seen as the way in which the gods and humans communicated. The yogi may be making a ritual offering to the fire.

MUSLIM DEVOTEE

The turban suggests that this may be a Muslim Sufi devotee (see pp.172–73). In India, the exchange of ideas between holy people of different religions is common.

THE YOGI

The yogi is shown in the lotus position with his hands in the teaching position. Buddha and Shiva are also often shown in this way in front of a tree, surrounded by followers. This tree iconography is older even than Buddhism (see pp.54–55).

NEW DEVOTEE

The shaved head is a penance that devotees undergo when they first become a sadhu, or wandering ascetic. This devotee is offering a drink to his teacher to show his respect.

ASCETIC PENANCE

Ascetics often perform penances over many years, which sometimes harm their bodies. This devotee has a deformed arm resting on a wooden crutch, which may be the result of such a penance.

WATER POT

A water pot or begging bowl called a *lota* is the only item a sadhu is permitted to own.

SHAIVITE DEVOTEE

Shaivite devotees traditionally have matted hair, reminiscent of Shiva's own locks. Ascetics are often followers of Shiva, rather than of other gods, since Shiva, who is known for abandoning a settled life, is the greatest of all mendicants and is often shown as an ascetic.

SNAKE OF POWER

The snake is symbolic of Shiva's association with death and of his power to retain and control sexual energy. Part of an ascetic's penance is to refrain from physical relationships as a way of freeing him- or herself from the world.

Matted hair

Naked body

Sacred thread of Shiva

The Yogi

The yogi is sitting in the upright lotus, or padmasama, yoga position. Yoga, which means "union," plays an important role in worship, disciplining the body so that it complements the mind in its endeavors to reach a sublime state of consciousness. At the highest level, it refers to the union of the individual soul with the universal soul. Since the 19th century, yogis have brought their teachings to the West and have founded new cults or religions. An example is the Maharishi Mahesh Yogi and Transcendental Meditation.

TANTRIC HINDUISM

Tantric Hinduism is an unorthodox form of Hinduism in which followers do not seek to perform orthodox *dharma* in order to gain liberation, but try to gain this liberation (*jivan-mukti*) by acquiring *siddhi*, spiritual or supernatural power, and *bukhti*, pleasure in higher worlds. They also consider the body to be a microcosm of the cosmos and emphasize *shakti*, the dynamic female energy represented by the Mother Goddess (see pp.24–25). Male energy, represented by Shiva, is considered powerless without the presence of the female. Tantric Hinduism also teaches that gods can be worshiped only by other gods, so the worshiper is deified by reciting *mantras*, or prayers. These ideas come from Tantric ritual texts, which date from between the 7th and 11th centuries CE, although the ideas and traditions may be older. The texts often take the form of conversations between Shiva and his consort. Some forms of Tantrism are very extreme. Some of the less extreme forms have been absorbed into orthodox Hinduism in different parts of India. The more extreme forms seem to derive from the practices of ascetics living in cremation grounds (places considered polluted by orthodox Hindus). In order to gain power and make an offering to the god, some rituals may involve breaking orthodox taboos, such as sexual intercourse between people of different castes, or using wine, meat, fish, and parched grain in sacrifice or ritual.

FESTIVALS

Hindu festivals, which are based on the Hindu calendar and are often linked with seasonal changes, serve a cathartic role in releasing community tensions and temporarily suspending the distinctions of caste and class (see p.18). Festivals mix worship with pleasure and are used to avert malicious influences, to bond communities, and to stimulate the vital powers of nature. The main festivals are Holi, Diwali, and Dusserah, although many local festivals exist, usually dedicated to a regional deity. Holi, originally a fertility ceremony, celebrates the New Year in March and the return of spring. A bonfire is lit on the eve of Holi to symbolize the destruction of the old year, and on the following morning, festival-goers indulge in a spirit of playfulness, forget about normal codes of behavior, and throw red-colored water and red powder at each other.

Diwali Lights
Children in the home light lamps to welcome Lakshmi. Diwali, a five-day festival, is a festival of lights; houses and the neighborhood are lit with many lights so that Lakshmi will not lose her way.

DIWALI AND DUSSERAH

Diwali celebrates Rama's return from exile (see p.30). It is celebrated by inviting Lakshmi, goddess of wealth, into the house, thus linking Diwali with traders and marking the start of the financial year. *Puja* (see p.32) is performed to bring prosperity, gifts are exchanged, and lamps are lit to dive out Alakshmi, misfortune. Diwali is held between late October and mid-November. Dusserah, between late September and mid-October, lasts nine days and celebrates the triumph of good over evil. In south India it celebrates the story of the *Ramayana* (see pp.30–31). In east India and Bangladesh it is in honor of Durga slaying the buffalo demon (see p.23). A large image of Durga is paraded in the streets and immersed in a river on the last day.

HOLI FESTIVAL
This painting from Udaipur shows the Maharana Amar Singh celebrating Holi in his garden. It dates from between 1708 and 1710 and shows him celebrating with his friends and servants.

Red powder

Celebrating the Victory of Rama
In south India, the defeat of the demon Ravana by Rama, an incarnation of Vishnu, is celebrated at Dusserah. The story of Rama's victory is acted out with the aid of giant paper statues, and on the tenth night of the festival, an actor playing Rama fires a flaming arrow into a giant firecracker-filled statue of Ravana and reduces it to ashes.

The Red Powder of Holi
The red powder is symbolic of blood from the rite of sacrifice. Red is the color of fertility and is an auspicious color at weddings.

SPRING FLOWERS
Holi is primarily a celebration of spring, associated with the act of creation and renewal that marks the spring equinox and the wheat harvest.

THE PRINCE JOINS IN
A courtier is throwing red paint at the prince. The spirit of Holi is fun and playfulness, and it is common for people of a lower caste to throw powder and paint over those of a higher caste, so distinctions have to be temporarily forgotten.

THE FESTIVAL CALENDAR

January   **Lohri**: Celebrated in the Punjab, this marks the end of winter.

February   **Pongal-Sankranti**: A feast held in south India to celebrate the rice harvest.

March   **Holi**: The national celebration of spring and the New Year.
Shivaratri: A national honoring of Shiva. Worshipers fast during the day, and an all-night vigil is held at Shiva temples.

April   **Sri Vaishnavas**: An honoring of Vishnu and his consort Sri, celebrated in Madras at the beginning of the hot season. Images of Vishnu are taken from the temples to the seashore.

May   **Rathyatra**: The birthday of Lord Jagannath, celebrated with chariots in Puri.

August   **Janmashtami**: The birthday of Krishna, celebrated nationally. Worshipers fast during the day and break the fast in the evening, following a special *puja*, or worship.

September   **Dusserah**: A celebration of the triumph of good over evil, in honor of Durga or Rama.
Ganesh Chaturthi: The birthday of Ganesh, celebrated nationally throughout India. Huge images of Ganesh are paraded.

October   **Diwali**: A national celebration in honor of Rama and his consort.

SYMBOL OF GREATNESS
The imaginary solar disk in this otherwise realistic portrait of the Maharana tells us that he is a member of the Mewar clan, who claim descent from the sun.

SPRINGTIME APHRODISIAC
The red powder is traditionally believed to be an aphrodisiac, a reminder that the festival was once a celebration of Kama, the god of sexual desire. Kama relates to one aspect of Hindu tradition that states that the pursuit of love and pleasure, both sensual and aesthetic, is necessary for life. Kama was the inspiration for the *Kama Sutra*, a classic work of erotic technique.

The Role of Music
The elements of a festival are "rang, ras, and rag"; color, dance, and song. There are three main kinds of music used: the chanting of a **Veda** *that ritually relates to the festival; the singing of communal* **bhajans** *(devotional songs); and music made by a double reed instrument known as a* **Shehnai** *or a* **Nagasvara.** *This is played very loudly to drown out inauspicious sounds.*

A HOOKAH
A pipe used for smoking opium, tobacco, and hashish. Holi is traditionally a time for a release of tension, and intoxicating substances are often used.

MAKING A NOISE
The tradition of noisemaking at the festival relates to a story about the sorceress Holika, a name common to many tales of Holi. Holika demanded that she was provided with a child a day to eat. One day, the women and children hid in wait for Holika, and when she arrived, they screamed and shouted insults at her. She was so scared that she never bothered them again.

TRUTH AND THE UNIVERSE

INDIAN COSMOLOGY imagines the universe as oval with zonal divisions (see pp.26–27) or as a diagram called a mandala, a concentric arrangement with a square divided into a number of smaller squares around the supreme deity (see p.65). The deity is the source of all existence and is compared to a spider in a web, from which all things are emitted and into which all things are absorbed. The mandala links the world of gods with the temple, which is based on the same geometrical formula (see pp.32–33). Diagrams called *yantras* are based on the mandala and relate to various deities and uses. *Yantras* visualize patterns of force, which have an equivalent sound, and act as mechanical devices or meditational aids.

SRI YANTRA

The Sri Yantra, shown here, is used by the Tantrikas sect (see pp.24–25 and p.37). It expresses the powers and emanations of Shakti, the Mother Goddess, and is made up of nine interlocking triangles, centered around the *bindu*, the central point or deity. The *yantra* is created by superimposing five downward-pointing triangles, representing Shakti, the feminine principle, with four upright triangles representing the male god Shiva. The Sri Yantra depicts the universe, symbolizing the various stages of Shakti's manifestation. It represents the levels of the earthly and celestial universe and also the stages in the development of consciousness of the Tantrika in his search for enlightenment.

SRI YANTRA
This 18th-century Sri Yantra from Nepal is a symbolic pattern of the Mother Goddess. The devotee in meditation moves through chakras, points of spiritual power, and visualizes a journey to the center from the outer square.

The Goddess Parvati
Around the outside edge of the yantra are repeated figures of the goddesses Parvati, in yellow, and Kali, in red. They are the major peaceful and terrifying manifestations of Shakti, the female force, the subject of this yantra.

THE FIRST THREE CHAKRAS
The space between the square and the three circles is the *Trailokyanohana*. This is the first chakra where the adept one is still preoccupied by desires and distractions. It is usually white, red, and yellow. The 16 lotus petals of the two outer circles, the second and third chakras, indicate fulfillment of desire.

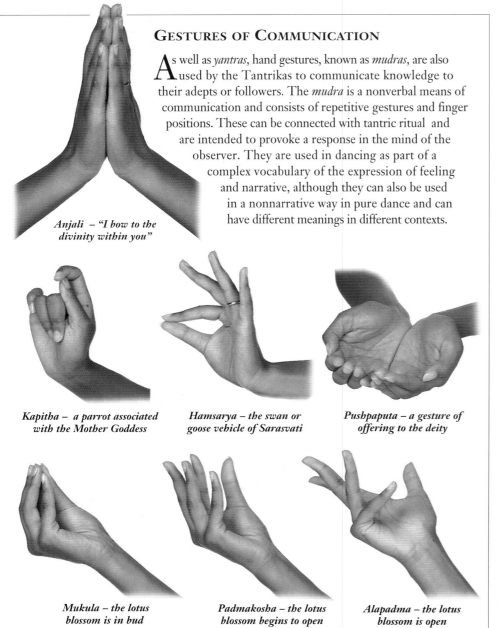

GESTURES OF COMMUNICATION

As well as *yantras*, hand gestures, known as *mudras*, are also used by the Tantrikas to communicate knowledge to their adepts or followers. The *mudra* is a nonverbal means of communication and consists of repetitive gestures and finger positions. These can be connected with tantric ritual and are intended to provoke a response in the mind of the observer. They are used in dancing as part of a complex vocabulary of the expression of feeling and narrative, although they can also be used in a nonnarrative way in pure dance and can have different meanings in different contexts.

Anjali – "I bow to the divinity within you"

Kapitha – a parrot associated with the Mother Goddess

Hamsarya – the swan or goose vehicle of Sarasvati

Pushpaputa – a gesture of offering to the deity

Mukula – the lotus blossom is in bud

Padmakosha – the lotus blossom begins to open

Alapadma – the lotus blossom is open

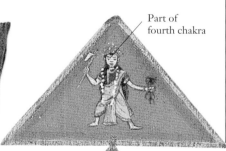

OUTER EDGE
The *yantra's* outer edge is a square with four gates facing the four directions of the universe: north, south, east, and west.

GUARDIAN DEITIES
There are eight protective guardian deities at the four gates and in the four corners outside the square (first chakra) of the *yantra*. Clockwise from here, they are: Indra, Agni, Yama, Nirriti, Varuna, Vayu, Kubera, and Ishana.

LINGA AND YONI
The *linga* emerging from the *yoni* is a sexual symbol of male and female energy as personified by Shiva and Shakti.

NINTH CHAKRA
The *bindu* or central point is the ninth and final chakra. In progressing around and through the nine interlocking triangles that make up the *yantra*, the devotee has undergone a process of "becoming" from the earthly stage to heavenly realization. The upright triangles represent the male force, and the downward-pointing ones represent the female force.

EIGHTH CHAKRA
The inverted triangle is the eighth chakra, the last stage before the final realization in the ninth chakra. All the triangles in the *yantra* are red, suggesting the power, fire, and intensity of this cosmic energy.

SEVENTH CHAKRA
The seventh chakra consists of eight triangles. At this stage the adept one is free from earthly bonds and is near the threshold of realization.

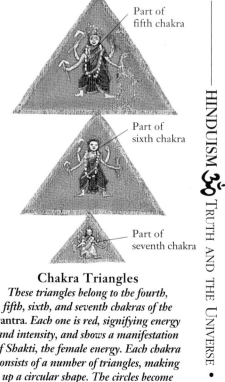

Part of fourth chakra

Part of fifth chakra

Part of sixth chakra

Part of seventh chakra

Chakra Triangles
These triangles belong to the fourth, fifth, sixth, and seventh chakras of the yantra. Each one is red, signifying energy and intensity, and shows a manifestation of Shakti, the female energy. Each chakra consists of a number of triangles, making up a circular shape. The circles become smaller as the devotee approaches ultimate bliss.

SCENES OF WORSHIP
Scenes of worship featuring naked tantrikas, a sacred fire, and the *linga* and *yoni*, representative of male and female energy, are repeated around the *yantra*.

FOURTH CHAKRA
This upward-pointing triangle belongs to the fourth chakra. Counting around, there are 14 triangles in this chakra, forming a circular shape. The number of triangles in each "circle" decreases nearer the center.

FIFTH CHAKRA
This is part of the fifth chakra, made up of ten triangles. The sixth chakra also has ten triangles.

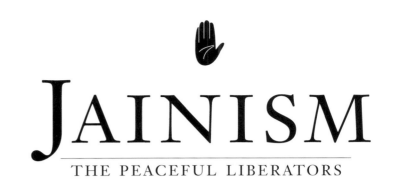

JAINISM

THE PEACEFUL LIBERATORS

A JAINA, OR JAIN, is a follower of the *Jinas*, the spiritual conquerors from whose lives and teaching the Jain religion in India is derived. They are human teachers who have attained the highest knowledge and insight, and who share with their followers the way to *moksha*, the release from rebirth in the worlds of ignorance and suffering. The *Jinas* are also known as the *tirthankaras*, the "builders of the ford" that leads souls across the river of rebirth, or *samsara*, to spiritual freedom. Jains believe that 24 *tirthankaras* appear in each half-cycle of time (see p.46) to teach this way of release of the soul, *jiva*, from its entanglement in material existence, known as *karma* (see below).

Of the 24 *tirthankaras* of the present half-cycle, little is known historically of any but the last two, Parsva and Mahavira, and even then legend prevails. But Parsva and Mahavira, together with the first *tirthankaras* Rsabha and Nemi, are objects of veneration and the equivalent of worship. Parsva lived in the 9th century BCE and Mahavira in the 6th century BCE.

JAIN BELIEFS

Jains believe that every soul is potentially divine and can reach its true goal by following the practices of purification and discipline laid down by the *tirthankaras*. The emphasis is on asceticism, because it is in this way that the soul is disentangled from *karma*, the material nature of the universe. For Jains, the understanding of *karma* is different from that of the Hindus and Buddhists, for whom it is a moral concept of cause and effect. The *tirthankaras* embody and teach the way of release. The released, liberated souls, or *siddhas*, reside at the apex of the universe in spiritual freedom.

Jains rely on teaching but not on any divine, or other, help – God or gods are recognized as part of the cosmos, but not

as supreme or as "outside" the cosmos or its processes. Jains, like Buddhists, do not believe in a creator god.

At the heart of the Jain way are the Great Vows, known as the *Mahavratas*, which are taken by the ascetics: these are nonviolence (*ahimsa*), speaking the truth (*satya*), abstaining from sexual activity (*brahmacharya*), not taking anything that is not given (*asteya*), and detachment from persons, places, and things (*aparigraha*). A sixth was added later: abstaining from eating after dark.

Laypeople take a parallel set of vows, known as *anuvratas*, or lesser vows, which apply the five vows to life in the world. These are that laypeople should be vegetarian and should not do work that involves the deliberate destruction of life, such as hunting or fishing. Being a farmer is acceptable because the destruction of life is unintentional. There are six occupations that are traditionally acceptable: government work, writing, the arts, farming, crafts, and commerce.

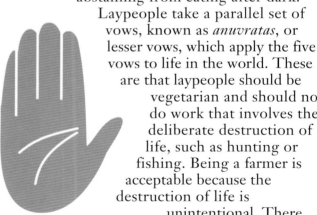

A Sign of Peace
The Jain religion adopted an open palm as its symbol in 1975, the 2,500th anniversary of the Jain spiritual leader Mahavira's enlightenment. The palm usually has the word ahimsa, *nonviolence, written on it.*

SECULAR LIFE

The life of a Jain layperson is clearly not a simple one if the vows and rules are kept strictly. Most Jains, therefore, do the best they can in their own circumstances. "The best that one can do" is not trivial, given the belief in rebirth: it means that the soul can make at least some progress on the path of

The Jain Cosmos
This detail (see pp.48–49) depicts the cosmos as a human body. At the top is the realm of liberated souls, and below that is the realm of the gods. The central disk is the realm of humans, and below this are the levels of hell.

spiritual growth. In an important text, the *Tattvartha Sutra*, which is revered by both the Digambara and Shvetambara sects (see below), this path of spiritual progress was laid out formally in 14 stages. "To do one's best" is always to make progress through the stages. Since the first stage, *mithyadrishti*, is one in which the soul is in a state of deluded sleep, it is not difficult to begin the climb upward with the help of the *tirthankaras*. Very few Jains accept the possibility of advancing beyond the sixth stage, and the model of the stages is, at any rate, largely theoretical. The 14th stage, *ayoga-kevali*, is one in which the soul, like a mountain rock, cannot be distracted in any way. All the *karmas* have been eliminated, and the soul is free from all involvement in life and the world – at death it attains liberation. Between the first and 14th stages, most laypeople in general practice a faith that concentrates on some aspects of the vows and on daily rituals or occasional public ceremonies. Since the *tirthankaras* are not present to the worshiper, there is no need for priests or any others to act as intermediaries. Laypeople can, therefore, engage in worship, either in temples or at home, as they choose. Concerning public occasions, the annual rite of Samvatsari, a Shvetambara festival, is of great importance. It is held during an eight- to ten-day period known as Paryusana-parva, during which laypeople abstain from various foods, following the Jain emphasis on fasting. Toward the end of the period,

The Art of Jainism
Jainism has a rich artistic tradition. Although painting was forbidden to monks and nuns, the commissioning of illuminated manuscripts and votive paintings, such as this one from south India, were a means by which a lay patron could gain religious merit. From the 11th century on, scenes from Jain narrative traditions constitute a major theme in Indian painting.

confession is made, not only to an ascetic teacher but also to family and friends. Pardon is also asked from any beings who might have been hurt: "I ask pardon of all living creatures. May all of them pardon me. May I have a friendly relationship with all beings and unfriendly with none."

Jain liberation is thus a well-established way of practice, based on instruction that overcomes ignorance. Especially important in reinforcing this is *Samayika*, a very ancient practice of meditation aimed at securing peacefulness of mind. It involves renouncing all possessions temporarily and sitting in meditation for 48 minutes (a *mahurta*, a thirtieth of a day, a standard unit of time in India, is often used for ritual purposes). It begins by forgiving and asking forgiveness from the entire world of living beings and includes the prayer: "Friendship to all living forms, delight in the qualities of the virtuous ones, unlimited compassion for all suffering beings, equanimity toward all who wish me harm, may my soul have these dispositions now and forever."

DIFFERENT SECTS

A major split occurred among the Jains around the fourth century CE. This created two major groups, the Digambaras and the Shvetambaras. Digambara means "sky-clad"; this sect believes that all possessions, including clothing, are a hindrance to liberation. According to the Digambaras, living without clothes means that you are detached from sexual feelings and notions of modesty, and that you can avoid killing

Devotion to the Tirthankaras
This votive meditation painting depicts a tirthankara, *one who has achieved a state of spiritual liberation and freedom from rebirth. Although* tirthankaras *cannot directly aid their devotees, it is believed that concentration on their iconic form will enhance spiritual progress.*

life-forms by not washing clothes. The Shvetambara claim that detachment is in the mind, and that equal destruction of life may occur without wearing clothes if, for example, fires are lit to keep warm. The four other main issues between them are the status of women – the Digambara believe that they must be reborn as men before they can attain liberation; whether certain writings have the authority of scripture; whether a bowl is allowed for begging and eating, and if it should be renounced along with everything else; and whether the fully enlightened and omniscient require continuing life-support like food.

JAINISM TODAY

In its early years, the Jain movement spread out from its place of origin in the Ganges basin, and in India it is now found mainly in Maharashthra, Madhaya Pradesh, Mysore, Gujarat, and Rajasthan. Outside India, the main communities are in the US. Although they make up less than 0.5% of India's population, the Jains have had a remarkable influence. One Jain leader, Raychandbhai Mehta, had a deep effect on the Indian political leader and holy man Mahatma Gandhi as he formulated his commitment to nonviolence and a truth-bearing life.

It is probable that the Jains are unlikely to expand in numbers in the near future, and that sectarianism will continue to play a part in dividing the community. Nonetheless, there seems no evidence for any diminishing of the hold of Jainism on the spiritual imaginations of its followers. The religion continues to evolve and adapt to changing circumstances, particularly in the West, without compromising its basic message, and will, without doubt, remain a faith with unique institutions and practices.

Srivatsa mark, a sign of divinity

Posture for meditation

THE FIVE SUPREME BEINGS

THE FIVE SUPREME BEINGS, or in Sanskrit, *Panca Paramesthin*, are the idealized types around whom the ascetic ideal of Jainism revolves. They represent both the practice and the goal of the religious path. The most supreme of the five beings are the *arhats*, "the worthy ones," also known as the great teachers (*jinas*), or ford-makers (*tirthankaras*). They teach the path to liberation and attain it themselves after having founded religious communities. Second are the *siddhas*, the liberated souls who live at the roof of the universe in a state of pure bliss (see pp.48–49). Third are the spiritual teachers who lead the monks and nuns; fourth are the teachers who instruct the monks and nuns in Jain scripture; and fifth are all other monks. They are all depicted here at the center of a *siddhachakra*, an esoteric diagram that serves as a focus of devotion and ritual. Each group of the five supreme beings is revered in a *mantra* called the *Panca Namaskara*, "The Five Homages." This *mantra*, which is known by all Jains, is recited in worship in the morning and at important devotional occasions. It is believed by many to have the power to cure illness and to destroy evil, and is considered highly auspicious.

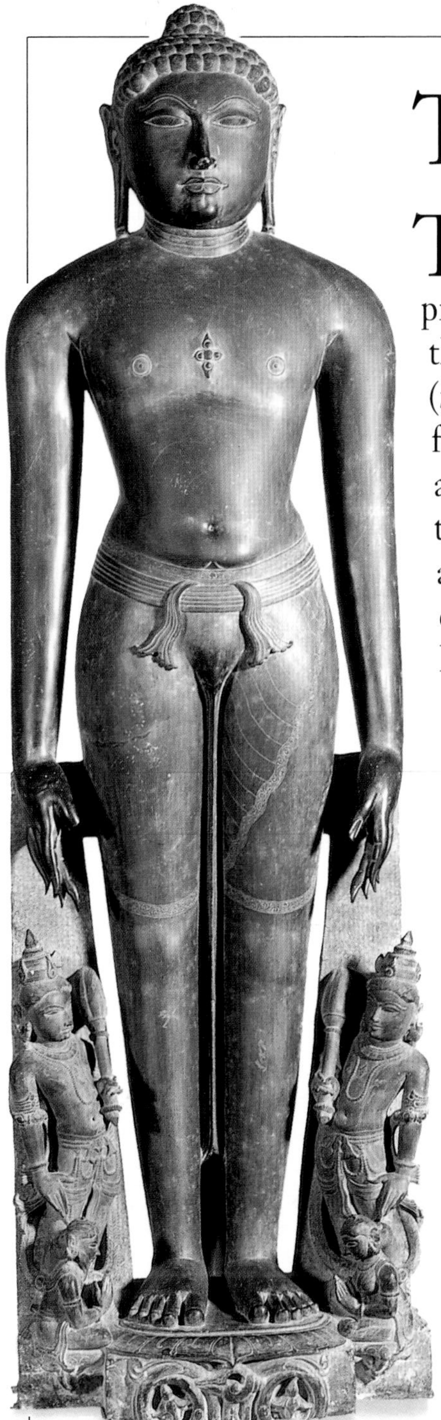

Shantinatha, 16th Tirthankara
Shantinatha is associated with social and personal peace (shanti) and the ability to avert danger. He is seated in meditation, attended by protecting deities. He hears the srivatsa mark, a sign of divinity. Prayers for world peace are often addressed to Shantinatha.

A SIDDHACHAKRA
This embroidered textile depicts a siddhachakra, a circle consisting of the five supreme beings and the four essentials of Jainism. It is much revered, especially during the Siddhachakrapuja festival in March or April. The mantra used to worship the five supreme beings represents the essence of the scriptures. It is seen as existing throughout time and without an author. It may have evolved from the 1st century BCE.

THE SIDDHA
Above the *tirthankara* (see below) is the *siddha*, a liberated soul who is the second of the five supreme beings. Liberation is attained in Jainism after a lengthy process of rebirth, in which spiritual merit is gained through positive religious action. The *siddha* state is without gender preference.

THE FOUR ESSENTIALS OF JAINISM
The four essentials or jewels of Jainism are written in *mantras* on the lotus petals between the five supreme beings. These are, clockwise from the top left: Right Knowledge, Right Faith, Right Conduct, and Right Penance, or Austerity.

Parsvanatha, 23rd Tirthankara
Parsvanatha is the 23rd tirthankara or ford-maker. He lived in Varanasi in India around 800 BCE and is the most popular object of Jain devotion. He is closely associated with compassion, although free from the world of rebirth, like all tirthankaras, and therefore unable to aid his devotees personally.

THE NINE EMINENT POSITIONS
The nine eminent positions are made up of the five supreme beings and the four essentials of Jainism.

SPIRITUAL CONQUEROR
At the center of the *siddhachakra* is the first supreme being, the *arhat* or *tirthankara*, the great Jain teacher who paves the way to liberation for others. The *arhat* is separate from the *siddha* in that he does not need a teacher to understand the Jain doctrine of liberation.

HEAD OF AN ORDER
Located in the east of the *siddhachakra* is the *acharya*, the head of an order of Jain monks and the third of the five supreme beings.

TEACHER OF THE SCRIPTURES
The *upadhyaya*, the fourth of the supreme beings, is the monk who instructs others in the scriptures.

PREDICTIONS OF GLORY
Along the edges of the *siddhachakra* are the symbols of the 14 dreams of Mahavira's two mothers, which foretold the future savior's noble nature. Each saw an elephant, a bull, a lion, the goddess Sri, a garland, the moon, the sun, a banner, a vase, a lotus pond, an ocean of milk, a celestial chariot, a jewel, and a smokeless fire shown left to right from the top.

Empty silhouette representing a liberated soul

A Liberated Soul
According to Jain belief, the soul adopts the outward appearance of the body in which it resides. Since the last existence before the attainment of spiritual liberation must be human, the siddha or liberated soul that resides at the roof of the universe is regarded as assuming a human shape, despite being free from a body and without material form. The metal icon of the disembodied siddha depicted can serve as a meditative focus upon the goal of the Jain religion: to become less concerned with existence in this world and free the soul from material possessions.

Symbols of the 14 Dreams
The sun is a symbol of one of the 14 dreams dreamed by Mahavira's two mothers (see p.46). These foretold the nobility of nature that would be a characteristic of the 24th tirthankara.

THE MONK
The figure of the monk, the fifth supreme being, is located at the west of the center of the *siddhachakra*. According to the Digambara sect of Jainism (see pp.50–51), women cannot attain liberation but have to be reborn as males.

MYSTIC SYLLABLE
Above the four essentials of Jainism are the mystic syllables *om hrim*, the sound of which is believed to have a divine power.

EXALTED HUMANS
Neither the *arhats* nor the *siddhas* are gods, and thus cannot directly influence human affairs or destinies. They are exalted human beings who have attained the goal of liberation.

JAIN TEXTILE
The *siddhachakra* is embroidered and painted on cloth, and is used as an object of devotion, hung on a temple wall, or used in esoteric ritual by Jain Shvetambara monks.

CROWNED DEITIES
Outside the central lotus containing the five supreme beings are four crowned deities in celestial chariots. Deities have a role in Jainism but are subject to rebirth in the same way as humans.

PAST, PRESENT, AND FUTURE
The five supreme beings represent the ideal beings of the past, the present, and the future. An infinity of these have existed in the past and will exist in the future.

❝ *The liberated is not long or small or round . . . he is without body, without contact of matter; he is not feminine or masculine or neuter; he perceives, he knows, but there is no analogy whereby to know the nature of the liberated soul; its essence is without form; there is no condition of the unconditioned.* **❞**

MAHAVIRA, THE 24TH TIRTHANKARA

THE LIFE OF MAHAVIRA

IN JAIN THOUGHT time is infinite and made up of a series of upward or downward movements that last for millions of years. During each movement, 24 teachers appear in succession. These are the *tirthankaras*, or "makers of the ford across the ocean of rebirth", who reactivate the Jain religion when humanity has spiritually declined. Mahavira is the 24th *tirthankara* in the current time motion. For Jains, all of Mahavira's predecessors are historical figures. Mahavira himself is traditionally dated 599–527 BCE, and was a contemporary of the Buddha. Born in the Ganges basin in India as a princely member of the Hindu *kshatriya* warrior caste (see p.18), Mahavira renounced the world at the age of 30 and became a wandering ascetic. After 12 years of denial of the body, he achieved enlightenment. He then converted 12 disciples, who structured his teachings into the Jain scriptures, and built up a community of followers. Mahavira died in meditation and became a liberated soul.

The Samavasarana of Mahavira
Every tirthankara *delivers his first sermon in a* samavasarana. *This is a circular structure constructed by gods that consists of linked tiers with surrounding balustrades, in which an audience listens to the* tirthankara *who is seated on a dais in the centre.*

THE KALPA SUTRA
The Kalpa Sutra, *the Book of Ritual, is one of the two principal texts of Shvetambara Jainism (see pp.50–51). It is the earliest known account of the life of Mahavira, the 24th* tirthankara, *and places him in relation to his 23 predecessors. This folio records Mahavira's birth to Queen Trishala.*

QUEEN TRISHALA
Queen Trishala was Mahavira's second mother. The Shvetambara sect believes that Mahavira's embryo was mistakenly placed in the womb of Devananda, a woman belonging to the priestly brahmin caste, by one of the god Indra's servants. As all *tirthankaras* must be born into the warrior caste, the embryo was transferred to Queen Trishala by the messenger Harinegameshin.

NEW-BORN MAHAVIRA
Before his birth, both Mahaviras's mothers experienced prophetic dreams, in which 14 auspicious symbols indicated that he would be a great religious leader (see pp.44–45). Tradition has it that in Mahavira's devotion to the principle of not causing harm to others, he did not kick while in his mother's womb, and when he grew up he postponed his renunciation of the world until after his parents' deaths, lest he distress them.

FRIEND OF THE GODS
Before his birth, Mahavira resided in the Pushpottara heaven. The *Kalpa Sutra* says that at his conception, Indra, king of the celestial beings, stepped off his throne and praised the *tirthankaras* for attaining liberation and bringing to humanity the religion that overcomes suffering and death.

SHVETAMBARA SCRIPTURE
The *Kalpa Sutra* is thought to have been written in the first century BCE. This scripture is particularly important to the Shvetambara sect. The text is read and the illustrations are displayed for their annual *Paryushan* ceremony.

JAIN LANGUAGE
The language of the *Kalpa Sutra*, and the other Jain scriptures, is called *Ardhamagadhi*. This was probably based on a popular vernacular and could be contrasted with the Sanskrit language used by the priestly Brahmins (see p.18).

Mahavira and Indra
Mahavira was born with the help of the god Indra. This illumination from the
Kalpa Sutra depicts the infant Mahavira sitting on the lap of Indra at the top
of the cosmic mountain Meru, surrounded by divine attendants. It is prior
to the human birth of the tirthankara *Mahavira.*

INDRA'S HEAVEN
Mahavira's previous birth had been as a god
in one of Indra's heavens. Indra is said to
have recited a hymn in praise of the *Jinas*
at the time of Mahavira's conception.

INDRA, THE WARRIOR GOD
Indra is the king of the Hindu Vedic
gods. In Jainism, however, he is little
more than a ceremonial figure who
validates the birth of Mahavira.

“*On the night when Mahavira was born, countless gods and goddesses glided resplendently in ascending and*
descending movements. The whole world was awed and there arose from it a mighty tumult of wonder.”
FROM THE KALPA SUTRA

COSMOLOGY

ACCORDING TO JAIN SCRIPTURES, Mahavira and other *tirthankaras* (see pp.44–45) had, through their attainment of enlightenment, discovered the nature of the universe, which is known in Sanskrit as the *loka*. Much effort was devoted by Jain monks to understanding the *loka*, and cosmography became an elaborate branch of scholarly knowledge. The *loka* has three main sections and is vast in extent. At the bottom are the eight hells, each of which is successively more unpleasant. At the top is a series of heavens of increasing brightness, above the highest of which is the home of the liberated souls. In the middle is *Madhya Loka*, "the Middle World," a narrow band where concentric continents and oceans are located. Within this is the continent of Jambudvipa. Only on Jambudvipa and the one and a half continents nearest to it is human existence possible. Toward the end of the medieval period, it became common for the *loka* to be represented in human form. These images serve as objects of reverence and remind Jains of the importance of making use of the rare achievement of human birth.

Jambudvipa
Jambudvipa, "the continent of the rose-apple tree," is crossed by six mountain ranges that divide it into seven regions, with Mount Meru in the center. The most important areas are Bharata, or India, in the south; Airavata in the far north; and Mahavideha in the middle region. These are the realms where religious action may bear fruit and spiritual deliverance can be obtained.

REALM OF THE JINAS
At the top of the *loka* is Ishatpragbhara, the realm of the *siddhas*, or liberated souls. *Siddhas*, who have attained the goal of liberation from the world, are separate and isolated; they have no unity with the world that they inhabit, or with each other.

LEVELS OF REBIRTH
Gods do not have a central role in the Jain universe and, like all other creatures, will be reborn into the human realm when their merit runs out. It is possible to develop correct religious impulses in the heavens and thus take new existence in a pious Jain family, ultimately attaining liberation.

THE INNER CONTINENT
Jambudvipa is the inner continent of the mortal world. It is believed to be orbited by two suns and two moons, and is surrounded by two oceans and two additional continents.

Lord Bahubali
According to the Digambara sect of Jainism (see pp.50–51), Bahubali is the first person of our present age to achieve spiritual liberation. Having defeated his half-brother in battle, Bahubali refrained from killing him and renounced the world to become an ascetic. Every 12 years, in a spectacular ceremony, the 54-ft (16.5-m) statue of Bahubali in the south Indian town of Shravana Belgola is worshiped by hundreds of thousands of pilgrims.

THE COSMIC WORLD
The Jain cosmos, or loka, is represented here in human form. The loka has not been created by any entity, and it is eternal; it has and always will exist.

HIERARCHY OF GODS
The various categories of gods are envisaged in human terms, with their powers and luster more pronounced in each successive heavenly realm. Gods of the highest level are beyond the experience of desire, whereas those of the lower levels, with their palaces, retinues, and armies, are not dissimilar to worldly kings.

THE NONUNIVERSE
There are three layers of wind outside the confines of the *loka*. Beyond these is the *aloka*, the "nonuniverse," where nothing whatsoever exists.

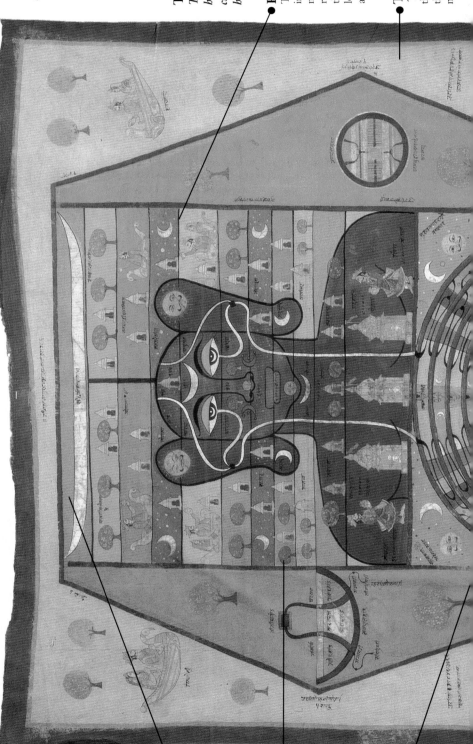

NONRELIGIOUS REALMS
Not all of the realms of Jambudvipa are suitable for religious activity. Four and a half of its outer regions are realms of sensory pleasure whose inhabitants are, by their nature, incapable of gaining merit to advance on the religious path.

MOUNT MERU
At the center of Jambudvipa lies the cosmic mountain Meru. Jambudvipa is named after the *jambu*, or rose-apple tree, that is said to be northwest of the cosmic mountain.

MAHAVIDEHA
Jains often wish to be reborn in the region of Mahavideha, because it is believed that the *tirthankaras* are currently teaching there.

GEOGRAPHICAL CORRECTNESS
Two substantial scale models of the *loka* (cosmos) have been constructed in India at the towns of Hastanapur and Palitana. Many traditionally minded Jain monks and nuns argue that their religion's cosmographical model is more authentic than conventional Western geography.

Jambudvipa and the Salt Ocean
Jambudvipa is represented here in a simplified form. It is surrounded by a salt ocean, Lavanasamudra, which is represented by the outer circle. The salt ocean is filled with aquatic animals and human beings.

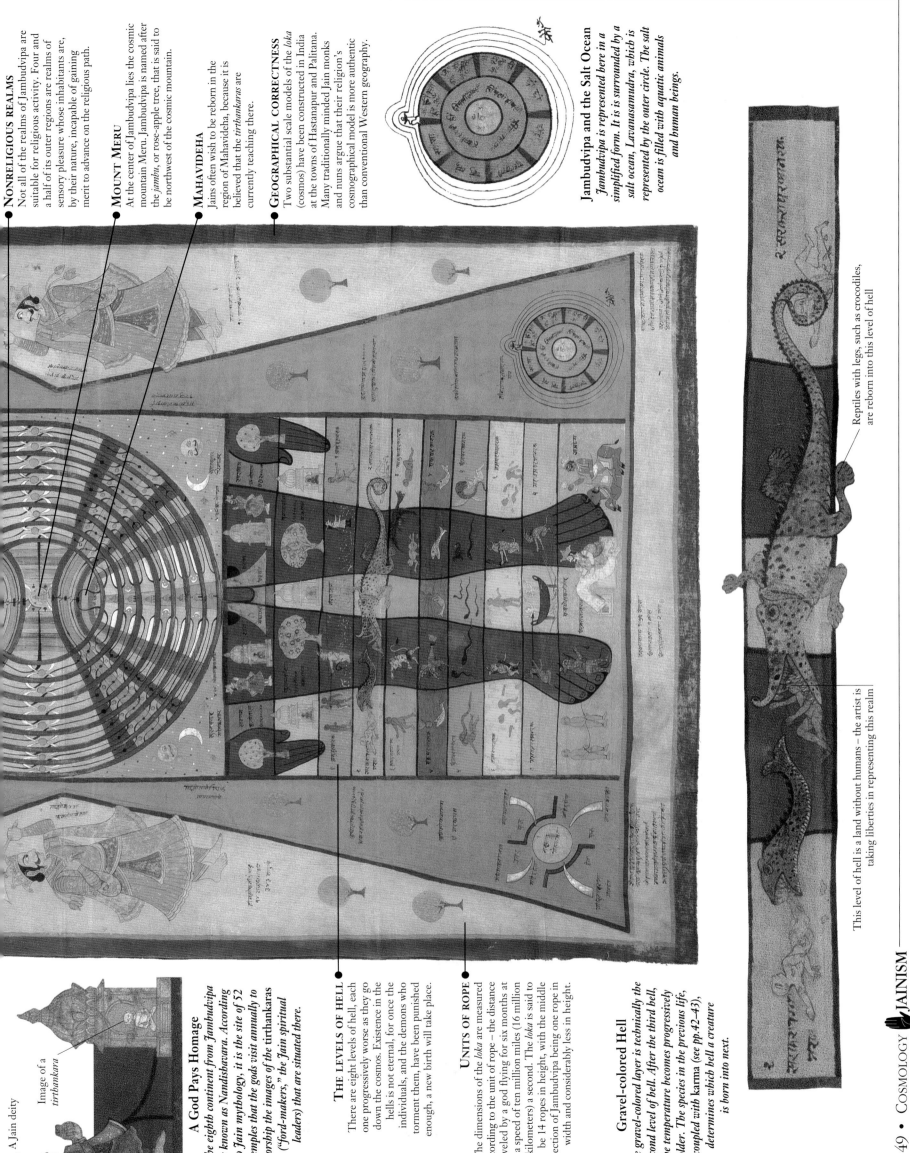

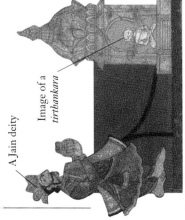

A Jain deity

Image of a
tirthankara

A God Pays Homage
The eighth continent from Jambudvipa is known as Nandisbavara. According to Jain mythology, it is the site of 52 temples that the gods visit annually to worship the images of the tirthankaras ("ford-makers," the Jain spiritual leaders) that are situated there.

THE LEVELS OF HELL
There are eight levels of hell, each one becoming progressively worse as they go down the cosmos. Existence in the hells is not eternal, for once the individuals, and the demons who torment them, have been punished enough, a new birth will take place.

UNITS OF ROPE
The dimensions of the *loka* are measured according to the unit of rope – the distance traveled by a god flying for six months at a speed of ten million miles (16 million kilometers) a second. The *loka* is said to be 14 ropes in height, with the middle section of Jambudvipa being one rope in width and considerably less in height.

Gravel-colored Hell
The gravel-colored layer is technically the second level of hell. After the third bell, the temperature becomes progressively colder. The species in the previous life, coupled with karma (see pp.42–43), determines which bell a creature is born into next.

Reptiles with legs, such as crocodiles,
are reborn into this level of hell

This level of hell is a land without humans – the artist is
taking liberties in representing this realm

ASCETICISM

ALTHOUGH THE VAST MAJORITY of the Jain religion's adherents today are laypeople, Jainism has, to a large extent, taken its identity from those men and women who have chosen to follow the path of ascetic renunciation. This is undertaken in adherence to the Jain goal of attaining complete liberation from the effects of *karma* (see p.42). Most broadly, initiation as a Jain monk or nun involves acceptance of and conformity to the five "Great Vows" that enjoin nonviolence, not lying, not taking what has not been given, abandonment of sexual relations, and nonpossession. A variety of subsidiary vows relate to the curbing of other potentially harmful physical and mental activities, while the standard mode of life is that of a wandering mendicant, punctuated by preaching, fasting, and study. Jain ascetics are disciplined by a senior Jain monk called an *acarya*, who is also entitled to interpret the scriptures. Jain laypeople do not follow the Great Vows, but all are strict vegetarians, in accordance with the vow of nonviolence.

DIGAMBARA AND SHVETAMBARA

Different emphasis has been given to the ascetic vow of nonpossession. One of the two main sects, Digambara, meaning "Sky-clad," claims that the total renunciation suggested in Jain scriptures involves the abandonment of clothes by male, but not female, ascetics. The Shvetambara, "White-clad" sect holds that monks and nuns can wear robes. Both these approaches have been authenticated in ancient Jain scriptures, although the evidence is that Mahavira, the founder of the Jain faith (see pp. 46–47), spent almost all of his ascetic career as a naked monk. One story tells how, near the start of his wanderings, he was so deep in contemplation that he did not notice or care when his robe was pulled off by a thorn bush.

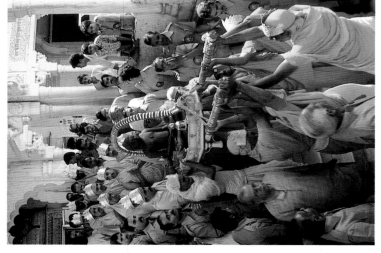

Installation of a Tirthankara
The tirthankaras, or guides, of the Jain religion (see pp.44–45) were all ascetics before they reached enlightenment. The installation of an image of a tirthankara in a Jain temple involves the symbolic reenactment of the main events of his life and ascetic career: anointing in heaven, birth, renunciation, enlightenment, and final release. Here, laymen dressed as Indra, the king of the gods, process with an image within a temple at Mahavirji in Rajasthan, symbolizing the tirthankara's ascetic wanderings.

A NAKED ASCETIC

A naked Digambara monk approaches a Jain statue

A naked Digambara, or "Sky-clad" monk, walks in front of a Jain image in south India. He holds in his hand a whisk of peacock feathers, which can serve the practical purpose of removing small insects before he sits down so as not to crush them, and also functions as a sectarian emblem, signifying total adherence to the principle of *ahimsa*, or nonviolence. Digambara monks do not have alms bowls, using their cupped hands as a receptacle for food. The only other possession they are allowed is a pot containing water for washing. According to the Digambaras, all possessions are a hindrance to liberation, therefore they wear no clothes at all. Today there are only a few hundred Digambara monks, as opposed to almost 2,000 monks of the Shvetambara sects.

Shvetambara Nuns on Pilgrimage
Nuns of the Shvetambara Sthanakavasi sect are pictured here on pilgrimage. The Sthanakvasis emerged in the 17th century, and advocate the wearing of mouth guards by ascetics in order to minimize the chances of breathing in insects and microbes. Today there are three times as many Shvetambara nuns as there are monks. Digambara nuns, unlike their male counterparts, are obliged to wear clothes, and Digambara teaching holds that women are incapable of liberation, thus obliging them to be reborn as men before they can attain it.

• **A MONK'S PORTRAIT**
This portrait of a Shvetambara monk was commissioned by the Mughal Emperor Akbar. Akbar is recorded as having had close relationships with several Jain monks. As a result he temporarily banned hunting and the eating of meat within his kingdom.

PORTRAIT OF A JAIN ASCETIC
This 16th-century portrait of a Shvetambara Jain ascetic was painted by a Hindu artist, Basawan, for a Muslim, the emperor Akbar, who was very impressed by Jain holy men. It is the only known surviving example of an imperial portrait of a Jain ascetic.

> *He who controls his hands, feet, speech, and senses, turns his mind inward, has a calm soul and knows the holy texts and their meaning; he is a true monk.*
>
> FROM THE DASHAVAIKALIKA SUTRA

THE SEASON FOR WANDERING

The wandering life of a Jain ascetic is suspended during the four-month period of the Indian monsoon. During this period he lives in the midst of the lay community within a monastic lodging house called *upashraya*, preaching and studying the scriptures. Ascetics are not encouraged to stay in one place, since this develops attachment, although permission to do this may be given in certain circumstances.

POSSESSIONS OF A MONK

Shvetambara monks are allowed to carry with them a whisk, a staff, an alms bowl, and a copy of a scriptural text. Some monks also carry a tiny image of the *tirthankaras* (see pp.44–45) for devotional purposes.

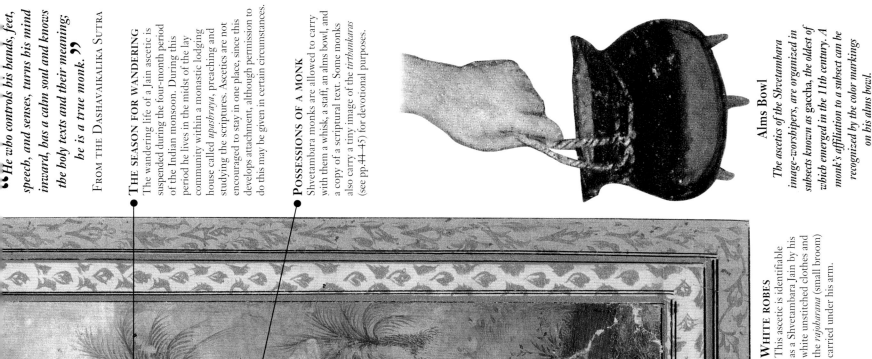

Alms Bowl

The ascetics of the Shvetambara image-worshipers, are organized in subsets known as gaccha, the oldest of which emerged in the 11th century. A monk's affiliation to a subset can be recognized by the color markings on his alms bowl.

WHITE ROBES

This ascetic is identifiable as a Shvetambara Jain by his white unstitched clothes and the *rajoharana* (small broom) carried under his arm.

COLLECTING FOOD

It is forbidden for Jain monks to cook or grow food. The action of begging for food by Shvetambara ascetics is called *gocari*, "grazing like a cow," and should be conducted in silence, without any requesting or importuning involved. Food is collected in the alms bowl and taken back to the monastic residence, where it is eaten out of sight of the laity. Giving food to an ascetic is an important way for lay Jains to earn spiritual merit.

> *He should forever give up dwelling in the body, this unclean and transitory house, his mind standing firm in the eternal good. A monk who has cut off the fetter of birth and death goes to liberation, that place from which there is no return.*
>
> FROM THE DASHAVAIKALIKA SUTRA

BARE FEET

Ascetics spend much of their lives wandering. Their vow of renunciation means that even the "White-clad" sect may not wear shoes. This vow extends to other things, including being unable to wash with running water. This makes monks impure and only able to perform "inner worship," such as singing hymns, or performing *darshan* (see p.52) or movements of homage. Direct contact with an image is forbidden because of their impurity. Modern monks are thought to clean themselves with damp rags, but in the past they would have been very dirty.

> *Without fixed abode, walking from house to house as a beggar, gleaning that which was left by other mendicants, using a limited number of utensils and avoiding quarrels and arrogant behavior in a crowd of people: this is proclaimed as the monkish life of the wise ones.*
>
> FROM THE DASHAVAIKALIKA SUTRA

LONE MONK

During the 19th century, the number of Jain monks was extremely low. Among the Shvetambaras the teacher Atmaramji played an important part in the latter part of the century in resuscitating the tradition, and the Digambara monastic lineage was reactivated by the charismatic Jain leader Shantisagar (1873–1955).

SPARSE HAIR

Jain ascetics are encouraged to pluck their hair out at regular intervals. According to the scriptures, on renouncing the world Mahavira tore out his hair in five handfuls. In the ascetic initiation carried out today, the hair is usually shaved off, apart from five small tufts that are removed by hand.

TEMPLE AND IMAGE WORSHIP

THE EARLIEST WRITINGS OF JAINISM say nothing about temples and images. However, evidence of a devotional cult having developed by at least the second century BCE, which centered on worship of the *tirthankaras*, has been found in Mathura in northwest India, where many ancient images of the great Jain teachers have been excavated. Usually Jain temples are not dissimilar to Hindu ones (see pp.32–33), with a standard main tower, or *shikhara*, and an outer concourse, or *rang mandap*. Jain temples always have an inner sanctum housing the image of the *tirthankara* who presides over them. Every temple is regarded as the equivalent of the preaching assembly, or *samavasarana*, of the *tirthankara*, and to enter brings the devotee into immediate contact with Jain teachings. Worship can involve the quiet intoning of a *mantra* accompanied by simple eye contact with the image, called *darshan*, or more elaborate forms of ritual, involving the anointing and decoration of the image, called *puja*. Because *tirthankaras* have achieved spiritual liberation and freedom from wordly affairs, they cannot directly assist their devotees. Image worship is regarded as effecting an inner, spiritual transformation, calling to mind the qualities of the *tirthankaras* and instilling a desire to emulate them.

Ambika, the Mother Goddess
For help in wordly and material matters, Jains can call upon a variety of goddesses, whose images are normally located in the outer concourses of the temples of the tirthankaras *with whom they are linked. Ambika, the Mother Goddess, is one of the most popular of these deities. According to legend, Ambika was a pious Jain laywoman who leapt into a well with her two sons to escape her Brahmin husband, who was angry with her for having given alms to a monk. Subsequently reborn as a goddess, Ambika is associated with childbirth and prosperity, and is usually portrayed with children. She is associated with Nemi, the 22nd* tirthankara.

THE JAIN TEMPLE, SITAMBAR, CALCUTTA
The Badridas temple complex at Sitambar, Calcutta, was built in dedication to the tenth tirthankara *Shitala. An image of Shitala sits at the center of the temple complex. Its construction was undertaken by the Jain Raibahadur Badridas, after a dream showing him where the image of the* tirthankara *Shitala was buried.*

TEMPORAL ACCOMMODATION
Most large Jain temples have ancillary buildings attached to them. These can include libraries and lodging houses where monks and nuns can stay during the monsoon period.

"Whatever is called a shrine in the heavenly, hellish or human realms, however many images of the tirthankaras *there are, I praise them all."*
FROM THE OVANDANA SUTRA

ATTITUDES TOWARD WATER
Although lay people are expected to wash and wear clean clothes before visiting the temple, Jainism places its main emphasis on "inner cleanliness" and rejects Hindu claims about the possible purifying nature of sacred rivers and temple tanks (see pp.32–33).

The Use of Flowers
Flowers are frequently used in temple ritual. Although they are living, it is not considered a sin to cut them for this purpose. However, some Jains claim that only flowers that have already fallen should be used in worship.

INSIDE THE TEMPLE
When the worshiper enters the temple, he or she takes *darshan*: seeing the image of the *tirthankara* and believing him- or herself to be in his presence. *Darshan* is a practice also central to Hindu worship (see pp. 32–33).

TEMPLE CLEANLINESS
Large Jain temples are kept clean by servants called *pujaris*. They carry out daily duties such as lighting devotional lamps and providing materials for worship. They are often paid with the remainder of the offerings that sometimes include money.

At the Feet of Lord Bahubali

To the Digambara sect of Jainism, Lord Bahubali is as important as the tirthankaras. The son of a king, he gave up his life and retired to the forest, meditating for years while vines grew up his body, and birds built a nest in his hair. However, he realized complete knowledge only after he had forgiven his brother, who had tried to kill him. Here, a devotee anoints the feet of the huge image of Bahubali at the Digambara holy site of Shravana Belgola, India. Jain tradition records that the very first anointing of this image, carried out in 981 by the general Camundraya who erected it, could only be completed with the aid of the goddess Kushmandini, who was disguised as an old woman.

CENTRAL SHRINE
The image of the tenth *tirthankara* Shitala is housed within the central shrine of the Badridas temple.

WORSHIPING AT HOME

Among the duties of a Jain is to worship images and to build temples, helping to satisfy the individual's need for achieving the proper mental attitude for spiritual guidance. Image worship in Jainism does not necessarily require the assistance of a priest, and many Jain households maintain domestic shrines for private use. This was particularly common in earlier centuries during occasional periods of Muslim persecution in western India. Home shrines are usually made of wood and are modeled on stone temple shrines. Most include a rich iconography, with carvings of deities and celestial musicians. As in temples, male worshipers should ideally wear fresh, unstitched clothes.

A boy worships at a home shrine

CENTRAL CHAMBER
Upon entering the central chamber of the temple, the worshiper makes offerings of eight "substances": water, sandalwood, flowers, incense, lamp, rice, sweets, and fruit. Offering these implies renunciation of worldly things by the worshiper, and they are symbolic of a spiritual path.

ELABORATE DECORATION
Jain temples tend to be very elaborate. This is because they came to be regarded as replicas of the celestial assembly halls, or *samasavarana*, of the *tirthankaras*. In this way Jainism differs from Hinduism, in which the temple is considered to be the actual residence of a deity.

JAIN WORSHIPERS
Once pure, Jain worshipers may touch the *tirthankara* image when annointing it or making offerings. Monks and nuns, however, may not come into direct contact with an image because of their renunciation of worldly behavior, which renders them "impure" (not washing with running water) and unfit to touch holy things.

IMAGE WORSHIP
Not all Jains are image-worshipers. Two important Shvetambara sects, the Sthanakvasis and the Terapanthis, reject temples and idols, and instead concentrate on devotion to senior monks.

ENTRANCE HALL
The entrance hall to most Jain temples is decorated with images of deities from the Jain pantheon, including Lakshmi, the Hindu goddess of wealth, who has been appropriated by the Jain religion, probably because so many Jains are traders and merchants.

Yama and the Wheel of Life
Yama, the Lord of Death (see pp.64–65), holds the Wheel of Life, a symbol of the cosmos. At the center of the wheel are three animals symbolizing the cardinal faults: greed (the pig), hatred (the snake), and delusion (the cock).

BUDDHISM

THE PATH TO ENLIGHTENMENT

BUDDHISM BEGAN HISTORICALLY in North India in the 6th or 5th century BCE, when a man called Siddhartha Gautama attained "enlightenment," the ultimate truth by which people are freed from the cycle of rebirth (see below). He became the Buddha, meaning "enlightened one," who taught others the way to escape from constant rebirth and therefore from suffering. The truth of the Buddha discipline or *Buddha sasana*, which involves meditation and spiritual exercise, and the teachings of the Buddha or *Buddha dharma* have, according to the followers of Buddhism, always been in existence.

The life of Gautama or Gotama (Buddhist words and names have two forms, in Sanskrit and in Pali) is not known in verifiable detail. However, the combination of historical facts, poetry, and legend have produced a narrative that Buddhists believe in as their model for the human search for enlightenment. Gautama was brought up in a royal household, protected from the suffering in the world, but against his father's wishes he went outside the palace grounds on chariot rides. On separate occasions he saw a sick man, an old man, a corpse, and a wandering holy man (see pp.36–37). These four events, known as the Four Signs, led to Gautama's inner struggle to search for a meaning to life. He left his wife and family and lived an ascetic, homeless existence, known as the Great Renunciation. During this period, he attained all the goals that extreme discipline can attain, but it was not enough: he still had not escaped from the world of suffering and death. Sitting in despair in Bodh Gaya under the Bodhi tree he passed through the four stages of *dhyana/jhana* or meditative trance, and finally attained enlightenment. Although initially he decided to remain where he was, "seeing all things as they really are," the Hindu god Brahma (see p.18) persuaded him to teach others the truths that even the gods did not know.

THE FOUR NOBLE TRUTHS

What the Buddha saw is summarized in the Four Noble Truths. First, all existence is *dukkha*, unsatisfactory and filled with suffering; second, *dukkha* arises from *tanha*, a craving or clinging, which means a constant effort to find something permanent and stable in a transient world; third, *dukkha* can cease totally, and this is nirvana; and fourth, this can be reached by following the Eightfold Path. These eight steps do not have to be followed in order. Each is described as "right," or *samma*: right understanding, right directed thought, right speech, right action, right livelihood, right effort, right mindfulness, right concentration. Right understanding includes the vital understanding of "Conditioned Arising" or "Dependent Origination," a central theme in Buddhist thought. It is a 12-linked chain that explains how all things are connected, how error and attachment to error arise, and how, if the chain is unraveled, nirvana is attained. According to this belief, things that exist are dependent on each other, and only nirvana is independent.

The Wheel of Law
Buddha is said to have "set in motion the wheel of the dharma" when he explained the natural law of things to five ascetics during his first sermon at Sarnath, India. His teaching is often symbolized by a wheel.

Born in India, the Buddha accepted the general context of Indian ideas, but he radically altered many of them. He accepted that there is rebirth through many lives, *samsara*, with outcomes in new lives dependent on *karma*, the moral law of cause and effect. But his insight was that there is no soul or *atman* being reborn, because there is no permanence in anything. There is only the sequence of one moment of appearance giving rise to the next, so that death simply represents a new form of appearance, as human or animal, in heaven or hell. Even the gods (of which there are many) are only temporary forms of appearance. So the Buddha vigorously denied the worth of the Hindu sacrificial system, advising his followers to "work out your own salvation with diligence." Old ritual gains new form: sacrifice of animals becomes self-giving in service to others. His last reported words were, "Decay is inherent in all compounded things, so continue in watchfulness." The goal is neither absorption into Brahman – the Absolute – nor union with God: it is nirvana, which means the blowing out of the fires of longing and attachment. Nirvana can be attained in this life, but the residue of *karma* may sustain an appearance for a while longer. An *arhat*, one who is "worthy of honor," is a person who has attained the condition of nirvana.

After enlightenment, the Buddha engaged in teaching, wandering with a band of followers, but settling during the rainy season in one place. From this began the relationship in Buddhism between the monks, *bhikkhu/bhikshu*, in community or *Sangha*, and the lay people. Lay people supply the monks with material support, and the monks bring spiritual learning and merit to them and their ancestors. The Three Jewels summarize Buddhism: "I take refuge in the Buddha, in the teaching (*dharma/ dhamma*), and in the *Sangha*."

FORMS OF BUDDHISM

Buddhism died out in India, perhaps due to the Muslim invasions in the 11th century, spreading to Sri Lanka and then to southeast Asia, in a form staying close to the Pali canon (the Buddhist texts collected together in three baskets or *tripitaka*). This form is usually known as Theravada, although Theravada was originally one school among many in early Buddhism. But another form developed, claiming to reveal the further teaching of the Buddha at the appropriate time. This form calls itself Mahayana, or "Great Vehicle," referring derisively to Theravada as Hinayana or "Small Vehicle." The Mahayana spread into China, Mongolia, Korea, Japan, and Tibet, where it took the form of Vajrayana, the "Thunderbolt Vehicle" (see p.74).

Mahayana is distinguished by calling the Buddha "Shakyamuni," the enlightened one of the Shakya clan, and by its emphasis on *sutras*, texts containing the Buddha's teachings. They are revealed at the proper time according to the Buddha's "skill-in-means," teaching always to the capacity of the audience, initially in simple ways. Mahayana also

The Bodhisattva and the Soul
Bodhisattvas *are those who have attained enlightenment but have sworn to remain in this world to help others who are still suffering. In this 10th-century Chinese painting, the* bodhisattva *Avalokiteshvara leads a soul, portrayed as a fashionably dressed woman, to paradise. Avalokiteshvara is one of the most popular* bodhisattvas *of the Mahayana tradition and is seen as the embodiment of compassion.*

stresses the importance of *bodhisattvas*, those who have attained nirvana but who vow to remain active in helping those still unenlightened and suffering. For this reason, Mahayana is sometimes known as Great Compassion, Hinayana as Little Compassion. Mahayana emphasises the Buddha-nature in all things; everything already is the Buddha-nature, and has only to realize what it is in order to attain nirvana. This life, therefore, rightly seen, can be nirvana. It involves devotion to the many Buddhas and *bodhisattvas*, and many believe in the possibility of sudden enlightenment, as opposed to going through countless reappearances prior to achieving this.

Mahayana Buddhism has developed through schools and traditions, especially philosophically in Madhyamaka and Yogacara; and in Pure Land, Ch'an, T'ien-t'ai, and Hua-yen in China; in Japan, as Soto, Rinzai, Jodo (Pure Land), Zen, and Nichiren; in Tibet, as Nyingmapa and Sarmapa (including Kagyupa, Sakyapa and Gelugpa, to which the Dalai Lama belongs); and in Korea, as Popsong and Son (which were united in 1935 as Chogye).

The Hidden Buddha
This 9th-century bronze statue is of a stupa, a funeral mound originally built to contain the relics and remains of emperors and kings. After the Buddha's death, his relics were distributed in a number of stupas, and from this they came to be a symbol of the Buddha's final nirvana. For this reason stupas were worshiped. They were later used to house the relics of important monks.

THE LIFE OF THE BUDDHA

GAUTAMA BUDDHA LIVED SOMETIME BETWEEN the 6th and 4th centuries BCE, in northeast India. According to Buddhist traditions, Siddhartha Gautama, or Shakyamuni, as he was also called, was born into a royal family of the Shakya clan. His father, fearing that he might be distressed by unpleasant experiences, kept him confined within the palace. However, at the age of 29, Gautama saw human suffering for the first time in the shape of old age, sickness, and death. On seeing a wandering ascetic, he determined to follow this ancient path and stole away from his home at night, leaving his wife and family. After six years of severe austerity, he attained his goal. But he had not escaped from suffering. Sitting under the Bodhi tree, the tree of enlightenment, he passed through all the stages of meditation (*jhana*) and attained enlightenment, understanding the true nature of suffering. From this point on he was known as the Buddha, literally "the awoken one," and for some 40 years until he died, he taught others, preaching his first sermon in a deer park at Sarnath in northeast India. Gautama is held to be the 24th Buddha in the present stage of the world. When his teachings fall into decline, as inevitably they must in the present age of disorder, the future Buddha Maitreya will come.

The Birth of Buddha
Traditionally, the Buddha was the son of King Suddhodana and Queen Maya, who gave birth while she stood holding on to a Sala tree in Lumbini, Nepal. She died seven days later, like the mothers of all Buddhas, because no other child may be born from the same womb as a Buddha. She is said to have been reborn as a male in the Tusita heaven. This Thai manuscript shows her with human and divine helpers before the birth.

THE SHAKYA SCHOOL
A Lama, probably of the Tibetan Shakya school, suggests that this *thang-kha*, or temple hanging, probably hung in a monastery belonging to this school.

▸ TREE OF ENLIGHTENMENT
Historically, the Buddha reached enlightenment under the Bodhi tree in a deer park in Varanasi (see p.63). In legend, he reached it sitting at the foot of a tree in a forest surrounded by spirits called *devas*.

THE BUDDHA CONQUERS MARA
This temple hanging shows the Buddha when he was still a bodhisattva or "future Buddha" (see pp.68–69), although many of the details relate to his enlightenment shortly afterward. Here, he is at the point where he calls upon Mother Earth to witness his victory over Mara, the evil one (in Sanskrit, literally "death"), who, according to legend, was determined that Shakyamuni should not achieve enlightenment.

A Buddhist Master
It is customary for the central image in a Tibetan temple hanging (thang-kha) to be surrounded by subsidiary figures. Ranged above the Buddha's head are a group of Tibetan and Indian Buddhist masters. Judging by the wheel of dharma in his left hand and the scripture in his right, this particular figure is a skilled exponent of the Buddha's teachings.

Wheel of Dharma

Aura

BODILY SIGNS OF A "SUPERMAN"
The *ushnisa* or wisdom bump is one of the 32 bodily signs of a "Superman" or *mahapurusha*. In this picture it is surmounted by a gemstone. The small tuft of hair or *urna* between the eyebrows, the elongated ears, and the hair (difficult to see here; one strand from each pore, rising straight and then curling to the right) are also significant signs.

SYMBOL OF THE BUDDHA'S TEACHING

The eight-spoke wheel that lies in the Buddha's palm is symbolic of the teaching or *dharma*, which he formulated after reaching enlightenment. The spokes represent the stages of the noble eight-fold path that leads to enlightenment: right understanding, right view, right speech, right conduct, right means of livelihood, right endeavor, right mindfulness, and right contemplation.

PALMS AND SOLES

The palms of the hands and soles of the Buddha's feet are colored in red henna, a traditional mark of beauty in the Indo-Tibetan world.

"There is a sphere which is neither earth, nor water, nor fire, nor air, the sphere of nothingness. It is only the end of suffering."
THE BUDDHA, UDANA 80

Halo, a mark of spiritual advancement

Pallid skin

Emaciated Buddha

This statue shows the Buddha prior to his enlightenment. After Shakyamuni left his home and family, he spent six years accompanied by five other mendicants, devoting himself to strict asceticism, with practices such as severe fasting and holding of the breath. He gave this up after realizing that perfection comes by observing the middle path between the extremes of self-mortification and hedonism. The dull color of the lacquer on this image represents the traditional belief that excessive asceticism dimmed the natural luminosity of his golden skin.

AURA OF BUDDHAHOOD

Each Buddha possesses his own distinctive aura. Shakyamuni meditated through the night after he defeated Mara. At dawn he achieved enlightenment and became a Buddha. Then an aura or *rasmi*, 20ft/6m in diameter, composed of six colors, radiated out from his shining body. Afterward the Buddha meditated for another seven weeks. Hovering over his aura is the serpent king Mucalinda.

VICTORY OVER MARA

The Buddha touches the ground with his right hand. This is the gesture he made to call upon Mother Earth to witness his victory over Mara. Not wishing Shakyamuni to become enlightened and teach others how to reach nirvana, and escape the cycle of rebirth, Mara sent messengers to trick Shakyamuni into returning to his kingdom. He sent his beautiful daughters to tempt him, launched an army of demons upon him, and finally flung his magic discus, capable of slicing a mountain in two, toward him. But Mara was defeated.

LOTUS THRONE

The Buddha sits on a meditation throne. The lotus has its roots in the mud but it flowers in pure open space and symbolizes the state of enlightenment. Legend says that when the Buddha was born he took seven steps, and at each step a lotus bloom sprang up.

TREASURY OF DESIRE

A vase, symbolizing the treasury of all desires, stands on the low table for offerings below the meditation throne. All sense of desire must be lost before enlightenment can be reached.

World Protector

This figure is one of the four world protectors (lokapala) of Buddhism, probably Surya, the Hindu god of the sun. As Buddhism developed, Indian gods evolved as protectors of the Buddha's teachings. The Buddha was said to have been delivered upon his birth by the gods Brahma and Indra.

THE BUDDHA IMAGE

IN THE EARLIEST phase of Buddhist art, the Buddha is not depicted. He dissuaded his followers from speculating about his existence after death, and this may have led to a reluctance to represent him. Instead, he is indicated with various symbols, of which the most common are the wheel (representing the *dharma* – see p.54), his footprints, the stupa, and the tree of enlightenment. The first figurative depictions date from the 2nd century CE in northern India, although this rapidly spread throughout Buddhist Asia. The variety of styles of Buddha images today indicates the many differing cultures in which Buddhism has flourished. Traditionally, Buddhist artists have sought to depict 12 elements in the Buddha's life story (see pp.56–57): his prior existence in the Tusita Heaven; his conception, birth, education, marriage, and pastimes; his renunciation, his asceticism; the Bodhi tree; the defeat of Mara; his enlightenment, first sermon, and death.

Death of the Buddha

Buddha on a Lotus Throne
This complex and finely carved Burmese Buddha is seated on a lotus throne and surrounded by scenes from his life. The topmost scene depicting the Buddha's passing away, in which he lies on his right side attended by gods and monks, is particularly striking. A stupa for his relics is positioned above his body. The Buddha's last recorded words are: "Decay is inherent is all compounded things, so continue in watchfulness."

Gesture of defeat of Mara

Wisdom bump

Elongated earlobes

HAIR OF AN ASCETIC
The Buddha's hair is arranged in the characteristic topknot of an ancient Indian wandering ascetic. The sculptor probably borrowed this feature from earlier images of Greek gods.

MARKS OF A SUPERMAN
The *urna* or beauty spot of the Buddha is a small tuft of hair between the eyes. It is one of the 32 physical marks of a "superman." Others include legs like an antelope, skin so smooth that dust may not alight, intensely black eyes, eyelashes like a cow, 40 teeth, and genitals enclosed in a sheath.

Boon-granting gesture

GANDHARAN BUDDHA
This 2nd to 3rd-century CE image is typical of the Graeco-Buddhist art of Gandhara, a region of northwest India. Gandharan art was influenced by Greek styles that may have been introduced by Alexander the Great, who conquered the region. The area was considered holy because it was believed that events from the Buddha's former lives had taken place there.

BUDDHA HALO
This nimbus or halo is in the plain "solar disc" form, typical of a Gandharan Buddha figure.

MONASTIC CLOAK
A heavy monastic cloak covering both shoulders is typical of the Gandharan style.

The cobra Mucalinda opens his hood to shelter the Buddha from the rain

Buddha and Mucalinda
This image from Cambodia depicts the incident when, three weeks after enlightenment, the Buddha was protected from a rain storm by the serpent king Mucalinda, who wound his coils seven times around the Buddha's body with his hood

The Buddha-to-be

WHEEL-TURNING POSTURE

It is customary for Buddha images to be constructed with the hands in stylized poses or mudras. This looks rather like the *dharmacakra mudra*, the "wheel-turning posture," but since this is among the earliest of all Buddha images, it does not obey the conventions to the letter.

MEDITATION POSTURE

Since the legs are covered, it is impossible to be precise about the posture (*asana*) that the artist intended for this Buddha image. Most likely it is the *dhyanasana* or meditation posture, in which the legs are crossed with the soles of both feet turned upward and resting on the opposite thighs.

❝ Being dispassionate, he becomes detached; through detachment he is liberated. When liberated there is knowledge that he is liberated. And he knows: birth is exhausted, the holy life has been lived, what has to be done is done, there is no more to be done on this account. ❞

FROM THE FIRE SERMON;
THERAVADA SUTTA PITAKA

MEDITATION THRONE

The Buddha sits on a meditation throne. Such thrones were used as symbols of the presence of the Buddha in the earliest period of Buddhist art.

Bare feet of an ascetic

A Standing Buddha

Images of the Buddha standing are uncommon, perhaps because of the artistic difficulties involved in portraying contemplation in this posture. This 6th-century Indian image shows the Buddha in monastic robes covering his right shoulder. The elongated earlobes refer to the period when the Buddha, as a young prince, wore heavy earrings. The wisdom bump (ushnisa), one of the 32 traditional signs of a "superman," is prominently represented. The right hand is shown in the boon-granting gesture.

GREEK INFLUENCE

The style of this Buddha is influenced by Greek art and is very different from the Indian styles farther east. The rulers of the area did not suppress Buddhism and are said to have shown a great interest in the religion of the Buddha. A Pali text, the *Questions of King Milinda*, presents Buddhist doctrine in the form of a conversation between Nagasena, a Buddhist monk, and the Indo-Greek king Milinda.

Courtly Figures

A young courtly figure sits surrounded by attendants and devotees. The hairstyle and clothing of the central figure indicate that he is a bodhisattva or buddha-to-be. He is probably Maitreya, the future Buddha, although the scene may be one from Gautama's life prior to enlightenment. Maitreya frequently appears in Gandharan sculptures. He is a protector of Buddhism, especially of missionary monks, which may be a reason why he was popular in central Asia, where monks were often exposed to alien religions and hostile peoples.

THE FACE TOWERS OF THE BAYON

The Bayon, a spectacular ruined temple in Cambodia, contains huge face towers, and the identity of the faces has been much debated. The most likely explanation is that they represent the 14th-century king Jayavarman IV, who was regarded as the Buddha, the Hindu god Shiva (see pp.22–23), and the *bodhisattva* Avalokiteshvara (see pp.68–69) all rolled into one – a reflection of the way in which the Cambodian pantheon was a mixture of Hindu and Buddhist deities and deified persons. The temple itself represents a terrestrial version of Indra's heavenly palace. Its central image was a statue of Buddha with Mucalinda, the serpent king.

The face towers of the Bayon, Cambodia

Spire
representing
cosmological
hierarchy

STUPAS, TEMPLES, AND RELICS

STUPAS ARE ANCIENT INDIAN BURIAL MOUNDS containing relics of kings or heroes. In the Buddhist context, they are thought to contain relics of the Buddha himself—after his death his relics were divided and a number of stupas were raised to hold them. Later, stupas were used as burial mounds for other significant figures from the early Buddhist period. Although no ancient stupa stands fully intact today, many stupas were built during the great expansion of Buddhism under its imperial patron, the Indian ruler Ashoka (268–239 BCE). In time, some stupas became important pilgrimage sites, and as their prestige increased, they were encrusted with stone, often carved and depicting scenes from the life of the Buddha. In Tibet the stupa became the chorten, which has a dome that rests on a five-tiered base symbolizing the five elements of this world, and a sun resting on a crescent moon symbolizing wisdom and compassion at the top of the spire. In Southeast Asia, China, and Japan, stupas became pagodas, which represent the Buddhist cosmos.

A GOLD RELIQUARY

This gold reliquary, dating from the 2nd century BCE, was excavated from inside a stupa or burial mound at Bimaran, Afghanistan. The central niche contains the Buddha standing in the traditional teaching pose, flanked on either side by the Hindu gods Brahma and Indra in a posture of homage. The reliquary is studded with garnets and presumably contained the ashes of a Buddhist saint, although objects that holy people have used are also considered as relics. The rich materials used in this artifact demonstrate the success of early Buddhist missionary activity beyond the Indian subcontinent.

A reliquary used for holding the cremated remains of an important Buddhist saint

PARASOL
This stylized parasol is an ancient symbol of kingship, signifying the spiritual sovereignty of the Buddha, who is symbolized by the stupa. This structure is also said to symbolize the Bodhi (or Bo) tree in Bodh Gaya, India, under which the Buddha obtained his enlightenment.

THE STUPA
As an object of devotion, a stupa was often set within a complex ceremonial area. It was generally huge, solid domes mounted on cylindrical platforms, surrounded by great railings. This railing encircled the structure and had a number of gates through which pilgrims entered a walkway. The stupa itself was venerated as a symbol of the Buddha.

THE BUDDHA'S LIFE
A scene from the Buddha's life before his final enlightenment is depicted on the stupa image. At this period the Buddha was known as the *bodhisattva* – "Buddha-to-be."

RAILING
The *harmika*, a low railing surrounding a square area, recalls the enclosures often found around sacred trees.

CELESTIAL SPIRITS
Celestial beings carry garlands as offerings to the Buddha. Such garlands may be seen around the upper dome of the stupa.

THE WHEEL OF THE LAW
The wheel represents the cosmos and the Buddhist concepts of *karma* (see pp.58–59) and rebirth.

STUPA GATES
The pillars that make up the gates to the stupa are known as *ayaka* pillars.

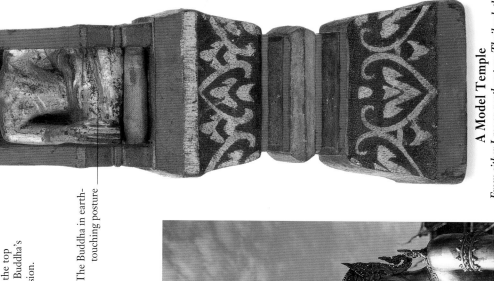

STONE LIONS

Two lions in the stupa railing guard the entrance to the gateway. Lions adorn many of the stupas and temples built during the reign of Emperor Ashoka. They are symbols of royalty.

MEDITATIONAL AID

By the 2nd century BCE, stupas were being used as a meditational aid. Thus the ground on which a stupa rests symbolizes generosity; the base is a symbol of moral restraint, and the top symbolizes the Buddha's moral compassion.

The Buddha in earth-touching posture

A Model Temple

From either Laos or northeastern Thailand, this model temple is an artifact of the Theravada form of Buddhism. The Buddha's right hand is touching the ground, recalling the time when he called on Mother Earth to witness his enlightenment after it had been questioned by Mara, the Buddhist personification of evil (see pp.56–57). The spire of the model represents the hierarchy of traditional Buddhist cosmology (see pp.64–65).

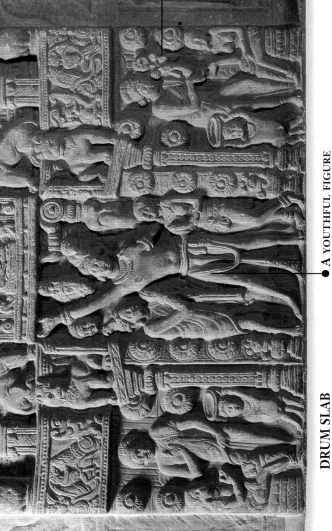

THE BUDDHA

The Buddha is symbolically at the center of the stupa, attended by devotees. He is represented in the fear-banishing gesture, his right hand raised with an open palm. According to the authority of an ancient Buddhist text (see pp.66–67), the Buddha recommended the laity obtain religious merit by worshiping stupas.

Lion guarding the entrance to the stupa

DRUM SLAB

This decorated slab, dating from about the 3rd century BCE, is from the drum of the stupa at Nagarjunakonda, southern India. It depicts a stupa, perhaps Nagarjunakonda itself, in its heyday.

A YOUTHFUL FIGURE

A youthful figure is dressed in princely garb and is attended by male and female followers in attitudes of reverence. The appearance of a wheel motif at the top right-hand corner of the frieze suggests that he is probably a universal Buddhist king. His raised hand is pouring out gold.

Pilgrim with offering of flowers

> ❝I have run through the course of many births looking for the maker of this dwelling and finding him not; painful is birth again and again. All your rafters are broken, your ridge-pole is destroyed, the mind has attained the extinction of desires.❞
>
> GAUTAMA, ON RECEIVING ENLIGHTENMENT

The Royal Palace, Thailand

Theravada Buddhism (see pp.54–55) is the state religion of Thailand, and it is the religion of the great majority of the country's people. The Royal Palace at Ayutthya was ruled over by a succession of progressive Thai kings. The Palace's stupas are bell-shaped, similar to the Sri Lankan style. After the destruction of Ayutthya in 1767, the Thai capital was moved to Bangkok, where kings of the Chakri dynasty, notably Rama IV (1851–68), did much to reshape and reinvigorate the Buddhist monastic community.

Bowl for receiving alms

Outside the Gates of the Stupa

Outside the gates of the walkway there are a variety of pilgrims, food vendors, and potbellied dwarfs holding trays on their heads for the reception of alms. Stupas were built by lay people and were primarily objects of devotion for the laity, to remind them of Buddha's nirvana.

BUDDHIST DEVOTION

IN THE WEST, BUDDHISM is often regarded as a religion in which monastic contemplation holds center stage. This view obscures the importance of popular devotion in the history of the tradition. It is known, for example, that soon after his death, burial mounds or stupas containing the Buddha's relics were visited as a way of gaining merit. Pilgrimages to places made sacred by the Buddha's presence in his lifetime, such as Bodh Gaya (see pp.56–57), also became popular. In time, devotional cults grew up around several significant celestial Buddhas and *bodhisattvas* such as Amitabha and Avalokiteshvara. In China, the lohan (a corruption of the Sanskrit word *arhat*, meaning "Worthy One"), who were the 18 disciples who became enlightened in the Buddha's lifetime, were also important.

Disciple of the Buddha

AUSPICIOUS ACTIONS

Texts were written and chanted for devotional purposes, and temples in which elaborate rites were performed began to multiply, especially because it was considered more auspicious to build a new temple than to renovate an old one. For lay Buddhists in particular, devotional acts have a great significance. By performing meritorious actions, such as making donations of food, clothing, lodging, and medicine to members of the sangha (the community of monks) the lay Buddhist is assured of a favorable future birth. In this, the maximum possible opportunity is given for acting on the Buddha's teachings.

Temple of the Jade Buddha, Shanghai

In this temple, the Buddha is venerated by the 18 Lohan. Celebrated in Chinese Buddhist texts and iconography, the Lohan exemplify particular Buddhist virtues and qualities, such as skill in meditation, magical powers, ability to memorize texts, skill in teaching dharma, and pacifying wild animals. The Buddha is holding a lotus, an ancient symbol of purity and illumination. The lotus rises unstained through the impurity of the world, or the "mud," and therefore represents enlightened beings: buddhas, arhats, and bodhisattvas.

The Buddha and Four Disciples

At his first sermon at Sarnath, near Varanasi in northeast India, the Buddha taught the Four Noble Truths (see pp.54–55), as well as the Middle Path between the extremes of self-indulgent pleasure and self-denial. Four of the five ascetics traditionally believed to have attended this sermon are represented on this carving from Afghanistan, once a Buddhist country. All are focused in adoration on the central figure of the Buddha, who sits above a wheel motif, representing the teachings of the natural law (dharma) that was set in motion on that day. The two deer at the bottom of the carving remind us of the setting of the sermon – a deer park.

THE BUDDHA'S FOOTPRINTS

This carved slab formed part of the decorated surface of the stupa at Amaravati, once an important monastery and pilgrimage site in Andhra Pradesh in India. It depicts the Buddhapada, or footprints of the Buddha. Before it was customary to depict the Buddha naturalistically, this was the way his presence was symbolized, conveying an idea of his transcendental nature and power. The Buddha's feet were supposed to have been imprinted with 108 auspicious symbols, although this example shows fewer. Elaborate cults developed around the Buddhapada,

MYTHOLOGICAL MONSTER ● The *makara*, a mythological sea monster made up of an elephant's trunk and a fish's tail, acts as a protector for the central image. The border of lotus blossoms and buds emerge from the monster's mouth.

MARKS OF A SUPERMAN ● One of the 32 marks of a "superman" in Buddhist tradition is that he possesses toes that are long and straight. The visible toenails show that the upper surface of the toes is depicted.

The Svastika

The svastika is a traditional Indian symbol of good fortune, usually found on depictions of the palms and soles of the Buddha. It was adopted by the Nazis and its meaning was perverted.

WHEEL OF DHARMA

The central wheel is symbolic of the Buddha's teachings, which set the wheel of *dharma* in motion.

THE TRIPLE JEWEL

This three-pointed symbol represents the triple jewel, or *triratna*. The three jewels are the Buddha, his teaching (*dharma*), and the community of monks (*Sangha*), who preserve and transmit the Buddha's teachings. One definition of a Buddhist is someone "who takes refuge in the triple jewel."

A LOTUS BLOSSOM

A lotus blossom joins the *triratna* symbol. The lotus has its roots in mud, but it flowers into pure open space, and as such symbolizes the state of enlightenment, as well as the doctrine of the Buddha.

The Lotus

The lotus has come to be the symbol of the doctrine of Buddhism. As the community of monks, or sangha, comes from the doctrine, a common image is of a monk rising out of a lotus.

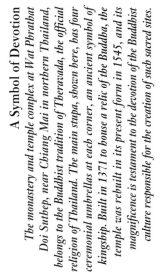

> "Having crossed over the turbulent sea of suffering on the vessel of Amida's great compassion, we are enabled to save every sentient being."
>
> YUI-EN, A DISCIPLE OF SHINRAN

A Symbol of Devotion

The monastery and temple complex at Wat Phrathat Doi Suthep, near Chiang Mai in northern Thailand, belongs to the Buddhist tradition of Theravada, the official religion of Thailand. The main stupa, shown here, has four ceremonial umbrellas at each corner, an ancient symbol of kingship. Built in 1371 to house a relic of the Buddha, the temple was rebuilt in its present form in 1545, and its magnificence is testament to the devotion of the Buddhist culture responsible for the creation of such sacred sites.

NOVICES OF THE PURE LAND SCHOOL

Young priests of the Pure Land school, one of the largest Buddhist sects in Japan today, are required to attend a ceremonial head-shaving. None of the boys are formally trained for a priesthood. The cardinal doctrine of the school, which was said to have been founded by the Chinese monk Hui Yuan (334–417 CE), is the saving power of Amitabha, the Buddha of the Western Region. This is at the root of a strongly devotional emphasis, in which the devotee must uproot all self-serving desires, even the desire for enlightenment itself, and abandon himself entirely to the power of Amitabha, who saves all those who have faith and trust in him. Another practice associated with the school is the chanting of the *nembutsu*, a simple *mantra* (sacred sound) in the form of "*Namu Amida Butsu*" or "Adoration to the Buddha Amitabha."

Young monks have their heads shaved

COSMOLOGY

BUDDHISTS SHARE THE SAME GENERAL UNDERSTANDING of the cosmos as other Indian religions. The cosmos is not permanent or created. At the summit are the four realms of purely mental rebirth, without form. Below them are the realms of pure form, where the gods dwell. Gods are prominent in ordinary Buddhist life, but they are not permanent, let alone eternal; they are themselves subject to rebirth and must seek enlightenment. At the lowest level is the realm of desire. This consists of the heavens, where the 33 Vedic gods of Hinduism dwell (see pp.20–21), including Indra, known as Sakka, who is the protector of Buddhism. Also included here are the levels on which animals, humans, and *asuras* (jealous gods) live. Below these are the realms of the hungry ghosts (*pretas*) and the hells.

Three Cardinal Faults

At the center of the Wheel of Life lie the three symbols of the cardinal faults of humanity: greed (the pig), hatred (the snake), and delusion (the rooster). The Buddha stated: "Consumed by craving, enraged by hatred, blinded by delusion, overwhelmed and despairing, man contemplates his own downfall, that of others, and both together."

WHEEL OF LIFE

The Wheel of Life, turned by Yama, Lord of the Dead, is depicted on a thang-kha, a temple hanging, dating from the 19th or 20th century. Thang-khas are used in meditation as a means of visualization.

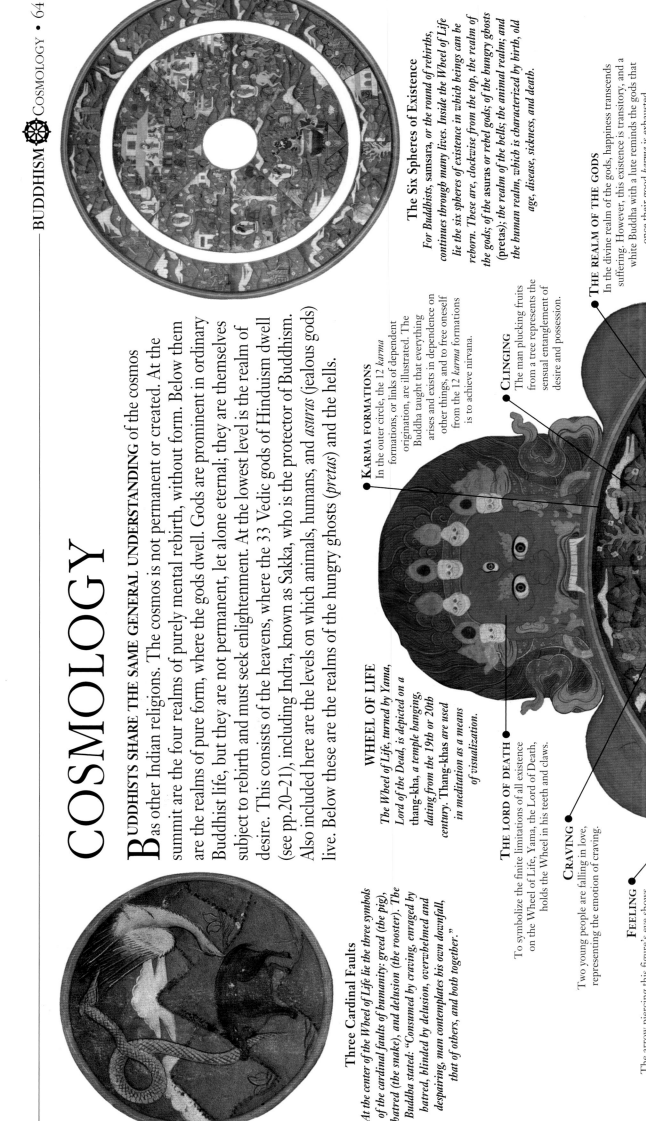

The Six Spheres of Existence

For Buddhists, samsara, or the round of rebirths, continues through many lives. Inside the Wheel of Life lie the six spheres of existence in which beings can be reborn. These are, clockwise from the top, the realm of the gods; of the asuras or rebel gods; of the hungry ghosts (pretas); the realm of the hells; the animal realm; and the human realm, which is characterized by birth, old age, disease, sickness, and death.

KARMA FORMATIONS
In the outer circle, the 12 *karma* formations, or links of dependent origination, are illustrated. The Buddha taught that everything arises and exists in dependence on other things, and to free oneself from the 12 *karma* formations is to achieve nirvana.

CLINGING
The man plucking fruits from a tree represents the sensual entanglement of desire and possession.

THE REALM OF THE GODS
In the divine realm of the gods, happiness transcends suffering. However, this existence is transitory, and a white Buddha with a lute reminds the gods that once their good *karma* is exhausted, they will leave this realm.

BECOMING
The man and woman are prisoners of the sensory stimulation of touch.

THE REALM OF THE ASURAS
The perpetual war in this realm is caused by the boundless envy of all creatures, often represented by people fighting over the fruit of the wishing tree. A green Buddha appears in warrior's armor, holding a flaming sword. He declares the virtue of moral restraint and orders the *asuras* to end their mighty struggles.

REBIRTH
The natural consequence of sensual contact and marriage is birth.

THE LORD OF DEATH
To symbolize the finite limitations of all existence on the Wheel of Life, Yama, the Lord of Death, holds the Wheel in his teeth and claws.

CRAVING
Two young people are falling in love, representing the emotion of craving.

FEELING
The arrow piercing this figure's eye shows the way in which emotions strike us.

THE REALM OF HUMANS
Suffering in the human realm is caused by egoism, ignorance, and desire. This gives rise to the perpetual cycle of birth, sickness, old age, and death. It is the most important of all the realms, because this is the only world in which a being has the power to control behavior, and to choose the Path of Bliss to enlightenment. A yellow Buddha preaches the virtue of willpower and dispensable energy, through which people may find the path to enlightenment.

CONTACT
The operation of the six senses results in contact with the things of the world and this in turn leads to the arising of feeling and desire.

THE REALM OF HUNGRY GHOSTS
Insatiable greed gives rise to the permanent hunger and thirst suffered in this realm, represented by grotesque figures with tightened throats and swollen stomachs. A red Buddha carries a vessel of celestial nourishment as a gift to the hungry ghosts or *pretas* and preaches the virtues of generosity and sacrifice.

OLD AGE AND DEATH
The inevitable consequence of birth is illness, anxiety, old age, and death.

IGNORANCE
Ignorance, represented here by a blind man, is the first in the traditional list of 12 factors.

THE REALM OF HELL
Cold-hearted hatred and burning anger transport creatures to the hell realms, the darkest of all worlds, to suffer the tortures of fiery heat and icy cold. An indigo Buddha appears with water (patience) and fire (the light of hope). He preaches the virtue of patience and reveals the way to the light.

ACTS OF VOLITION
The potters mold their own fate (*karma*) in the pots they produce, each one representing a deed, such as acting, thinking, or speaking.

THE SIX SENSES
The six senses acknowledged by Buddhism are sight, smell, taste, hearing, touch, and thought.

THE REALM OF BEASTS
The realm of beasts is ruled by ignorance, apathy, lethargy, instinctive action, and spiritual incapacity. This state brings suffering upon the animals: humans devour one another. A blue Buddha holds the Book of Insight in order to teach the animals the benefits of perfect wisdom, entry into the realm of knowledge, and the cosmic laws.

NAME AND FORM
The activity of consciousness conditions the arising of name and form, symbolized here by two figures.

CONSCIOUSNESS
The monkey swinging randomly from branch to branch represents the absence of control over consciousness, one of the goals of Buddhism.

> *"But what, O monks, is the noble truth of the origin of suffering? It is that desire which results in rebirth, that desire bound up with longing and greed, which indulges itself now here, now there; the desire of the senses, the desire to be, the desire to destroy oneself."*
>
> THE BUDDHA

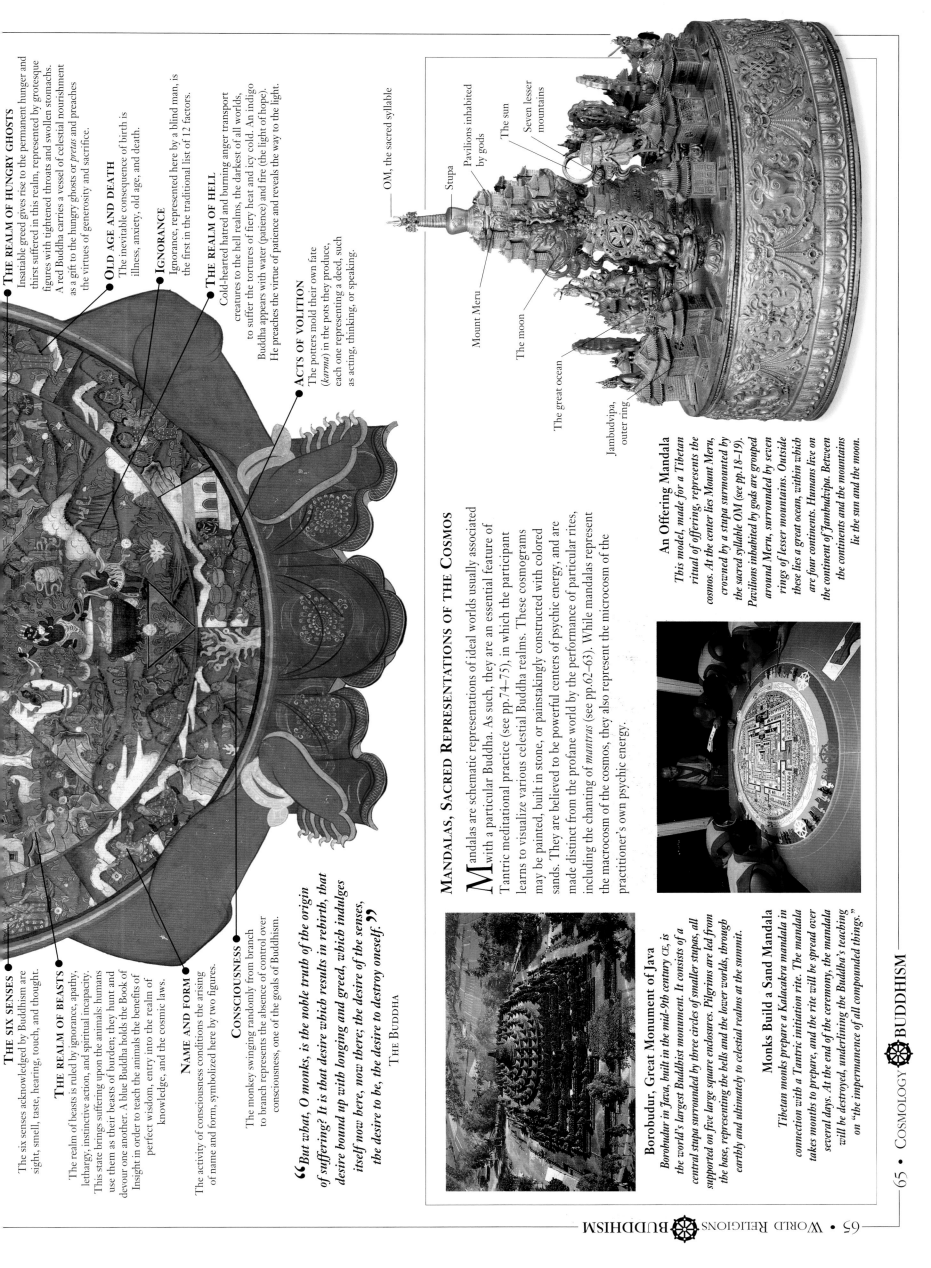

MANDALAS, SACRED REPRESENTATIONS OF THE COSMOS

Mandalas are schematic representations of ideal worlds usually associated with a particular Buddha. As such, they are an essential feature of Tantric meditational practice (see pp.74–75), in which the participant learns to visualize various celestial Buddha realms. These cosmograms may be painted, built in stone, or painstakingly constructed with colored sands. They are believed to be powerful centers of psychic energy, and are made distinct from the profane world by the performance of particular rites, including the chanting of *mantras* (see pp.62–63). While mandalas represent the macrocosm of the cosmos, they also represent the microcosm of the practitioner's own psychic energy.

An Offering Mandala
This model, made for a Tibetan ritual of offering, represents the cosmos. At the center lies Mount Meru, crowned by a stupa surmounted by the sacred syllable OM (see pp.18–19). Pavilions inhabited by gods are grouped around Meru, surrounded by seven rings of lesser mountains. Outside these lies a great ocean, within which are four continents. Humans live on the continent of Jambudvipa. Between the continents and the mountains lie the sun and the moon.

OM, the sacred syllable
Stupa
Pavilions inhabited by gods
The sun
Seven lesser mountains
Mount Meru
The moon
The great ocean
Jambudvipa, outer ring

Borobudur, Great Monument of Java
Borobudur in Java, built in the mid-9th century CE, is the world's largest Buddhist monument. It consists of a central stupa surrounded by three circles of smaller stupas, all supported on five large square enclosures. Pilgrims are led from the base, representing the hells and the lower worlds, through earthly and ultimately to celestial realms at the summit.

Monks Build a Sand Mandala
Tibetan monks prepare a Kalacakra mandala in connection with a Tantric initiation rite. The mandala takes months to prepare, and the rite will be spread over several days. At the end of the ceremony, the mandala will be destroyed, underlining the Buddha's teaching on "the impermanence of all compounded things."

Samye Monastery, Tibet
Samye is the oldest monastery in Tibet. It is alleged that it was only possible to construct the complex after the area had been exorcised from antagonistic forces by the Tantric yogi Padmasambhava. This involved the drawing of an enormous mandala (cosmic representation), which became the ground plan of the monastery. At the center is a temple that once contained golden images of the Buddha. The central temple is surrounded by four stupas (memorial mounds) at each corner. Samye has been significantly damaged since the Chinese occupation of Tibet.

SPIRITUALLY CLEANSING •
This preface to the main text requires the reciter of the *sutra* to purify his mouth with a *mantra*, a sacred sound. The opening passage of the *sutra* proper starts with the traditional phrase: "Thus I have heard . . ."

**THE DIAMOND SUTRA,
FROM THE PERFECTION OF WISDOM**
This Chinese Diamond Sutra, *dated 868 CE, is the oldest printed existing book. Recovered from the cave temples of Tun-huang at the beginning of this century, this 16-foot-long (nearly five-meter) scroll, printed with wooden blocks, is part of the* Perfection of Wisdom *text, a Mahayanist sermon preached by the Buddha. The picture shows the opening scene of the Buddha preaching to an audience.*

Monks at Mandalay, Burma
*Young Burmese novice monks stand before a ceremonial complex including a stupa or pagoda in the background. In the Theravada form of Buddhism found in Burma, ordination into the community of monks (*Sangha*) is a two-fold process. From the age of eight, a boy may be accepted as a "novice," then full membership of the* Sangha *is conferred by a higher ordination at about the age of 20.*

TEXTS AND MONASTERIES

T HE BUDDHA SAW HIMSELF as a physician and teacher who pointed the way to enlightenment. As a result, his teachings (and teachings derived from his teachings) are highly revered. The *Three Jewels* or *Refuges* state: "I take refuge in the Buddha, . . . in his *dhamma* (teaching), . . . in the *Sangha* (communities of monks)." Thus texts and monasteries are closely related. Buddhism does not have a collection of texts constituting a "Bible," but early collections were made especially for the *Sangha*. The *Pali Tripitaka*, or "Triple Basket," is among the earliest. Different areas of Buddhism produced their own canons or collections. Those of Tibet and China are notable. According to tradition, the canon began at the Council of Rajagrha after the Buddha was cremated, when Ananda and Upali recited his discourses and the regulations for monks, which became the *Suttapitaka* and the *Vinayapitaka*. The origin of a third collection, the *Abhidhammapitaka* (further teaching and analysis), is disputed. In Mahayana Buddhism (see pp.54–55), what is claimed to be more developed teaching of Buddha is preserved in *sutras*.

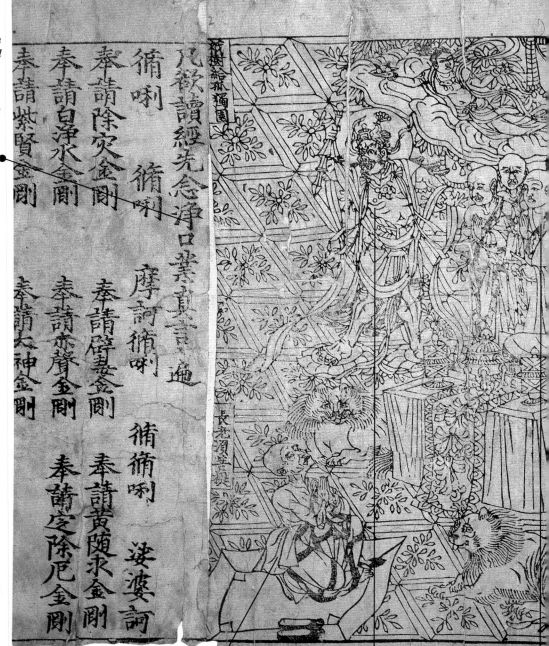

SUBHUTI, THE BUDDHA'S DISCIPLE •
Subhuti is one of the Buddha's most advanced disciples. It is Subhuti's request for the means of obtaining perfect wisdom that prompts the Buddha to preach the *Diamond Sutra*. Subhuti's stance suggests reverence for the Buddha.

OF LOWLY STATUS
A protector deity stands next to the Buddha. It is most probably an *asura*, a warlike, quarrelsome spirit that is far down on the chain of rebirths.

AN AUDIENCE OF MONKS
According to the text of the *Diamond Sutra*, 1,250 monks were present when the Buddha delivered his discourse.

Celestial Beings
Celestial beings fly above the Buddha. These are most probably gandharvas, *the lowest-ranking members of the divine realms.* Gandharvas *are heavenly musicians.*

THE BUDDHA
The Buddha sits on a lotus throne expounding the *Diamond Sutra*. His right hand is in the gesture of teaching and his left hand indicates meditative calm. His third eye, symbolic of inner wisdom, comprises a sun and moon, a famous Tantric symbol.

TWO BODHISATTVAS
Bodhisattvas are those believed to be well advanced on the path toward enlightenment. The majesty of these *bodhisattvas* is symbolized by their halos and crowns.

THE MANUSCRIPT OF THE PERFECTION OF WISDOM

These four palm leaves are from an 11th-century text called the *Perfection of Wisdom Sutra*, which has 8,000 verses. This Sanskrit text, bound between wooden boards and threaded with string, was prepared by a pious layman living in eastern India. Texts of this kind were very important in early Mahayana Buddhism (see pp.54–55). It seems that the copying of the text was commonly considered a means of acquiring religious merit at this period. The palm leaves are richly illustrated with scenes from the life of the Buddha, and with images of celestial *bodhisattvas* and divinities, including Prajnaparamita, the personification of perfected wisdom and the mother of all Buddhas.

The Buddha is born from the right side of his mother, Queen Maya, while she stands holding the branch of a tree. The Buddha was born to the warrior Suddhodana and Maya in Lumbini, southern Nepal, traditionally in about 566 BCE.

The Buddha preaches his first sermon (see pp.54–55) to two of the five ascetics present in the deer park in Sarnath, near what is now Varanasi in northern India. His hands are held in the classical teaching posture.

A celestial bodhisattva, *probably Maitreya, sits with his hands held in the teaching posture. Maitreya is a beautiful young man dwelling at present in the Tusita heaven. He will come to earth and become the next Buddha in time.*

Candraprabha is the "moonlight bodhisattva." For many, the bodhisattvas *are manifestations of the wisdom and compassion of the Buddha.*

GOOD FORTUNE
A *svastika*, a traditional Indian symbol of good fortune, is on the chest of the Buddha. It is usually found on the palms or footsoles of Buddha images.

PIOUS LAYMEN
Pious laymen and women, with servants in attendance, listen to the sermon, dressed in the regalia of Chinese dignitaries.

CELESTIAL BEINGS

MAHAYANA (GREAT VEHICLE) BUDDHISM (see pp.54–55) develops teachings of the Buddha not found in the earliest texts or found only in outline. They are believed to have been held back until people were sufficiently advanced in understanding to receive them. The Buddha used *upaya*, "skill-in-means," adjusting his teaching to the level of those listening, so Mahayana Buddhists see nothing strange in this elaboration of his teaching. An important belief is that the attainment of enlightenment or nirvana is not to be kept to oneself as an *arhat* (perfected one) but is to be shared with all suffering and striving beings. The celestial beings who help others are *bodhisattvas*, and they in turn are related to Buddhas who are manifestations of the Buddha-nature. Buddhas reign over Buddha-lands, where the faithful can come as the last stage before nirvana. Visualizing the Buddhas or *bodhisattvas*, and so attaining union with them, is a basic form of devotion. This was originally called *nembutsu*, "mindfulness of the Buddha." Pure Land Buddhists place emphasis on the grace of Amitabha, the Buddha of the western region of space. Faith in his power is said to result in rebirth in Sukhavati, where suffering is absent.

THE BODHISATTVAS

A *bodhisattva*, literally meaning "enlightened existence," is an advanced spiritual being who has chosen not to pass into nirvana, the state of complete enlightenment, but to continue in the round of rebirth in order to help others. Once a *bodhisattva* does enter nirvana, he or she is no longer in a position to help anyone, having no further links with the world. The career of a *bodhisattva* will last three, seven, or 33 eons, during which time they accumulate an inexhaustible store of merit through the perfecting of generosity, morality, patience, vigor, meditation, and wisdom. Beyond these six perfections, the *bodhisattva* progresses to four final stages of the path in which it becomes possible for him or her to manifest various supernatural powers. When the tenth stage, or "ground," is completed, the *bodhisattva* attains supreme enlightenment and becomes a Buddha.

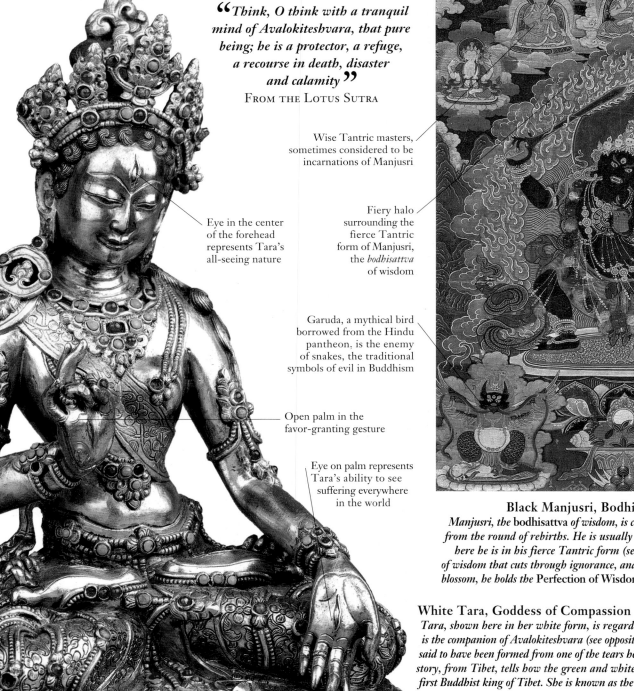

"Think, O think with a tranquil mind of Avalokiteshvara, that pure being; he is a protector, a refuge, a recourse in death, disaster and calamity"
FROM THE LOTUS SUTRA

Eye in the center of the forehead represents Tara's all-seeing nature

Open palm in the favor-granting gesture

Eye on palm represents Tara's ability to see suffering everywhere in the world

Wise Tantric masters, sometimes considered to be incarnations of Manjusri

Fiery halo surrounding the fierce Tantric form of Manjusri, the *bodhisattva* of wisdom

Garuda, a mythical bird borrowed from the Hindu pantheon, is the enemy of snakes, the traditional symbols of evil in Buddhism

Black Manjusri, Bodhisattva of Wisdom
Manjusri, the bodhisattva of wisdom, is concerned with helping people escape from the round of rebirths. He is usually depicted as a beautiful young man; here he is in his fierce Tantric form (see pp.74–75). He wields the sword of wisdom that cuts through ignorance, and in his left hand, balanced on a lotus blossom, he holds the Perfection of Wisdom Sutra, an important Buddhist text.

White Tara, Goddess of Compassion
Tara, shown here in her white form, is regarded as the mother of all Buddhas. She is the companion of Avalokiteshvara (see opposite), the bodhisattva of compassion, and is said to have been formed from one of the tears he shed over the suffering of others. Another story, from Tibet, tells how the green and white forms of Tara were the two wives of the first Buddhist king of Tibet. She is known as the "cheater of death," her devotees believe that she bestows a long life free from all dangers. In this statue, the eyes in the center of her forehead and on the palm of her hands indicate her all-seeing nature.

TIBETAN TEACHERS
Around the image of Avalokiteshvara are depicted Tibetan lamas – spiritual teachers – of the red-hat or Kagyudpa school.

ENLIGHTENMENT
Avalokiteshvara holds a lotus blossom, a Buddhist symbol of enlightenment.

THE BUDDHA
The Buddha shown here is the most recent of a line of 25 Buddhas. At some stage in the far-distant future, Avalokiteshvara will attain supreme Buddhahood.

Eleven-headed Celestial Being
Avalokiteshvara is shown with 11 heads. The red one at the top is Amitabha, the Buddha with whom Avalokiteshvara is especially associated. Avalokiteshvara is invoked by people in distress to save them and lead them to Amitabha, ruler of the Western region, one of the many worlds of Mahayana cosmology. There, Amitabha looks after them on their way to nirvana.

PRINCELY ORNAMENTATION
Avalokiteshvara wears the princely ornamentation associated with celestial *bodhisattvas*. The heavily bejeweled earlobes are particularly typical of Tibetan iconography.

BOW AND ARROW
The bow and arrow, suggesting the *bodhisattva*'s ability to aim at the heart of all beings, is a common Tantric symbol.

CUPPED HANDS
The central pair of hands are depicted in an attitude of homage.

AURA
The aura around Avalokiteshvara is made up of 1,000 arms symbolizing his inexhaustible compassion.

AVALOKITESHVARA
Avalokiteshvara constantly delays his entry into nirvana in order to help others attain enlightenment. The present Dalai Lama, spiritual leader of Tibet, is believed to be a reincarnation of Avalokiteshvara.

WHITE TARA
White Tara, one of the forms of Avalokiteshvara's female companion, is known as the Savioress. She is particularly popular in Tibet, of which she is the patron goddess.

BODHISATTVA AVALOKITESHVARA
This temple hanging, or thang-kha, depicts Avalokiteshvara, "the Lord who looks down." It is associated with the red-hat school and was used as an aid to visualization. Avalokiteshvara is the bodhisattva of compassion and probably the most popular of Buddhist celestial beings. He features prominently in the Lotus Sutra (see pp.110–11). Between births, not always in human form, he withdraws to Sukhavati – the Buddha realm of Amitabha (see above).

GREEN TARA
Green Tara, like White Tara, is Avalokiteshvara's companion. Although the symbolism of the two often differs, here they differ only in terms of color.

EIGHT-SPOKED WHEEL
Avalokiteshvara is said to have 108 forms. Here he is depicted with a thousand arms, and in a right hand he holds the eight-spoked wheel symbolic of the Buddha's teaching (see pp.62–63).

EYE OF COMPASSION
The eye at the center of Avalokiteshvara's prominently exposed hand is symbolic of his all-seeing nature as well as his compassion.

Cross-legged meditation posture

Elongated earlobes, one of the signs of an enlightened being

CHINESE BUDDHISM

BUDDHISM FLOURISHED IN CHINA during the T'ang dynasty (618–907CE) and is still a major religious and cultural influence. It appealed because the concept of enlightenment, rebirth, and *karma*, the moral law of cause and effect, offered individuals responsibility for their own fate and an opportunity for salvation. Through meditation, ritual, chanting, teaching, and the study of Buddhist texts, monks and nuns were seen as gaining merit for future lives, and even gained merit for their families and lay supporters. The sophisticated philosophy of Buddhist texts attracted many scholarly Chinese, while the opportunity for an improved rebirth, or birth in the Buddha Amitabha's Western Paradise, and the use of art and architecture appealed to ordinary people. Buddhist funeral rites helped dispel anxieties about the fate of dead relatives, and many emperors supported Buddhism because it was seen as encouraging moral and peaceful citizens.

Celestial Infants Pay Homage
Infants paying homage to Kuan Yin confirm her association with children. Their hands are held in the Buddhist mudra (hand sign) of respect, which also represents the union of the spiritual with the physical.

The Worthy One
This ceramic statue of a Lohan is from 10th- or 11th-century China. A Lohan is a "Worthy One", a person who is enlightened. The 18 Lohan were disciples of the Buddha who became enlightened during his lifetime. They were celebrated in Chinese Buddhist texts and paintings, and often exemplify particular Buddhist virtues, such as skill in meditation, magical powers, the ability to memorize texts, skill in teaching the dharma (see pp.54–55), and taming wild animals. The Buddha's own son was one of them. The Lohan depicted reflects a meditative, peaceful quality and inner strength, and may be the 14th Lohan, Vanavasa.

FLAMING JEWEL
Kuan Yin holds a flaming jewel symbolizing her role as "Granter of Desires and Petitions." The jewel is a key symbol in Buddhism. It represents the brilliance and purity of the *dharma* (see pp.54–55), the teachings of the Buddhas, and the truth that underlies those teachings. The Buddha, the *dharma*, and the *Sangha* (the spiritual community) are known as the Three Jewels.

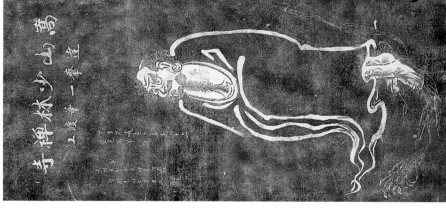

Bodhidharma, First Patriarch of Ch'an
This stone rubbing from the Ming dynasty (1368–1644CE) depicts Bodhidharma, the first patriarch of Ch'an Buddhism, whose name is associated in China with serious meditation, ascetic discipline, and psychic power. He was a south-Indian prince who became a monk and traveled to China in the late 5th century. Having condemned the practice of merit-making as materialistic, he meditated in a cave for nine years. His ascetic practices are associated with yoga and the Shaolin school of martial arts.

BUDDHA OF THE WESTERN PARADISE
In Kuan Yin's crown is Amitabha, Buddha of the Pure Land or Western Paradise. Those showing devotion to either will be reborn there

MEDITATIONAL AID
Kuan Yin is elaborately dressed in the style of a royal *bodhisattva*, evident in the large jeweled rosary she is wearing. The rosary is a fundamental aid to Buddhist prayer and meditation. Her right hand makes a *mudra* or hand sign that signifies the teaching of the Buddha.

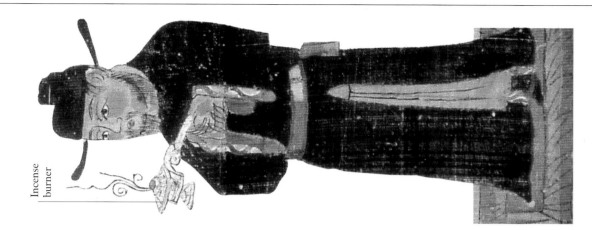

Incense burner

CELESTIAL ATTENDANTS

Kuan Yin's two celestial attendants are holding scrolls that are almost certainly the text of the Kuan Shih Yin chapter of the *Lotus Sutra* (see pp.110–11), one of the most important scriptures in Chinese Buddhism. They are dressed in the style of royal attendants.

KUAN SHIH YIN

This 10th-century painting depicts Kuan Shih Yin, a form of Avalokiteshvara, Bodhisattva of Compassion (see pp.68–69). She is the goddess of mercy and the giver of children, and is said to appear as a young woman to help people in distress. It is said that those in danger should call on Kuan Yin by name, and anyone undertaking a dangerous journey will make offerings to her.

THE LOTUS

The lotus is one of the oldest Buddhist symbols. Because the stem produces a beautiful flower with its roots in the mud, it represents purity and perfection rising through and above the mud of worldliness and impurity. It serves as the throne for Buddhas and *bodhisattvas*.

“*If there be countless myriads of millions of beings, suffering pain and torment, who bear the name of Kuan Shih Yin Bodhisattva and single-mindedly recite the name, Kuan Shih Yin will bear their cries and all shall be delivered.*”

FROM THE LOTUS SUTRA, CHANTED IN CHINESE BUDDHIST CEREMONIES

OFFERING TO KUAN YIN

The painting is in the form of an offering to Kuan Yin. A senior official, Mi Huang Te, commissioned it to commemorate his family pilgrimage to Tun huang, a temple complex in Chinese Central Asia. He undertook the journey because he had to make an official tour of inspection to Tai Han Shan in the Western Province. As a devout Buddhist, he is requesting Kuan Yin's protection.

THE CHINESE BUDDHAS

Buddhism entered China around the 1st century CE, and by the 4th century many Buddhist works were translated from Sanskrit into Chinese. This meant that the Buddhas and *bodhisattvas* of India came to have their own forms: Avalokiteshvara (see pp.68–69) became Kuan Shih Yin; Maitreya the Buddha-to-be, usually depicted as a beautiful young man, became the overweight Laughing Buddha, and Amitabha, the Buddha of the Pure Land, was believed to have come from the Kun-lun mountains of China.

The Donor of the Painting

An official is depicted holding an incense burner, paying homage to Kuan Yin. He is the donor of the painting, Mi Huang Te. The inscription says: "Donor Mi Huang Te eternally and wholeheartedly pays homage." His younger brothers have accompanied him to pay their respects.

Children of the Donor

On the lower level of the painting are the children and grandchildren of the painting's donor, Mi Huang Te, depicted as respectful devotees of Kuan Yin. Above them is the wife of the donor and her sisters-in-law. The compassion and kindness of Kuan Yin are seen as female virtues.

Relatives of the painting's donor

JAPANESE BUDDHISM

BUDDHISM ARRIVED IN JAPAN ABOUT **1,000** YEARS after the time of the Buddha, by way of Korea. Since the 7th century CE, waves of Buddhism, principally of the Mahayana variety (see p.55), reached Japan from China. These were mainly introduced by Japanese monks who had sojourned in Chinese monasteries. The most widely known forms that arrived in this manner are Tendai; Shingon, a Tantric variety; the Pure Land schools (see p.110); and the three major sects of Zen, the Japanese version of Chinese Ch'an Buddhism: Rinzai, Soto, and Obaku. In the 13th century the monk Nichiren established a purely Japanese form based on an interpretation of the *Lotus Sutra*, a central text of Tendai.

❝At an old temple, in cold weather, he spent the night. He could not stand the piercing cold of the whirling wind. If it has no sacred ashes, what is there so special about it? So he took the wooden Buddha from the hall and burned it. ❞
POEM FROM THE PAINTING BELOW,
BY CH'U-SHIH FAN-CH'I, ZEN MASTER

The Zen of Calligraphy
*Calligraphy (*shodo*) is one of the Rinzai Zen arts imported from China during the Kamakura period (1185–1333). Above is an example of the work of a Zen master of the 17th century. Putting brush to paper is in itself to enter into the single Buddha-nature (see pp.68–69) of all things.*

NEW SCHOOLS OF BUDDHISM

In the last century new forms of Buddhism have emerged, most notably Soka Gakkai, a lay movement with origins in Nichiren Buddhism. Along with many Japanese new religious movements, Soka Gakkai has a high profile and emphasizes individual and social reform. About three-quarters of the Japanese population are Buddhist, although many of these are equally at home venerating the divine spirits (*kami*) of Shinto.

A ZEN PAINTING

This fragment of a much larger scroll was painted in the 13th to 14th century by Yin-t'o-lo. Although not Japanese but more probably Indian or Chinese, this picture was much admired by the Japanese because it articulates one of the central teachings of Zen.

THE IMPORTANCE OF TEA

Tradition says that the Japanese monk Eisai (1141–1215) brought seeds of the tea bush back from China in 1168 and planted them in the grounds of his temple. Since that date the "way of tea" (*chado*) has been connected with Eisai's Rinzai school of Zen; it is an element of Chinese culture cultivated and transformed by Rinzai. In China, tea had already been used to harmonize the various organs of the body. Although not strictly religious, *chado* is intimately bound up with the spirit of Zen – it is said that "Zen and tea have the same taste." Eisai introduced the Rinzai form of Zen to Japan, which seeks a spontaneous form of *satori* – a Japanese expression for the reaching of enlightenment – gained through a meditative absorption in all things.

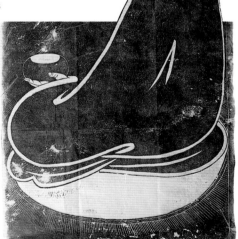

Bodhidharma
Bodhidharma was an Indian monk who founded the Ch'an – or Zen – form of Buddhism. His form of spirituality based on meditation influenced Japanese arts such as calligraphy, garden-making, and the tea ceremony.

The Tea House
The tea room and its garden are based on the design set by Sen no Rikyu (1521–91), the master who is generally considered to have brought the tea ceremony to its present form. Drinking tea is seen as "an adoration of the beautiful among the sordid facts of everyday existence."

古寺天寒度一宵不堪風泠雪聲
嗟若何專特些取堂中木佛燒

SEAL OF THE ARTIST
The seal of the artist Yin-t'o-lo states: "Children do not know that snowflakes in heaven are just willow flowers." To the left of it is the seal of the poet Ch'u-shih.

> **"*A special tradition outside the scriptures; No dependence on words and letters; Pointing directly into the mind; Seeing into one's own nature and the attainment of Buddhahood.*"**
>
> A VERSE ATTRIBUTED TO
> BODHIDHARMA, THE FOUNDER OF ZEN

THE MONK

The monk from Tan-hsia keeps warm on a cold day. This is a traditional Zen story. When criticized by the abbot of the monastery for burning a Buddha image, he responded that it was simply a piece of wood. The story underlines Zen's indifference, perhaps even hostility, to the worship of images.

Buddhism in Modern Japan

Japanese Buddhism has undergone significant changes in recent times. The most traumatic period was between 1868 and 1875 when an officially sanctioned Shinto-inspired "Exterminate Buddhas and Destroy Shakyamuni" movement led to the destruction of many Buddhist temples and sacred objects. In retrospect, what seemed like a grave setback at the time led to a substantial resurgence and modernization of Buddhism in Japan, in spite of the fact that many monasteries lost their traditional landholdings as a result of agrarian reform at the end of World War II.

SOURCE OF MEDITATION

This genre of painting attempts to capture the essence of the teachings of Zen masters of the past. Such stories were very popular and provided suitable topics for monastic meditation.

LANDSCAPE ART

This fairly typical ink-painted Chinese landscape style was copied in Japanese Buddhist art, and although few works by the artist survive, he was greatly admired by the Japanese.

ZEN BUDDHISM

Although not as popular as the Pure Land and Nichiren-derived schools of Buddhism, Zen is probably the most widely known form of Japanese Buddhism in the West. It has undergone significant development and sectarian division throughout its 800-year history in Japan. The two most prominent schools of Zen today are Rinzai and Soto. Both have their origins in China. Rinzai is sometimes termed the "shouting and beating school." This designation derives from the manner in which its founder, Lin-chi, gained enlightenment. Many stories circulate concerning the exuberant behavior of its masters, often acting in ways not usually approved of. The central meditative practice of Rinzai focuses on *Koan*, an enigmatic saying or question. The Soto school, on the other hand, stresses *zazen*, "sitting in meditation." According to Dogen (1200–1253), the most important figure in Soto history, *zazen* is understood not as a means to enlightenment but rather as an expression of the enlightened state.

IMAGE OF THE BUDDHA

A wooden image of the Buddha is wreathed in smoke and fire. Pious Buddhists would have regarded this act as the epitome of sacrilege, although the monk here is clearly unconcerned.

THE ABBOT

The abbot from the monastery is remonstrating with the monk for burning an image of the Buddha in order to keep warm.

TANTRIC BUDDHISM

THE WAY OF TANTRA arose in the 6th century CE, based on texts known as Tantras. It uses meditation, ritual, symbolism, and magic. Although magic was not part of the Buddha's teaching, Tantric practitioners regard Tantra as a faster way of attaining the Buddha-nature than the path of the *bodhisattvas* (see pp.68–69). The forms of Tantra using *mantras*, powerful sacred sounds, are known as Mantrayana. Tantra tries to realize the continuous connection between all human states and conditions, including ones that are usually thought polluting or dangerous; all are the Buddha-nature, if perceived and experienced rightly. Thus hatred and revulsion, which are the oppositions of love and desire, dissolve in the realization that all states are equally the undifferentiated Buddha-nature and are without real characteristics of their own.

VEHICLE OF THE THUNDERBOLT

Another name for Tantric Buddhism is *Vajrayana*, the Vehicle of the Thunderbolt. The *vajra* is a double-headed ritual implement, used with a bell. Held in the right hand, it represents the masculine, skillful means, and compassion. The bell in the left hand represents the feminine, wisdom, emptiness, and nirvana. It is especially common in Tibet. In the *Vajrayana* the five *Jinas*, eminent ones, also known as *dhyani-Buddha*, are a major focus of meditation. They are Akshobya, Amitabha, Amoghasiddhi, Ratnasambhava, and Vairocana.

A State of Being
The central image, the Buddha Kalacakra, is not a god. He represents a state of being that the initiate wishes to achieve.

Nairatmya, Hevajra's consort, is the personification of freedom

A *vajra* chopper

Passionate embrace, representing the enlightened bliss that comes from the union of wisdom and compassion

Hevajra tramples on his own form, showing conquest over egoism

SECOND PALACE
The second palace or enclosure contains eight eight-petaled lotuses that contain the 64 goddesses of speech, the mothers of all mantras. In the center of each lotus we find a divine couple in which the female is dominant.

Hevajra and his Consort
In the Tantric system, the many-headed Hevajra is one of the wrathful manifestations of Aksobhya, the Imperturbable Buddha (see opposite). These wrathful forms symbolize the transformation of the poisons, in this case anger, that bind us to the world of becoming (samsara). He is depicted in embrace with his consort Nairatmya.

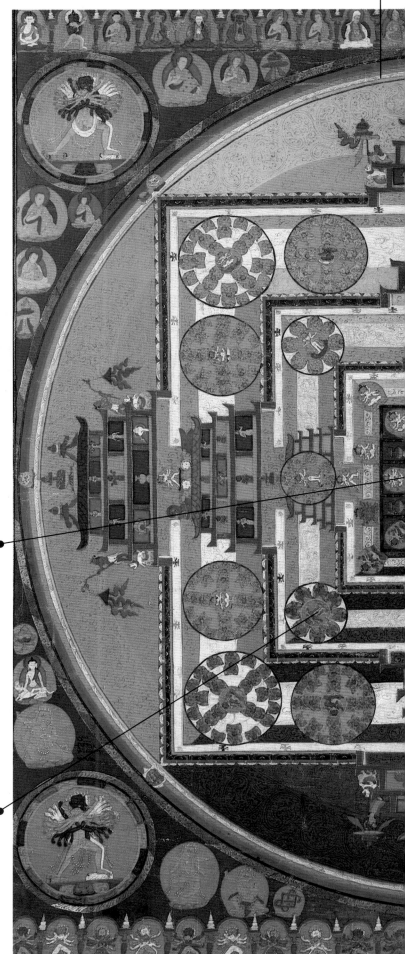

THE BURNING GROUND ENCLOSURE
The burning ground enclosure lies beyond the boundaries of the three palaces. The four differently colored segments represent the four elements from which all things are made.

EIGHT FEMALE DEITIES
Around the central couple are eight female deities with four faces and eight arms, each on the petal of a lotus.

MANDALA OF THE KALACAKRA TANTRA

This mandala is an expression of the teachings of the Kalacakra (Wheel of Time) Tantra, a prominent text in the Supreme Yoga class of tantras. It shows the purified universe of the all-embracing Buddha Kalacakra attended by 722 deities, all regarded as emanations of the central couple. It is both a depiction of the ideal world and a meditational device. The practitioner visualizes Kalacakra's world in every detail until the subtle psychology of their body is in harmony with the structure of the mandala.

PROTECTOR DEITIES

Images of protector deities, both wrathful and benign, are contained in the outer section of the mandala. The expressions of rage or passion that these fierce deities exhibit signify an immense degree of energy.

Tantric staff, topped by crossed bolts of thunder or *vajras* and three skulls and a trident

Elaborate head-gear with an eagle's feather, unique to Padmasambhava

Vase containing the elixir of immortality

Vajra, a thunderbolt symbolizing compassion

Padmasambhava, the Lotus-Born
Padmasambhava helped establish Buddhism in Tibet in the mid-8th century by exercising his Tantric powers to subdue demons. Believed to be an emanation of Amitabha Buddha (see below), he is said to have emerged from a lotus blossom. After his time on earth, he withdrew to the Copper Mountain Paradise, home to the cannibal trolls, where he reigns as a second Buddha. The crossed vajras on his trident signify the union of wisdom and compassion, and the trident and three skulls are the symbols for mastery of the three subtle channels of Tantric physiology.

CENTRAL PALACE
In the middle of the central palace is the Buddha Kalacakra in an eternal embrace with his female consort Visvamata ("all-mother"). They are in the Tantric *yab-yum* ("mother-father") posture. This is the heart of Buddhahood, which is gradually revealed through the practice of visualization and yoga.

THIRD PALACE
The third, outermost palace houses twelve 28-petaled lotuses on which rest 360 deities, representing the days of the year. The 12 lotuses represent the months of the year. Each one has a deity couple, with the male dominant, at its center.

BELIEF IN MANY BUDDHAS

Buddhism has always held that the historical Buddha was one in a line of enlightened beings, all of whom preached the same religious message of liberation. In time this idea was elaborated into the view that the number of Buddhas were "as numerous as there are grains of sand on the banks of the river Ganges." Some of these celestial Buddhas, such as Amitabha, Vairocana, Aksobhya, and Amogasiddhi, became objects of popular devotion, and detailed descriptions of their Buddha-lands feature in many Mahayana texts. Tantric Buddhists see each one as a particular manifestation of the Buddha-essence. Tantric practitioners, under a guru's supervision, learn to visualize and identify with one of these aspects of the Buddhahood. The techniques involved include mantra recitation and meditation on the deity's mandala. These may be supplemented by yogic techniques aimed at altering the balance of subtle forces within the body.

THREE PALACES
The path to the central chamber passes through three concentric palaces, each one punctured at the middle of its four sides by increasingly ornate triumphal gates, which are protected by both fierce and benign deities. The path to the central chamber represents the journey of the initiate to the Buddhahood that rests in the heart of all beings. Entry through the gates may be achieved through the correct use of mantras and other tantric techniques.

Masters of Tantra
Along the edges of the mandala are Indian and Tibetan masters of Kalacakra Tantra. It is common for Tantric practitioners to focus on the mandala of a particular Buddha, and the course of an individual's spiritual history may demand that he or she learn and assimilate a given mandala for a special occasion.

SIKHISM

DEVOTION TO THE GURU

LIKE RELATED WORDS in many Indian languages, the Punjabi word *sikh* means "learner." In the religious sense, a Sikh is someone who believes in one God, *Sat Guru*, or "true teacher," and follows the Gurus who reveal his teachings. In Indian religion, a guru is any religious teacher or guide, but for the Sikhs, the Gurus are more specific. They are God as *Sat Guru*; the ten leaders of the Sikh faith, from the founder, Guru Nanak (1469–1539), to Guru Gobind Singh (1666–1708); and the Adi Granth, the "original volume," which is revered as Guru Granth Sahib, the Sikh scripture that became the final Guru after the death of Guru Gobind Singh.

According to Rahit Maryada, an authoritative guide on Sikh life, "A Sikh is any woman or man whose faith consists of belief in one God, the ten Gurus, the teachings of the Guru Granth Sahib and of the ten Gurus, who has faith in the *amrit* of the tenth Guru, and who adheres to no other religion."

Amrit (literally "undying," the nectar of immortality) is holy, sweetened water that is used in the ceremony of initiation into the dedicated Sikh community, the Khalsa (see pp.86–87). The Khalsa began in 1699, when it was instituted by Guru Gobind Singh. The members are given rules of discipline and are outwardly marked by their keeping of the five "Ks" – five items beginning with the letter K: *Kesh*, uncut hair, showing acceptance of God's will; *Kangha*, the comb, showing controlled spirituality; *Kirpan*, the steel dagger, showing determination to defend what is true; *Kara*, the steel bangle worn on the wrist, showing unity with God and binding to the Guru; and *Kachh*, an undergarment, showing moral strength.

Sikhism began in North India in the 15th century CE, with the life and teaching of Guru Nanak. At that time there was tension between the Hindus and the Muslims (it was the beginning of the Mughal Empire) and some holy people, especially the poet Kabir, and various religious movements, especially the Vaishnavites, the Hindu followers of the god Vishnu (see pp.26–27), sought a love of God beyond religious conflict. Guru Nanak was influenced by these groups, and stated: "There is no Hindu or Muslim, so whose path shall I follow? I shall follow the path of God." But Guru Nanak was moved even more by his own profound experience of God.

As a result, he made sure that there would be a movement to follow his way by appointing a Guru to succeed him.

Guru Nanak emphasized the absolute unity and sovereignty of God. He believed that God created all things, and that all things are dependent on God's will or *hukam*. God does not become manifest in the world (unlike the *avatars* of Hindu belief – see p.27), but his will becomes known through the Gurus. For this reason meditation (*nam simaran*, remembrance of the name) is of the highest importance for Sikhs, especially in conjunction with the *mul mantra*, which forms part of Sikh prayer at the beginning of each day. This theological poem was composed by Guru Nanak,

The Khanda
The Khanda is the symbol of the Khalsa. The central double-edged sword symbolizes belief in one God, as well as the protection of the community from oppression. The two swords represent spiritual and temporal power.

Guru Nanak
Guru Nanak (1469–1539) was the founder of Sikhism. A Hindu by birth, he traveled widely in search of spiritual truth. He emphasized the oneness of God, and the fact that all things are created by, and dependent on, God.

Fresco from the Atal Rai Tower
This 19th-century fresco comes from the Baba Atal Rai tower next to the Harimandir, or Golden Temple, in Amritsar, the center of Sikh worship. The frescos generally show scenes from the Janam sakhis, stories of Guru Nanak's life. The tower itself commemorates the early death of Guru Hargobind's youngest son, Atal Rai, who at the age of nine was said to have brought a dead friend to life. Guru Hargobind scolded him for using magic, and Atal Rai gave up his own life to make amends.

and although it cannot be directly translated, it means something like: "God is One, whose name is truth, the immanent creator, without fear, without hostility, immortal in form, unborn, self-sustaining, known by the grace of the Guru."

Humans are bound by *karma* or *karam*, the moral law of cause and effect, which is worked out through rebirth. God gives them help (grace, *prasad*) to move through five stages, from being a wrong-doer or *manmukh* to being devoted to the Guru and absorbed in him or *gurmukh*. The *manmukh* indulges in the five deadly evils, which are similar to the Christian deadly sins (see pp.158–59), and is lost in *maya*, which means for the Sikh error that gives a higher value to the material things in life than to the spiritual. (This is different from the Hindu concept of *maya* as appearance – the power of God to bring the Universe into appearance.) The final stage is utter bliss, or *sachkand*, which is beyond words and beyond rebirth.

Prayer Beads
Guru Nanak, the first of the ten Gurus of the Sikh religion, is always depicted with prayer beads or mala. This is a symbol of his status as a holy man, in contrast to the later Sikh Gurus, who were depicted as community leaders. Many Sikhs use a rosary, often made of white wood or steel, in order to meditate by repeating the word "Satnam" or "Vahiguru" on each bead.

LIFE IN THE COMMUNITY

Sikhs are not required to renounce the world; they must find the way and the will of God in their everyday life. Thus in contrast to the Hindu ideal of four stages of life or *ashramas*, which are student, householder or family person, forest-dweller, and renunciant, Sikhs see householders as the ideal throughout adult life. There is a strong emphasis on communal life—community service (*seva*) is highly valued, and the gurdwara, the Sikh temple, is the center of Sikh life. The gurdwara houses the Guru Granth Sahib, the Sikh scripture, which is a focus of reverence within it (see pp.82–83). The community assembles there for worship, especially for the singing of hymns or *kirtan*, but it is also important for community purposes, above all for the *Guru-ka-Langar*, usually known as *langar*. This is the practice of cooking and serving vegetarian food for free, without distinctions of race or caste or religion, although men and women usually sit apart. The voluntary work and donations required for *langar* summarize the demands and privileges of community service.

Guru Nanak did not regard other religions as worthless, but he did believe that their attention to the detail of ritual and outward observance was a severe impediment to a relationship with God, who can be found better within. Under the first four Sikh Gurus, there was no real conflict with the surrounding majority religions, but marks of Sikh identity were developed. Guru Ram Das built the "pool of Nectar," or Amritsar, hence the place of that name with the Golden Temple near it (the Harimandir), the major place of Sikh devotion (see pp.84–85). Increasing opposition from the Mughals led to further definitions of Sikh identity, including the formation of the Khalsa (see above), but also to more cooperation with Hindus in defense against Muslim expansion. Some Sikhs began to observe Hindu practices of which the early Gurus would have disapproved, and this led to the reformist Singh Sabha movement. In the 1920s this developed into the Akali movement when radical Sikhs struggled to regain control of historic gurdwaras. The Sikh political party, the Akali Dal, strongly campaigned for a Punjabi-speaking state, which was created in 1966. During their campaign in the 1980s for greater autonomy from the Indian government, some Sikhs advocated creating Khalistan, the land of the Khalsa, as an independent Sikh state.

THE LIFE OF GURU NANAK

GURU NANAK WAS BORN IN 1469, in a small village, Talwandi. He was married at the age of 12 and worked as an accountant, but he always showed interest in a spiritual quest. In 1499, while he was bathing in the Bein River, he experienced the call of God. He was given a cup filled with *amrit* (see pp.86–87) and commanded: "Nanak, this is the cup of devotion of the Name: drink this . . . I am with you, and I bless you and exalt you. Whoever remembers you will receive my blessing. Go, rejoice in my Name and teach others to do the same . . . I am bestowing on you the gift of my Name. Let this be your vocation." When he emerged from the river after three days, he gave away his possessions and said, "There is neither Hindu nor Muslim." This can be interpreted as "the majority are not true to their faith" but is often taken to mean that God is greater than the divided opinions of religions. Nanak began to travel, especially to pilgrimage centers, where he taught and chanted hymns and established centers of worship known as *dharamsalas*. He settled in Kartarpur with his followers. The date of his death was probably in September of 1539. He designated one of his followers, Lahina, to be his successor as Guru, and the Sikh movement thus continued beyond his death with a succession of Gurus (see pp.80–81).

FIRST AMONG GURU
Guru Nanak is the most honored of the ten Gurus. His status is suggested in the illustration by the overhanging tree, which represents the royal canopy of authority

GURU NANAK
Popular prints such as this are an important part of every Sikh home and gurdwara, or place of worship. This modern print of Guru Nanak is distinctive in showing him as he appeared in a vision to a devotee called Baba Nand Singh. Sikh art came into being with the Janam-sakhis, the reverent accounts of Guru Nanak's life. The earliest surviving examples date from the 17th century CE.

SAFFRON ROBE
Guru Nanak wears a saffron robe (*jama*) and a shawl (*chaddar*). These are traditionally the clothes of one who has chosen a spiritual path, and they remind us of Guru Nanak's foremost role as a spiritual teacher, who humbles the proud and enlightens the devout. His cross-legged position is suitable for his saintly role.

Guru Nanak and the Rich Man
Guru Nanak came to Lahore in Pakistan, where there was a rich man, Duni Chand, who was holding a sharadh, a feast offered to Brahmins. He believed that whatever he offered to the Brahmins would reach his father in heaven. Guru Nanak gave Duni Chand a needle and said that he must give it back to him in heaven. Duni Chand asked Guru Nanak how it would be possible for him to take a needle to heaven when he died. Guru Nanak told him that it is not possible to take anything with us; it is more important to be charitable to those living.

Guru Nanak Visits Mecca
Guru Nanak and his companions arrived at the Muslim city of Mecca (see pp.168–69). They lay down to sleep in the precincts of the Great Mosque, and a passing Muslim official was shocked to find that the visitors were sleeping with their feet pointing towards the Ka'ba, the sacred shrine. At the Muslim's command, an attendant seized the offending legs of the visitors and dragged them away, and the Ka'ba moved too. Guru Nanak said to the official, "God does not live in one place. He lives everywhere."

THE GURU'S HALO AND MUKAT
Guru Nanak is portrayed wearing a *mukat*, a crown-shaped hat. The *mukat* and the halo that surrounds it are symbolic of the Guru's holiness.

HALF-CLOSED EYES
The half-closed eyes of Guru Nanak represent spiritual ecstasy, the divine intoxication of mystical meditation. In this way, Guru Nanak is represented not only as a teacher of spiritual wisdom but also as a mystic.

A Pastoral Setting
Paintings of Guru Nanak sometimes depict him set against a rich background of trees, plants, flowers, and waterfalls. This emphasizes the Guru's role as a wandering ascetic who spent most of his life preaching his doctrine – as well as searching for spiritual truth – across Asia and beyond. After many years of traveling, Guru Nanak finally joined his family in Kartarpur, India.

> **If the heavens should hold a hundred moons, if a thousand suns should shine, without the Guru their light would be dim in a darkness dismal and cold.**
> FROM THE GURU GRANTH SAHIB

FLOWING WHITE BEARD
Guru Nanak is almost always portrayed with a flowing white beard. The whiteness gives the impression of a wise old sage, and the length of the beard is in accordance with the Sikh ideal of uncut hair (see pp.86–87).

NANAK'S NECKLACE
Guru Nanak has round his neck a *seli*, the necklace worn by an ascetic or fakir. This is almost always included in any depiction of Guru Nanak, as are the prayer beads (*mala*) that he holds as a rosary. In many paintings, the *mala* is also around his turban or hat.

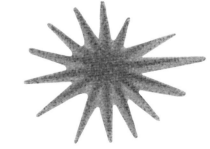

Symbol of Greatness
The mark on Guru Nanak's foot is an indication of his special status. The mark is of Hindu origin.

ਧੰਨ ਗੁਰੂ ਨਾਨਕ ਤੂੰਹੀ ਨਿਰੰਕਾਰ

DECLARATION OF DEVOTION
The Punjabi inscription below Guru Nanak states, "Blessed Guru Nanak, You alone, the Formless One."

THE TEN GURUS

GURUS IN INDIAN RELIGIONS are spiritual guides. The word "guru" means "weighty one," and gurus are those who bear the weight of wisdom and knowledge. Originally they were teachers and parents, but the word gradually came to be applied to those who convey spiritual insight. Among Sikhs, the word takes on another meaning because the Gurus do not simply teach and guide individuals; they are community leaders as well. From the time of Ram Das (see below) they were called *Sachapadshah*, a term used for the Mughal rulers meaning "true emperor." But Guru Nanak was suspicious of gurus in general, having met some during his lifetime. He realized that many were acting fraudulently as gurus, as a kind of career: "Some sing religious songs without knowing God; others have their ears pierced and turn into yogis; others become beggars to conceal their caste." In contrast, Guru Nanak insisted that the true guide is one who "eats what he earns through honest work, and gives from what he has to those in need – he alone knows the true way to live." (Adi Granth 1245).

GURU GOBIND SINGH AND HIS FAMILY

The Sikhs were severely persecuted under the Mughal empire. Active resistance to this oppression became prominent under the later Gurus. Guru Tegh Bahadur, his son Guru Gobind Singh, and Gobind Singh's four sons were honored for giving up their lives in this struggle but not their faith. Guru Tegh Bahadur (top left) was beheaded in Delhi in 1675 after refusing to convert to Islam. Guru Gobind Singh (top right) was the second most important Guru and the founder of the Khalsa (see pp.86–87), the foremost institution of the Sikh community. In 1708 he was wounded by an arrow from a Mughal assassin and died a few days later. Guru Gobind Singh lost his four children within his lifetime: his elder sons (center) were killed in battle against Mughals, and his younger sons (bottom) were bricked up alive in a wall after refusing to give up their faith. Martyrs are honored within the Sikh tradition; the Guru Granth Sahib states that "they attain glory both here and hereafter."

Guru Har Krishan
Guru Har Krishan is the only Guru portrayed without a beard. He had been summoned to Delhi by the emperor Aurangzeb, but in obedience to his father's command, he refused to see him. Instead, he showed allegiance to his own people by visiting the Sikh community in Delhi, where he died of smallpox at the age of eight.

● **GURU NANAK**
Guru Nanak (1469–1539), the first Guru, belonged to the Hindu *kshatriya* caste (see pp.18–19). Following a mystical experience while swimming, he became a wandering preacher, teaching that everything is created by God, and the way to come close to him is through devotion and meditation, not ritual. Eventually he joined his family in Kartarpur in the Punjab and composed 974 hymns, expressing his realization of the command to constantly remember the name of God. His teachings were later set out in the Sikh holy book, the Guru Granth Sahib (see pp.82–83).

● **GURU GOBIND SINGH**
The tenth Guru, Guru Gobind Singh (1666–1708), is second only to Guru Nanak in stature and importance. The son of Guru Tegh Bahadur, he became Guru after his father was executed. He resisted oppression by Mughal authorities and Hindu kings, and he exemplified the Sikh ideal of a saint-soldier—someone in whom sanctity and heroism are combined. He was the founder of the Khalsa (see pp.86–87) as well as a poet, whose work is compiled in the *Dasam Granth*.

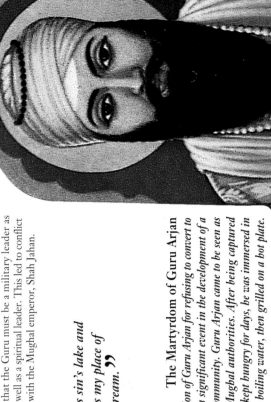

GURU TEGH BAHADUR

Guru Tegh Bahadur (1621–75) was made the ninth Guru by his grandnephew, Guru Har Krishan. Because he was barred from Amritsar by competing Sikh rivals, Guru Tegh Bahadur founded the Sikh center of Anandpur. He was beheaded in Delhi by Muslims after helping Kashmiri Brahmins against forcible conversion to Islam by the emperor Aurangzeb.

GURU HAR KRISHAN

The eighth Guru, Guru Har Krishan (1656–1664), was the son of Har Rai. The five-year-old Har Krishan became Guru in place of his older brother (see below). The young Guru's last words were "Baba Bakala." This indicated that his successor would come from the village of Bakala.

GURU HAR RAI

Guru Har Rai (1630–1661) was the seventh Guru and the grandson of Guru Hargobind. When Guru Har Rai was summoned by the Mughal emperor Aurangzeb to Delhi, he sent his son, Ram Rai, who agreed to reword a section in the Sikh scriptures that caused offense to Aurangzeb. This disqualified him from becoming a Guru in his father's eyes.

GURU ANGAD

Guru Angad (1504–52) was chosen by Guru Nanak as his successor. By choosing a follower rather than a son, Guru Nanak set a pattern for Guruship based on devotion rather than kinship. Angad composed Gurmukhi, the script used for the Punjabi language, as well as 62 hymns later included in the Guru Granth Sahib.

THE GURU GRANTH SAHIB

The authority of the Gurus was passed to the Guru Granth Sahib, the Sikh sacred scripture, by Guru Gobind Singh, the tenth Guru. In it the Gurus' spirit was manifest.

GURU AMAR DAS

Guru Amar Das (1479–1574) became the third Guru at the age of 73. He organized three annual gatherings for Sikhs on Hindu festival days, set up the first pilgrimage site at Goindval Sahib in the Punjab, and introduced Sikh rituals for birth and death that were distinct from existing Hindu ones. His most famous hymn, *Anand Sahib*, is part of Sikh daily ritual.

THE TEN GURUS

This modern print shows the ten Gurus and the Guru Granth Sahib, the sacred scripture which is the guiding force of Sikhism. Such prints are very popular and easily found in shops and markets in areas where Sikhs live.

GURU HARGOBIND

Guru Hargobind (1595–1644) was the sixth Guru. The son of Guru Arjan, he proclaimed that the Guru must be a military leader as well as a spiritual leader. This led to conflict with the Mughal emperor, Shah Jahan.

GURU ARJAN

The son of Guru Ram Das, Guru Arjan (1563–1606), became the fifth Guru. He collected the hymns of the previous Gurus, and, with his own 2,216 contributions, prepared the Guru Granth Sahib. He also built the Golden Temple, which was to house the holy book.

GURU RAM DAS

Guru Ram Das, the fourth Guru (1534–1581), is remembered for founding Amritsar, the most sacred city for Sikhs (see pp.84–85). His followers dug the pool that was to become the Harimandir Sahib, the holy lake that surrounds the Golden Temple, which became an important symbol of Sikhism. His Lavan marriage hymn is central to Sikh marriages.

> ❝ The Guru is my ship to cross sin's lake and the world ocean. The Guru is my place of pilgrimage and sacred stream. ❞
>
> GURU NANAK

The Martyrdom of Guru Arjan

The execution of Guru Arjan for refusing to convert to Islam was a significant event in the development of a militant Sikh community. Guru Arjan came to be seen as a threat by Mughal authorities. After being captured and kept hungry for days, he was immersed in boiling water, then grilled on a hot plate.

THE SINGLE FLAME OF THE GURUS

The concept of Guru is central to the Sikh faith, and applies to God, the human masters, the scriptures, and the community. Consequently, many Sikh names begin with *Gur*, as do important words such as *gurmukh* (one who is oriented toward the Guru); *Gurmukhi* (the script of the Guru Granth Sahib), and *gurdwara* (the place of worship). Guru Nanak described the Guru as the ferry across the ocean of existence, leading the pilgrim to God. He saw the Guru as the spiritual guide within, and God is often referred to as *Adiguru* (the original teacher). In Sikh belief, all the Gurus are one in spirit; their souls are indistinguishable, just as one flame must be lit from another and cannot be isolated from it. To emphasize the oneness of the Gurus, the authorship of the hymns is not ascribed to individual Gurus by name, but by their number in the succession of Gurus (see p.82).

THE GURU GRANTH SAHIB

In 1603, GURU ARJAN, THE FIFTH GURU, began to collect the inspired and inspiring poetry of both himself and the earlier Gurus. A *Granth* (from the Sanskrit, meaning "book") was needed, because the Sikh religion was spreading widely, and because hymns of doubtful authenticity were being attributed to the earlier Gurus. Guru Arjan and the faithful Bhai Gurdas went to a quiet place near Amritsar (now the pilgrimage site called Ramsar), and the Adi Granth ("the Primal Book") was compiled. Almost all the hymns are organized in 31 sections following musical scales (*ragas*). In each section, the poems follow the order of the Gurus who are indicated not by name but by *Mahalla* 1 (Guru Nanak), *Mahalla* 2 (Guru Angad) and so on. *Mahalla* is a code word usually meaning an abode. Each work is referred to by its *rag* and *mahalla* number and sometimes also by a title. For example, *Sodar Rag Asa Mahalla* 1 means "The Gate," in *Asa Rag*, written by Guru Nanak. Poems by Hindus and one Muslim are also included. In 1708 the tenth Guru, Gobind Singh, appointed the Adi Granth as his successor (so that after him there would be no human Guru), and it became the Guru of the Sikhs. The Adi Granth is therefore known as Guru Granth Sahib. Sikhs recite daily, "Acknowledge the Guru Granth as the visible body of the Gurus."

GURU GOBIND SINGH AND THE HOLY BOOK

Guru Gobind Singh was the tenth and last in the line of human Gurus. Before his death, he declared that the line of personal Gurus would end and the authority of the Gurus as religious and political leaders of Sikhism would be passed into the sacred scripture of the Guru Granth Sahib, as well as into the Sikh community of the *Guru Panth*. Although the Guru's own compositions do not appear in the holy book, he was a prolific poet, and much of his work is collected in the *Dasam Granth*, the second most important Sikh scripture, some of which is used in worship. Tradition holds that rival claimants to Guruship refused Guru Gobind Singh permission to see the original manuscript that was compiled by Guru Arjan, the fifth Guru, and so he dictated its contents from memory to his servant Bhai Mani Singh. Although the manuscript was lost in battle, copies of it survived. He also added to the original text hymns by his father Guru Tegh Bahadur, the ninth Guru.

Guru Gobind Singh, the tenth Guru

The holy book

Requirements for Reading
Unlike many other religions, both men and woman can officiate at Sikh ceremonies, and either can read the Guru Granth Sahib. There is no ordained or hereditary priesthood – only competence in Gurmukhi is required.

> *From the timeless one came the bidding by which the Panth was established. All Sikhs are commanded: Acknowledge as Guru the Granth. Acknowledge the Granth as Guru, the manifest body of the Gurus. You whose hearts are pure, seek him in the world.*
>
> THE LINES OF ARDAS, THE DAILY SIKH PRAYER

THE GRANTHI
Although anyone who is competent is allowed to read from the Guru Granth Sahib, for most congregational occasions a *granthi* or Sikh official reads from the book. A *granthi* also looks after the gurdwara.

READING THE BOOK
As the Guru Granth Sahib is honored in the same way as a human Guru would be, there are many respectful practices involved in reading from it. It is kept under a canopy and on top of a throne, and is laid to rest at a special place at night, covered in rumalas, or decorative cloths. A chauri, or whisk, is waved over the book as it is being read. Upon coming into its presence, all must prostrate themselves before it, be barefoot, and bare their heads covered. The book is wrapped in cloth and carried on someone's head – a sign of its honored status.

RANDOM READING
There are different ways of reading the Guru Granth Sahib. Practices include *akhand path*, a continuous 48-hour reading; and *vak*, guidance obtained by opening at random and reading the hymn on the left-hand page.

The Sacred Whisk
The sacred whisk, or chauri, is waved over the sacred book as a sign of respect. It is waved above the scriptures whenever they are being read or carried in procession. This dates back to a time when retainers would keep their dignitaries cool with a whisk, and so it came to be a symbol of sovereignty. The chauri consists of yak tail hair or artificial fiber set in a wooden or metal holder.

Yak tail hair

Metal or wooden holder

THE WORD OF GOD
The rituals that surround the Guru Granth Sahib, such as covering it with cloths and garlands and waving a *chauri* over it, are a way of showing respect for God and his teachings that are contained within the book. It is not the book itself that is worshiped.

"Such is the nature of the true believer that like the sandal tree be imparts bis fragrance to all."
ADI GRANTH P.721

COLLECTION BOX
Any offerings that are brought are left in front of the *manji*, the throne in which the Guru Granth Sahib is installed. Typical offerings are milk and fruit, or money for the collection box.

INSTALLATION
The Guru Granth Sahib has to be specially installed at the gurdwara and treated with great devotion. After making an offering, the worshipers move back, but without turning away from the holy book.

ORNATE EDITION
Despite the ornateness of most editions of the Guru Granth Sahib, it is always stressed in the Sikh faith that only what is contained in the book is important. Without the true name of God all ritualistic reading from the book is meaningless. Guru Nanak stated: "The only temple that matters is inside one's self" (Guru Granth Sahib, p.152).

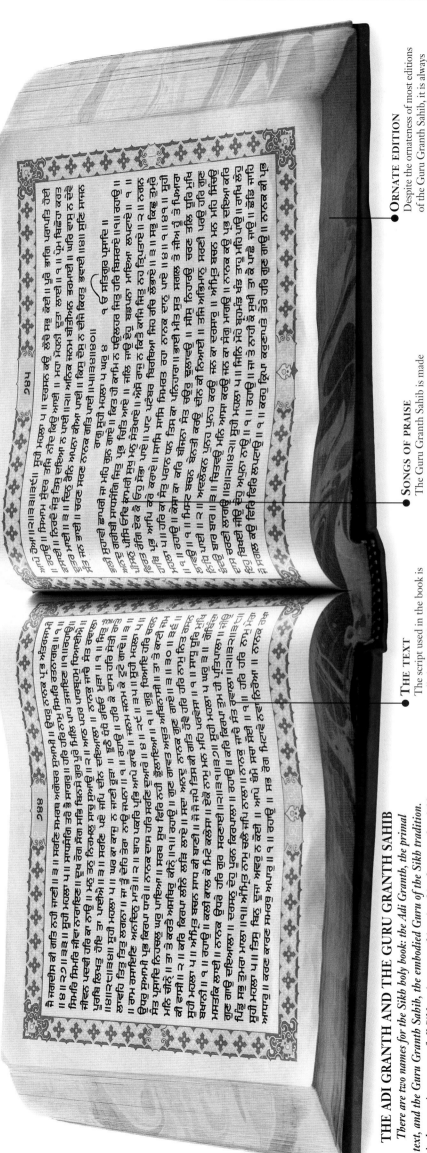

SONGS OF PRAISE
The Guru Granth Sahib is made up of hymns of varying lengths, all written in verse. The primary division of the contents is by their raga, or melody, and there are 31 ragas in the book. Sikhs are proud that the book has contributions by non-Sikhs – four early bhagats, or mystical poets, and 14 other Hindu and Muslim poets. The standard length of the book is 1,430 pages.

THE TEXT
The script used in the book is called Gurmukhi. The language is a form of Hindi that was used by saint-poets of the middle ages, and includes vocabulary from Persian, Punjabi, and Sanskrit.

THE ADI GRANTH AND THE GURU GRANTH SAHIB
There are two names for the Sikh holy book: the Adi Granth, the primal text, and the Guru Granth Sahib, the embodied Guru of the Sikh tradition. It is the most important of all Sikh scriptures and is primal in the sense that Sikhs believe it uncovers the truth about God, the Primal Being, which has been true for all eternity. It contains hymns of varying lengths, mostly conveying the message that spiritual liberation comes through a belief in the divine name, or Nam, not through external ritual. Because the volume has to be specially installed and treated with great devotion, most Sikhs keep a small manual at home, the Gutka, containing the passages used in daily prayer.

Taking Langar
The practice of langar, *eating a communal meal, is central to the Sikh community and reflects the Sikh ideal of charity and service, where each gives according to their capacity and takes according to their needs. A traditional Punjabi vegetarian meal is provided free to all who come, regardless of caste or status. Everyone present must sit on the ground, stressing equality. The practice was instituted by Guru Nanak (see pp.80–81), the first Guru, as a gesture against the caste system, which restricted communal eating. Langar, or "anchor," refers to the food, the eating area, and the kitchen it is prepared in.*

THE GOLDEN TEMPLE

For Hindus, god becomes manifest and available in many ways but especially in temples and at places of pilgrimage (see pp.32–35). In contrast, Guru Nanak recognized how easily temple worship and pilgrimage can become empty rituals, and he encouraged his followers to seek God where he may always be found – not outside in buildings, but within one's own being. The Name, *Nam*, dwells within everyone, as does the soundless Word of Truth, *anahad Shabad*: why search outside for what can be found within? But provided this is understood as the priority, it does not prevent Sikhs from building shrines to mark important places and events in Sikh history. Harimandir means "temple of the Lord," and it is the name of a number of Sikh shrines, including the gurdwara, or temple, at the birthplace of Guru Gobind Singh in Patna. But supremely it is the name of the central shrine for all Sikhs at Amritsar in the Punjab.

THE HOME OF THE BOOK
The Akal Takht houses the Guru Granth Sahib at night; only in the day can it be consulted in the main temple. Originally built by Guru Hargobind, the sixth Guru (see pp.80–81), and rebuilt in 1984, it once housed the weapons and relics of the last five Gurus and is used as a conference center for issues of political and religious importance.

THE CAUSEWAY
The 60-ft (196-m) marble causeway that connects the *parikrama* (the walkway that surrounds the lake) with the temple itself is always filled with pilgrims coming to the central shrine. From here the sound of *kirtan*—the singing of hymns—can be heard. The daily worship at the temple starts at four o'clock in the morning and continues until midnight.

❝*All places have I seen, none can compare to thee.*❞
GURU ARJAN, FROM THE ADI GRANTH

The Noblest of all Places
The Harimandir, the Golden Temple itself, serves as a symbol of the Sikh religion and is the most important pilgrimage site for Sikhs. It was declared by Guru Arjan to be the noblest of all places, and is so named because the Maharaja Ranjit Singh commissioned the covering of the upper part of the walls with sheets of gilded copper in the early 19th century. The architectural style follows a Sikh tradition, and the arches of the temple are decorated with floral engravings and lines of religious hymns.

THE WISH OF GURU ARJAN

Guru Arjan, the fifth Guru, wanted the Golden Temple to be open for worship to all, regardless of caste, color, country, or sex. He declared all occupations sacred and all classes equal, and stated:

"If I go to a temple, I see men boasting;
If I enquire of Brahmins, I find them proud.
O my friends, show me that place
Where only God's praises are always sung."
GURU ARJAN, FROM THE GURU GRANTH SAHIB

Guru Ram Das and the Golden Temple
Guru Ram Das, the fourth Guru, excavated the pool of Amritsar that now surrounds the Golden Temple. He then founded the city of the same name, after being granted the land by the emperor Akbar. Guru Ram Das began excavations that were to produce two sacred pools; the first was called Santokhsar, and the second pool received the name Amritsar, or "Lake of Immortality." After excavating the pool, Guru Ram Das invited men of 52 different trades to settle and open business in the Guru's market, the "Guru ka Bazaar," and so a center of Sikh civilization was born. Out of respect for the Guru, Sikhs who enter the confines of the Golden Temple state: "Great is the city of Guru Ram Das."

THE HARIMANDIR
The temple itself, the Harimandir, houses the Guru Granth Sahib, the holy book of the Sikhs, which is installed here at five o'clock every morning. It has four entrances, signifying openness to people of every social class, unlike the single doorways of Hindu and Muslim shrines. It is said to have been built on the site where Guru Nanak (see pp.78–79) meditated.

THE LAKE OF IMMORTALITY
A popular story tells of how the life-giving qualites of the Lake of Immortality were first revealed. After being taken by his wife from one pilgrimage center to another, a leprous cripple arrived at the lake of Amritsar. Upon noticing that black crows plunging into the lake emerged as white doves, he crawled into the lake and found himself cured. Next to the lake still stands the Ber tree under which the sick man crawled into the water.

THE GOLDEN TEMPLE
The Golden Temple, which was completed in 1601 by Guru Arjan, the fifth Guru, stands at the center of the holy lake of Amritsar and houses the sacred book of the Sikhs, the Guru Granth Sahib (see pp.82–83). In Punjabi the temple is known as **Harimandir Sahib** *(House of God) or* **Darbar Sahib** *(Royal Court). Sahib is a title of respect that Sikhs use for places as well as for people.*

ENTRANCE TO THE TEMPLE
The gateway is called the *Darshani Deorhi*. Over this is a treasury containing four sets of golden doors, jeweled canopies, and the golden spades that were used to dig the pool while the foundation was laid. Behind the two watchtowers next to it is where *langar* is taken (see p.84).

The History of the Golden Temple
This 19th-century manuscript painting of the Golden Temple illustrates the Sikhs' most revered shrine after it had been rebuilt. It was first built in 1601 under Guru Arjan, and the Guru Granth Sahib was installed in 1604. Always a political as well as a religious center, the temple has been the scene of many conflicts. Afghan invaders seized Amritsar in 1756 and desecrated the temple. In response, Baba Dip Singh gathered 500 horsemen and proceeded toward Amritsar, his army slowly growing until it numbered 5,000. A battle against the 8,000 Afghan troops raged, and Baba Dip Singh's head was cut off. He allegedly continued to fight with his head in his hand. Another Afghan attack came from Ahmad Shah, who in 1762 destroyed the temple and polluted the sacred lake with the bodies of slaughtered cows. The temple was rebuilt in 1764. The latest conflict at the temple was in 1984, when the Akal Takht (see opposite) was seriously damaged following conflicts between Sikhs and the Indian government.

SPECIAL OCCASIONS

THE SIKH RELIGION IS HISTORICAL, founded in the lives and teachings of Guru Nanak and the succeeding Gurus (see pp.78–81). As a result, its festivals are tied closely to events connected with them. *Gurpurbs* (see below) commemorate events in the Gurus' lives. Some are therefore celebrated mainly at the site of the original event, such as the birthday of Guru Har Krishan in Delhi in July, or the anniversary of the installation of the Guru Granth Sahib (see pp.82–83) at Amritsar in September. Most of the festivals are celebrated throughout the world in Sikh communities. Because Sikhs follow a lunar calendar, the dates do not remain the same according to the solar calendar, so that outside India Sikhs tend to observe a festival on the nearest public holiday. By special readings of the Guru Granth Sahib, the progress of the year itself is made into a special occasion. The *Barah Maha* (Guru Granth Sahib 1107–10) follows the year as a spiritual journey: "The 12 months, the seasons, the dates, and all the days are blessed: each hour, minute, second leads naturally to the True One: meeting the Beloved, all one's deeds reach their purpose and fulfillment."

A SIKH WEDDING

A Sikh marriage is considered not only as a union between two people but also between families. The customs surrounding marriage, such as the bride's red clothing and the presents of money, derive from Punjabi culture. The bride and bridegroom sit in front of the Guru Granth Sahib, the Sikh holy book, and the duties of married life are explained to them by the *granthi*, the official. The *Lavan*, the verses written by Guru Ram Das on the soul's union with God, is read and the couple circle the Guru Granth Sahib after each verse. As the ceremony takes place in front of the Guru Granth Sahib, no contract is necessary. The ideal marriage is described in the Guru Granth Sahib as "husband and wife who have one spirit in two bodies."

A Sikh bride and bridegroom

A Festival Procession
Processions often form part of a Sikh festival. Here, the Guru Granth Sahib is carried on a decorated vehicle, led by the Panj Pyare, five committed Sikhs in yellow and white.

UNIFORM OF THE KHALSA
When the men who had offered their lives to the Guru came out of the tent, they all carried swords and wore the same saffron uniform as he did. The Guru said to them: "My brothers, I have made you the same as I am." They wore swords and turbans, which is used for covering uncut hair (*kesh*), one of the symbols of the Sikhs.

THE FOUNDING OF THE KHALSA

The founding of the Khalsa, the community of Sikhs, was a pivotal event in Sikh history. It was instituted in 1699 on Vaisakhi day, the spring harvest festival, by Guru Gobind Singh, the tenth and last of the Gurus. He founded the Khalsa as a reaction to constant persecution by Mughal authorities and aimed to create a brave and loyal community with a strong identity.

REGAL AUTHORITY
Guru Gobind Singh's kingly status is emphasized by the regal umbrella or *chatri* under which he sits. His royal authority is also symbolized by the *kalgi* or plume on his turban, his own special symbol of greatness.

FIVE BELOVED ONES
In 1699 Guru Gobind Singh invited all Sikhs to a fair at Anandpur where he asked if anyone was willing to die to prove their faith in him. One by one, five Sikhs entered his tent. Each time, the Guru came out with his sword wet with blood. When the crowd thought they were all dead, he revealed the *Panj Pyare* – five beloved ones – alive.

GURU GOBIND SINGH IS INITIATED
Having initiated the five Sikhs into the new community, he asked them to initiate him, then declared: "The Khalsa is the Guru and the Guru is the Khalsa." In this way the Guru emphasized the equality of all Sikhs.

Throne of the Guru

From a cushion throne, Guru Gobind Singh performed the ceremony that became the formal initiation for all who joined the Khalsa and declared the *rahit* (code of conduct) that all Sikhs were to adhere to.

Kirpan, the dagger; a symbol of resistance against evil

The Symbols of the Khalsa

When Guru Gobind Singh founded the Khalsa in 1699, he asked all Sikhs to wear five symbols, the five "Ks," as an indication of their allegiance to the new Sikh community. The symbols are a reminder to the wearer to use the Gurus' actions as a model for their own. They also emphasize the equality of all Sikhs. Not shown here is Kesh, the uncut head and body hair, which is symbolic of an acceptance of God's will.

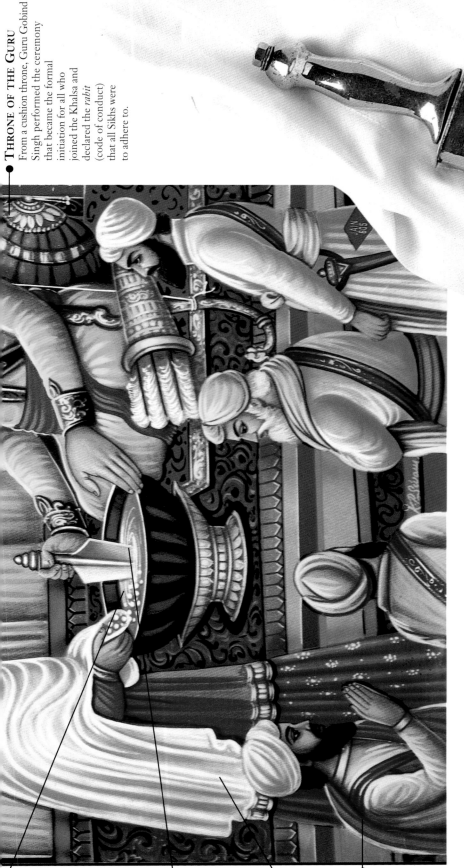

Kangha, the comb; a symbol of personal care and cleanliness

Kara, the steel bangle; a symbol of responsibility and allegiance to God

Kachh, undergarment; practical in battle and a symbol of chastity

Holy Water

After the five Sikhs had emerged from the tent, Guru Gobind Singh initiated them into the new community or Khalsa with *amrit* (blessed water sweetened with sugar cakes). They were to be called Singh (lion), instead of their caste-derived names. They agreed to follow the Guru's code of conduct by not cutting their hair, consuming alcohol or tobacco, engaging in sexual relations with Muslims, or eating Halal meat, meat killed according to Islamic law.

The Khanda

Guru Gobind Singh stirred the blessed water that was used for initiating Sikhs with the *khanda*, the double-edged sword that came to be the symbol of the Sikh community. The *khanda* represents the Sikh belief in one God.

The Guru's Better Half

Guru Gobind Singh's wife helped him in the initiation of the first Sikhs into the Khalsa. The Guru intended men and women to be treated as equals, and Sikh women are called *Ardhangi* (the better half).

Paying Homage

When Guru Gobind Singh asked for the heads of five followers, many thought he had gone mad and left him. Someone even called his mother. But when they heard the cheers of the crowd after the five men came out of the tent, hundreds returned to pay homage to the Guru.

The Sikh Festival Calendar

The important festivals are *gurparbs*, which mark the birth or martyrdom of a Guru. The others are *melas* or fairs. Most festivals involve an *akhand path*, a ritual 48-hour reading of the Guru Granth Sahib, preaching, prayer, and congregational worship, including singing.

December/January

Guru Gobind Singh's Birthday: Guru Gobind Singh, founder of the Khalsa and the tenth Sikh Guru, was born in 1666.

February

Holy Maholla: A *mela* in Anandpur on the Indian festival of Holi in memory of Guru Gobind Singh.

April

Vaisakhi: Originally a festival of thanksgiving, now a celebration of the Khalsa, which traditionally dates to Vaisakhi day in 1699.

May

Martyrdom of Guru Arjan: Arjan, the fifth Guru (see pp.82–83), was tortured and killed by the emperor Jahangir in 1606.

August

Celebration of the Guru Granth Sahib: A remembrance of the completion of the sacred scripture in 1606.

October

Diwali: A Hindu festival (see pp.38–39) appropriated by Sikhs to mark the release of Guru Hargobind, the sixth Guru, from prison in 1619.

Guru Nanak's Birthday: Guru Nanak, the first Guru and founder of the Sikh faith, was born in 1469 in what is now Pakistan.

November

Martyrdom of Guru Tegh Bahadur: Guru Tegh Bahadur, the ninth Guru, was executed in 1675 by the emperor Aurangzeb.

CHINESE RELIGIONS

THE LAND OF THE THREE WAYS

CHINESE RELIGION is not a single religion like Judaism or Islam. It is made up of many different religions and philosophies, of which four are particularly important. Three are known as *San-chiao*, the three ways, and they themselves are made up of many different strands. Together with them, popular or folk religion is so extensively practiced (although it is even more diverse) that it makes up a fourth way. Chinese people do not, in general, feel that they must choose one religion or philosophy and reject the others. They choose whatever seems most suitable or helpful – whether at home, in public life, or for one of their rites of passage.

Of the *San-chiao*, three ways, the first is the way of Confucius (also known as K'ung Fu-tzu, Master K'ung), which rests not only on the *Analects* containing the teaching of Confucius, but also on the Five Classics: the Books of Change, History, Poetry, Rites, and the Spring-Autumn Annals. The way of Confucius regulates ethics and rites of passage (such as being born, getting married, or dying), and seeks to create and practice order and harmony (balancing the opposite forces of *yin* and *yang*) in family and society. Respect for teachers and tradition is fundamental. Confucianism does not emphasize God and revelation, but teaches a kind of humanism open to an agent or principle of moral order. It insists on the observance of correct relationships between ruler and ruled, husband and wife, father and son in filial piety (see pp.90–91), and encourages respect for ancestors through ritual sacrifices. The elaboration of the correct relationship between ruler and ruled is achieved through the worship of *T'ien*, or heaven, as the source and guarantor of order. This enabled rulers to regard themselves as exercising the Mandate of Heaven (see pp.92–93).

TAOISM

The second of the three ways is Taoism. *Tao* means "the way," but the *Tao* is the source and guarantee of all that there is in this or any other universe. This means that the *Tao* is the "unproduced Producer of all that is" – the source of all things.

Taoism is so called because it shows how to live according to the *Tao*, by going with the flow and not struggling against the tide. *Tao* is related to *Te*, the power to bring the *Tao* into realization in all things. As the Taoist Liu Ling said, "I take the whole universe as my house and my own room as my clothing." The great virtue is active nonacting, or *wu-wei*: "*Tao* invariably does nothing, and yet there is nothing that is not done." Traditionally, Taoism goes back to Lao Tzu (though nothing certain is known of him) and the *Tao Te Ching*. That work is now read as mystical and personal, but it was originally addressed to the needs of society. Where a Confucian asks, "What shall I do?" a Taoist asks, "What kind of person should I be?" A second major work is *Chuang Tzu*, which

Unity of the Yin and Yang
The opposite forces of yin *and* yang *are interdependent and contain the seed or potential of one another.* Yin *is associated with darkness, water, and the female;* Yang *with light, activity, air, and the male.*

A Taoist Paradise
This silk tapestry depicts a Taoist paradise. In the sky is the Queen of the Western Heavens, and at the railing stand the gods of longevity, prosperity, and happiness. Descending the stairs are the Eight Immortals of Taoism.

was influential in the development of philosophical Taoism (*Tao-chia*). But Taoism also developed religiously with rituals, especially in healing and exorcism, and festivals. In religious Taoism, called *Tao-chiao*, the quest for immortality is very important. Because all nature is united in *Tao*, immortality cannot be achieved by setting free some part of oneself, like the soul. It can be achieved only by the proper directing of the natural forces within the body, through breathing exercises called *ch'i*, through control and direction of sexual energy, through alchemy, through behavior, and through the quest for the way of the Immortals and the Isles of the Blessed (see pp.96-97). *Tao-chiao* is made up of many movements and sects and has a large canon or official collection of authoritative texts. In traditional China, Taoism regulates many festivals in the community, as well as performing healing and exorcism through the ritual expertise of the religious officials, usually spoken of as priests. In exorcism, the priests

Scholars study the Yin-Yang
This 17th-century painting depicts three Taoist and popular deities studying the T'ai chi (Great Polarity) symbol, which depicts the interaction of yin and yang qualities. Shou Hsing, God of Longevity, is on the right; Fu Hsing, God of Happiness, is in the center; and Lu Hsing, God of High Rank, is on the left. A positive state is suggested by the presence of children, especially sons, and by the deer, which is a popular Chinese symbol of longevity and good fortune. The seriousness and dignity of the gods suggests scholarship and reflection, while the deer and the children suggest more popular or worldly concerns.

ritually confront troublesome ghosts or spirits and seek to control the dangerous excess of *yin* forces by invoking the superior *yang* forces, thereby ensuring cosmic, social, and personal harmony. It is only for the rare adepts or masters that Taoist harmony is achieved through the total channeling of energies and the attaining of immortality. Immortality may be interpreted literally (the attaining of an enduring subtle body) or symbolically (the attaining of spiritual freedom and effortless spontaneity).

BUDDHISM

Buddhism is the third of the three ways. It entered China at about the beginning of the Christian era, reaching its height during the T'ang dynasty (618–907 CE). Not only did Buddhism offer to the Chinese an analysis of the transitory and suffering nature of life, it also offered a way of release, and it introduced the possibility that the ancestors might be tormented in hell. Rituals for acquiring and transferring merit to the dead became important, whether through the correct performance of funerals or through other rituals. Particular care began to be taken for unhappy or unfortunate ghosts – the wandering, unplaced dead and the hungry ghosts who are not being cared for as ancestors. This has been a work undertaken especially by Buddhist monks and nuns. In order to introduce Buddhism into China, Buddhists undertook immense programs of translation – literally of

Cranes and Pine Trees
The subjects depicted in this 18th-century watercolor by the painter Chu Chi-i are symbolic of long life, an important theme within Chinese religion. Taoist beliefs can be expressed in paintings of the natural world, and this explains the predominance of Chinese landscape art. In both animate and inanimate things, painters sought to express the "life" in things and the harmonious unity between humanity and nature.

texts, but also of Indian ideas, deities, and other figures. Thus the Buddha-to-be, Maitreya, became the laughing Buddha of China with children climbing all over him; Avalokiteshvara (see pp.68–69), the *bodhisattva* of compassion, became the female Kuan Yin, the giver of children (see pp.72–73). Schools of devotion and meditation appeared, notably Pure Land and Ch'an. Pure Land says that all beings, no matter how depraved or wicked, can attain the salvation of the Western Paradise by simple, total faith in the help of Amitabha/Amida, the Buddha who rules over the Western Paradise (see pp.68–69). According to some, for this to happen it is necessary only to murmur the formula of faith, the *nien-fo*, better known in the Japanese form of *nembutsu*, which means "mindfulness of the Buddha." It states, "I take refuge in the Buddha Amida." Ch'an or "meditation" Buddhism cuts through rituals, devotions to Buddhas, and the study of texts, called *sutras*, and teaches that sitting in meditation is the only thing necessary to achieve enlightenment. In Japan, Ch'an became Zen.

POPULAR RELIGION

There is a fourth "way"; popular religion of daily life, with dramatic festivals, spirit-worlds, techniques of magic (dealing with everything from illness to buying a house), and care of the dead and the ancestors. Of importance is *Feng Shui*, or geomancy, the siting of habitations, for the dead as much as the living, in locations that catch the currents of vital breath or *ch'i* as they circulate. Cities may be built on these principles, which seek to harmonize the *yin* and *yang* energies, from whose interaction the universe and its diverse forms emerge.

CONFUCIANISM

CONFUCIANISM IS THE DOMINANT ethical influence on the traditional religious and social life of China and Japan. It is derived from the teachings of the sage K'ung Fu-tzu (551–479 BCE), known in the West as Confucius. He was a social, ethical reformer, at a time of growing disorder in China. Confucius was sceptical or indifferent to many traditional religious ideas, but a firm advocate of filial piety and ancestor rites (see p.93) as a basis for a strong society. It was not until the Han dynasty (206–221 CE) that his teachings were formalized into a political and religious system, designed to maintain the balance and harmony between heaven, earth, and humanity, and his works became official texts. These are the Five Classics (see left), and the Four Books: *The Analects*, *The Doctrine of the Mean*, *The Great Learning*, and *Mencius*.

Confucius
Confucius carries the Five Classics of the Confucian canon. They are the Classics of History, Poetry, Rites, Changes (I Ching), and the Spring and Autumn Annals. These texts became the basis of Chinese education and the means of training state officials from the Han dynasty until the end of Imperial China in 1911.

THE TEACHINGS OF CONFUCIUS

Confucius's basic moral rule was "What you do not want done to you, do not do to others." He also placed a great emphasis on learning and correct ritual as forms of moral education. He believed heaven was the source of the human potential for goodness and correct conduct, but taught that heaven rarely communicated with people directly. People should look to the past to deepen their understanding of how they should behave.

Teacher's Day
In Confucianism teachers are highly valued, and their authority is almost as absolute as that of the father. Teacher's Day is still celebrated in Taiwan on September 28.

HARMONY IN THE HOME
The traditional Chinese values of harmony and order are perfectly represented. Harmony in the family, as shown in this 12th-century painting, is the Chinese/Confucian ideal. It was valued both in itself and as the indicator of harmony in the state and in the cosmos.

CONSULTING THE I CHING

The *I Ching*, or *Classic of Changes*, is a work of divination based on rituals probably dating from 3000 BCE. Divination is fundamental to traditional Chinese life and is a way of establishing heaven's approval or anticipating disruption in the human and natural order (see pp.92–93). Based on the changing relationship between *yin* and *yang* forces in the universe (see pp.88–89), the *I Ching* depends on the reading of 64 hexagrams made up of broken (*yin*) and unbroken (*yang*) lines, which are determined by six stalks drawn from a container.

Confucius consulting the I Ching

FILIAL PIETY
An elderly couple is served by their son and daughter-in-law. In the *Analects*, Confucius insists that in all circumstances sons should support their fathers and fathers should support their sons.

OBEDIENT SON
The son is serving his parents. In Imperial China (pre-1911), children were expected to serve and be obedient to their parents above all else. This led to children being unable to testify against their parents in court and being expected to serve a parent's sentence even if it incurred death.

— Filial children

The Importance of Children
The importance of children and grandchildren in traditional Chinese family life cannot be overstated. A mother with a child represents harmony and fertility. In Chinese the character for "good" (hao) is understood to depict a mother with her child.

❝ *In guiding a state of a thousand chariots, approach your duties with reverence and be trustworthy in what you say; avoid excesses in expenditure and love your fellow beings; employ the labor of the common people only in the right season.* **❞**

FROM THE ANALECTS

The Work Ethic

The farmer and the gentleman scholar/official were the cornerstones of traditional Chinese society. Farmers and scholar/officials were expected to work unstintingly in the service of family and state. Together they embody the Confucian work ethic. The farmers' labors fed the population of traditional China. Their close relationship to the earth was expressed and celebrated at the seasonal festivals, which were supported and regulated by the Confucian state.

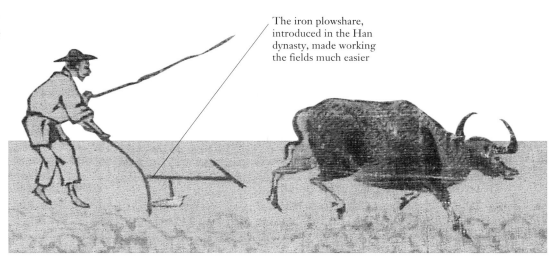

The iron plowshare, introduced in the Han dynasty, made working the fields much easier

● WET-FIELD CULTIVATION
The farming technique used here is wet-field cultivation. This was introduced by scholar/officials who wrote treatises advising farmers on land organization and agricultural methods. The treatises quoted liberally from the Confucian classics and popular morality books, and praised farmers for their labors.

● FAMILY LABOR
Each rural family had to support itself, with all the members working together in the Confucian ideal pattern. Cooperation with friends and neighbors was also essential for the upkeep of irrigation ditches and terraces.

● GOOD WATER
The water around the family compound is good *Feng Shui*. *Feng Shui*, which literally means "wind and water," is the Chinese practice of determining auspicious sites for buildings and graves in accordance with the natural forces or *ch'i* of the landscape (see p.89). If a building or grave has bad *Feng Shui*, it is not in alignment with the landscape, and the flow of *ch'i* is disturbed. This means that unfortunate things are bound to happen to anything or anyone associated with it.

● PROSPERITY
The full rice bin is a symbol of prosperity to which all Chinese families aspire. Prosperity and plenty indicate that the universe is in harmony and evil or negative forces are under control.

● OPEN DOOR
The door opens from the family compound onto the rest of the world, where each member of the family will perform his or her tasks following the morality and ideals that they have learned within the family.

● BASIS FOR ETHICAL REFLECTION
In Confucianism, respect for one's parents and demonstration of filial piety is the starting-point for ethical reflection. It is also the practical basis for the development of an ordered and harmonious society. For Confucians, good government and an ordered society begin with filial piety.

● FAMILY COMPOUND
The enclosed family compound is central to the Confucian ideal. Growing up within a virtuous environment, showing proper respect for parents, family, and ancestors, the individual is educated to be an honorable citizen, upholding the harmony of the state and, by association, the cosmos.

● HARMONY OF YIN AND YANG
The rooster and hen are embodiments of *yin* and *yang*, the negative and positive forces that must be kept in balance in order to achieve harmony within the home and the rest of the universe (see pp.88-89). They are also symbols of a prosperous and therefore balanced household.

THE HEAVENLY MANDATE

THE CHINESE NOTION OF KINGSHIP was rooted in the belief that royal ancestors had became divinities and must be worshiped. If Chinese rulers gained the approval of heaven and the ancestors, then they ensured the regularity of the seasons, a good harvest, the correct balance of *yin* and *yang* in the community (see pp.88–89), and the maintenance of the royal hierarchy. This was called the Heavenly Mandate. The earliest texts, preserved in the *Shu Ching* (*Classic of History*), reveal a notion of "divine right." The Chou people, who overthrew their rulers in 1027 BCE, were eager to show that heaven approved of their succession. The Confucian philosopher Mencius (371–289 BCE) helped to support their power by stating that, if the ruler was just and if he carried out sacrifices to heaven and worshiped the ancestors, then cosmic, natural, and human order would be maintained, and the ruler would retain the Heavenly Mandate.

The Emperor
The emperor eats a meal while attended by courtiers. Despite the typically Chinese formality, the emperor was actually a Manchu, a descendant of the nomadic tribes from the north of China.

NEGLECTING RITUAL DUTIES

If the ruler neglected his ritual duties and moral responsibility to the people, then social and natural disorder would follow, and the Heavenly Mandate would be withdrawn. Rebellion would then occur and a new ruler would emerge. It could only be known retrospectively, however, whether the ruler possessed the Mandate or not, by the next ruler establishing correct order.

THE EMPEROR AND HIS ATTENDANTS
This painting depicts the Ch'ing Imperial Court during the 19th century, with the formality of the emperor and his attendants reflecting Confucian imperial tradition. The Ch'ing came to power in 1644 and ruled China until the collapse of the Imperial system in 1911.

THE PHOENIX
The phoenix is an indication that the land is being ruled justly and that the ruler has the Heavenly Mandate. There is a female and male phoenix, indicating that the *yin* and *yang* qualities are in harmony within the empire. In later Chinese art the female phoenix came to represent an empress, and a woman who wore a phoenix on her wedding dress was regarded as empress for a day.

EUNUCHS
Eunuchs had two important roles in the Ch'ing Imperial Court. They were in charge of the emperor's concubines and also acted as food tasters. The Ch'ing emperors were very fearful of being poisoned, and every court had a eunuch to fulfill this role. In these two capacities, eunuchs came to exert considerable influence within the court.

Bureaucratic Rank
The court ministers were highly trained bureaucrats who had spent years studying the Confucian classics (see p.90) to prepare themselves for grueling written examinations. There were five levels of examination, and success in the highest exam, which was conducted in the Imperial Palace in the Forbidden City, qualified the scholar as a jinshi, *a presented scholar. This gave the minister potential for courtly influence, but the tradition of deference to the emperor meant that even senior officials had to be very diplomatic in giving advice.*

INFLUENCING POLICY
Ministers advised the emperor using divination with the *I Ching* (the *Classic of Changes*), as a way of gaining influence. This was seen as an acceptable part of state procedure.

SYMBOLIC GUARDIANS
Lions served as symbolic guardians, and have been featured in Chinese architecture from the 3rd century CE. Live lions were brought as gifts to emperors.

The Ch'ing Manchu Imperial Court

In this painting of the Ch'ing Manchu Imperial Court, hundreds of officials are depicted prostrating themselves before the emperor. It illustrates the concept, central to Confucianism, that society should be highly stratified, and that different standards of propriety would be required for different groups. It was expected that a gentleman's behavior would be appropriate to the situation and to the rank of the person he was dealing with. The large canopies that are held by attendants are symbolic of Heaven, and were modeled on the canopies that covered the war chariots of the rulers and the warrior nobility. It was believed that the cosmos was a huge royal chariot, with the canopy as the heavens and the chariot as the earth. The canopy therefore indicates high status and prestige.

FEATHER FAN
The feather fan was considered auspicious, because in Chinese it is pronounced in the same way as the word for "good." Deities and spirits were often depicted with fans, which they used in exorcism and healing. The emperor always had the finest fan, which was carried for him and was made with silk or fine paper and feathers.

THE INNER SANCTUM
The only people allowed into the inner sanctum, with direct access to the emperor, were the empress and the emperor's consorts or secondary wives, senior ministers, eunuchs, and women servants.

> **"***The three dynasties won the empire through benevolence and lost it through cruelty. An emperor cannot keep the empire unless he is benevolent; a gentleman or commoner cannot preserve his four limbs unless he is benevolent.* **"**
> MENCIUS ON THE MANDATE OF HEAVEN

REVERENCE FOR ANCESTORS

According to Confucianism, reverence for ancestors as an expression of filial piety (see pp.90–91) was fundamental to good order. Here, two dutiful sons make offerings and pay respects at their father's grave. The grave is crescent-shaped, considered auspicious as this represents *yin* and *yang* qualities in balance. Sons and daughters would also make offerings to an ancestor tablet in the home shrine. The bowing of the head was used to show reverence to the father in the same way as it was to the emperor; Confucianism emphasizes the importance of the correct relationship between father and son as well as ruler and official. This was laid out in the Confucian text *The Doctrine of the Mean*. This respect was fundamental in holding society together.

THE MANCHU IMPERIAL GUARD
The Imperial guard was dedicated to the protection of the emperor and fought against attacks such as the T'ai Ping rebellion of 1851–60 and many foreign invasions.

HIGHEST RANKS
Senior officials pay their respects. State ceremony was seen as an expression of *Li* – ritual propriety and the proper ordering of life, a concept fundamental to the Heavenly Mandate and Confucian ethics.

POPULAR RELIGION

POPULAR RELIGION AS PRACTICED in China, Taiwan, Malaysia, and among Chinese communities around the world is communal, festive, and participatory, rather than doctrinal or theological. Identification with the family lineage is achieved by participating in life-cycle rituals and ancestor offerings (see p.93), and identification with the wider community is achieved by participating in annual festivals, renewal rites, and the birthdays of important gods. The three other religions in China—Confucianism, Taoism, and Buddhism—are accepted as complementing popular beliefs and each other. Much of popular religious activity can be seen in terms of regulating and harmonizing the fundamental forces in nature, society, and the individual. These forces are classified as *yin* and *yang* (see pp.88–89). Like all other phenomena in traditional Chinese thought, people may be seen as consisting of varying combinations of *yin* and *yang* qualities. *Yin* is associated with heaviness, water, and passivity, while *yang* qualities are associated with lightness, fire, and activity.

Happiness, Wealth, and Longevity
The gods of Happiness (Fu Hsing), Wealth (Tsai Shen), and Longevity (Shou Hsing), are surrounded by children, who complete this picture of prosperity and good fortune. Of the three, Shou Hsing, on the right, is the most popular. He is a star god associated with the south, the most auspicious direction in Chinese cosmology.

Hell Scroll
Hell scrolls are used at funerals, during Ghost Month, and when making offerings to the dead. They remind people of the dangers of leading sinful lives and encourage them to smooth the passage of the recent dead through the hells, with correct rites and offerings. This scroll depicts the seventh hell presided over by King Tai Shan. There are usually nine hells and a tenth final court. The dead pass through all ten levels, their actions assessed and punished appropriately.

FORCE OF THE TALISMAN
These characters indicate the talismanic power of this picture, protecting the family from evil influences. It is a command that spirits and evil forces must obey.

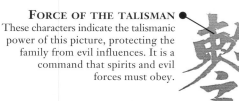

TALISMAN SEALS
This seal says: "Divinely empowered talisman controlling the wind." It indicates the status of this document in governing malevolent forces. The seal opposite reads: "Drive out evil, bring in blessings."

T'AI CHI, SUPREME ULTIMATE
This symbol represents the fundamental complementarity of *yin* and *yang* forces and *pa kua* (eight trigrams around the edge), which are made up of the combination of *yang* (unbroken) and *yin* (broken) lines. Here the *T'ai Chi* and *pa kua* are employed for their exorcising power in driving out evil forces.

THE DEMON TRAP
Chung K'ui holds a demon trap, into which the five noxious creatures, the spider, centipede, snake, toad, and gecko, are sucked. These animals are th[e] embodiment of the *yin* principle, which is perceive[d] as negative. In northern China, people try to exp[el] them on the fifth day of the fifth Chinese mont[h.] This is close to the summer solstice, a time of transition when people are said to be particularly prone to danger.

CHUNG K'UI'S SWORD
Chung K'ui wields his sword against the forces of evil. There are many stories about how he became a demon-slayer. One tells how he dies on the steps of the Imperial palace, thus making it vulnerable to demons. As a result, the red demon enters and the emperor becomes ill. Chung K'ui's ghost appears and kills the demon with his sword, thus curing the emperor. The emperor gives Chung K'ui's body a state funeral and names him demon-slayer for the whole empire.

CHUNG K'UI THE DEMON-SLAY[ER]
Chung K'ui and the stories about him demonstrate the dramatic and even viol[ent] nature of exorcism in Chinese popul[ar] religion. In one common account he [is a] poor scholar who commits suicide a[fter] passing the state examinations but [does] not get a state job because of his ex[treme] ugliness. In hell, he is given control [of a] large spirit army to help him slay dem[ons.]

CHUNG K'UI TALISMAN
Talismanic pictures, such as this one depicting Chung K'ui the demon-slayer, are put up in traditional Chinese homes to protect the household against demons. They are especially popular at New Year, an important festival concerned with cleaning out yin *forces and welcoming those of* yang *for the year ahead.*

YANG TIGER
Chung K'ui rides a tiger, which is regarded as a powerful *yang* animal and therefore a useful ally in the exorcism of *yin* forces.

HOUSEHOLD GODS

This paper print depicting the Kitchen God and his wife dates from the 9th century and would have been placed above the stove in the kitchen. This deity reports everyone's deeds to heaven at New Year. Just before New Year, honey is spread on his mouth, either to sweeten his tongue or to make it sticky and prevent him from speaking at all. The print is burned to dispatch him to heaven and a new print is put up at Chinese New Year.

Heavenly Dragon
The heavenly dragon represents the power of heaven and the yang force at its highest.

SOLAR AND LUNAR CALENDAR
This calendar incorporates the lunar and solar system of measuring the year. This is vital to people for working out the key dates for festivals and agricultural work.

TSAO CHUN, THE KITCHEN GOD
The Kitchen God controls each person's destiny and lifespan. He and his wife observe everybody during the year and at New Year report their deeds to the Jade Emperor, the chief deity and the popular embodiment of the more abstract principle of heaven.

EXHORTATIONS TO TSAO CHUN
This vertical panel and the one opposite read: "Report Good Things to Heaven" and "Return from the Heavenly Place with Blessings."

REPORT OF DEEDS
Tsao Chun and his wife hold plaques that record everyone's conduct during the year. This will be delivered in an oral report to the Jade Emperor when they ascend to heaven.

GOOD AND EVIL
Two servants hold vases representing the stores of merit accruing to good and evil actions.

Dress of an official

IDEAL HOME
The full money pot, the domestic animals, servants, and support of officials represent the ideal Chinese household. Invoking the ideal helps bring it into one's own household.

YANG AND YIN ANIMALS
The rooster and the dog opposite are embodiments of *yang* and *yin*. A rooster crowing in the morning is sometimes seen as the power of *yang* driving away the *yin* forces of night, often represented by a dog howling at the moon.

Divine Civil Official
This official, and the military official opposite him, serve Tsao Chun and the Jade Emperor. The popular heavenly structure reflects, to some extent, the structure and ranks of Imperial bureaucracy on earth.

RELIGIOUS TAOISM

RELIGIOUS TAOISM (*Tao-chiao*) refers to religious sects, movements, and lineages that seek access to the *Tao* ("the way") as the supreme reality, and consequently immortality, through meditational, liturgical, alchemical, and philosophical means. It draws on two key texts, the *Tao Te Ching* and the *Chuang Tzu*. Some sects were concerned with the ritual control of spirits and the cosmic currents of *yin* and *yang*; others specialized in inner disciplines of meditation or breath control and mind-body exercise regimes. Taoist training manuals were collected together as the Taoist canon, a huge collection of writings, which even in its reduced form still consists of 1,120 volumes. All religious Taoists share a concern with harmonizing the fundamental energies in the universe. Some channel their powers to perform healing and exorcism; others seek to harmonize *yin* and *yang* forces internally to achieve immortality. This may be interpreted literally in terms of cultivating an imperishable subtle body, or metaphorically as a state of spontaneity and spiritual freedom.

SPIRITUAL RENEWAL

This Taoist nun is sounding the bell to punctuate the chanting of a Taoist text. As in Buddhism, the chanting of key texts is an important ritual activity. It serves the community and wider society by effecting a moral and spiritual renewal. It also serves as a meditative procedure for the participants and frequently involves visualization exercises. It focuses the minds of the participants on the central teachings of the tradition of Taoism – the importance of the balancing powers of *yin* and *yang*, and the importance of harmony with nature. In both Buddhism and Taoism it is seen as an inherently beneficial action, producing great merit for those sponsoring or participating in it.

Taoist nun performing a daily temple ritual.

The Heavenly Empress
The Western Heavenly Empress holds the peach of immortality and invites the gods and immortals to her Feast of Peaches. When the peaches ripen, after 1,000 years in the palace gardens of the Kun-lun mountains, the Empress holds a great feast.

A TAOIST PARADISE
This silk tapesty, which dates from the 18th century, depicts the Eight Immortals of Taoism, the three star gods, and the Western Heavenly Empress.

THE PEACH OF IMMORTALITY
In the 16th-century novel *The Journey of the West*, the monkey king is put in charge of the heavenly peach garden, but steals and eats all the peaches that bring immortality. When he is captured, his immortal state protects him from execution, so he is brought before the Buddha to be disciplined. Kuan Yin, goddess of compassion (see pp.72–73), persuades the Buddha to release Monkey, providing he reforms and becomes servant to the monk Hsuan Tsang on his dangerous 14-year pilgrimage to India, in order to bring the Buddhist scriptures to China.

THE THREE STAR GODS
The Star Gods are, from left: Shou Hsing, God of Longevity; Tsai Shen, God of Wealth; and Fu Shen, God of Happiness. Shou Hsing, holding a peach, is a very popular god. Tsai Shen, a high-ranking god, is dressed as a senior official. Fu Shen was a judge who petitioned Emperor Han Wu Ti (502–550 CE) not to enlist dwarfs into his service, because he believed that it disrupted families, and the Emperor did so.

THE IMMORTAL CHUNG LI CH'UAN
Chung Li Ch'uan was an alchemist in the Han dynasty (206 BCE–220 CE), who used his skills to feed thousands of people in a famine.

THE IMMORTAL LU TUNG-PIN
Lun Tung-pin was an official turned sage. He traveled to Ch'ang An, where the immortal Han Chung-li taught him immortality. He then traveled for about 400 years, exorcising evil forces and helping people.

THE IMMORTAL LAN TS'AI-HO
Lan Ts'ai-ho was originally a cross-dressing poet and singer. He sang about the transience of life, and when given money he shared it with the poor. One day, when he was drunk outside an inn, he ascended on a cloud to heaven, leaving his few possessions behind.

THE IMMORTAL CHANG KUO-LOA
The immortal Chang Kuo-lao travels on an ass that he can turn into paper. He was traveling to see Empress Wu (684–705CE) when he died. His body decayed, but he was later seen alive and well in the mountains.

THE IMMORTAL TS'AO KUO-CHIU

Ts'ao Kuo-chiu's brother was executed for killing someone, so Ts'ao Kuo-chiu left home in shame, to cultivate himself in "the way" or the *Tao*. Two immortals discovered him and asked him where "the way" was, and he pointed to the sky. When they asked him where the sky was, he pointed to his heart. He was admitted as an immortal within days.

THE EIGHT IMMORTALS

The Eight Immortals of Taoism are examples of how all can obtain immortality. Taoist texts contain many accounts of their deeds, and as inspirational and spiritual role models, they are like the Lohan (see pp.72–73), the enlightened followers of Buddha. The two groups are often represented together on altars and temple murals.

Ho Hsiang-ku was a Taoist ascetic in the T'ang dynasty in the late 7th century

FLUTE-PLAYING IMMORTAL

The immortal Han Hsiang-tzu is renowned for his flute playing. He was the nephew of the scholar Han Yu (768–824 CE), and renounced worldly success to study the *Tao* with Lu Tung-pin, another of the eight immortals. He can make flowers bloom at his command.

> *Beings that are forcefully vigorous simply age. This is called going against the Tao. To go against the Tao is to be destroyed.*
>
> FROM THE TAO TE CHING

The Immortal Ho Hsiang-ku
Ho Hsiang-ku is the only female immortal. The contemporary of Empress Wu (684–705 CE), she vowed never to marry, and lived an ascetic life in the mountains. There the secrets of immortality were revealed to her by a spirit in a dream. She could cloud-walk and used to fly over mountains gathering fruit for her mother, no longer needing food for herself. Her fame spread to the T'ang court, and Empress Wu invited her there, but she disappeared while traveling, having been summoned by Lu Tung-pin to the Eight Immortals.

The Immortal Beggar
The immortal Li T'ieh-kuai appears as a lame beggar with an iron crutch. The story behind this is that once, he allowed his spirit to wander while he slept. His disciples found him, and, thinking that he was dead, cremated his body. When the spirit returned it saw that it had no body, so it entered the body of a lame beggar who had just died of hunger. Li T'ieh-kuai has great powers as a healer and is said to have been trained in healing and immortality by Hsi Wang Mu, Queen of the Western Heavens and keeper of the peach of immortality.

Deer of longevity and good fortune

Controlling the Ghosts
The image of Ta Shih Yeh, the wrathful aspect of Kuan Yin, goddess of compassion, is placed by Taoist priests in front of temples at the start of Ghost Month, usually in August. He controls the many ghosts for whom the rites are performed.

TAOISM—BODY AND MIND

THE PIVOTAL TEXT FOR TAOISM is the *Tao Te Ching*, the "*Classic of the Way and its Power*," traditionally ascribed to the sage Lao Tzu, from the 6th century BCE. Central to it are the beliefs that the *Tao* is the unchanging principle behind the universe, and that the secret of life is to live in accordance with the *Tao* "which never acts, yet nothing is left undone." *Tao* integrates a mystical path of naturalness and unconstrained spontaneous action with a political philosophy of creative inaction or *wu-wei*, in which the ruler does not seek to impose and dominate affairs of national and state concern. The *Tao Te Ching* endorses a spiritualized version of immortality, which is seen as arising from a natural and harmonious life with little importance attached to material gain. Mystics, philosophers, and poets were greatly attracted to and inspired by its teachings, interpreting the model of the detached, nonmaterialistic Sage Ruler as a guide to life at whatever level they found themselves.

Longevity Character
Longevity is one of the ancient Chinese ideals. It is valued as the mark of one who follows the "way of heaven and earth," flowing with the natural order of things, accepting fame or misfortune with equanimity.

Lao Tzu carries a scroll of one of his texts

TAOIST SCHOLAR DREAMING OF IMMORTALITY
This 15th-century handscroll by Chou Ch'en is concerned with themes central to Taoism: solitary reflection, immortality, and the importance of nature. It depicts the artist in his mountain retreat, dreaming that he is immortal. The Chinese character for immortality depicts a person and a mountain.

The Legend of Lao Tzu
The sage Lao Tzu retired from official service after seeing the decline of the state of Chou in the 6th century. Traveling on an ox, he wrote the text of the Tao Te Ching upon leaving the state, and departed from civilization to realize the Tao.

> **❝***Idly leaning on the desk over my books I fell asleep. Having earlier had a drink, I dreamed I was in a beautiful world. I saw the face of the Sage. When I woke I realized that to become immortal and see reality, you must encounter him face to face.***❞**
> T'ANG YIN (1470–1524CE) REFLECTS ON IMMORTALITY

● **MOUNTAINS OF IMMORTALITY**
The agelessness of the mountains was associated with immortality and spirituality. Immortality, conceived either as infinite life or as a state of detachment, spiritual liberation, and freedom from the fear of death, was a major concern for many Taoists.

● **DREAMS AND ECSTATIC FLIGHT**
Immortality can be encountered in a dream, where anything is possible, including flight, although immortals themselves do not dream. Chang San-feng, the founder of the martial art T'ai chi ch'uan (Great Polarity Boxing), is said to have discovered T'ai chi in a dream.

THE BODY IN TAOISM

The human body in Taoist theory is regarded as an energy system consisting of patterned flows of *ch'i* or vital energy and blood. The flow of *ch'i* in the body is regarded as closely parallel to the flow of *ch'i* over the landscape, and *ch'i* in the body is as subject to change as the forces in the weather. If *ch'i* is solidified and congealed it is called *ching* or seminal essence. The gross forms of *ching* include sexual fluids, but *ching* also refers to subtle sexual energy, the emotional and psychological equivalent of these substances. In its more refined form, *ch'i* is subtle air or breath. Even further refined *ch'i* is *shen*, spirit or consciousness. There is a close interconnection between body, mind, and environment in Taoist thought, and from this developed the many medical techniques and psychophysical disciplines in Chinese tradition.

Meridian Lines
Meridians are the invisible channels carrying blood and ch'i through the body. They nourish the vital organs and regulate yin *and* yang *(see pp.88–89). The dots mark points where acupuncture can help regulate the flow of ch'i.*

T'ai chi ch'uan at the Temple of Heaven
T'ai chi ch'uan incorporates the Taoist principles expressed in the Tao Te Ching. *It uses focused energy or* ching *to overcome attacks, drawing on the strength of the earth and the ch'i of the heavens.*

THE SCHOLAR DREAMS
The scholar, poet, or mystic in his mountain retreat is a common theme in Chinese art. This interest in solitary reflection could be seen as a respite from the bureaucracy of office in which so many scholars and officials were involved.

PINE TREE
Pine trees are a symbol of longevity and endurance in Chinese art. In the Taoist classics the *Tao Te Ching* and the *Chuang Tzu*, longevity is valued as the mark of those not selfishly pursuing their own interests and goals.

THE CH'I OF THE LANDSCAPE
In the *Chuang Tzu*, the flow of wind as *ch'i* over the contours of the mountains and trees, and the sounds it makes, are compared to the *ch'i* of the flow of breath across the throats of people, producing different opinions and designations.

THE IRREGULAR LANDSCAPE
The ever-changing nature of the landscape expresses an important notion in Taoism: that the flow of *ch'i* as experience produces different opinions, which explains conflict. Wisdom consists of not taking as fixed the relative viewpoints that we reach.

 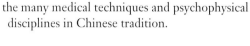

JAPANESE RELIGIONS

THE WAY OF THE KAMI

RELIGION IN JAPAN is a rich tapestry of interwoven traditions and religions, which has been developing for over 2,000 years. Some of the strands are indigenous; others have been introduced during the course of history. In general, Japanese people do not choose between the different religions, but like the Chinese participate in several for different occasions and purposes (see pp.88–89). Common to all is an emphasis on the sacredness found in nature, respect for ancestors in strong family associations, local cults and festivals, and the unity of religion and the nation of Japan.

The main sources of Japanese religion are indigenous folk beliefs and practices, organized Shinto, Confucianism, Buddhist and Taoist teaching, and some Christian influence.

The indigenous folk tradition of Japan was later called Shinto. Shinto was a name produced in the 6th century CE from the Chinese *shen*, "divine being," and *tao*, "way," but in native Japanese it translates as *kami no michi* (sometimes *kannagara no michi*), "the way of the *kami*" or "the way that accords to the *kami*." The *kami* are sacred powers present throughout the cosmos (sometimes simply the sacredness present in an object), worshiped especially in shrines or *jinja*. In a famous definition, Motoori Noringa (1730–1801, who worked to revive Shinto) wrote: "I do not yet understand the meaning of the word *kami*. In its most general sense, it refers to all divine beings on earth or in heaven that appear in the classic texts. More specifically, the *kami* are the spirits

abiding in, and worshiped at, shrines. In principle, humans, birds, animals, trees, plants, mountains, oceans, can all be *kami*. In ancient usage, anything that was out of the ordinary, or that was awe-inspiring, excellent, or impressive was called *kami* . . . Evil and mysterious things, if they are extraordinary, are called *kami*." There are innumerable *kami*, in Japanese *yaoyorozu no kami*, vast myriads of *kami*, divided into those that are heavenly and those that are earthly. The most important are the creators Izanami and Izanagi, and the sun *kami*, Amaterasu. The *kami* are vital in mediating *musubi*, the creative potency in the universe. To deal with the *kami*, religious specialists called shamans and diviners play a part, and correct ritual is more important than "correct" doctrine. In early religion each clan or *uji* had its guardian *kami* or *ujigami*. When the emperor's clan became dominant, a sacred national "clan" was formed with the emperor as the divine head.

Reinforcing the imperial status and cult was the contribution from Chinese and Korean influences. There was no formal missionary movement from China, but by the 6th century CE, the Japanese were sending delegations to

The Torii
The way into a Shinto shrine is marked by a torii. This gateway, which consists of two columns crossed by two beams, separates the sacred area of the shrine from the ordinary world outside.

Amaterasu, the Sun Goddess
Amaterasu the sun goddess is the supreme kami, or sacred power, of the Shinto pantheon. She is said to be the daughter of Izanami and Izanagi, the creators of the Japanese world. Japan's imperial line is said to be descended from her.

learn about Chinese political and social organization. From China, Japan derived two major ideas: first, that a good human (one who exhibits *jen*) will live according to the norms of society made public in rites; second, that the emperors have received the Mandate of Heaven (see pp.92–93) to bring that desirable and required order into the nation. Prince Shotoku (573–621CE) acted as regent for his aunt the empress Suiko, and allegedly drew up the Seventeen Article Constitution (604) to apply his own Buddhist and Confucian beliefs to Japan. The Taika reforms, which began in 645, carried the process much further, so that the emperor became the Son of Heaven, the descendant of the sun goddess Amaterasu, and thus the divine ruler or *Tenno*.

CHINESE INFLUENCE

The influence of China was not restricted to the imperial cult. At times, Chinese Buddhism (see pp.72–73)

dominated the religion of Japan. It developed important movements and schools, such as Shingon, Pure Land, Nichiren, Tendai, and Zen. At other times, Confucianism (see pp.90–91) or neo-Confucianism was dominant, especially in public life. As in China, people were happy to draw on different religions for different purposes: Shinto for birth and marriage, Buddhism for funerals. However, there were also repeated attempts to bring order into the religious scene and to insist on Japan's own religion, Shinto, at least as the official or state religion.

As the central power and authority of the emperor gained ascendancy, the supporting myths became more universal and were gathered into two collections, the *Kojiki* and the *Nihonshoki*. These became a resource of authority for later Shinto and contained the major themes of the religion. These themes are: the three-layered cosmos; the creation by Izanagi and Izanami; the forces of life and fertility; pollution and purification; the supremacy of Amaterasu from whom the imperial line descends; and the rituals and chanting of *norito*, which is the invocation and praise of the *kami*.

Shinto received much from Confucianism and Buddhism—in the medieval period they were largely indistinguishable—it also perpetuated some from the earlier forms of Japanese religion. These early forms laid emphasis on nature and divination, and on many aspects of worship. *Harai/harae* and *misogi*, for example, are two cleansing rituals; exorcism, in the case of *harai*, goes back to the very earliest days. As

all these varied influences were absorbed, so Shinto took different forms or went through different transforming stages. The stages were the National Learning movement of the 18th and 19th centuries, restoring Shinto to the center; Imperial or Koshitsu Shinto, confined to the rites of the emperor; Shrine or Jinja Shinto, of popular devotion; State or Kokka Shinto, created by the Meiji government and lasting to the end of World War II, to control shrines and rituals to serve government purposes; Sect or Kyoha Shinto, new religious movements that were recognized by the government; New Sect or Shin Kyoha Shinto, new religious movements that have developed since the war; and Minkan or folk Shinto, which coexists with the other forms.

Although State Shinto lost its official status in 1945, and worship is now more private, the wider tradition still occupies a significant position in Japanese life. It is not a religion of systematic theology and practice but of participation in tradition and ritual, especially at shrines and in the home. It lends itself to the emergence of new religious movements, of which there have been many since the end of World War II. As well as the important folk festivals, a devout follower of Shinto regards daily life as *matsuri*, service to the *kami*. Shinto emphasizes gratitude to the *kami* and to the ancestors, from whom life and all its blessings come. The purpose of Shinto is to realize and carry out the will of the *kami* and the ancestors in the family, the community, and the nation. Humans, like the whole of nature, are children of the *kami*. They are, therefore, inherently good and need only to have their defilement removed for the natural goodness to shine through.

An Ema for Success
One of the most conspicuous sites at Shinto shrines is the wall full of wooden placards or ema *with requests to the gods written on them. The* ema *often use pictorial symbols to express the request. Here we see a target pierced through the center by an arrow with the words "prayer to passexam." The* ema *also contains a pun; the word for pentagon (gokaku), the shape of an* ema, *also means to pass an exam.*

Thunder Gods
The eight thunder gods of Japanese mythology do not so much represent heavenly thunder as the earthly thunders of earthquakes. They are mentioned in connection with the creators of Japan, Izanagi and his sister and lover Izanami. When Izanami dies and Izanagi goes to find Izanami in hell, her decomposing body is protected by eight thunder gods. Offended that he came for her, Izanami ordered the thunder gods to pursue Izanagi, but he escaped.

THE ORIGINS OF SHINTO

THE ORIGINS OF SHINTO cannot be accurately traced; they lie far back in the period of prehistory, emerging from the traditions and practices of Japanese folk religions. The records of the earliest times, the *Kojiki* and *Nihongi* (see p.101) were compiled as late as the beginning of the 8th century CE and were already much influenced by Chinese traditions. They describe the creation of the cosmos out of chaos in the shape of an egg, which then separated. As the way of the *kami* (see p.100), Shinto has no founder, no collection or canon of sacred texts making up scriptures, and no agreed or fixed system of doctrine. It is often viewed as the way in which society is bound together in common values and attitudes, in which the myths and religious practices are seen as the rope that ties things together. Shinto is a religion of participation in traditional rites and festivals, in the shrines and by extension in the home. The early prayers are simple and direct; the worshipers at a harvest festival prayed to the Great Heaven Shining Deity who dwells at Ise: "As you have blessed the ruler's reign, making it long and enduring, so I bow down my neck as a cormorant in search of fish to worship you and give you praise through these abundant offerings on his behalf."

The Making of Japan
Izanagi and Izanami, the last of the seven generations of the gods, were commanded by the heavenly deities to "complete and solidify the drifting land." So Izanagi dipped the jewel-spear of heaven into the ocean, drew it out, and the brine that dropped from it coagulated and formed the first island Ono-goro-jima. Here, Izanagi and Izanami became man and wife and gave birth to the islands that make up Japan, as well as various gods, such as those of the wind, trees, mountains, and fire.

AMATERASU APPEARS
This picture depicts one of the most famous stories in Shinto mythology. It is the story of Amaterasu, the sun goddess daughter of Izanagi (see above), who goes into a cave after her brother, Susanoo, the sea god, has thrown a skinned piebald colt through the roof of the hall where she does her weaving. When she disappears inside, the world is thrown into eternal darkness, which makes it easier for the wicked gods to do evil deeds and create chaos. Determined to restore order and light, the gods follow a plan thought up by Omohi-kane, the "Thought-combining" deity, who suggests making her curious about what is going on outside her cave.

Heavenly Offerings
The gods have tied white streamers to poles and to the branches of a 500-branched sacred sakaki tree, which they have dug up from Heavenly Mount Kagu. They have also hung up a large mirror, or Yata Kagami in Japanese. At the Ise shrine (see pp.106–7) it is an object of worship. It is also one of the three imperial regalia.

AMATERASU EMERGES
Amaterasu emerges when she hears laughter outside her cave even though she knows the world is plunged in darkness, and there is nothing to laugh about. The gods are laughing at Ama no Uzume, the "Terrible Female of Heaven," possibly the woman on the left, who is performing a dance that involves taking off all her clothes. The artist probably thought that it would be too shocking to show the exact details of the story as described in the ancient text, the *Kojiki*.

ROYAL REGALIA
Amaterasu holds the necklace given to her by her father, Izanagi when he entrusted her with *Takama no Hara*, or rule of the heavens. She is also holding the sword that was passed on to her grandson's great-grandson, the emperor. It now makes up part of the imperial regalia and is kept in the Atsuta shrine, near Nagoya.

MOUNTAIN DEITIES

Sengen-Sama, goddess of Mount Fuji

In Japan almost every mountain has its own deity worshiped by the local people. One of the ancient mountain gods is O-Yama-Tsu-Mi, who was born when Izanagi cut the fire god into five pieces (see below). Four other major mountain gods are those of the high slopes, low slopes, steep slopes, and the mountain base. Of individual deities relating to specific mountains, the goddess Sengen-Sama, the deity of Mount Fuji, the most magnificent mountain in Japan, is among the most important. Many people from all over Japan worship her and visit her on pilgrimage each year, climbing to the peak at dawn to worship the rising sun. Here, dressed in ancient, rich clothes, Sengen-Sama holds a magical jewel in her right hand and a branch of the sacred *sakaki* tree in her left.

AND THEN THERE WAS LIGHT . . .
Emerging from her cave, Amaterasu dazzles the gods with light. One story says she comes out intrigued by the noise, another that the gods trick her with a mirror, making her believe there is a brighter god than herself outside.

NO REENTRY
To stop Amaterasu from returning to her cave, the gods have roped it off. These ropes, called *Shimenawa*, are used today to show that something is sacred.

Ancestor of Emperors
Amaterasu, the sun goddess, is the most central female deity in Shinto mythology. Her grandson's great-grandson was the first emperor Jimmu. Her shrine, which was once in the Royal Palace, was moved to Ise in the 1st century CE to prevent her priestesses from inhibiting the emperor's powers through her oracles.

MUSIC OF THE GODS
This reads, *Iwato kagura*, music of the gods. Kagura is a type of Shinto ritual or performance, which is said to originate from this story and the dance of Ama no Uzume. It is essentially the invocation of gods followed by song or dance or both. It has been widely performed since ancient times at the imperial court and major Shinto shrines. Throughout history, Kagura performances were believed to pacify spirits as well as entertain the gods.

CAUSING A COMMOTION
The gods purposefully cause a commotion, banging drums, reciting, causing the cocks or "long-singing birds" who welcome the dawn, to cry to one another in an attempt to attract Amaterasu out of her cave, bringing light and order back into the world. The drum, called a *dadaiko*, can still be heard at *Gagaku* or court music performances.

AMATERASU THE SUN GODDESS
Amaterasu was born when her father Izanagi washed his left eye after going into hell to search for his wife Izanami, who had died giving birth to the god of fire. The moon goddess was born when he washed his right eye.

THE HAND-STRENGTH-MALE DEITY
The "hand-strength-male" deity Ta-jikawa-wo, heaves aside the rock door, eager to welcome Amaterasu back into the world. He then takes her by the hand and leads her out.

CLOTHES FOR A GOD
All the gods wear aristocratic clothes that have been woven by Amaterasu and her weaving women. Traditionally, this was one of her roles and is now carried on by Shinto priestesses who are also employed in weaving garments for great ceremonies.

ADDRESSING THE GODS

JAPANESE RELIGION is a rich texture of different traditions, in which the *kami*, the ancestral spirits, the Buddhas, and the *bodhisattvas* (see pp.68–69) are extremely close to everyday life. Japanese people talk to these figures naturally and involve them in their lives. When they go to a Shinto shrine and choose a number and then receive a slip of paper with advice, warning or blessing, this is not a matter of chance: the *kami* are so close that they know each person's needs and direct the choice. Many of these figures have specialized functions, like Jizo (opposite), Fudo, who protects against danger, or Yakushi (Bhaisajyaguru), who heals both mind and body. The Japanese do not have to choose between religions in order to address the gods: all are equally available, so much so that at various times attempts have been made to show how the figures of one religion really belong to all. What is known as *honjisuijaku* ("original substance manifest traces") claims that the original truth has left different traces in the world. Thus, for example, Yoshida Kanetomo (1435–1511) held that Shinto is the original trace and that the Buddhas are the fruit of its teaching.

PICTORIAL VOTIVE OFFERINGS
Ema, illustrated here, are pictorial votive offerings that can be found at most major religious centers. The word "ema" means "horse picture" and derives from an old notion that horses were messengers to the gods or kami (see pp.102–03). People write their wishes and often their names and addresses on the back. The ema are then hung up as a petition or message to the deity until they are eventually ritually burned to symbolize a liberation of the request.

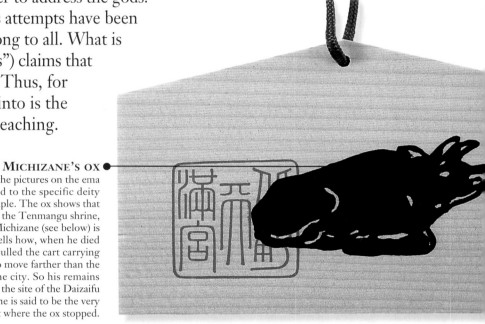

Writing an Ema
Any type of request can be written on an ema, ranging from stopping smoking to finding the right partner for marriage, or luck in gambling. For young people, academic success, especially in passing the entrance exams of schools and universities, is very common.

MICHIZANE'S OX
Frequently the pictures on the ema are motifs related to the specific deity of the shrine or temple. The ox shows that this ema comes from the Tenmangu shrine, where Sugawara no Michizane (see below) is honored. Legend tells how, when he died in exile, the ox that pulled the cart carrying his remains refused to move farther than the northeast corner of the city. So his remains were buried there, and the site of the Daizaifu Tenmangu shrine is said to be the very spot where the ox stopped.

Hishaku

Oke

White clothes, symbolic of purity

PATRON OF SCHOLARS
Sugawara no Michizane, pictured here, was a 9th-century scholar, poet, and political figure. After his death in exile misfortunes in the capital were attributed to his angry spirit. To honor Michizane and placate his spirit, shrines were dedicated to him in Kyoto and Daizaifu. Today there are numerous shrines around Japan where he is worshiped as Tenjin, patron saint of scholarship. These shrines, known as Tenmangu, are visited by countless Japanese students, who come to pray for success in passing their school entrance exams.

ANCIENT STAMP
The name of the religious site is often stamped on ema, as here, in ancient Chinese characters.

Scooping Nectar
A shrine maiden or miko performs part of the "yutate," literally "immersion in hot water" ritual. The miko symbolically scoops nectar from the land of the kami into the wooden bowl raised above her head. The bowl is then filled with sacred hot water and passed to one of the priests, who offers it to the kami at the altar of the inner shrine.

JIZO'S ATTRIBUTES ●
In Jizo's right hand he holds a *shakujo*, or staff with dangling metal rings, typical of traveling monks. When shaken they make a ringing noise that supposedly clears the road of poisonous snakes and noxious insects. In his left hand he holds the *hoju* or magical jewel, which has the power to remove misfortune.

● **BUDDHIST EMA**
Ema can be found at Buddhist temples as well as Shinto shrines. This ema is from the famous Zen temple Kenchoji in Kamakura. It pictures the *bodhisattva* Jizo who, in popular Japanese religion, is considered to be the protector of children and travelers.

鎌倉

建長寺

身代り地蔵尊

豊川閣靈積順守護攸

Protective Fuda

Fuda or amulets can be obtained at most religious centers. They can both ward off evils or misfortunes and bring good luck. They are usually placed on a Buddhist altar, or butsudan, or on the "god shelf," or kamidana, at home to protect and bring good fortune to the family. They are also occasionally seen on trains to protect them from accidents. The name of the religious center or the deity are usually written on the fuda .

❝*When the east wind blows***
Let it send your fragrance
Oh plum blossoms
Although your master is gone
***Do not forget the spring.*❞**
MICHIZANE

● **AUSPICIOUS PLUM TREES**
The Dazaifu shrine is famous for its plum trees. Plums or *ume* have been a popular motif in Japanese poetry since the 8th century. With bamboo and pine, plums are used during the celebration of auspicious occasions.

SHRINES AND FESTIVALS

JAPANESE WORSHIP is summarized in the word *matsuri*, from a verb meaning "to entertain" or "to attend to." It came to mean "to serve the *kami*" (see pp.100–01), or a person in authority, or the souls of the departed. *Matsuri* thus implies an attitude of respect and obedience, a willingness to listen and obey. In Japanese religion, *matsuri* may be public or private. In public, *matsuri* is expressed in the many festivals held at shrines (for some examples, see opposite), at which the *kami* is received as a guest of honor and is revered through ritual acts of thanksgiving. The shrines differ from each other in their history, in the *kami* they honor and enshrine, and in the nature of the rituals performed, but many of them share a belief that the *kami* are revitalized at the shrine, especially at the New Year.

The Heian Shrine
This Kyoto Shrine was built in 1895 to mark the 1,100th anniversary of the founding of the Heian capital. The shrine is dedicated to the spirits of Emperor Kammu (781–806). In October the shrine sponsors the Jidai festival, when marchers wear costumes representing periods of history.

TRANSLATING THE WILL OF THE KAMI

Matsuri also involves translating the will of the *kami* into life, and in this way *matsuri* becomes the private practice and faith of individuals, the bringing of the power of the *kami* into everyday life. *Matsuri* also has its effect on political and public life; the old word for "government" was *matsurigoto*, "*matsuri* affairs." Thus shrines and festivals give a focus to a profound attitude in Japanese life, which continues to the present.

A SHINTO SHRINE
Shrines serve as a dwelling for one or more kami or deities. They are visited throughout the year and attract large numbers on festival days. At major shrines like this Yoshida Jinja shrine in Kyoto, there is often more than one sanctuary building. However, the main hall (honden) where the principal deity is enshrined cannot be approached directly, but only by priests. In contemporary urban Japan, shrines are not only a place of worship but also a quiet space to escape from the bustle of the city.

Worshippers praying at the *haiden*

The Hall of Worship
*At the shrine, people line up at the **haiden** or worship hall to pray. Individual prayers conducted at the **haiden** consist of a four-step process: money is put in an offering box; two deep bows are made before the shrine; worshipers clap their hands twice; and finally, one deep bow is made. From the **haiden** offerings and petitions to the **kami** can be made, and on special occasions, worshipers enter the **haiden** to be ritually cleansed by a priest.*

MAKING PETITIONS TO THE GODS
Worshipers come to the shrine to make petitions to the *kami*. The shrine still serves as the basis for Shinto worship, from the shrines found in homes (*kamidana*) to national shrines, such as the one dedicated to the goddess Amaterasu at Ise.

THE DAIGENGU BUILDING
The *Daigengu* is dedicated to the pantheon of Shinto deities mentioned in the *Engishiki* text of the tenth century. It is unique to this particular shrine in Kyoto, which was built in 1484 by Yoshida Kanetomo.

A Portable Shrine

During festival times the kami *(deity) of a shrine is temporarily transferred into the* mikoshi *or portable shrine, and paraded through the community. The procession of the* mikoshi *signifies a visit of the deity to the community that the* kami *protects, and allows for a blessing of the entire community. During festivals the* mikoshi *is bounced up and down, vitalizing both the* kami *and the participants in the festival.*

The Star Festival of Agonshu

The Hoshi Matsuri, or Star Festival, held by the new religious movement Agonshu, attracts over half a million visitors each February. There are two huge fires, which represent the two mandala worlds of esoteric Buddhism (see pp.74–75). These are fueled by millions of wooden sticks or gomagi, *which have prayers and requests written on them.*

THE FESTIVAL CALENDAR

Nara Yamayaki: During January at twilight, the grass of the Naga hillside is burned by people wearing warrior monk costumes, to celebrate the resolution of a dispute between two local temples.

Kasuga Matsuri: Held in March for the deity of the Kasuga shrine, it features ritual dances.

Kanda Matsuri: In May, floats filled with portable shrines and dancers are paraded through Tokyo in honor of deities at the Kanda shrine.

Gion Matsuri: Held at Kyoto in July, large floats carrying musicians and smaller floats with tableaux of historical and mythological people are paraded.

Nebuta Matsuri: Associated with the August Bon festival, Nebuta features paper floats of famous people, accompanied by singing and dancing.

Chichibu Yo Matsuri: Held in December to honor the Chichibu deities, this festival features fireworks and a parade of floats.

THE OUTSIDE ARCADE
The outside arcade acts as a corridor (*kairo*) to link buildings together. There are many buildings within the wall, for example, storehouses for implements such as the portable shrine or *mikoshi* used by the *kami*. Halls for sacred dances are also common.

THE SHRINE ROOF
The roofs of shrines are usually made with thatched cyprus bark. The cross above the roofing (*chigi*) and the short logs (*katsuogi*) were designed in ancient times to secure the shrine roofs.

CLEANSING PROCESS
Near the entrance, and before worshiping at the main hall, it is proper for worshipers to purify themselves by washing hands and gargling with water.

The Sacred Bridge

On the approach to the shrine, before its gate, there is sometimes a pond or another body of water over which a sacred bridge or shin-kyo *is erected. This, like the* torii *(see p.100) separates the sacred world within the shrine from the profane world outside. Many Shinto shrines were originally sacred areas set up around sacred objects, such as trees, ponds, or rocks, and are now often built in groves of trees in the Japanese countryside.*

RELIGIOUS ACTION

JAPANESE RELIGIONS are unified by the way they draw people into common values; the emphasis is on action rather than a conformity of beliefs. The actions that are held to be desirable depend on the circumstance and the nature of the religions involved. State Shinto looked for actions that reinforced the emperor's status and the authority of the government. In the Meiji reform of the 19th century, religious freedom was bestowed on Japanese citizens, but only "within limits not antagonistic to their duties as subjects." Shrine Shinto puts emphasis on action, not belief: to be grateful for the blessings of the *kami* in rituals gladly undertaken; to help others with deeds of service; and to live in harmony with the will of the emperor, seeking the peace and prosperity of the country. Pilgrimages, which are important in all Japanese religions, draw people together in common values.

Japanese Jizo Dolls
Stone figures similar to these are often seen at Buddhist temples. Jizo, Ksitigarbha in Sanskrit, is a bodhisattva that is believed to protect children and help the souls of dead fetuses. The dolls are commonly bought and taken care of by women who have had abortions or parents who have lost their children. In this way mothers can look after their children even when they have died.

THE PURPOSE OF PILGRIMAGE

Pilgrimages were undertaken in order to receive help from the deities in obtaining worldly benefits, such as good health or an abundant harvest. For many, however, pilgrimages offered a chance of escape from mundane, stifling village life. For most peasants, going on a pilgrimage was the only means of obtaining permission to travel outside of the village where they lived. The desire to make a pilgrimage was so strong that leaving home without permission, or *nuke mairi*, was a considerable problem for authorities in the early modern period.

ALONG A PILGRIMAGE TRAIL
This wood-block print by the 19th-century artist Hiroshige depicts the station town of Fujisawa and the famous Tokaido highway. The development of station towns like Fujisawa, and the improvement of highways, led to a significant increase in the number of people who went on pilgrimages during the Edo period (1600–1868). Pilgrimages to Ise, Mount Fuji, and Saikoku and Shikoku were particularly popular.

FAVOR OF THE DEITY
Pilgrims were often given food by the people of the towns they passed, since it was believed that by helping a pilgrim one could win the favor of the deity of the place to where the pilgrim was traveling.

Pilgrims carried belongings in a sack

Traveling Pilgrims
Since travel was rough and often involved walking great distances, peasants from the Edo period making a pilgrimage would bring only a walking stick (tsue) and bare necessities tied in a cloth or furoshki.

THE TORII
The way to the Shinto shrine is marked by a *torii*. This symbolically separates the sacred enclosure of the shrine from the profane world outside. Often the *torii* are situated a long way from the shrine itself.

A Funeral Procession

On the 49th day after death, the ashes of the deceased are taken to be buried in the family tomb. Behind the priest, who is wearing white vestments, is a procession of the next of kin. At the front of the procession a picture of the deceased is carried, followed by his or her ashes, which are enclosed in a box, and a memorial tablet with the name of the dead person on it. The memorial tablet will later be placed in the Buddhist family altar and given offerings of food and water. The tomb is visited particularly at higan, *which occurs twice a year, at the spring and autumn equinoxes. Although rituals vary between sects, a cremation and a stone memorial are universal.*

A Buddhist Pilgrimage

Buddhist pilgrimages usually have a route consisting of 33 or 88 temples. The pilgrims pictured are on the 88-temple pilgrimage, which covers 932 miles and the island of Shikoku. This pilgrimage focuses on the cult of Kukai, the founder of Shingon. The staffs used by the pilgrims represent him, and the white attire symbolizes a separation from the profane world.

● VISITING A TEMPLE

The Yugyoi temple was often visited by *daimyo* or noblemen on their way to Edo. *Daimyo* would visit the temples as a way of avoiding a *daimyo* of a higher rank, to whom they might have to make some form of formal acknowledgment.

> ❝ *My daily activities are not different, Only I am naturally in harmony with them. Taking nothing, renouncing nothing. In every circumstance no hindrance, no conflict.* ❞
> ZEN IN DAILY LIFE

THE ROAD TO EXCESS

The Tokaido road was used by thousands of pilgrims, who were often thought to be a nuisance. They were habitually loud, drunk, and in more than a few cases engaged in either buying or selling sexual services.

The Head Temple of the Ji Sect

The Yugyoi temple, established in 1325, has been one of the main temples of the Ji sect. The sect was founded by Ippen (1239–89), who was famous for handing out talismans to lay people in the country and for dancing while reciting the name of Amida Buddha.

NEW RELIGIONS

JAPANESE RELIGION DOES NOT HAVE a strong central authority or creed. It encourages people to recognize and realize the religious in every aspect of life as, for example, Buddha or *kami*. Many movements have therefore arisen to help people to do this, and at different times attempts have been made to classify these "new religions" (or in Japanese, *shinko shukyo*). Many "new religions" have a long history. The earliest are those like Tenrikyo and Konkokyo, which have roots in the Tokugawa period (1603–1868) and developed in the Meiji period (1868–1912). Next are those, such as Omoto, Hito no Michi, or Soka Gakkai, that appeared between 1868 and 1945. Finally, there are religions that have emerged since 1945, like Aum Shinrikyo or Ananaikyo, often called "new new religions." Soka Gakkai, one of the largest new religions, was founded in 1930 by Makiguchi Tsunesaburo and Toda Josei. Until recently Soka Gakkai was associated with Nichiren Shoshu, an exclusive Buddhist sect based on the teachings of Nichiren, a 13th-century monk. Daisekiji, their central temple, was founded in 1290. Nichiren had based his sect on absolute faith in the *Lotus Sutra*.

Western Soka Gakkai Followers
Chanting is central to many new religions. Soka Gakkai (Value-Creating Society), has many members in the West. It teaches that a person's inherent Buddha-nature can manifest itself by chanting namu myoho renge kyo: *"Devotion to the Lotus Sutra."*

The Saving Hand of Kannon
Here, the hand of Kannon catches and saves someone from falling off a mountain. The Lotus Sutra *states: "If from the peak of (Mt.) Sumeru, People would hurl him down, Let him think of the Cry-Regarder's power, and like the sun he will stand firm in the sky."*

PROSPERITY OF THE NATION
On the cover is a supplication for the prosperity of the nation and the *dharma*. The recitation of the *Lotus Sutra* has been used to protect the nation. In Japan the text was counted as among the "Three Sutras for the Protection of the Country" (*Chingo Kokka no Sambukyo*).

HOKKEKYO, THE LOTUS SUTRA
The Lotus Sutra, *an ancient Mahayana Buddhist text, has been one of the most important and influential religious texts in Japan since the 7th century. It is very influential among several of the largest lay religious movements such as Soka Gakkai, Rissho Koseikai, and Reiyukai. The message of the sutra is that all sentient beings can attain Buddhahood and that simple devotion is a means to enlightenment. The text also illustrates the various expedient devices used by the Buddha to save sentient beings.*

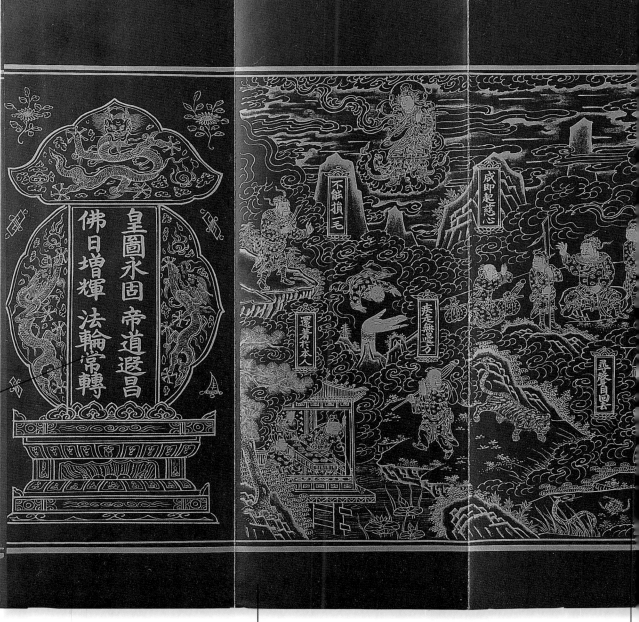

CHAPTER 25, KANNONKYO SUTRA
Chapter 25, shown here, has often been treated as a separate *sutra* – *Kannonkyo*. The chapter exalts the grace of the *bodhisattva* Kannon and her power to save sentient beings who call on her for assistance.

TRANSFORMED APPEARANCE
The transformation (*henso*) of the doctrines and ideas of a *sutra* into pictures is used to explain the meaning of the *sutra* and as images of worship in religious services and rituals. In Nichiren-based religious movements, the *sutra* is used for ancestral ritual and to destroy bad karmic influences.

RELIGION OF DIVINE WISDOM

Most new religions hold several festivals and conventions each year. At these gatherings, the new religion's group identity and beliefs are expressed through clothing and rituals. Conventions are also held for specific groups. This picture shows the Tenrikyo students' association spring convention attended by 4,000 members. Tenrikyo, literally "religion of divine wisdom," has two million members and teaches that God, who is called Tenri-O-no-Mikoto, literally "Lord of Divine Wisdom," appeared through Nakayama Miki (1798–1887), the movement's female founder. According to its doctrine, God created people to be happy and live harmoniously. In order to discover the true self, one must rid oneself of selfish desires and realize that one's body is "a thing lent, a thing borrowed" from God.

Tenrikyo Student Spring Convention

KANNON, SAVIOR OF BELIEVERS
Kannon is believed to appear in this world in various forms to save those who call out her name. In China she is known as Kuan Yin (see pp.72–73).

KANNON
Kannon, "Regarder of the Cries of the World," is one of the most popular *bodhisattvas* in Japan. In popular religion Kannon is usually shown as a woman.

Praying for Help
In times of crisis, if one prays to Kannon for assistance she will, according to the Lotus Sutra, *surely come to the rescue. Among the new religions, praying for assistance is common and is usually for this-worldly benefits, gense riyaku, such as health or a prosperous business.*

HAIL FALLS AND RAIN STREAMS
In the *Lotus Sutra* it says: "Clouds thunder and lightning flashes, Hail falls and rain streams: He thinks of the Cry-Regarder's (Kannon's) power and all instantly are scattered."

SOURCE OF ENLIGHTENMENT
In the 13th century, a reformer named Nichiren (1222–82) concluded that the *Lotus Sutra* contained the highest truth. Nichiren proclaimed that by simply reciting its title, *Namu-Myoho-Renge-Kyo*, it would lead the believer into the highest state of enlightenment.

HANDS TOGETHER IN PRAYER
As with Christians, Buddhists kneel and bring their hands together in prayer. This action, called *gassho*, is a sign of reverence and respect and is also used as an expression of gratitude for blessings received.

Rescue at Sea
A man shipwrecked in a storm calls on the name of Kannon and is saved by the **bodhisattva's supernatural powers.** *The* Lotus Sutra *states that if a single person on a ship calls on the name of Kannon, all will be saved.*

SAVED FROM EXECUTION
In the most dire circumstances, trust in Kannon is all that is needed: "If meeting suffering by royal command, his life is to end in execution, and he thinks of the Cry-Regarder's power, the executioner's sword will break in pieces."

JUDAISM

JUDAISM BEGAN "in the beginning," *bereshith bara Elohim:* "in the beginning God created." These are the first three words of the Jewish Bible, called Tanach, from T, N, and K, the first letters of the Hebrew words for *Torah* (guidance and instruction), *Nebi'im* (prophets), and *Ketubim* (writings). There are at least five different stories of creation in Tanach, but from Genesis (or *Bereshith* in Hebrew) Jews see a purpose and providence in the work of God in creating the world and humans within it. "In the beginning God saw that all was very good." The Book of Genesis also shows how the original peace and harmony became disrupted and destroyed.

The story is told of how conflict arose between humans and God, husband and wife, parents and children, town dwellers and country dwellers, finally culminating in God so regretting his creation that he decided to end it. Only Noah (see p.114) found favor with God, who saved him and made a covenant or promise with him, thereby beginning the repair process.

Tanach is the story of God's work of repair in successive covenants, involving the call of particular individuals, and eventually of an entire people, to specific roles in that process. Of particular importance are Abraham (see pp.114–15) who, in obeying God's command to "arise and go" to a promised land (Genesis 12:1), was the father of the people of Israel as the people of God's purpose, who are often called "the Chosen People"; Isaac and Jacob (the Patriarchs; Jacob was the father of the 12 tribes of Israel); Moses, through whom the covenant on Mount Sinai was made (see pp.116–17), which introduced the Law as the marker of the Covenant agreement; and David (see pp.118–19). When David captured Jerusalem, he introduced kingship as a way of mediating God's purpose to his people: the king is anointed, so is known

as *haMashiach*, the anointed one, in English "the Messiah." When the kings failed the people, the messianic hope went to a future king who would come to inaugurate God's kingdom on earth. David's son Solomon built the first Temple as the center of worship, devotion, and pilgrimage. The second Temple was built in the fifth century BCE after the exile of the Jews in Babylon. The Romans destroyed this Temple in 70 CE (see below).

GOD AND HIS PEOPLE

During the biblical period there was a conflict between God as he revealed himself and the inclination of the people to follow other gods. Prophets spoke powerfully for God who makes himself known as YHWH (Exodus/ Shemot 6:2–8). Jews do not attempt to pronounce this name – it is too holy, and they say instead *HaShem*, the Name; but it is conventionally written as Yahweh. The basic command on Israel is, "Be holy, as I am holy" (Leviticus/ Wayyiqra 19:2); and the fundamental creed is the Shema (Hebrew for "hear"): "Hear, O Israel, the Lord your God is one. . . ."

Tanach, and especially Torah, the first five books of the Bible, shows and tells Israel what it means to be holy. Torah is often translated as "Law," but is really guidance that includes law. There are 613 commands, of which 248 are positive and 365 are negative. In keeping these, Jews are saying "Yes" to God's purpose

Temple Candlestick
The Menorah, a seven-branched candlestick, is an ancient Jewish symbol deriving from the candlestick that originally stood in the Temple in Jerusalem built by David's son Solomon in the 10th century BCE.

Passover Meal
This detail from a stained-glass window (see pp.120–21) shows the Seder Pesach or Passover meal, which celebrates the Exodus. This revealed God's power to rescue the Israelites from slavery in Egypt.

of using Israel to begin his work of repair. Jews do not have to find a reason for the laws. Laws, such as not eating certain foods, do not have to be explained by saying that some food spoils in hot countries. Even without a reason, the laws are an enacted language of love, a visible way of accepting that God has chosen Israel to be a healed community, demonstrating in advance what will one day be the case for everybody, "when the knowledge of God shall cover the earth as the waters cover the sea" (Habakkuk 2:14). Festivals in Judaism celebrate the saving purpose of God in Jewish history.

DIFFERENT INTERPRETATIONS

The healed and obedient community has not always been apparent in practice. When Jesus was alive, there were many conflicting interpretations of how the covenant should be observed. A Jewish revolt against Rome in 66 CE ended in defeat in 70 CE and in an even greater defeat in 135 CE. The Temple was destroyed, and Jews were scattered from the Promised Land into a wide dispersion, known as the Diaspora. This led to two major communities that developed differently: the Ashkenazim, who lived mainly in central Europe, but who, after many persecutions, especially the Holocaust (see pp.134–35), were scattered worldwide, founding a large community in the US; and the Sephardim, who built communities in Spain and around the Mediterranean.

The reconstruction of Judaism was achieved by the rabbis, the masters or teachers, who built up through oral

Torah Mantle
The scrolls of the Torah, part of the Jewish Bible, are covered with a mantle and kept in the Ark of the Covenant behind a curtain in the synagogue, facing in the direction of Jerusalem. The Hebrew text at the top of the mantle shown here reads: "Crown of the Torah." The crown on the mantle is symbolic of the Torah being the crowning glory of Jewish life; the lion is a common Jewish symbol associated with the tribe of Judah.

transmission an interpretation of what the commandments of the Torah should mean in life, without a Temple and in a new exile, and based on family and synagogue. These interpretations were eventually committed to writing, in collections that are known as Mishnah and Talmuds (of which the Babylonian Talmud has particular authority). These were later organized in codes, of which the code of Maimonides (1135–1204) and of Joseph Caro (1488–1575), known as *Shulchan Arukh*, are paramount. Application of the tradition to new circumstances continues to the present.

As well as in law or *halakah*, "that by which one walks," Judaism was graphically expressed in stories or *aggadah* (sometimes spelled *haggadah*) and in biblical interpretation, or *midrash*. Jews also went deeper into the love and worship of God in *kabbalah* (an esoteric exploration of God's dealings with the world – see pp.124–25) and in Hasidism (see p.126), which arose in Eastern Europe in the late 18th century. A Hasidic leader is known as *zaddik*, meaning "righteous." Well-known *zaddikim* were Ba'al Shem Tov (the Besht), Dov Baer, and Jacob Joseph. Around them gathered disciples who entered with them into profound, and often ecstatic, experience of God. The Lubavicher are a well-known group of Hasidic Jews.

Babi Yar Sculpture
This glass sculpture, by Lucio Bubacco, expresses the horror and tragedy of the Holocaust (see pp.134–35). At Babi Yar, on September 29, 1941, 33,771 Jews – entire families from Kiev – were murdered. The artist comments: "This work recalls their final contact with each other, their last touch with life. The red is not from the glow of the sun. It is their blood which flows together." It is from the collection of the American Interfaith Institute, **Artists Confronting the Inconceivable.**

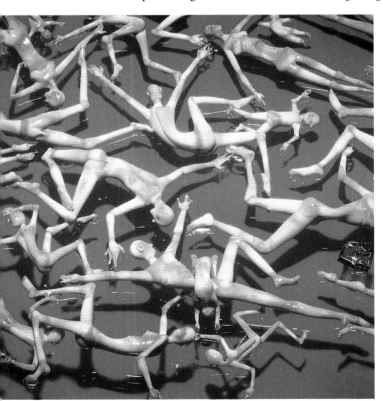

ZIONISM

Through this whole period of *Galut*, or exile, the memory of Zion, the traditional name of Jerusalem, has endured. The Zionist movement (see pp.132–33) began to work for the return of the Jews to Jerusalem in the 19th century. Not all Jews agree, because they believe that only the Messiah can restore Jerusalem. But the vicious cruelty of anti-Semitism, especially in the Holocaust, before and during World War II, led many to see the restoration of Israel as a Jewish State as essential. Whether Israel should coincide with the boundaries of the original promised land remains an issue in dispute.

Jews are by no means united in their various interpretations of laws, customs, and practices and these interpretations vary from country to country, community by community. But whether Orthodox, Reform, Conservative, or Liberal, Jews are held together by their age-old group identity, a fundamental belief in God and his Commandments and a yearning to return to Israel, their promised homeland.

In the words found inscribed on the wall of a cellar where a Jew had been hiding from the Nazis: "I believe in the sun, even when it is not shining; I believe in love, even when I am not feeling it; I believe in God, even when he is silent."

THE ORIGINS OF JUDAISM

THE **JEWISH PEOPLE BELIEVE** themselves to be descended from a tribe that lived in Canaan, which is normally understood to be an extensive area in the eastern Mediterranean encompassing most of modern Israel, Jordan, and Syria. In the days of the Patriarchs, Abraham, his son Isaac, and Isaac's son Jacob, it lay between the great Middle Eastern centers of civilization: Egypt to the south; Mesopotamia to the east; and the land of the Hittites to the north. It was a natural corridor for both traders and invading armies. The Jews believe they are descended from Abraham, a "wandering Aramaean," who became the father of a great nation. God made a covenant or agreement with him and promised him a land "flowing with milk and honey." Although they have never throughout recorded history been the sole possessers of the territory, the land remains crucial to their understanding of themselves.

ABRAHAM'S TRAVELS
This 16th-century map of Canaan and the nearby nations is surrounded by roundels illustrating episodes in Abraham's life. They should be read clockwise. The Latin inscription reads "The wanderings and life of the Patriarch Abraham." Abraham's life is recounted in the Book of Genesis. He is said to have been the great, great, great, great, great, great, great, great-grandson of Noah, whom God had saved from the flood (see below). Abraham was the first Jew – God's covenant or promise was with him and his descendants, rather than with the whole of humanity.

Noah and the Survival of the Human Race
According to the Book of Genesis, soon after the creation of the earth and the founding of the human race, God sent a great flood to destroy what he had made because people were so wicked. Only the righteous Noah, his family, and a pair of each animal species were saved, safe in a great ark that God had told Noah to build. Here Noah sends out a raven and a dove to see whether the waters have subsided.

THE COASTAL PLAIN •
West of Canaan lies the fertile coastal plain, providing a communication line between north and south. It was the location of various independent city-states that extended up the Mediterranean coast. Archaeological evidence indicates they achieved a high level of civilization.

THE LAND OF EGYPT •
Canaan lies next to Egypt. Abraham is said to have spent time there (Genesis 12:10–20). Later the Jews were held as slaves by the Egyptians and were led to freedom in the Promised Land by Moses (see pp.116–17).

THE PROMISE
The Latin inscription records God's promise to Abraham: "And I will give to you, and to your descendants after you, the land of your sojournings, all the land of Canaan, for an everlasting possession" (Genesis 17:8).

BIRTH OF ISAAC
Abraham was 100 when Isaac was born. Isaac was the heir to God's covenant, making possible God's promise that Abraham would be the father of a nation.

SODOM AND GOMORRAH •
The cities of Sodom and Gomorrah were destroyed, as the angels said, because they were so evil. Abraham asked God to spare them if ten good men were found. Ten were not found, so God destroyed them, rescuing only Lot and his family.

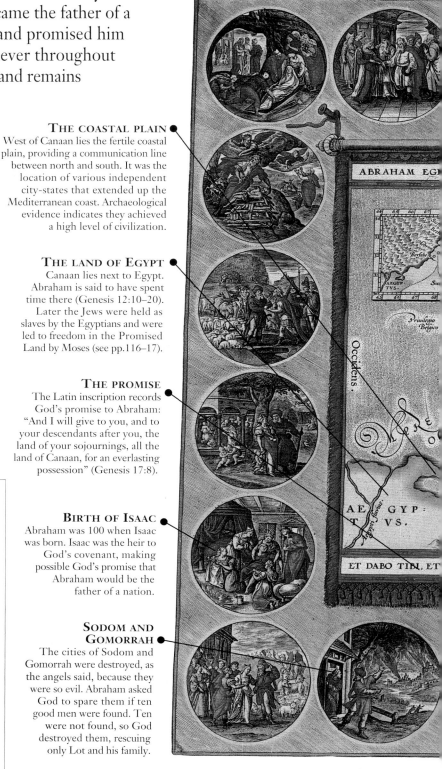

JACOB, WHO WAS RENAMED ISRAEL

Jacob, Abraham's grandson, was a wily character. He bought his older twin Esau's birthright and tricked Isaac, his blind dying father, into giving him Esau's blessing as the eldest son. As a result, he fled to his uncle's house to escape Esau's anger. On the way, he had a vision of a ladder with angels on it. Then God spoke to him, promising that the land he lay on would be given to him and his descendants forever. Years later Jacob returned with his household to submit to his brother. Again he met with God; this time he seemed to be wrestling all night with a stranger who put his hip out of joint. At dawn, the stranger told Jacob, "Your name shall no more be called Jacob, but Israel, for you have striven with God and with men, and have prevailed" (Genesis 32:28).

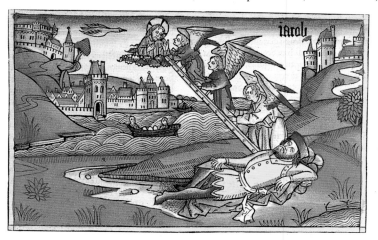

Jacob dreams of a ladder with angels going up and down

Hagar and Ishmael Are Cast Out
Hagar, Sarah's servant and mother of Abraham's son Ishmael, was cast out with her son once Isaac, Abraham's son by Sarah, was born. However, God protected them, and Ishmael grew up to be the father of a great people. The Ishmaelites have been identified with the Arabs. Thus the enmity between the Jews and the Arabs has legendary origins.

> *A wandering Aramaean was my father; and he went down into Egypt and sojourned there, few in number; and there he became a nation, great, mighty, and populous.* "
> DEUTERONOMY 26:5

The Sacrifice of Isaac
As a final test of obedience, God told Abraham to sacrifice his son Isaac, the precious heir to God's promise. Abraham obeyed; he built a fire and tied up the boy. Only at the last minute did God tell him to spare the lad. Instead Abraham sacrificed a ram caught in nearby undergrowth.

OBEDIENCE TO GOD
Abraham, his father, his wife Sarah, and orphaned nephew Lot moved from Ur in Mesopotamia to Haran. But when Abraham was 75, God told him to leave, promising that he would be the father of a nation. Even though he had no children, Abraham obeyed God and left his home.

The Covenant
For much of his life Abraham had no children, but God repeatedly promised him that he would be the father of a great nation; that his descendants would be as numerous as the stars of heaven, as the sand on the shore, and the dust of the earth.

ABRAHAMI PATRIARCHAE PEREGRINATIO, ET VITA. *Abrahamo Ortelio Antverpiano auctore.*

A TVA, ET DE COGNATIONE TVA, ET VENI IN TERRAM QVAM MONSTRAVERO TIBI.

TE, TERRAM PEREGRINATIONIS TVAE, OMNEM TERRAM CHANAAN, IN POSSESSIONEM AETERNAM.

SOJOURN IN EGYPT
Driven by famine in Canaan, Abraham, Sarah, and Lot went to Egypt. Unaware that Sarah was married, the Pharaoh took her as his wife. In punishment God afflicted the palace with plagues, so Pharaoh sent Abraham and Sarah back to Canaan.

A QUARREL WITH LOT
After Abraham left Egypt, his men and Lot's quarreled because the land could not support so many animals. This can be seen as the first threat to God's promise that Abraham would own the land. So they compromised – Lot went east, near the city of Sodom, and Abraham went toward Canaan.

THE DESERT
Abraham seems to have been a rich wandering herdsman, guiding his flocks through the desert. In the Jewish story the desert was often the place for revelation and renewal. It was in Sinai that Moses received the Ten Commandments (see pp.118–19).

RESCUE OF LOT
The next crisis came after a war in which Lot was captured by kings hostile to the kings of Sodom and Gomorrah. Abraham and his men rescued him and his household by attacking the enemy at night.

BLESSING OF MELCHIZEDEK
After his victory, Melchizedek, priest and king of Jerusalem, gave Abraham bread and wine, declaring: "Blessed be Abram by God Most High, maker of heaven and earth; and blessed be God Most High, who has delivered your enemies into your hand" (Genesis 14:19–20).

SIGN OF THE COVENANT
When Abraham still had no child by Sarah, God established his covenant with a sign. He told him that "every male among you shall be circumcised . . . it shall be a sign of the covenant between me and you" (Genesis 17:10–11). Today, all Jewish boys are circumcised at eight days old, symbolizing their inheritance of Abraham's covenant.

ALTERNATIVE HEIR
Many years passed and still Sarah did not have a child. When he was 86 Abraham had a child by Sarah's servant Hagar. Hagar gave birth to a son, Ishmael – but Ishmael was not the heir to God's promise.

Receiving God's Messengers
Seeing three strangers, Abraham offered them hospitality. They promised him that Sarah, despite her great age, would bear a son. Later, the messengers, described as angels, warned Lot that the cities of Sodom and Gomorrah would be destroyed.

> " *. . . because you have done this, and have not withheld your son, your only son, I will indeed bless you, and I will multiply your descendants as the stars of heaven and as the sand which is on the seashore.* "
> GENESIS 22:16–17

THE LAWS OF GOD

JEWS ARE OFTEN DESCRIBED AS "people of the Book" because they base their lives on the Bible and, as such, hold in special reverence the revelation of God in Torah. Torah is often translated as "Law," but it means "instruction" or "guidance." Torah is contained in the first five books of the Bible, which, as well as history, contain the 613 commandments fundamental to Jewish life. Jews believe God gave these laws to Moses, the prophet who led the Israelites out of slavery in Egypt in about the 14th century BCE. They include ritual laws, rules of hygiene, and moral laws. Jews believe that the laws form part of a covenant relationship with God – as God's Chosen People, they should keep them all. This does not suggest superiority to others; the role of the Jews is to bring other nations to the knowledge of the one true God. Of the 613 laws, the Ten Commandments (Exodus 20), said to have been inscribed by God on stone tablets, hold a central place. The tablets, kept in the Ark of the Covenant, built in Moses' time, were housed in the Temple in Jerusalem (see p.119).

Moses on Mount Sinai
After Moses led the Israelites out of slavery, they camped in the wilderness of Sinai. Leaving his people at the bottom, Moses climbed the mountain. There was thunder and lightning, and the mountain was shrouded in smoke. Here, with the young Joshua as a witness, God spoke with Moses and gave him the tablets on which were written the words of the Law.

THE ORAL LAW

Written Torah contains much guidance and instruction, but it does not deal with every human situation. The application and meaning of Torah were passed on by word of mouth. They became Torah *she be'al peh*, "Torah which is by mouth." This Oral Law, consisting of interpretations of Torah, is called Mishnah. It was written down by Rabbi Judah ha Nasi in about 200 CE. Over the next three centuries, Jewish scholars debated and reinterpreted the contents of Mishnah; this was written down in about 400 CE as the Gemara, or "completion." Around 500 CE, a Babylonian rabbi, Rav Ashi, combined the Gemura with the Mishnah; this was called the Talmud. Several summaries were compiled to help readers understand it; the most famous were by Maimonides in the 12th century and Joseph Caro in the 16th. Keeping these laws is seen as a religious duty, and Jews have maintained a single community by practicing the rituals laid down in them (see pp.126–27).

Holy Trinity Chapel on the summit of Mount Sinai, built on the spot where Moses received the Ten Commandments.

Mount Sinai
God's revelation to Moses on Mount Sinai is regarded as the supreme unveiling of God. The Book of Deuteronomy (34:10–12) declares that ". . . there has not arisen a prophet since in Israel like Moses, whom the Lord knew face to face . . . for all the mighty power and all the great and terrible deeds which Moses wrought in the sight of all Israel." On Sinai, God revealed his will to the Jews and, in keeping with his commandments, they are accomplishing his work in the world.

NO GRAVEN IMAGES ●
The first and second Commandments state that Jews must worship the one true God; they may not worship idols or bow down to the idols of other nations. The real God is too overwhelming to be contained within an image; He can be worshiped only in spirit and in truth.

● **GOD'S SACRED NAME**
The third Commandment reminds Jews that God is too great for his name to be taken in vain. Traditionally Jews do not use his name at all, but speak of *Adonai* (the Lord) or *HaShem* (the Name).

● **PRESERVING PROPERTY**
The eighth Commandment states: "Thou shalt not steal." The rabbis interpreted this to mean that theft of all property is wrong, including plagiarism, the stealing of ideas. Complicated systems of compensation were devised, and the thief could not be forgiven until he had recompensed the victim.

● **RESPECTING THE MARRIAGE BOND**
The seventh Commandment forbids adultery. It is adultery (extramarital relationships) rather than fornication (premarital relationships) that is so condemned. This is because traditionally, Jews married very young, and adultery can call into question the legitimacy of children.

Plague of flies

Plague of frogs

Plague of animal deaths

Pharaoh frees the Israelites

The Jews had been slaves in Egypt for years. The Book of Exodus teaches that God had chosen Moses to be his agent in freeing the Jews and leading them out of Egypt. Not surprisingly, the Egyptians were most reluctant to lose their source of free labor. In order to persuade them, God sent ten plagues to Egypt. The Nile River turned to blood; frogs from the river overran the land; there was a swarm of gnats and then a plague of flies, and all the Egyptian cattle died. The Egyptian people were then struck down with sores and boils; there were hail storms; a plague of locusts; and darkness fell for three days. Finally, all the first-born of the Egyptians died. This convinced Pharaoh to free the Israelites. God had demonstrated his power. He stated as the first Commandment: "I am the Lord your God who brought you out of the land of Egypt, out of the house of bondage. You shall have no other gods before me" (Exodus 20:2–3).

THE HOLY SABBATH
The fourth Commandment states that Jews must keep the Sabbath holy. Just as God did on his seventh day of creation, they should rest after six days of work.

HONORING ONE'S PARENTS
The fifth Commandment states that children should honor their parents. In many societies, parents in their old age are dependent on their children, just as all children, when young, are dependent on their parents.

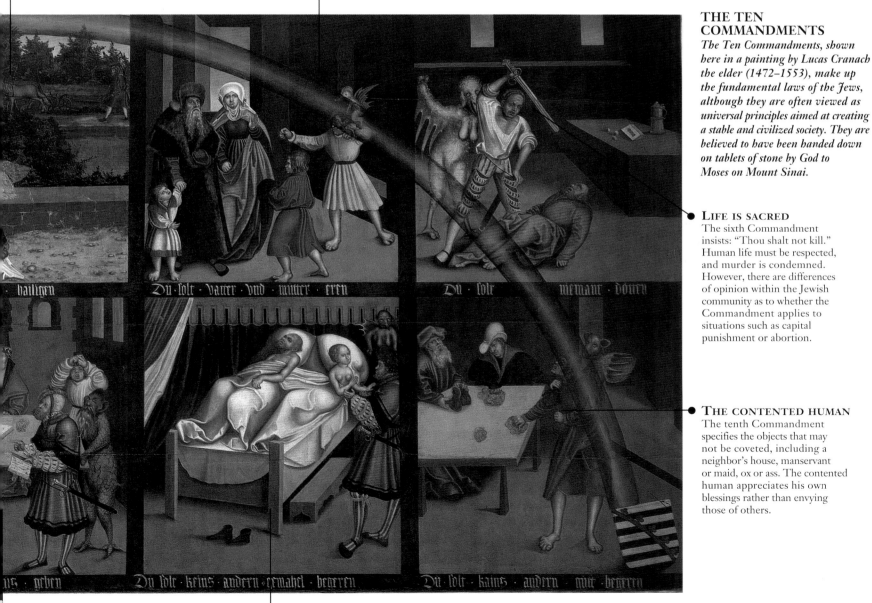

THE TEN COMMANDMENTS
The Ten Commandments, shown here in a painting by Lucas Cranach the elder (1472–1553), make up the fundamental laws of the Jews, although they are often viewed as universal principles aimed at creating a stable and civilized society. They are believed to have been handed down on tablets of stone by God to Moses on Mount Sinai.

LIFE IS SACRED
The sixth Commandment insists: "Thou shalt not kill." Human life must be respected, and murder is condemned. However, there are differences of opinion within the Jewish community as to whether the Commandment applies to situations such as capital punishment or abortion.

THE CONTENTED HUMAN
The tenth Commandment specifies the objects that may not be coveted, including a neighbor's house, manservant or maid, ox or ass. The contented human appreciates his own blessings rather than envying those of others.

THE IMPORTANCE OF TRUTHFULNESS
The ninth Commandment states: "Thou shalt not give false testimony against your neighbor." In a civilized society, the law courts must be incorruptible, and fundamental honesty has to be observed in everyday dealings between individuals.

AVOIDING ENVY AND JEALOUSY
In the tenth Commandment, God commands his people to avoid covetousness. This includes avoiding the temptation to covet a neighbor's wife.

❝If you will obey my voice and keep my covenant, you shall be my own possession among all peoples . . . and you shall be to me a kingdom of priests and a holy nation. ❞
EXODUS 19:5–6

WAITING FOR THE MESSIAH

IN HEBREW, "MESSIAH" means "the anointed." Of old, kings were anointed as a sign of their divine election. As 2 Samuel states, "great triumph He gives to His king, and shows steadfast love to His anointed." It was believed that God had chosen King David and his descendants, but when there ceased to be kings in Israel and the land was dominated by foreign powers, hope persisted that God would send another king like David to right all wrongs and put an end to earthly wars. The king would make a covenant with the righteous and kill the wicked, and his arrival would end history and establish God's kingdom on earth. For many centuries, the Jewish people have remained faithful to this vision, and the belief in the coming of the Messiah is enshrined in their liturgy or worship. In modern times, the expectation has faded in some quarters; today, for some Jews, the founding of the state of Israel has proved a substitute for the old hope; for others, the true Israel cannot exist until it is inaugurated by the Messiah: for many the traditional hope continues.

The Messiah Enters His Kingdom

According to the prophet Zechariah (9:9), the Messiah will enter his kingdom "meek and riding upon an ass." Here the Messiah is entering Jerusalem introduced by a herald, traditionally identified with the prophet Elijah. As promised by the biblical prophets, the Jewish people can then gather from all corners of the earth. Their exile is over and God's glory will go forth from Jerusalem.

THE STORY OF DAVID

This English illumination, dating from the late 12th century, shows part of the story of King David, the first of the great kings in the history of the Jews. His story is told in the two books of Samuel in the Jewish scriptures.

> ❝ Then David said to the Philistine, You come to me with a sword and with a spear and with a javelin; but I come to you in the name of the Lord of hosts, the God of the armies of Israel, whom you have defied. ❞
>
> 1 SAMUEL 17:45

● DEATH OF GOLIATH OF GATH

Goliath was said to be almost 10 feet (nearly three meters) tall, with a brass helmet, a coat of mail, greaves of brass, a shield of brass, and a spear. After David killed Goliath, he cut off his head, and the Philistine army fled.

● THE PROPHET SAMUEL

Samuel was the first of the prophets and the last of the judges of Israel, the rulers who were appointed periodically by God to rescue the Israelites from the consequences of their sins. He was told by God to appoint Saul as first king of the Israelites, but Saul became displeased with God and sent Samuel to Bethlehem, to the household of Jesse. Samuel recognized David, the youngest, as Saul's successor. "He was ruddy and had beautiful eyes and was handsome. And the Lord said 'Rise,

The clothing is medieval, the period from which the illumination dates

David and Goliath

David, youngest son of Jesse, was delivering cheeses to three of his brothers in the Israelite army when the Philistine giant Goliath issued a challenge to personal combat with any soldier who dared confront him. No one stepped forward until David appeared with a sling and five smooth stones. He felled the giant with a single

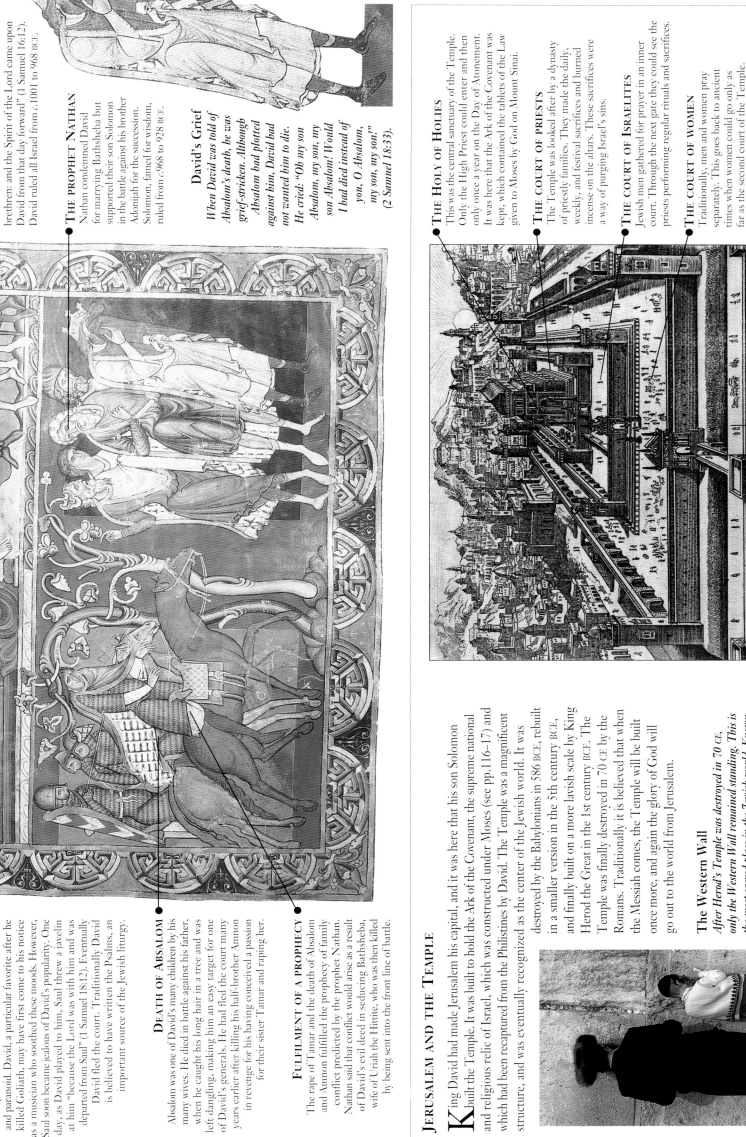

and paranoid. David, a particular favorite after he killed Goliath, may have first come to his notice as a musician who soothed these moods. However, Saul soon became jealous of David's popularity. One day, as David played to him, Saul threw a javelin at him "because the Lord was with him and was departed from Saul" (1 Samuel 18:12). Eventually David fled the court. Traditionally David is believed to have written the Psalms, an important source of the Jewish liturgy.

DEATH OF ABSALOM

Absalom was one of David's many children by his many wives. He died in battle against his father, when he caught his long hair in a tree and was left dangling, making him an easy target for one of David's generals. He had fled the court many years earlier after killing his half-brother Amnon in revenge for his having conceived a passion for their sister Tamar and raping her.

FULFILMENT OF A PROPHECY

The rape of Tamar and the death of Absalom and Amnon fulfilled the prophecy of family conflict predicted by the prophet Nathan. Nathan said that conflict would arise as a result of David's evil deed in seducing Bathsheba, wife of Uriah the Hittite, who was then killed by being sent into the front line of battle.

brethren: and the Spirit of the Lord came upon David from that day forward" (1 Samuel 16:12). David ruled all Israel from c.1001 to 968 BCE.

THE PROPHET NATHAN

Nathan condemned David for marrying Bathsheba but supported their son Solomon in the battle against his brother Adonijah for the succession. Solomon, famed for wisdom, ruled from c.968 to 928 BCE.

David's Grief

When David was told of Absalom's death, he was grief-stricken. Although Absalom had plotted against him, David had not wanted him to die. He cried: "Oh my son Absalom, my son, my son Absalom! Would I had died instead of you, O Absalom, my son, my son!" (2 Samuel 18:33).

JERUSALEM AND THE TEMPLE

King David had made Jerusalem his capital, and it was here that his son Solomon built the Temple. It was built to hold the Ark of the Covenant, the supreme national and religious relic of Israel, which was constructed under Moses (see pp.116–17) and which had been recaptured from the Philistines by David. The Temple was a magnificent structure, and was eventually recognized as the center of the Jewish world. It was destroyed by the Babylonians in 586 BCE, rebuilt in a smaller version in the 5th century BCE, and finally built on a more lavish scale by King Herod the Great in the 1st century BCE. The Temple was finally destroyed in 70 CE by the Romans. Traditionally it is believed that when the Messiah comes, the Temple will be built once more, and again the glory of God will go out to the world from Jerusalem.

The Western Wall

After Herod's Temple was destroyed in 70 CE, only the Western Wall remained standing. This is the most sacred place in the Jewish world. Known as the Wailing Wall, because Jews used to stand by it lamenting the loss of the Temple, it is still a major center of pilgrimage. Here, a member of a strictly orthodox Jewish sect prays with his son. Jews pray, especially at the end of Passover (see pp.128–29), "Next year in Jerusalem!"

THE HOLY OF HOLIES

This was the central sanctuary of the Temple. Only the High Priest could enter and then only once a year on the Day of Atonement. It was here that the Ark of the Covenant was kept, which contained the tablets of the Law given to Moses by God on Mount Sinai.

THE COURT OF PRIESTS

The Temple was looked after by a dynasty of priestly families. They made the daily, weekly, and festival sacrifices and burned incense on the altars. These sacrifices were a way of purging Israel's sins.

THE COURT OF ISRAELITES

Jewish men gathered for prayer in an inner court. Through the next gate they could see the priests performing regular rituals and sacrifices.

THE COURT OF WOMEN

Traditionally, men and women pray separately. This goes back to ancient times when women could go only as far as the second court of the Temple.

The Temple in Jerusalem

This 19th-century engraving shows what the Temple in Jerusalem probably looked like, although there are no authentic depictions of it.

THE COURT OF GENTILES

The outer court of the Temple was open to everyone. Over the gate into the next court was a notice warning non-Jews to come no farther.

THE PRECINCTS

The Temple was not a single building, but a series of courtyards, one leading to another. It had its own administration, led by the High Priest who was a descendant of Moses's brother Aaron.

JEWISH WORSHIP

THE HOLINESS AND MAJESTY OF GOD evoke worship and prayer. After the Temple in Jerusalem was destroyed in 70 CE, the sacrificial rituals that could no longer be performed were replaced by prayer in the morning, afternoon, and evening. The liturgy (prayer service) is described as "the service of the heart." It includes the *Shema*, the Jewish declaration of faith: "Hear O Israel, the Lord our God, the Lord is One," and the *Amidah*, a series of benedictions that use the formula "Blessed are you O God, King of the Universe." Attaching oneself to God through prayer is the ideal; the 13th-century philosopher Nahmanides stated, "Whoever cleaves to his Creator becomes eligible to receive the Holy Spirit." Ideally, set prayers are recited in a *minyan*, a group of at least ten men. Prayer can take place at any time and in any place, but throughout the Jewish world, the synagogue (derived from *sunagoge*, the Greek word for "congregation" or "assembly") has become the center for worship and study. Three times a day the faithful attend formal services, classes take place, and the buildings frequently include communal offices, social halls, and accommodations for visitors.

SEPARATION OF MEN AND WOMEN

Traditionally, men and women pray separately in Judaism, and in the synagogue there is a partition between the seating allocated for men and for women. According to the Talmud, the 6th-century Jewish law book, this separation goes back to the days of the Temple in Jerusalem, and it is enforced because women are perceived as a distraction to prayer. Women, unlike men, are not expected to attend daily services, and if they do go, their presence, except for Reform Jews (see p.127), does not count toward a *minyan*. A woman's responsibility is to keep a Jewish home, an important focus for Jewish life, and to bring up her children in the traditional way. Jewishness is passed down through the mother.

Blowing the Shofar

A shofar is a trumpet made out of a ram's horn. It is blown on Rosh Hashanah (the New Year) and on Yom Kippur (the Day of Atonement). As the great 12th-century philosopher Maimonides explained, it calls sinners to repentance: "Awake you sinners, and ponder your deeds; remember your Creator, forsake your evil ways and return to God . . ." In modern times in Israel, the shofar is blown on Friday afternoons to announce the Sabbath.

A STAINED-GLASS WINDOW

This modern window depicts the festival of the Passover (see pp.128–29). The Hebrew inscription at the top of the window indicates that it is the festival of unleavened bread. It is usually celebrated at home with a ritual family meal.

THE FESTIVAL LIGHT

The lighting of the Sabbath and festival candles is central to Jewish worship. The inscription is an abbreviation of the benediction: "Blessed are you Lord our God, King of the Universe, who has commanded us to light the lights of the festival."

THE ETERNAL LIGHT

While candles are lit in the home on the Sabbath and on festivals, a candle or lamp is left perpetually burning in the synagogue to indicate God's eternal presence. Known as the *Ner Tamid*, it is also a reminder of the golden candlestick that burned continually in the Jerusalem Temple.

THE LIGHT OF GOD

"By your light, we shall see light." In prayer, God is often compared with light. We cannot grasp light, but through it the whole world is illuminated. Similarly, we cannot directly know or understand God, but through worship and prayer all spiritual realities can be revealed.

CEREMONIAL CLEANSING

According to Jewish law, the hands must be ceremoniously washed after rising from sleep, touching a corpse, urinating or defecating, and before eating, praying, or performing rituals such as lighting candles. It is generally the mother of the household who lights the Sabbath or festival candles. After the flame is lit, the hands are waved over the flame, and the mother covers her eyes in a moment of silent prayer.

THE LANGUAGE OF PRAYER

All of the inscriptions of the window are in Hebrew. This was the language of the ancient Israelites. Although it was superceded by Aramaic in the second century BCE, it continued to be used for prayer and for reading from the scriptures. Yiddish later became the vernacular language of Eastern European Jews, and Ladino was used by Orientals, but Hebrew remained essential for worship and is an important element in Jewish education today.

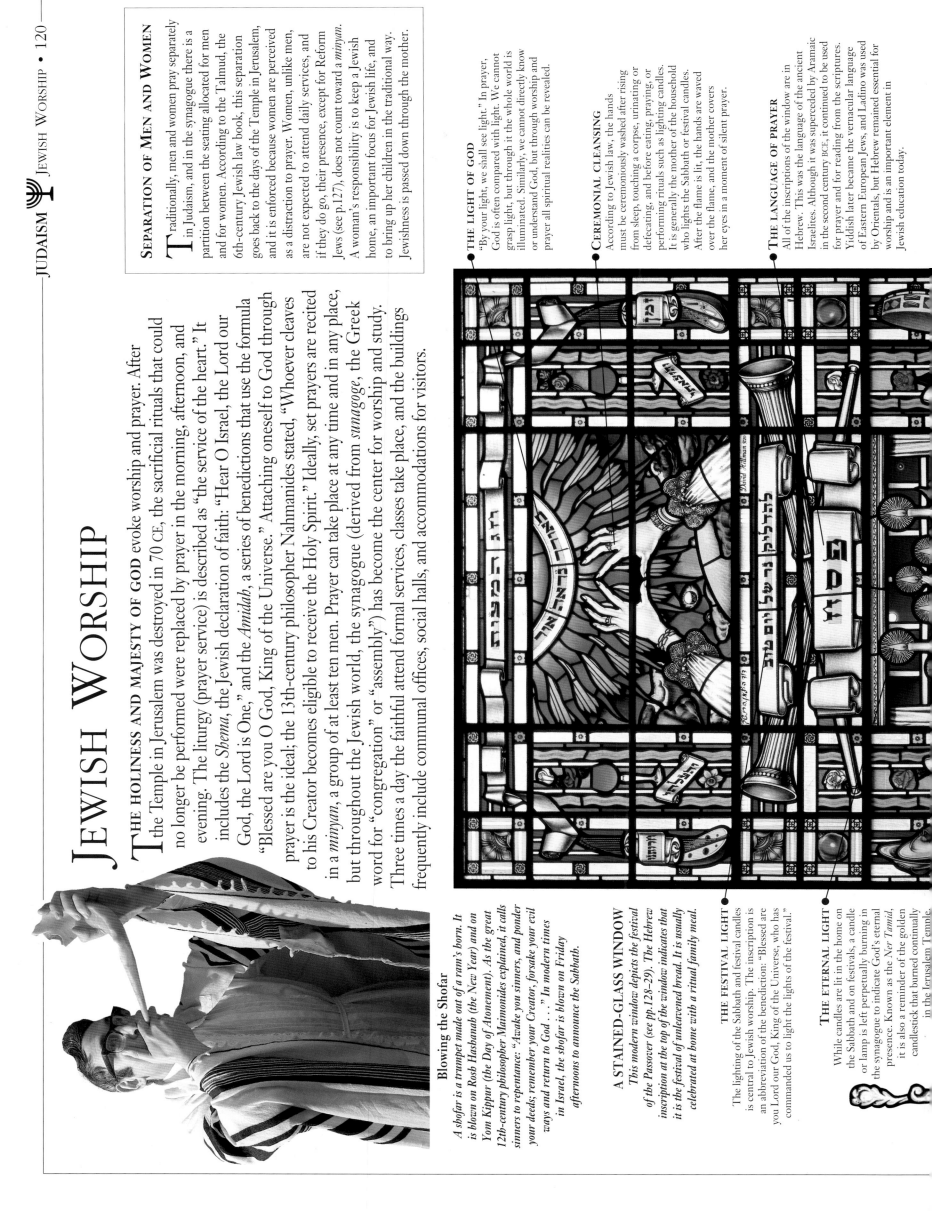

Wine and Worship

Wine plays an important part in Jewish worship. In the days of the Jerusalem Temple, it was poured over the altar with the sacrifices. Today it is used both to welcome and to conclude the Sabbath, and it is an essential part of both the Passover and the circumcision ceremonies (see pp.128–29).

PRAYER BOOKS

For centuries, all the liturgical prayers were known by heart, and prayer books were only used after the 9th century. The book containing the daily prayers is known as the *Siddur*, and the one containing the festival prayers is the *Mahzor*. Today they are generally printed with Hebrew on the right hand side of the page, with a translation on the left.

SEPARATE DISHES

Kosher dietary laws state that meat and dairy products must be served in separate dishes and may not be served at the same meal. This safeguards the religious purity of the home, the most important religious center for a Jewish family.

Incense Burner

Incense was commonly used in ritual in the Temple in Jerusalem. The smoke it produces is symbolic of prayer.

KOSHER FOOD

Every aspect of life can be seen as an opportunity for worship. The extensive Jewish food laws that outlaw certain foods and dictate methods of preparation are a means of sanctifying the individual and maintaining the separation of God's chosen people from gentile communities.

BREAD

Bread is shared as part of Jewish worship. On the Sabbath, a plaited loaf or *hallah* is blessed, sprinkled with salt, and eaten. At Passover, unleavened bread or *matzos* is an essential part of the ritual.

"TELL TO YOUR SON . . ."

For many centuries, Jews have lived as a minority group within a largely hostile alien culture. Thus there has always been a great emphasis on survival and on the importance of handing down the tradition to children and children's children.

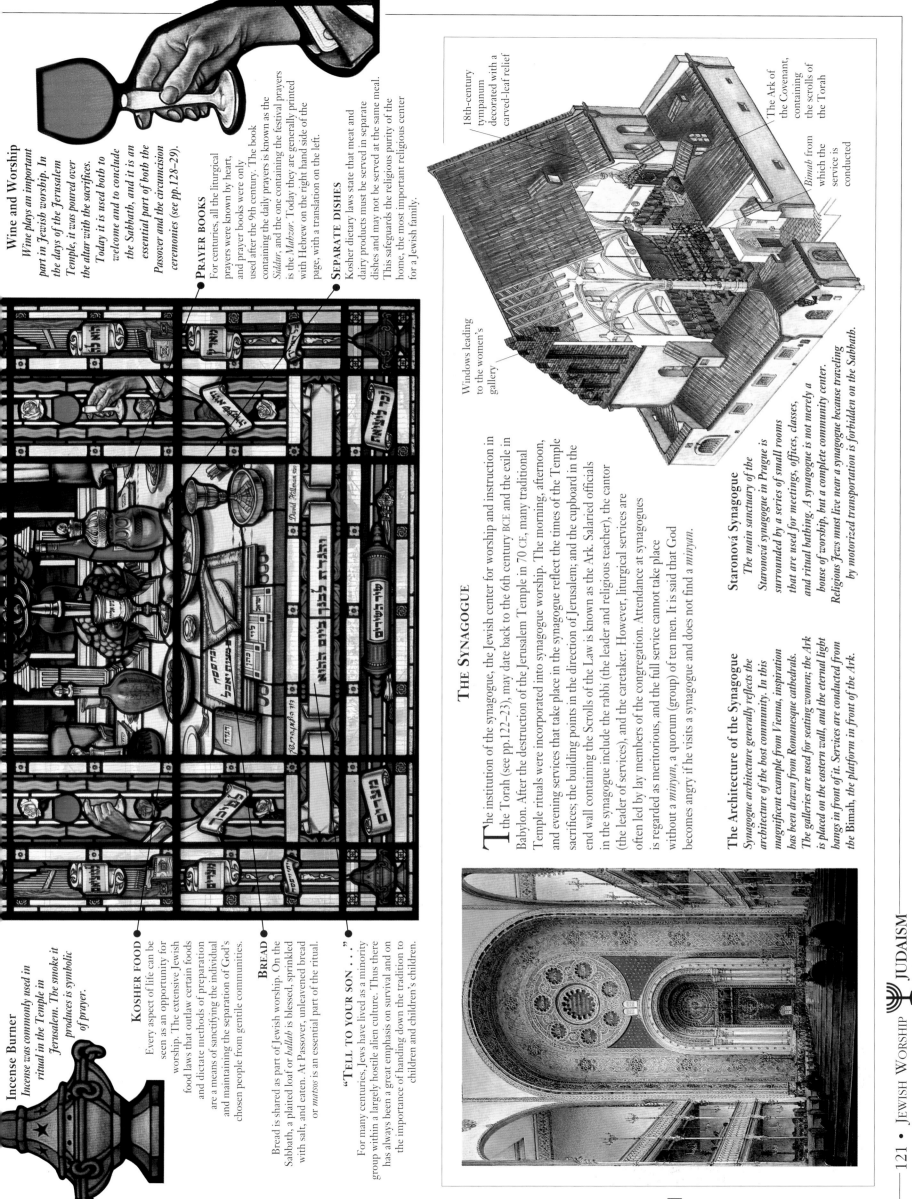

18th-century tympanum decorated with a carved-leaf relief

The Ark of the Covenant, containing the scrolls of the Torah

Windows leading to the women's gallery

Bimah from which the service is conducted

THE SYNAGOGUE

The institution of the synagogue, the Jewish center for worship and instruction in the Torah (see pp.122–23), may date back to the 6th century BCE and the exile in Babylon. After the destruction of the Jerusalem Temple in 70 CE, many traditional Temple rituals were incorporated into synagogue worship. The morning, afternoon, and evening services that take place in the synagogue reflect the times of the Temple sacrifices; the building points in the direction of Jerusalem; and the cupboard in the end wall containing the Scrolls of the Law is known as the Ark. Salaried officials in the synagogue include the rabbi (the leader and religious teacher), the cantor (the leader of services), and the caretaker. However, liturgical services are often led by lay members of the congregation. Attendance at synagogues is regarded as meritorious, and the full service cannot take place without a *minyan*, a quorum (group) of ten men. It is said that God becomes angry if he visits a synagogue and does not find a *minyan*.

The Architecture of the Synagogue

Synagogue architecture generally reflects the architecture of the host community. In this magnificent example from Vienna, inspiration has been drawn from Romanesque cathedrals. The galleries are used for seating women; the Ark is placed on the eastern wall, and the eternal light hangs in front of it. Services are conducted from the Bimah, the platform in front of the Ark.

Staronová Synagogue

The main sanctuary of the Staronova synagogue in Prague is surrounded by a series of small rooms that are used for meetings, offices, classes, and ritual bathing. A synagogue is not merely a house of worship, but a complete community center. Religious Jews must live near a synagogue because traveling by motorized transportation is forbidden on the Sabbath.

STUDYING THE TORAH

THE EDUCATION OF CHILDREN is a primary duty of parents. Scripture contains many references to the process: " . . . you shall teach them [the commandments] diligently to your children, and shall talk of them when you sit in your house, and when you walk by the way and when you lie down, and when you rise." If children are to grow into pious Jews, it is considered essential that they know the 613 precepts of the Torah, the Jewish law that, according to the Book of Exodus, was given to Moses by God. They must be familiar with the many opinions and interpretations of them. Holiness therefore requires learning. From ancient times, Jews were conspicuous for their education. Literacy was universal, at least among men, and schooling began at an early age. Boys learned to read Hebrew so they could study the Bible. Later they studied Aramaic, the language of the great 6th-century Babylonian law book, the Talmud. In the past, the holy books were the sole subject of study, and it was not uncommon for young men to continue their education into their early twenties and beyond. Today most young Jews do not embark on such an extensive religious education, but the tradition of respect for learning, both religious and secular, has continued.

Studying in a Yeshiva

A yeshiva is an academy for Talmudic study. Young men traditionally study in pairs, poring over the text of the Talmud together and discussing it in Yiddish, the language of the Eastern European Jews. It is an exclusively masculine environment – women do not usually study the Talmud. For many, this yeshiva experience will be the start of a lifetime in the Orthodox establishment as teachers, scribes, or rabbis. Others regard it as an important interlude in their lives before they start earning a living in the secular world.

Raising the Scrolls

During a synagogue service, the Torah scrolls are ceremoniously lifted while the congregation stands and declares: "This is the Law which Moses set before the children of Israel" (Deuteronomy 4:44). Among Eastern European Jews (see pp.126–27), it is raised after the reading; Jews of Spanish and Oriental origin raise it before. As is usual in the morning service, this man is wearing his prayer shawl and skull cap.

Torah Scroll

THE SCROLLS OF THE TORAH

The Torah is traditionally written on scrolls, which are kept in the synagogue in a container called an ark. When not in use, the Torah scrolls are wrapped up and kept in a cover. Usually crowns are placed over the finials of the scrolls once they are encased. Known as the Keter Torah (the Crown of the Law), these crowns symbolize the sovereignty of the law in the Jewish way of life. They are often cast in silver and provide an elegant finish.

Writing the Scroll

There is a long scribal tradition in Judaism. In prerabbinic Judaism, scribes were a class of experts on Jewish law. From them a class of lay Torah scholars arose, who preserved and interpreted the biblical laws. This professional scribe is checking a handwritten Torah scroll that must be perfect before it can be used for reading the scriptures in the synagogue. There are many laws concerning the scribal arts, and every aspiring scribe must be thoroughly familiar with them.

The Inscription

"This is the law which Moses set for the Congregation of Jacob." These words inscribed on this particular scroll reflect the essential Jewish belief about the Torah. As recorded in the Book of Exodus, it was given by God to Moses on Mount Sinai as part of the covenant with the Jewish people. Jacob was one of the early patriarchs of the Jews – his other name was Israel, meaning "He who strives with God" (see p.114).

THE TORAH CASE

The Torah is enclosed in a wooden case called a tik. These are used by Spanish and Oriental Jews. Eastern Europeans usually keep their Torah scrolls in extensively embroidered cloth bindings.

THE TREES OF LIFE

The staves of the Torah scroll are known as the *Azei Hayym*, the Trees of Life. This is a reference to a passage in the traditional liturgy that describes the Law of God as the "tree of life to which we cling."

READING FROM THE SCROLL

In contrast to European languages, Hebrew is written from right to left. This picture shows the Torah scroll unrolled near the beginning of the text. It is an honor to be called up to read the scrolls. Before reading, the scrolls are carried around the synagogue, then a benediction is recited. At least seven men are called up to read during the morning service.

The Yad or Pointer

The word *yad literally means "hand," and the pointer used for reading the Torah scroll is often cast in the shape of a hand. The yad is used to avoid touching or dirtying the sacred text, to direct the reader's attention to the precise word be is reading, and to encourage him or her to look at it and pronounce it correctly.*

Hebrew Text

The Torah is made up of the books of Bereshith, Shemoth, Wayyiqra, Bemidhar, and Deharim, the first five books of the Bible. It therefore contains the earliest history of the Jewish people as well as the 613 commandments of the law.

> **This book of the law shall not depart out of your mouth, but you shall meditate on it day and night, that you may be careful to do according to all that is written in it.**
>
> JOSHUA 1:8

THE HEBREW LANGUAGE

Hebrew is traditionally written with no vowels – all the letters are consonants. In order to read and understand the sacred text, it is necessary to be very familiar with the language, since without such familiarity it is impossible to know how each word is pronounced.

The Torah Binder

After the scroll is rolled, it is tied with a binder, known as a *mappah*, before it is placed in its case. Traditionally the *mappah* is made from swaddling clothes. Once a child reaches Bar Mitzvah age (see pp.130–31), the material is embroidered and presented to the synagogue for ritual use.

The Hebrew script is decorative and informative

The scrolls are raised in the synagogue

A marriage service conducted under a canopy

Inscription expressing loyalty to the Torah of God

Hebrew inscription and embroidered scenes

THE KABBALAH

KABBALAH IS THE NAME given to Jewish mystical knowledge, originally transmitted by word of mouth. Within the great treasury of the Talmud, the law book of the 6th century CE, there are hints of mystical speculation. Stories are told that indicate how these doctrines were kept secret, since it was believed that such powerful knowledge should be restricted to a small group. It was said that the hidden name of God should only be revealed to a man "who is modest and meek, in the midway of life, not easily provoked to anger, temperate, and free from vengeful feelings." Perhaps the most famous mystical work was the *Zohar* ("Divine Splendor"). Compiled by Rabbi Moses de León of Granada in the late 13th century, it is set in the early 2nd century. It purports to be a treasury of ancient knowledge, and it explains God's relationship with the world in terms of *sefirot*, the attributes of God, known as emanations, through which he created the universe. There were ten *sefirot*, and they were often portrayed as a tree, as concentric spheres, as a man, or as a branched candlestick. These doctrines were not intended merely as a theoretical system; the *Zohar* emphasized that human action has an effect on the higher world and that, through serving God, the pious soul will achieve union with the Divine. The candlestick below shows the hierarchy of the *sefirot* – God's attributes from the highest to the lowest with their corresponding qualities in human beings.

> ❝ As for the sefirot, each one has a known name and You are the perfect completion of them all. ❞
> FROM THE ZOHAR

The Tympanum of St. Trophime, Arles
This 12th-century Christian sculpture draws on Kabbalistic imagery. The center figure, the Messiah, Savior of the World, is surrounded by the four creatures mentioned by the prophet Ezekiel: the man is the cosmic man, representing the sefirot (see above); the eagle is the airy level of cosmic creation; the lion is the watery level of the heart; and the bull is the earthy level of the world of action.

The Mystical Messiah
Kabbalistic speculation was at its climax in the 16th and 17th centuries. Many scholars believed that they were living in the final days, and welcomed the arrival of the self-proclaimed messiah, Shabbetai Zevi, shown here. The Jewish world was in a state of excitement upon his arrival. But in 1666 he was captured by Turks and given the choice of death or conversion to Islam. By choosing the latter, he was discredited.

KETER, THE FIRST SEFIRAH
Keter, or Crown, is the point of equilibrium. It is the first revelation of God, and states his divine name. It contains everything that was, and is, and continues to be.

HOKHMAH, THE SECOND SEFIRAH
Hokhmah is the first attribute on the Pillar of Mercy. It is the intellect of the divine mind and the flash of genius in the human. It is balanced by *Binah*, Understanding, on the Pillar of Severity opposite.

HESED, THE FOURTH SEFIRAH
Hesed, Mercy, is the second attribute on the Pillar of Mercy. It represents the divine and human qualities of tolerance, generosity, and love, which are balanced with *Gevurah*, Judgment, on the Pillar of Severity.

BINAH, THE THIRD SEFIRAH
Binah, Understanding, is the third *sefirah* and the first attribute on the Pillar of Severity. It represents the divine intellect, and in humans it stands for acceptance of tradition and the use of reason.

GEVURAH, THE FIFTH SEFIRAH
Gevurah, Judgement, represents divine justice, as well as human rigor, discrimination, and discipline. On the other side of the Pillar of Equilibrium, it is complemented by Mercy, the fourth *sefirah*.

HOD, THE EIGHTH SEFIRAH
Hod, Reverberation, is the lowest attribute on the Pillar of Severity, the three arms to the left of the central stand. Traditionally translated as Splendor, it refers both to the controlling role of God's hosts and the passive, cognitive

NEZAH, THE SEVENTH SEFIRAH

Nezah, Eternity, is the third attribute on the Pillar of Mercy. Traditionally translated as Victory, it represents the expanding role of God's hosts and the active, instinctive, and impulsive qualities in humanity.

THE TWO PILLARS

The three right arms make up the Pillar of Mercy, the left arms the Pillar of Severity. The right arms are *Hokmah*, Mercy, *Hesed*, Wisdom, and *Nezah*, Eternity. They are constantly expanding, and are held in balance by the opposing forces on the Pillar of Severity: *Binah*, Understanding, *Gevurah*, Judgement, and *Hod*, Reverberation.

This spicebox reflects another pattern of laying out the *sefirot*

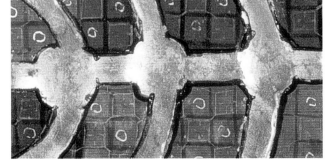

Like the candlestick, the spicebox stands on a Pillar of Equilibrium

The Spicebox

The scents of spices are inhaled at the conclusion of the weekly Sabbath. According to kabbalistic teaching, this lifts sadness as the "extra Sabbath soul" departs until the following week. Jewish life is governed by the yearly festivals and the rhythm of weekly Sabbaths, which reflects the rhythm of the sefirot.

THE PILLAR OF EQUILIBRIUM

The trunk is the Pillar of Equilibrium. On one side the Pillar of Mercy expands, while on the other the Pillar of Severity constrains. It is the divine will, expressed in the Pillar of Equilibrium, which holds the whole in balance and organizes the *sefirot* into its hierarchy.

THE HIERARCHY

God's creative activity is visualized as a beam of light and is manifest in the *sefirot*, which express divine attributes eternally held in balance and sustain all existence.

BRANCHED CANDLESTICK

According to Exodus 25:31, the specifications of the seven-branched candlestick were given by God to Moses on Mount Sinai. It was made of a single piece of gold and, in the kabbalistic tradition, its seven holders and three joints represent the unified and unchanging world of the ten sefirot. The arms to the left of the center make up the Pillar of Severity and those to the right the Pillar of Mercy. Both are centered on the Pillar of Equilibrium and their qualities balance each other.

Sixth and Ninth Sefirot

The three joints on the central pillar are, from the top, Daat, Knowledge, (not a sefirah), Tiferet, Beauty, the sixth sefirah, and Yesod, Foundation, the ninth. Although Daat, knowledge, will pass away, it illustrates the void where the absolute may enter at will. Tiferet, over which hovers the Holy Spirit, is the heart of hearts, where the essence of things resides. Yesod is the basis of everything that exists. In humans, it represents the ego, the basis of consciousness.

MALKHUT, THE TENTH SEFIRAH

The final sefirah, Malkhut, or Kingdom, represents the presence of God within matter. Traditionally, it was regarded as having a fourfold nature representing the elements: earth, air, fire, and water. It is within the combination and tension of the four elements that God manifests himself in the world.

DIVISIONS IN JUDAISM

AS A RESULT OF THEIR HISTORY of dispersion and exile, there are Jewish communities in most countries of the world. Over the centuries, different customs have developed in different communities, and although Jews have a strong sense of being one people, there are also many divisions between them. In addition to national distinctions, in the early 19th century in Western Europe and the US some Jews wanted to update tradition and adapt it to the conditions of modern life. This was the start of today's Orthodox movement (for the traditionalists) and the Reform (for the modernizers).

THE SEPHARDIC AND ASHKENAZIC JEWS

In the late 17th to early 18th centuries, Amsterdam was one of the major centers of the Jewish world and contained many thriving synagogues. The community was made up of two main groups. The Sephardim were the descendants of Spanish Jews who had been expelled from Christian Spain in 1492, and the Ashkenazim were descendants of German and Eastern European Jews. Both groups retained their own distinctive customs, even though their synagogues stood close to one another in the Jewish quarter of Amsterdam. The ceremonies of both were recorded in the engravings of the French artist Bernard Picart, which were produced in the 1730s. Most Jews in the US are generally Ashkenazim; Sephardim continued mainly in the Mediterranean world; both are found in Israel.

ASHKENAZI SYNAGOGUE ON THE DAY OF ATONEMENT
This engraving by Bernard Picart shows the Day of Atonement being celebrated by the Jews of German origin in Amsterdam. This is the holiest day of the Jewish year, which explains why the synagogue is so full.

WOMEN'S GALLERY
As in all Orthodox synagogues, men and women sit separately. Here the women are together in the women's gallery, above the men's heads. The Germans were stricter about such things than the Spanish. In their synagogue men and women are seen chatting together.

HASIDISM IN EASTERN EUROPE

Hasidism is a religious movement, characterized by great enthusiasm, religious ecstasy, and strong personal devotion to the individual leaders, which emerged in Eastern Europe in the late 18th century. The Hasidim are clearly visible since the men wear black suits, black hats, side-curls, and beards; the women dress modestly and the married women wear wigs. They are intensely Orthodox and live in separate communities, following their own customs. Today there are large groups in Israel and in some cities of the US. Although at first the Orthodox establishment disliked them, they are now seen, in the face of the threat from the Reform movement, as practicing a legitimate form of Judaism.

COMMUNITY SUPPORT
Each community supported its own synagogue. From the engravings it seems that the German synagogue was much smaller than the Spanish one, which was magnificent. Almost certainly the German Jews were poorer and less assimilated into the commercial life of Amsterdam than their Spanish counterparts.

GERMAN PIETY
The German community was known for its intense piety and its dedication to Jewish education and learning. It is notable that all Jews in the engraving can clearly read and follow the Hebrew of the prayer book. This was in an era when literacy among Christians was by no means universal.

Jews in Far-flung Places

This scroll of the Book of Esther *is from Kaifeng Fu in China. Small Jewish communities have existed in China since at least the 11th century. The origin of Jewish communities in India is unknown and, until the 18th century, the several groups did not know of each other's existence. In 1975 the Ethiopian Beta Israel (called by others the Falasha community) was recognized as Jewish by the Israeli rabbinate. Many now live in Israel. These groups have adopted customs from their neighbors and practice different forms of Judaism.*

> **"** . . . when you are scattered through the countries, then those of you who escape will remember me among the nations where they are carried captive . . . **"**
>
> EZEKIEL 6:8–9

HEAD COVERINGS

As in all Orthodox synagogues, the men keep their heads covered throughout the service. In Picart's pictures of the Spanish synagogue, the men wear fashionable tricorn hats, but the Germans mostly wear simple caps or their workaday hats.

REFORM JUDAISM

Reform Judaism arose in Western Europe in the early 19th century, and it quickly spread to the US. Its leaders accept the findings of modern biblical scholarship and emphasize the moral laws in Torah. They adapted the traditional liturgy, rejected the customs that they perceived as offensive to modern sensibility, and introduced new prayers in the vernacular. In recent years they have even ordained women as rabbis. This photograph shows the first woman rabbi ordained in Great Britain holding the Torah scroll. The Orthodox completely reject the movement, regarding Reform laypeople as sinners, their rabbis as laypeople, and their converts as non-Jews.

GERMAN JEWS

The German Jews maintained their differences from those of their host nation. Assimilation into a host nation is generally seen as the greatest threat to Jewish survival. Despite the very different forms of Judaism that have been practiced at different times and places, the Jews still strongly believe themselves to be a united people and have a strong sense of their own identity.

NIGHTTIME CANDLES

The candles indicate that it is nighttime. The Day of Atonement begins on the sunset of the previous day; it includes the night as well as the day until the following sunset. The artist was very impresssed that many of these German Jews passed the whole night and sometimes the next day without shifting their places, lamenting their sins.

The prayer book contains the Ashkenazic rite, which is different from the Sephardic rite

Prayer shawl

BEARDS AND CLOTHING

Following the Jewish tradition, these German Jews all wear beards. Because it is Yom Kippur, the Day of Atonement, they are wearing a distinctive white garment known as a *kittel*. These are worn only by Ashkenazic Jews. In Picart's picture of the Spanish synagogue, the men are clean-shaven and are dressed very fashionably.

Laws of Fasting

The Day of Atonement is the most solemn fast of the Jewish year. No food or drink is taken and, as shown here, shoes are not worn except out of necessity.

FESTIVALS

TRADITIONALLY, JEWISH LIFE is measured by the regular weekly day of rest, the Sabbath, and the annual rhythm of the festivals. The Sabbath begins on Friday evening and ends on Saturday night, and the Jewish year has approximately 354 days, so although the festivals always fall at roughly the same time of year, the secular date varies. According to the Book of Deuteronomy in the Bible, Jews are to celebrate three pilgrim festivals each year: "Three times a year all your males shall appear before the Lord your God at the place which he will choose: at the Feast of Unleavened Bread, at the Feast of Weeks and at the Feast of Booths." Pesach (Passover and Unleavened Bread, illustrated below), Shavuot (Weeks), and Sukkoth (Booths), are connected with Israel's history and the agricultural year; Rosh Hashanah (New Year) and Yom Kippur (the Day of Atonement) are times for reflection, repentance, and prayers for forgiveness; Purim (Lots) and Chanukah (Lights) celebrate the saving of the Jews from particular perils; Yom Ha'atzmaut is a modern innovation – a rejoicing at the creation of a political state in 1948.

The Festival of Unleavened Bread
When the Israelites fled from slavery in Egypt, they were in such a hurry that they baked their bread before it was leavened. In accordance with God's commandment to Moses, no leaven is to be eaten during future Passover seasons, and special unleavened bread, or matsos, must be baked.

THE FESTIVAL OF CHANUKAH

Chanukah is celebrated for eight days in the winter. It commemorates the victory over the Hellenizing Seleucid kings by the pious Maccabees, a noble family who dominated Palestine from 164 to 63 BCE. The Seleucids had desecrated the Temple in Jerusalem (see p.119), and after a three-year struggle Judah Maccabaeus, a member of the rebel family, took possession of the city and reconsecrated the altar. According to legend, one day's worth of holy oil miraculously kept the great Temple lamp burning for eight days. The festival is celebrated by lighting one candle on the first night, two on the second, three on the third, until all eight are lit. In modern times children receive presents (the festival occurs near the Christian celebration of Christmas), and games are played. Here, a young boy celebrates the Sabbath as well as the fifth night of Chanukah. The Sabbath candles are already burning, and five Chanukah lights are kindled.

A boy lights the Chanukah candles

PESACH PREPARATIONS
Pesach, or Passover, is the first pilgrim festival. It commemorates the exodus of the Israelites from Egypt and derives its name from the tenth plague of Egypt (see p.117) when the firstborn of the Egyptians all died, while the Angel of Death "passed over" the homes of the Israelites. This manuscript illustration comes from the Golden Haggadah, and dates from 1320.

SYMBOLIC FOODS
Symbolic foods are set for the *Pesach Seder*, or ritual meal. These include bitter herbs symbolizing the bitterness of slavery in Egypt; green herbs associated with spring; an egg commemorating festival sacrifice; a roast shankbone symbolizing the sacrificial lamb; salt water recalling the tears of the Israelites; and a mixture of apples, nuts, cinnamon, and wine as a reminder of the mortar that the Jews were forced to mix in Egypt.

AN AGRICULTURAL FESTIVAL
In the days of the Temple in Jerusalem, Pesach commemorated the beginning of the barley harvest. Seven weeks later Shavuot, the second pilgrim festival, celebrated the offering of the first fruits and the giving of the law to Moses on Mount Sinai.

UNLEAVENED BREAD
Three pieces of unleavened bread are placed in a pile. The upper and lower pieces represent the double portion of manna, the food given by God to the Israelites in the wilderness. The middle piece represents the "bread of affliction."

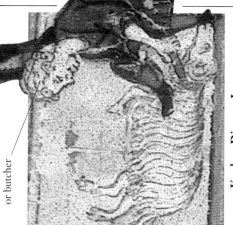

Trained *shochet*, or butcher

Blood is drained quickly from the body

LOOKING TO THE FUTURE

It is believed that the Messiah will reveal himself at the time of Pesach, and that he will be preceded by the Prophet Elijah. A cup of wine is set out for Elijah, and the service ends with the toast: "Next year in Jerusalem!"

Kosher Dietary Laws

According to laws believed to have been given to Moses on Mount Sinai, Jews may eat only Kosher (ritually fit) food. These include eating only animals that both chew the cud and have a cloven hoof, which excludes pigs, for example. Animals must have their throats cut with a clean stroke and the blood drained out, a method that causes the minimum of suffering. Also, meat foods may not be eaten with dairy produce. The dietary laws have had the effect of keeping the Jewish people separate from their neighbors and preserving the unique Jewish tradition.

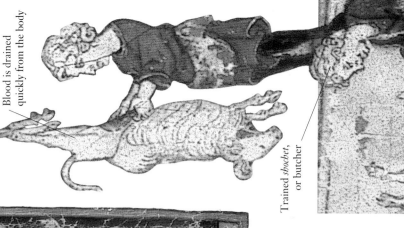

STRICT CLEANING

Passover today is essentially a family celebration, and requires a great deal of preparation. Since no leaven may be eaten during Pesach, the house must be thoroughly cleaned and scrubbed to remove all traces. All standard kitchenware must be put away and a special Passover set is to be used.

THE QUESTION

The youngest person present at the Pesach table asks the oldest why this night is different. It is explained that the Israelites were slaves in Egypt, but because God led them out, they can now live in freedom.

THE SEARCH FOR LEAVEN

On the evening before Pesach, it is customary to go around the house with a candle, looking for the last traces of leaven. The final crumbs are symbolically swept up with a feather.

SPECIAL SACRIFICES

Before the Jerusalem Temple was destroyed in 70 CE, special sacrifices were made on festival days. Slaughtering a lamb is associated with Pesach; during the tenth plague of Egypt the Israelites killed a lamb and smeared its blood on their doorposts, so that the Angel of Death would spare their houses.

> 66 *And you shall tell your son on that day, 'It is because of what the Lord did for me when I came out of Egypt.'* 99
> EXODUS 13:8

The Festival of Sukkoth

Sukkoth, also known as the Feast of Tabernacles, is the third pilgrim festival. Jews are commanded to dwell in booths to remember their sojourn in the wilderness. During the daily services, a sheaf of palm, myrtle, and willow is waved, and an etrog – a type of citrus fruit – is carried around the synagogue, symbolizing the presence of God in the four corners of the world.

Palm sheaf, myrtle, and willow

Etrog citron

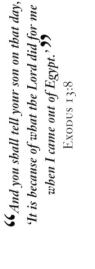

THE FESTIVAL CALENDAR

Every Saturday

Shabbat (Sabbath): A day of rest and cessation of labor. Candles are lit to signify the climax of God's creation, when his work was finished.

Spring

Purim: The Festival of Lots; a thanksgiving commemorating the victory of Esther over Haman.

Pesach (Passover): A celebration of freedom commemorating the exodus of the Israelites from Egypt, and the spring barley harvest.

Yom Ha'atzmaut: A festival of independence, commemorating the return to Israel in 1948.

Summer

Shavuot: The Festival of Weeks commemorating God giving the Ten Commandments to Moses on Mount Sinai, and also the offering of the first fruits.

Autumn

Rosh Hashanah: The Jewish New Year; a time for reflection and spiritual renewal. A ram's horn trumpet is blown as a call to repentance.

Yom Kippur: The Day of Atonement when sins are confessed directly to God and prayers are made for forgiveness.

Sukkoth: A seven-day harvest festival during which participants set up booths or tents to commemorate God's care of the Israelites in the wilderness after they fled from Egypt.

Winter

Chanukah: The Festival of Lights, which commemorates the rededication of the Temple in Jerusalem to God, following the victory of Judah Maccabaeus over the Syrians in 165 BCE.

RITES OF PASSAGE

VARIOUS CEREMONIES MARK THE STAGES in a Jewish lifetime. Traditionally, Jews have lived within their own communities, distinguished from their non-Jewish neighbors by their religious practices. They ate different food (see p.129), observed different festivals, and in the Middle Ages wore different clothes. Through these distinctions, the Jews managed to maintain their special identity. If one was born into the community, one expected to be educated within it, to marry within it, to raise a family within it, and to die within it. All these life-cycle events were marked by special ceremonies, emphasizing Jewish uniqueness. Through the rites of passage, Jews learn to identify themselves as members of the Chosen People, with special duties and responsibilities.

THE ROLE OF MEN AND WOMEN

Judaism is essentially a patriarchal religion with defined roles for men and women. Although Jewishness is passed on from the mother, Jews are described as sons or daughters of their father, as in "Isaac son of Abraham," or "Dinah daughter of Jacob." The birth of a son is celebrated with ritual circumcision; the birth of a daughter is recorded by a baby blessing during the course of a normal service. Boys have a coming of age ceremony, and each day men thank God in the liturgy that he has not created them as women (who are exempt from some commandments); women thank God that he has created them according to his will. Women have an honorable position as the custodians of the Jewish home, but nonetheless, many Jewish women today are unhappy with the traditional role assigned to them.

THE KETUBAH

The Ketubah is the traditional marriage contract between a husband and wife. According to Jewish law, the couple may not live together until the Ketubah has been drawn up. Like the 18th-century one depicted here, the Ketubah is frequently a richly decorated document.

CITY OF JERUSALEM
Jerusalem is the spiritual home of all Jews. Each year at Passover, the new couple will end the ritual meal with the hope "Next year in Jerusalem!"

SACRED CANDELABRUM
A seven-branched candlestick or *menorah*, used to stand in the Temple in Jerusalem and is a traditional symbol of the Jewish religion. It is a sign that the couple will be setting up a Jewish home and following the ways of their ancestors.

COMING OF AGE

Jewish boys come of age at 13. This means they should fulfill all the commandments (see pp.116–17). After this, the boy is known as a Bar Mitzvah ("Son of the Commandment"). Here a young man is saying the weekday morning prayers by the Western Wall in Jerusalem. He has phylacteries (small boxes containing verses of the Law) bound to his head and his arm, in accordance with the verse: "You shall bind them as a sign upon your hand and they shall be as frontlets between your eyes." A boy's transition to maturity is marked by his being called to read from the scroll of the Law during the Sabbath morning service. This takes much preparation and is often celebrated with a large party. Girls come of age at 12, but since women are not expected to keep the commandments of Jewish law, it is not as great an event. Progressive Jews, however, usually have a similar ceremony in the synagogue for girls, which is known as a Bat Mitzvah ("Daughter of the Commandment").

Bar Mitzvah boy at the Western Wall in Jerusalem

❝Behold you are consecrated to me with this ring according to the Law of Moses and Israel. Blessed are you O Lord who makes bridegroom and bride to rejoice.**❞**
FROM THE TRADITIONAL JEWISH WEDDING SERVICE

THE ZODIAC
The small circles each contain one of the signs of the zodiac with its Hebrew title above. There is a tradition of astrology within Judaism, and at an early period each Hebrew month was assigned one of the zodiacal signs. A correlation was also seen between the signs, the 12 tribes of Israel, and the 12 organs of the human body. The implication of the zodiac is that the couple are to share all future months together.

WEDDING CANOPY
The pillars represent the Jewish marriage canopy or *huppah*, symbolizing the marriage chamber. It is open at the sides, and the couple and their parents stand beneath it during the ceremony. Finding husbands and wives for people within the community is very important, since marriage to non-Jews is traditionally thought of as a tragedy. In the past, professional matchmakers were employed. Although regarded as a great sadness, divorce is sanctioned within the Jewish faith provided that the husband gives his wife a *get*, a formal document of release: this can create huge difficulties for wives whose husbands have run away or who refuse a divorce.

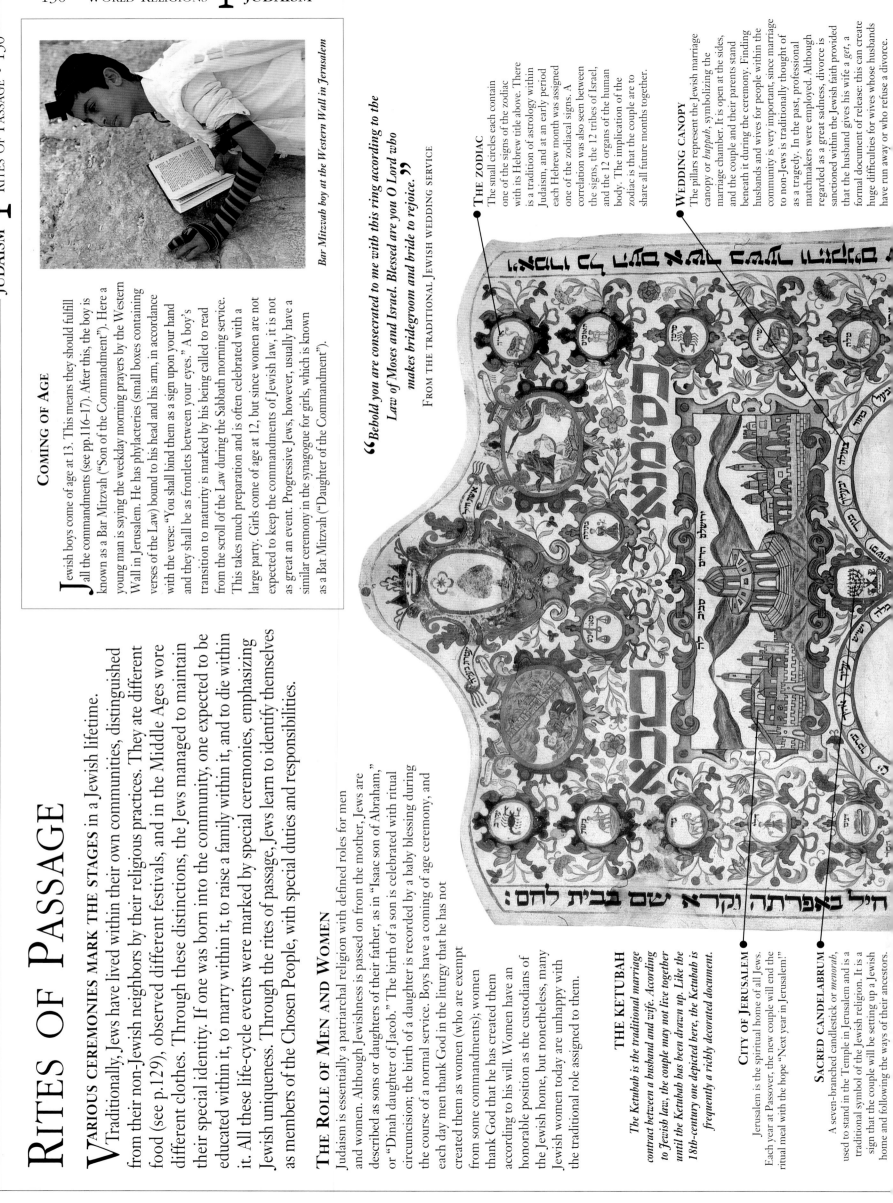

BIBLICAL SCENES

This is an Ashkenazi Ketubah (it comes from a European community). Along with the signs of the zodiac, it is decorated with representations of biblical scenes and surrounded by a suitably uplifting Hebrew text.

WITNESS SIGNATURES

The Ketubah must be signed by witnesses. Traditionally a member of the bride's family would hand over a kerchief to the groom, and then the witnesses would sign their names on the right of the Ketubah.

> *May my death be an atonement for the sins, transgressions and violations which I have sinned before you. And set my portion in the Garden of Eden, and let me merit the World to Come reserved for the righteous. Hear O Israel the Lord our God, the Lord is One.*
>
> PRAYER ON A DEATHBED, FROM A TRADITIONAL JEWISH PRAYER BOOK

ARAMAIC TEXT

Traditionally the text is written in Aramaic, and states the husband's obligation toward his wife. It is written according to regulations set down in the Talmud and in the codes of Jewish law. Its provisions are binding and serve to protect the position of the woman. It provides, for example, for the repayment of the bride price in the event of death or divorce.

ADDITIONAL PROVISIONS

Additional conditions are also agreed by the couple and laid out in the Ketubah. For example, in a country in which polygamy is usual, the groom often promises not to take another wife. In Syria it was customary for the groom to be released from this provision if his wife proved to be barren after a period of ten years.

CELEBRATION

Weddings are a time of great celebration, and it is customary to hold a party. Different communities follow different traditions for this, but invariably the ceremony is followed by as large a feast as the bride's family can afford.

SIGNATORIES

It is usual among Eastern European Jews for the bridegroom to sign the Ketubah on the left side of the document. Male literacy was universal among Jews from very early times. The bride was not expected to sign.

Circumcision – a Sign of God's Promise

The circumcision of male children goes back to the time of the patriarch Abraham. It takes place when the child is eight days old, when he is given his Hebrew name. Circumcision does not make a child Jewish. Any child of a Jewish mother is born Jewish, so circumcision is a sign that he is a member of the covenant between God and his people. These are the instruments used at the ceremony of circumcision, or Brith Milah.

Funnel to give a sip of wine to the baby after the ceremony

Death and Burial

Jewish burials take place as soon as possible after death. The body is washed, dressed in a white linen shroud, and placed in a plain wooden coffin with no ornaments. The deceased is carried to the grave, and biblical and liturgical verses are chanted by the rabbi as he leads the funeral procession to the graveyard. It is customary to stop on the way for the mourners to express their grief. Traditionally a eulogy is given either in the funeral chapel or as the coffin is lowered into the grave. Then the male mourners help fill the grave with earth. The traditional memorial prayers are recited, and the mourners offer words of consolation to the bereaved. This is the cemetery at the Jesefov synagogue in Prague.

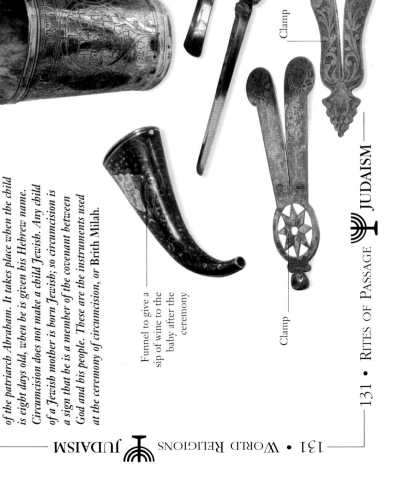

Bowl

Beaker

Knife

Knife

Clamp

Clamp

JERUSALEM – CITY OF ZION

EXILE, KNOWN AS GALUT, IS A FUNDAMENTAL CONCEPT for the Jews. Throughout their long history, from the time Israel was conquered by the Babylonians in 586 BCE, most of the community has lived far away from Jerusalem. Even earlier, in 722 BCE, ten of the 12 tribes of Israel had been captured by the Assyrians and assimilated with the surrounding peoples. Yet the Jews believe that God's promise was to all the people of Israel, and therefore, it was believed that one day all 12 tribes would be restored once more to the Promised Land. Jerusalem, the City of David, would again be the capital of the Jewish world. This hope was kept alive until the end of the 19th century when, increasingly, Jews realized that the only protection against anti-Semitism would be to have a land of their own. The modern State of Israel was created in 1948. Jerusalem was partitioned, but united under Jewish rule in 1967 and become the capital of the state. Jews are returning to the homeland – victims of the European Holocaust (see pp.134–35), Beta Israel from Ethiopia, Russian Jews who have suffered under the Soviet system, and those from Arab lands whose situation has become impossible. It seems to many Jews as if the long-promised gathering of the exiles has begun.

THEODORE HERZL

Theodore Herzl (1860–1904), a Viennese journalist, is remembered as the founder of modern Zionism. Initially he had believed that assimilation into the majority culture would solve the Jewish problem, but later he realized that anti-Semitism was endemic in Europe. In *Der Judenstaat* (The Jewish State), he advocated the founding of a Jewish state, and Palestine was the obvious location. He was opposed both by assimilationists, who believed in being good citizens of the host country, and by the Orthodox, who condemned him for anticipating the Messiah. Nonetheless many young Jews were inspired, and in 1897 Herzl conducted the first Zionist Congress. The world Zionist movement was founded and Herzl devoted his energy to building up international support.

Theodore Herzl, founder of modern Zionism

> "... the mountain of the house of the Lord shall be established as the biggest of the mountains, and shall be raised above the hills; and all nations shall flow to it, and many people shall come and say: 'Come, and let us go up to the mountain of the Lord, to the house of the God of Jacob; and he may teach us his ways, and we may walk in his paths.' For out of Zion shall go forth the law, and the word of the Lord from Jerusalem."
>
> ISAIAH 2:2–3

JERUSALEM AT THE CENTER
This 14th-century map shows the city of Jerusalem at the center of the world. It is the Holy City, the City of David, and the focus of Jewish prayer. A typical saying of the rabbis is that ten measures of beauty were given to the world, of which Jerusalem took nine. That Jerusalem was at the exact midpoint was a widespread belief, and it was said that the Holy Land was bigger than all other lands, and Jerusalem was built on its biggest point.

The Temple
Despite the destruction of the Temple by Babylonians in 586 BCE and by the Romans in 70 CE, it remains the focus of the Jewish world. Pilgrims come from every nation to pray at the surviving Western Wall, and Jews still pray for its restoration in the days of the Messiah.

INDIA AND CHINA
Far to the east, there are old communities of Jews in both India and China, who have maintained their own particular customs. Many of them have made new lives in the State of Israel.

SOVIET JEWRY
In recent years, the greatest number of immigrants to the Jewish state have come from the countries of the former Soviet Union. There is a long history of Russian anti-Semitism, and the creation of the State of Israel provided an opportunity to escape from prejudice and the rigors of the Soviet system.

BABYLONIA
Perhaps the most important community of the early Middle Ages was that of Babylonia, now Iran and Iraq. Because of increased anti-Semitism in the Muslim world, there are now almost no Jews left in that area. They have all fled and made their home in Israel.

EGYPT
Egypt was another important early medieval community. Jews here were particularly harassed after the Suez affair of 1956; most left for Israel. Those who remain are too small in number to maintain the splendid synagogues.

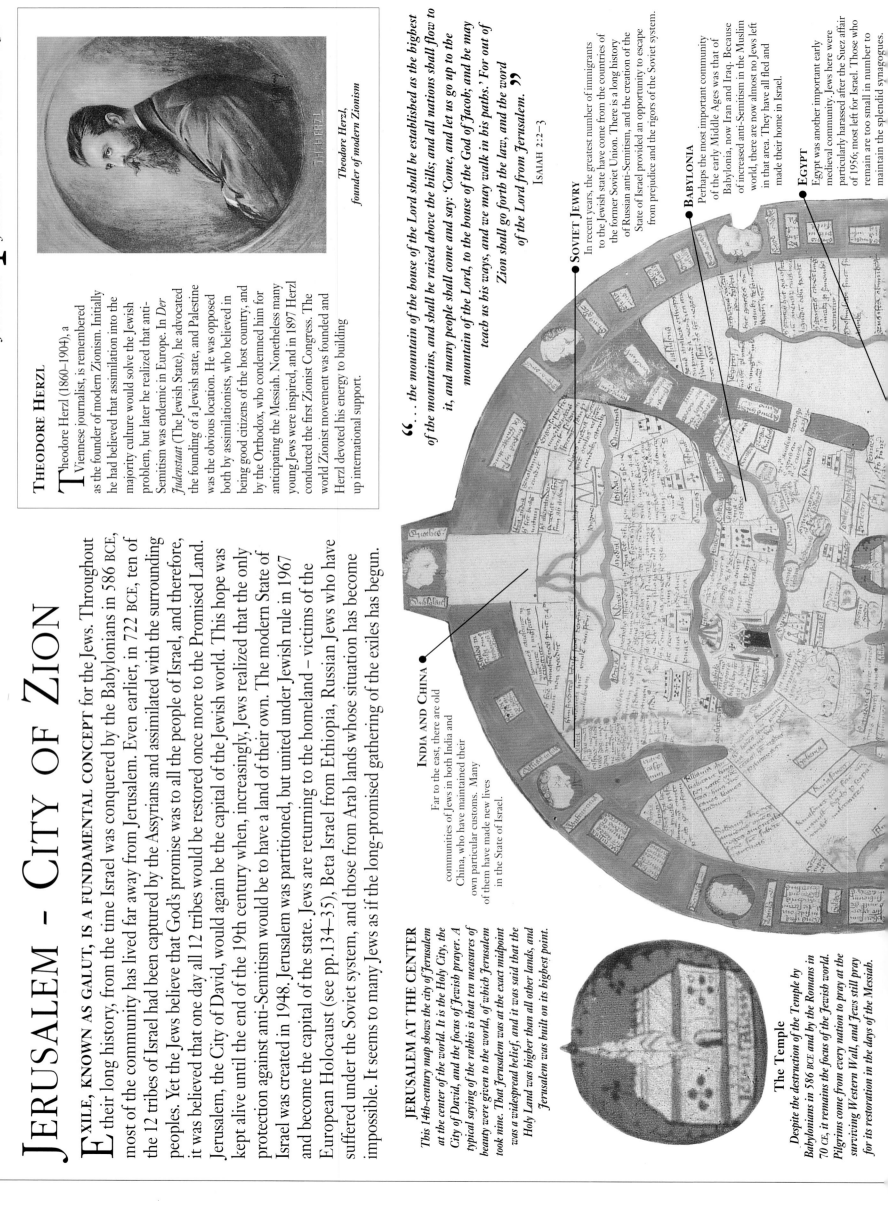

THE ETHIOPIANS
The community that has captured the imagination of the world is that of the Black Jews, Beta Israel, of Ethiopia. In the 1980s, in the face of war and famine, thousands were airlifted by the Israeli government to the Promised Land.

SPAIN
The rich and successful community in Spain was driven out by King Ferdinand and Queen Isabella in 1492. They were scattered all over North Africa, southern Europe, and Asia Minor, but they retained a sense of special identity.

THE PILLARS OF HERCULES
In medieval times, the rock of Gibraltar, or the Pillars of Hercules, was regarded as the western point of the world. Since the discoveries of Columbus in 1492, the map of the earth has changed. Today the largest Jewish community is that of the United States. Although most do not want to leave the US, the community is dedicated in its support of the State of Israel.

> **If I forget you, O Jerusalem, let my right hand wither! Let my tongue cleave to the roof of my mouth if I do not remember you, if I do not set Jerusalem above my highest joy!**
> PSALM 137: 5–6

A Nation at War
The Arab nations were opposed to the creation of the State of Israel in what they regarded as their territory. Israel defended her existence in 1948, 1967, and 1973. Despite Israeli victories, there have increasingly been calls for a just settlement to the Palestinian problem, and in recent years peace negotiations between the Jews and the Arab Palestinians have been widely welcomed. Nonetheless Israel remains a nation ever prepared for battle.

EUROPE
About six million Jews died at the hands of the Nazis in Hitler's Europe. The United Nations accepted the necessity for a Jewish state after the appalling carnage of the Holocaust was revealed (see pp.134–35). Many of the early immigrants to the new state in 1948 were concentration camp survivors for whom Israel was their only home.

The wall is all that remains of Herod's Temple after its destruction by the Romans in 70 CE

The text of the Torah, studied continually throughout the Jewish world

Praying for the Peace of Jerusalem
Jews are commanded to pray for the peace of Jerusalem. Here a group is standing before the Western Wall, the last remnant of the Temple and the most sacred place in the Jewish world. The holy scrolls are held up so that they can be read aloud and heard by the faithful. Since the Temple was built by King Solomon, pilgrims have come to this spot to learn the law of the Lord and to pray where their ancestors prayed before them.

THE HOLOCAUST

THROUGHOUT HISTORY, Jews have been subject to persecution. As a minority group, they have been seen as alien and sinister. The term "anti-Semitism" was first used by the German journalist Wilhelm Marr in the 1870s. He argued that Jews were a biologically alien people and that history should be understood as an "ongoing struggle between Semite and Native Teutonic stock." After Germany's defeat in World War I (1914–18), the country lurched from one economic crisis to another. In 1933 Adolf Hitler, the leader of the National Socialist party, became Chancellor. He was convinced that all Jews were degenerates, and that Germany had lost the war because of a worldwide Jewish conspiracy. He was determined to reestablish a German empire and to rid Europe of the Jews. During World War II (1939–45), the German army occupied most of Europe. Jews were rounded up, transported to the east, and systematically murdered in concentration camps. By 1945 European Jewry was destroyed, and it was estimated that six million Jews had been killed. Jews call the Holocaust *Shoah*, which means "catastrophe."

" The Stormtroopers were joined by people who were not in uniform; and suddenly with one loud cry of 'Down with the Jews,' the gathering outside produced axes and heavy sledgehammers . . . The little synagogue was but a heap of stone, broken glass and smashed-up woodwork . . . Where the well-cared-for flowerbeds had flanked both sides of the gravel path leading to the door of the synagogue, the children had lit a bonfire, and the parchment of the scrolls gave enough food to the flames to eat up the smashed-up benches and doors, and the wood, which only the day before had been the holy Ark for the scrolls of the Law of Moses. "

EYEWITNESS ACCOUNT OF
THE DESTRUCTION OF THE SYNAGOGUE
IN AACHEN, GERMANY, IN 1933

Shield of David

The six-pointed star was the device on the shield of King David (see pp.118–19). Under the Nazis, Jews were compelled to wear the yellow star to proclaim their Jewishness.

THE WHITE CRUCIFIXION

The White Crucifixion, painted by the Russian-Jewish artist Marc Chagall, was painted in 1938. It reflects the persecution of the Jews in Europe, which had started in Germany in 1933 with the looting and pillaging of Jewish shops and businesses.

KRISTALLNACHT

The synagogue has been set alight. In 1938 on Kristallnacht, "the night of broken glass," synagogues and other buildings owned by Jews were set on fire all over Germany. Above the two tablets of the Law containing the Ten Commandments, which Moses brought down from Mount Sinai (see pp.116–17). These are revered by both Christians and Jews. It is clear from the picture how little they were respected during the time of the Holocaust.

DESTRUCTION OF THE JEWISH RELIGION

The Ark, the container of the scrolls of the Law within the synagogue, is being plundered. The rest of the synagogue furniture is scattered. During the Holocaust period, thousands of synagogues were desecrated and destroyed.

LAMENTATION

Above the cross are lamenting figures. The man on the right is wearing phylacteries, the ritual boxes that male Jews put on their heads and left arms during the weekday morning prayer. The lower figure covers his eyes, blinded by the horror of what he sees. Most people in Germany, gentiles (non-Jews) as well as Jews, were unwilling to see where Hitler's policies were likely to lead. All the men here are fulfilling the Jewish rule not to shave the corners of their beards.

EARLY ATTACKS

A rabble of soldiers storms over the peak of a hill. Their red flags and hammer and sickle indicate that they are Russians. Russia had a long history of anti-Semitic attacks, known as pogroms, on Jewish settlements. Thus the Holocaust was only an extreme form of many earlier atrocities.

DESTRUCTION OF JEWISH SETTLEMENTS

A village burns, the result of a Russian pogrom that was to be repeated so often. Possessions are scattered and houses set on fire.

THE CRUCIFIED JEW

As Jews do not accept Jesus as the Messiah, Chagall's use of the Christian image offended some, since Christians have persecuted Jews for centuries. But Chagall called his paintings "the breath of prayer for redemption and resurrection." Jesus the Jew (words originally painted on his chest) wears the Jewish prayer shawl and embraces the suffering of all.

THE CREMATORIA

A scroll of the Law burns. European Jews were burned in the crematoria of the Nazi concentration camps. This period is known as the Holocaust, meaning "something burned up." Originally it was applied to sacrifices totally consumed by fire, then to sacrifices with many victims, and so to the destruction of European Jews between 1939 and 1945. The Hebrew terms are *Shoah*, "catastrophe," and *Hurban*, "destruction," a term also used for the destruction of the Temple (see p.119).

PLIGHT OF THE VULNERABLE

A young mother flees with her baby. Her head is covered, as is customary with observant married women. The Holocaust spared neither women nor children.

DESTRUCTION OF THE TEMPLE

At the foot of the cross is the *menorah*, the traditional candelabrum from the Temple. All the ritual objects of the Temple were lost when the building was sacked and burned by the Romans in 70 CE. Here, however, the candles can be seen burning, illuminating the terror of the scene.

JEWISH REFUGEES

A boatload of screaming men and women drift across a river. The casualties include children. All are now destitute with no anchor in their lives. During the Holocaust period many Jews tried to emigrate, but in a time of economic depression, very few found countries that would take them.

JEWISH PERSECUTION THROUGH THE AGES

An old man in blue flees from the scene. The white placard he wears is reminiscent of the breastplate worn by the High Priest in the days of the Temple in Jerusalem (see p.119). Originally, the words "I am a Jew" were written across it, but Chagall later painted them out.

THE SCROLLS OF THE LAW

An old man looks back at a burning synagogue. His head is covered, as is usual among observant Jews, and he is clutching the scrolls of the Law, the source of Judaism, to his chest. The handwritten parchment scrolls, which contain the Hebrew text of the first five books of the Bible, are wrapped in a white cover. On the cover is the six-pointed star of King David.

The End of the Line

The infamous railroad that led to the entrance of Auschwitz was journey's end for more than two million people. When the Allied troops finally liberated the camps at the end of World War II, they were horrified at what they found.

THE FINAL SOLUTION

By mid-1942 Germany had conquered most of Europe, and the decision was made to destroy the Jews systematically. To that end, death camps were built in the east: Chelmno, Auschwitz, Treblinka, Sobibor, Majdanek, and Belzec. Transported to the camps in cattle trucks, the Jews and other undesirables were sorted out on arrival. The young and fit became slave labor; the old and weak were killed immediately. Very few survived the terrible conditions in which prisoners were beaten, starved, and tortured. The question that has troubled Jewish theologians since 1945 is "Where was God?" Some have decided God simply cannot exist; others point to the existence of the State of Israel as a homeland for Jews everywhere and argue that although humans were responsible for the Holocaust, God created Good out of Evil. Still others view it as a punishment for religious laxity. But, in the words of the philosopher Emil Fackenheim, God issued a 614th commandment out of the ashes of Auschwitz: "You shall not grant Hitler a posthumous victory; Judaism and the Jewish people must survive."

"May God Remember . . ."

In 1943 German troops entered the Warsaw ghetto to deport the Jews to Treblinka. Although the Jews held out for several weeks, the end was inevitable. Here soldiers force the last survivors from their hiding places.

CHRISTIANITY

LOVE YOUR NEIGHBOR AS YOURSELF

CHRISTIANITY BEGAN IN THE LIFE, ministry, death, Resurrection, and Ascension of Jesus, a Jew whom Christians believe to be the Son of God. Its roots lie farther back in the Jewish tradition (see pp.112–35), with Christianity understanding itself as the New Covenant, or Testament, between Man and God, building on the Old Covenant. The story and early interpretation of Jesus' life are recorded in the New Testament, which includes Gospels, Epistles or letters, and other early writings; here he is portrayed as the Christ, or Messiah (see pp.138–39), and all these writings recognize that Jesus was, and is, the personal action of God in restoring his power and effect to the world.

God's power in the world was restored by Jesus through teaching, forgiveness of sins, and healing – so much so that it seemed to be God who was speaking and acting through him: in Jesus' words, "Anyone who has seen me has seen the Father" (John 14:9). Yet Jesus spoke of, and to, God as "Abba," "Father" – distinct from himself – giving rise to the Christian belief that Jesus was both God and man.

This belief that "God was in Christ reconciling the world to Himself" (2 Corinthians 5:19) led to basic Christian doctrines: that of the Incarnation (see pp.138–39), Christology, the Trinity, and Atonement (see pp.144–45). The doctrine of the Incarnation states that God was present in every moment and aspect of the life of Jesus and yet did not destroy or overwhelm a real human life; the doctrine of Christology says that Jesus was, therefore, one person in whom the two natures of the human and the divine are always and consistently present; the doctrine of the Trinity holds that God is always that which has been revealed through Christ: Father, Son, and Holy Spirit. Atonement is the belief that the things that Jesus did during his lifetime in healing people and restoring them to God,

no matter how great their sins may have been, is now done for everyone who has the faith that it can be so; his death on the cross overcomes the separation from God that sin and death create.

Because Jesus was born as a true human being (he called himself "the Son of man," which in Jewish scripture means "One who is born to die, but who will be saved by God beyond death"), many Christians have a special devotion to his mother Mary through whose obedient acceptance of the conception and birth of Jesus the Incarnation became possible.

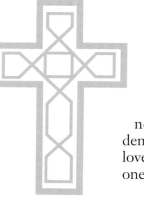

Christian Cross
The cross, a symbol of the Crucifixion of Jesus (see pp.144–45), represents his love for humanity in dying for its sins. The empty cross shows that he has risen from the dead (see pp.146–47).

JESUS' TEACHING
The teaching of Jesus was simple. He summarized it from the Jewish Bible (which Christians call the Old Testament) as the love of God and of one's neighbor. But it was also demanding – a life of *agape*, or the love of God for man, the love for one's fellow man. Before he died, Jesus enacted for his disciples his conviction that even after his death, he would continue to mediate for them, and for many after them, all that they had come to know of God through him during his life: he took bread and said, "This is my body," and wine and said, "This is my blood." In this way he promised in more than words to be with them to the end of time. In a second enacted sign, called a sacrament (see pp.150–51), men and women are made part of the living "Body of Christ" (the community of Christians in relation to Christ and the Church) by baptism,

The Church
This detail (see pp.150–51) shows part of a medieval church with the Crucifixion in the foreground and the sacrament of the Eucharist taking place behind it. The sacrament of the Eucharist is the reenactment of Christ's promise to remain with his followers forever.

which takes them through death to new life even before they die. Christianity teaches that this "good news" (or Gospel from god/good spell/message, that is, God's good news) of safety from sin and death must be shared: during the 19th century, known as "the century of mission," Christianity spread worldwide. It is now the religion of over a quarter of the world's population.

THE EARLY CHURCH

In the early Church, the Body of Christ was originally understood as a metaphor of many equal parts under one Head. By the second century, the metaphor had changed to one of the Roman army, with strong human chains of authority and command, ending up, in Roman Catholicism, with a pope (spiritual head of the Church), cardinals, bishops, priests, monks and nuns, and the laity. Other denominations of Christianity, such as the Presbyterians and Congregationalists, have tried to retain the earlier democratic model of the Body.

At first, Christianity was a small movement, confident because of its experience of the Holy Spirit and its trust in the Resurrection (see pp.146–47). From the time of the emperor Constantine (c.280–337) to that of Theodosius I (379–95), it became the religion of the Roman

Baptism of Christ
Before he traveled preaching the "good news" of God, Jesus was baptized in the Jordan River by his cousin John the Baptist: "And at once, as he was coming up out of the water, he saw the heavens torn apart and the Spirit, like a dove, descending on him. And a voice came from heaven, 'You are my Son, the Beloved; my favor rests on you'" (Mark 1:10–11).

Empire and took much from that context: for example, the Greek figures, Orpheus and Hercules, became the good shepherd and a metaphor for Christ. This absorption of local culture is characteristic of Christianity wherever it has spread.

DIVISIONS

Christians have never agreed on faith and practice. In the early centuries, councils established creeds as minimal statements of true belief. Two, still used, are the Apostles' Creed and the Nicene Creed, although the first was not written by the apostles and the second did not come from the Council of Nicaea. But major divisions appeared, especially between Western and Eastern or Orthodox Christianity. Attempts to reunite failed. Orthodox Christians reject claims of the Bishop of Rome (the pope) to universal authority, claims made more absolute at the first Vatican Council (1869–70), which stated that the pope is infallible when defining faith and morals. The second Vatican Council (1962–65) sought a more consultative style of Church, but this has not yet been attempted in practice. Orthodox Christianity is made up notably of the Greek and Russian Churches. Western Christianity was divided in the Reformation (see pp.156–57) and the Reformed Churches have continued to

Ceremonial Vestments
When officiating at a service or Mass (see p.142), priests may wear clothes called vestments. The color depends on the liturgical season. Green vestments are for everyday use; white is for joyful occasions, such as Easter (see pp.146–47); purple for mournful ones, such as Good Friday; and red symbolizes blood and and is worn for services that commemorate martyrs.

divide over doctrine and practice, leading to denominations such as Lutheran, Baptist, and Methodist. Attempts at ecumenism or reunion, especially through the World Council of Churches, have increased friendship but have not achieved union.

CHRISTIAN LIFE

The involvement of the Church in the world has led some people into monastic and religious orders, where they concentrated on prayer and took vows of poverty, chastity, and obedience (see pp.152–53). The preservation of ancient learning enabled schools and universities to be set up. Churches became centers of music, art, and architecture and gave rise to such styles as Romanesque, Perpendicular, Gothic, and Baroque.

Many Christians follow the liturgical year, which not only celebrates Jesus' life, death, Resurrection, and Ascension but also observes the lives of saints and martyrs (see pp.148–49). The quest for holiness and the desire to be "in touch" with holy things made pilgrimages to shrines and relics popular. Prayer and worship are basic to Christian life.

So too is commitment to the poor. Christians have been vital in bringing education and healing to the world. Christianity should be the answer to the question, "Good Master, what must I do to inherit eternal life?" (Mark 10:17). Jesus replied, by total generosity of self and substance. God judges everyone by one criterion: "In as much as you have done it to the least of one of these, you have done it to me" (Matthew 25:40).

THE INCARNATION

THE INCARNATION, from the Latin *in carne*, means "in the flesh" or "body," and is the Christian belief that God came to earth as a man. This man was Jesus, a wandering teacher living in Palestine in the 1st century CE. Christians believe that the eternal and unchanging nature of God was bound up in the humanity of Jesus, but that its presence did not overwhelm or destroy his human nature – he was both truly God and truly human. This belief in the divine and human nature of Jesus arises from his own insistence, chronicled in the Gospels of the New Testament (see pp.140–41), that it was not himself but God the Father, who was the source of the power that enabled him to heal and restore people, forgive them, and sometimes judge them.

THE PRESENCE OF GOD

The presence of God the Father in Jesus' life is made clear in the claims "The Father and I are one" (John 10:30; 14:9). From the earliest writings, the letters of St. Paul, Christians recognized that "God was in Christ reconciling the world to Himself"(2 Corinthians 5:19). Jesus called himself "the Son of man," an ordinary man who must die but who will be rescued by God. The Resurrection and Ascension (see pp.146–47) were that rescue, tying his humanity, and that of the human race, to God forever.

God's Messengers
Angels in the Bible are messengers between heaven and earth. They are said to have been present at the birth of Jesus. It was Gabriel who, according to Luke's Gospel, was sent to Mary, the mother of Jesus, to announce that she was to have a son – evoking from her the response of faithful trust, "Be it unto me according to thy word."

MARY IN GLORY
This painting by Jan Provost II dates from 1524 and depicts Mary, the mother of Jesus, in relation to the three persons of the Trinity (see above). They are worshiped by King David (see pp.118–19), and seers and sibyls from the Greco-Roman world (see pp.14–15).

THE INFANT KING
The Roman poet Virgil, writing at the time of Augustus, just before the early Christian period, wrote of the great longing that all people had for a king who would turn the age of iron into an age of gold: "The jarring nations he in peace shall bind, And with paternal virtues rule mankind: Unbidden earth shall wreathing ivy bring, And fragrant herbs (the promises of Spring), As her first offerings unto her infant king" (Eclogue of Virgil). Some Christians apply this to the birth of Jesus.

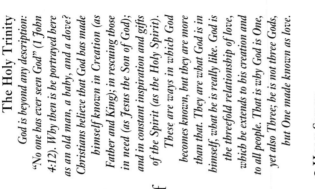

The Holy Trinity
God is beyond any description: "No one has ever seen God" (1 John 4:12). *Why then is he portrayed here as an old man, a baby, and a dove? Christians believe that God has made himself known in Creation (as Father and King); in rescuing those in need (as Jesus the Son of God); and in constant inspiration and gifts of the Spirit (as the Holy Spirit).*

These are ways in which God becomes known, but they are more than that. They are what God is in himself; what he is really like. God is the threefold relationship of love, which he extends to his creation and to all people. That is why God is One, yet also Three; he is not three Gods, but One made known as love.

HOLY SPIRIT
The dove is a symbol of the Holy Spirit, the third person of the Trinity, and appears at the baptism of Jesus (Mark 1:10). In the same way that the dove returned to Noah's Ark after the flood (see pp.114–15) as a sign of peace between humanity and God, so it appears here pointing to Jesus as the new declaration of peace.

THE VIRGIN MARY
Mary is believed to have been a virgin, who conceived Jesus through the Holy Spirit. For Christians the virgin birth is a sign that through Mary, an ordinary person, God is restoring the lives of all people to the state in which sin and death are overcome. According to Paul (Romans 5:17), the first Adam brought sin and death into the world. Jesus, the second Adam, brings new life.

❝ *The angel answered, 'The Holy Spirit will come upon you, and the power of the Most High will cover you with its shadow. And so the child will be holy and will be called Son of God.'* ❞

LUKE 1:35

The magi brought gifts of gold, frankincense, and myrrh. Their coming is celebrated at the feast of the Epiphany, which celebrates "the manifestation of God to the whole world"

Jewish prophets are set beside Gentile (non-Jewish) sibyls and seers to show that they have also longed for a savior and that Jesus is born to bring salvation to all, regardless of race or religion.

"Let this mind be in you, which was also in Christ Jesus: Who, being in the form of God, thought it not robbery to be equal with God: But made himself of no reputation, and took upon him the form of a servant, and was made in the likeness of men."
PHILIPPIANS 2:5–7

● **KING DAVID**

David was the first messiah, the first king of the Jewish people (see pp.118–19), who traditionally sang psalms to praise God. The Gospels of Matthew and Luke indicate that Jesus was a descendant of David, and the angels refer to this when they announce his birth to the shepherds: "Today in the town of David a Savior has been born to you; he is Christ the Lord" (Luke 2:11).

● **THE EMPEROR AUGUSTUS**

Augustus was the great Roman emperor (27 BCE–14 CE) under whom the "Roman peace," the *Pax Romana*, brought prosperity, law, and order to the empire. But here Augustus kneels to a greater king, one who conquered the Roman Empire itself, when Christianity spread over the Roman world.

● **PRAYING FIGURE**

Christian prayer is addressed to God, that is, the Trinity: Father, Son, and Holy Spirit. Prayer is a way of entering into or sharing the life of the Trinity. It starts with the Holy Spirit within us, urging us to pray and cry out "Abba, Father," and is offered "through Jesus Christ our Lord," who taught his disciples to pray. "Abba" is the word that Jesus used to address God in prayer. It is a word of affectionate respect, such as a child might use to its parent.

● **SCROLL**

On the scroll are written the Latin words: "*Gremium virginis erit salus gentium*" – "The womb of the virgin will be the salvation of the nations."

"Our Father in Heaven, Hallowed be Your name, Your kingdom come, Your will be done, on earth as it is in Heaven, Give us this day our daily bread, and forgive us our trespasses as we forgive those who trespass against us, and lead us not into temptation but deliver us from evil. For the kingdom, the power and the glory are Yours, now and forever."
THE LORD'S PRAYER, MATTHEW 6:9

Joseph and Mary had traveled from Nazareth to Bethlehem in Judea to register for the census. Tradition says that Jesus was born in a stable or cave in Bethlehem because there was no "room at the inn" (Luke 2:7)

The three magi were Zoroastrian priests (see p.13). In the 2nd century, they were thought to have been kings, and in the 6th century they were given the names Caspar, Melchior, and Balthasar

The Birth of Jesus

The Gospels of both Matthew and Luke tell the story of the birth of Jesus, using different traditions. Both emphasize that Jesus was born miraculously of a virgin according to the purpose and will of God. In Luke, shepherds are drawn to the stable where he was born. This shows how the birth of Jesus matters to people on the edges of society, as shepherds were at that time. In Matthew, the wise men or magi surrender their ancient powers and strength to Jesus.

THE ROLE OF MARY

This window in Canterbury cathedral shows how God gives his grace through Mary to women and through them to men – and women. The role of women in Christianity is profound. It was to Mary that Gabriel came, and through her faithful obedience, becoming the mother of the Savior, Jesus, salvation became possible. Throughout his life, Jesus was cared for by a number of women, and at the crucifixion (see pp.144–45) they stayed when most men ran away. It was to women that the risen Lord first appeared. Women have continued since in the work of salvation and in some denominations are ministers and priests. Gratitude to Mary by many Christians is expressed in the prayer: "Hail Mary, full of Grace, the Lord is with thee, Blessed art thou among women, and blessed is the fruit of thy womb, Jesus. Holy Mary, Mother of God, pray for us sinners, now and at the hour of our death."

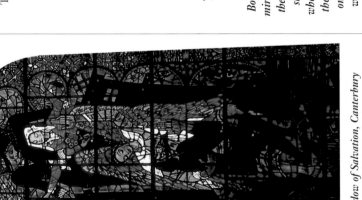

The window of Salvation, Canterbury Cathedral, England

THE LIFE OF CHRIST

IT **IS IMPOSSIBLE** to write a biography of Jesus, because the Gospels (see right) concentrate on his ministry – the three years that he was a wandering teacher. They portray him as someone who taught about God at work in the world, especially by using parables, "earthly stories with heavenly meanings." Jesus spoke of God's authority, but also of his compassion, particularly in forgiving sins and in creating new life. Jesus is also portrayed as someone who works miracles, above all healing, in which the power of God is revealed. In general, Jesus discouraged people from talking about him as superhuman (as, for example, the Messiah or Christ – see pp.118–19). He insisted he was an ordinary man, but one through whom the word and the will of the Father were being expressed in the world. Therefore, he spoke of himself as the Son of man. In the Bible this means that the son of Adam, one who, like all people, has to die, but will be saved by God after death (Daniel 7). Challenged (as teachers then often were) to make a *kelal*, or summary, of the Torah (see pp.122–23), Jesus said, Love God wholeheartedly, and your neighbor as yourself (Mark 12:30–31): "Always treat others as you would like them to treat you" (Matthew 7:12).

THE GOSPELS

The four Gospels are attributed to the evangelists or Gospel writers, Matthew, Mark, Luke, and John. The first three use the same material (or each other) to tell Jesus' story and are known as the Synoptic Gospels. Based on oral tradition, they were written from the mid-1st century and agree on many things. Their differences show how early Christians applied Jesus'

teachings to their own lives. Jesus, they believed, continued to live among them through these words. John's Gospel is a deeper reflection on the meaning of Jesus as the Word of God spoken and lived in the world. Each Gospel has a sign taken from both Ezekiel 1:4–10 and Revelation 4:6–7: the four are called tetramorphs ("four signs.")

The Gospel of Mark
St. Mark's sign is a lion. Mark, a disciple of Jesus, was associated with Peter and may have been the author of the Gospel. Its rough style and vivid detail have led scholars to suppose it the earliest Gospel, written between 65 and 75CE.

The Gospel of John
St. John's sign is an eagle. Some assume John was "the disciple whom Jesus loved." This Gospel may have been written particularly for churches around Ephesus. It probably dates from the end of the 1st century, but some think it may be earlier.

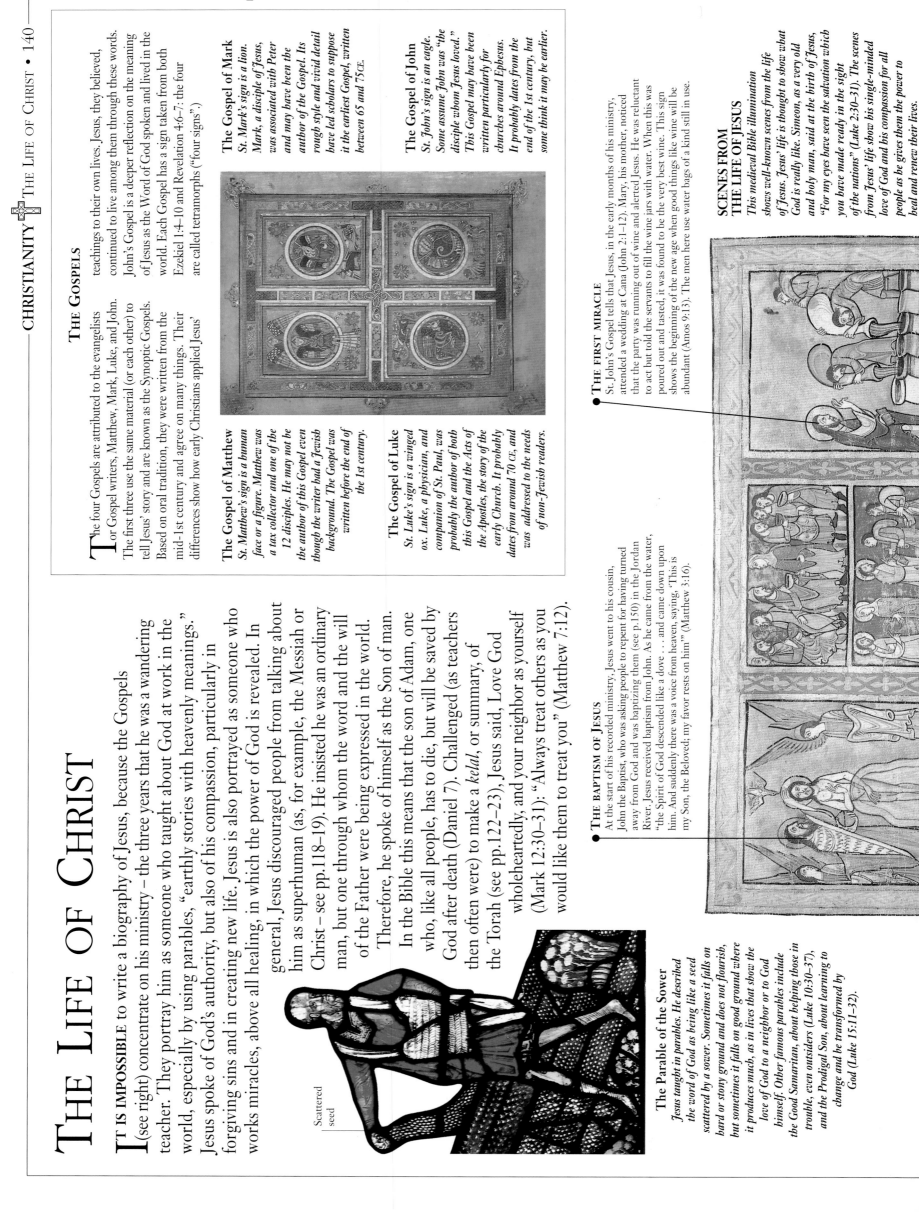

The Gospel of Matthew
St. Matthew's sign is a human face or a figure. Matthew was a tax collector and one of the 12 disciples. He may not be the author of this Gospel even though the writer had a Jewish background. The Gospel was written before the end of the 1st century.

The Gospel of Luke
St. Luke's sign is a winged ox. Luke, a physician, and companion of St. Paul, was probably the author of both this Gospel and the Acts of the Apostles, the story of the early Church. It probably dates from around 70 CE, and was addressed to the needs of non-Jewish readers.

The Parable of the Sower
Jesus taught in parables. He described the word of God as being like a seed scattered by a sower. Sometimes it falls on hard or stony ground and does not flourish, but sometimes it falls on good ground where it produces much, as in lives that show the love of God to a neighbor or to God himself. Other famous parables include the Good Samaritan, about helping those in trouble, even outsiders (Luke 10:30–37), and the Prodigal Son, about learning to change and be transformed by God (Luke 15:11–32).

Scattered seed

THE BAPTISM OF JESUS
At the start of his recorded ministry, Jesus went to his cousin, John the Baptist, who was asking people to repent for having turned away from God and was baptizing them (see p.150) in the Jordan River. Jesus received baptism from John. As he came from the water, "the Spirit of God descended like a dove . . . and came down upon him. And suddenly there was a voice from heaven, saying, 'This is my Son, the Beloved; my favor rests on him'" (Matthew 3:16).

THE FIRST MIRACLE
St. John's Gospel tells that Jesus, in the early months of his ministry, attended a wedding at Cana (John 2:1–12). Mary, his mother, noticed that the party was running out of wine and alerted Jesus. He was reluctant to act but told the servants to fill the wine jars with water. When this was poured out and tasted, it was found to be the very best wine. This sign shows the beginning of the new age when good things like wine will be abundant (Amos 9:13). The men here use water bags of a kind still in use.

SCENES FROM THE LIFE OF JESUS
This medieval Bible illumination shows well-known scenes from the life of Jesus. Jesus' life is thought to show what God is really like. Simeon, as a very old and holy man, said at the birth of Jesus, "For my eyes have seen the salvation which you have made ready in the sight of the nations" (Luke 2:30–31). The scenes from Jesus' life show his single-minded love of God and his compassion for all people as he gives them the power to heal and renew their lives.

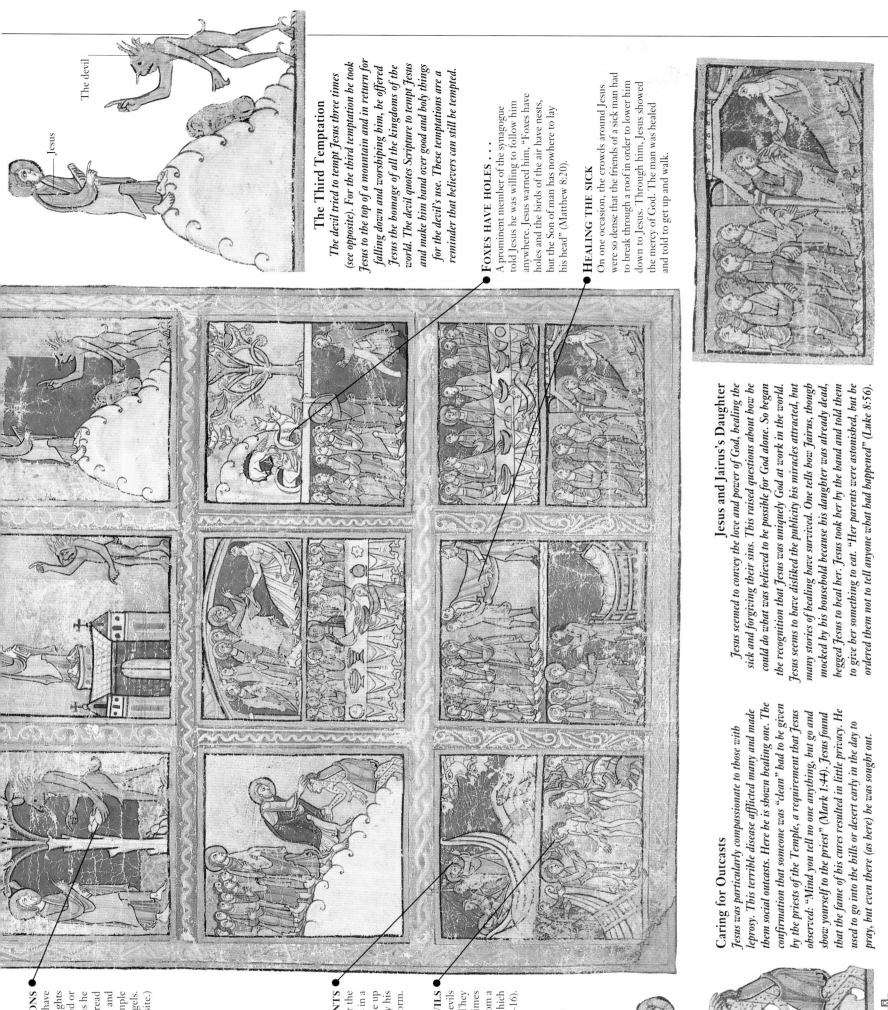

The Third Temptation

The devil tried to tempt Jesus three times (see opposite). For the third temptation he took Jesus to the top of a mountain and in return for falling down and worshiping him, he offered Jesus the homage of all the kingdoms of the world. The devil quotes Scripture to tempt Jesus and make him bow over good and holy things for the devil's use. These temptations are a reminder that believers can still be tempted.

FOXES HAVE HOLES . . .

A prominent member of the synagogue told Jesus he was willing to follow him anywhere. Jesus warned him, "Foxes have holes and the birds of the air have nests, but the Son of man has nowhere to lay his head" (Matthew 8:20).

HEALING THE SICK

On one occasion, the crowds around Jesus were so dense that the friends of a sick man had to break through a roof in order to lower him down to Jesus. Through him, Jesus showed the mercy of God. The man was healed and told to get up and walk.

THE FIRST TWO TEMPTATIONS

At the start of his ministry, Jesus is said to have gone into the desert for 40 days and 40 nights (Matthew 4:3–11). There he was tempted or tested by the devil in three ways: first, as he was hungry, to use his power to make bread from a stone; second, to attract admiration and acclaim by throwing himself off the Temple roof in Jerusalem and being saved by angels. (The third temptation is shown opposite.)

> ❝ *At sunset all those who had friends suffering from diseases of one kind or another brought them to him, and laying hands on each he cured them.* ❞
>
> LUKE 4:40

POWER OVER THE ELEMENTS

Jesus was seen as having power over the elements. On one occasion, when he was in a boat to escape the crowds, a storm came up while he was asleep. He was awakened by his terrified companions and stilled the storm.

CASTING OUT DEVILS

Those who were possessed by devils or unclean spirits sought out Jesus. They roamed wild places and were sometimes violent. In one story, the devils cast from a man were sent into a herd of pigs which then stampeded into a lake (Mark 5:1–16).

A crowd follows Jesus

The halo is a symbol of holiness

Jesus lays his hands on a leper to cure him

Jesus and Jairus's Daughter

Jesus seemed to convey the love and power of God, healing the sick and forgiving their sins. This raised questions about how he could do what was believed to be possible for God alone. So began the recognition that Jesus was uniquely God at work in the world. Jesus seems to have disliked the publicity his miracles attracted, but many stories of healing have survived. One tells how Jairus, though mocked by his household because his daughter was already dead, begged Jesus to heal her. Jesus took her by the hand and told them to give her something to eat. "Her parents were astonished, but he ordered them not to tell anyone what had happened" (Luke 8:56).

Caring for Outcasts

Jesus was particularly compassionate to those with leprosy. This terrible disease afflicted many and made them social outcasts. Here he is shown healing one. The confirmation that someone was "clean" had to be given by the priests of the Temple, a requirement that Jesus observed: "Mind you tell no one anything, but go and show yourself to the priest" (Mark 1:44). Jesus found that the fame of his cures resulted in little privacy. He used to go into the hills or desert early in the day to pray, but even there (as here) he was sought out.

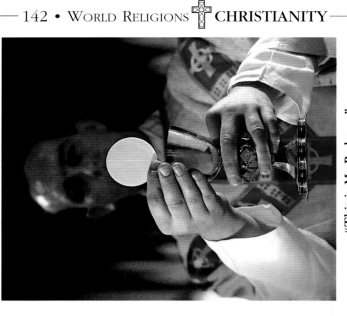

THE LAST SUPPER

THE LAST SUPPER was the last meal that Jesus ate with his disciples before his death (see pp.144–45). Jesus had gone to Jerusalem for Passover with his disciples, knowing that death probably awaited him because he taught without the acceptance of the Temple authorities. He told his disciples this and tried to impress on them that everything that he had taught them about God would remain with them even after he was dead. At this last meal shared together, he broke the bread, poured the wine, and told them, "Take it and eat; this is my body . . . Drink . . . for this is my blood of the covenant, poured out for many for the forgiveness of sins" (Matthew 26:26–28). Later he promised, "I am with you always; yes, to the end of time" (Matthew 28:20). Christians believe that Jesus' death opens the way to eternal life for all. Christians of all kinds reenact the Last Supper, but understand it differently. This is reflected in its many different names such as Communion, Eucharist, Mass, Last Supper, or Memorial Meal.

The Disciple Jesus Loved
The disciple whom Jesus especially loved is said to have been leaning on Jesus at supper (John 13:23). It was he who asked who would betray Jesus. His name is not given, and some have thought that this disciple was St. John, possibly the writer of the Gospel that bears his name.

ST. PETER

Peter was with Jesus at most of the important events described in the Gospels. He was the first to understand Jesus's divine status and was given the responsibility of continuing his teachings on earth: "You are Peter and on this rock I will build my community . . . I will give you the keys of the kingdom of Heaven" (Matthew 16:18–19). At the Last Supper he assured Jesus, "Even if all fall away from you, I will never fall away." But, as Jesus foretold, by morning he had denied three times that he knew him. When he realized this, Peter "went outside and wept bitterly" (Matthew 26:5).

THE LAST SUPPER
This early 16th-century portrayal of the Last Supper shows Jesus with his 12 disciples. The names of some of them are debatable, but it is suggested they were Peter, called Simon Peter, on Jesus' right; Andrew, Peter's brother; James (the greater), son of Zebedee, and his brother John, in Jesus' lap; Philip, Bartholomew, Matthew, Thomas, and James (the less), son of Alphaeus; Judas Iscariot, with the money bag, facing Jesus, Simon the Canaanite, and Thaddeus, also known as Judas, son of James.

"This is My Body . . ."
Some denominations, such as Roman and Anglo-Catholics, call the Last Supper the "Mass," from the Latin missa, derived from mittere, to send away. This emphasizes that although there was only one sacrifice of Jesus on the cross, each Eucharist "is a sacrifice because it re-presents, that is, makes present, the sacrifice of the cross . . . The sacrifice of Christ and the sacrifice of the Eucharist are one single sacrifice" (Catholic Catechism). Here a priest makes the offering of the host, from the Latin hostia, meaning sacrificial victim.

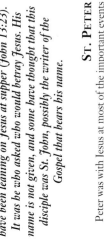

JESUS BETRAYED
Jesus sits with his 12 disciples, knowing the fate in store for him. After he has broken the bread and given thanks for the wine, he tells them that one of them will betray him. "They were greatly distressed and started asking him in turn, 'Not me, Lord, surely?' He answered, 'Someone who has dipped his hand into the dish with me will betray me.'" (Matthew 26:20–23).

PASSOVER MEAL
Jesus and his disciples celebrate the Jewish festival of the Passover (see pp.128–29). In Luke's Gospel, Jesus asks his disciples to break bread "in remembrance of me" (Luke 22:19). Most Protestants interpret the Eucharist in this way.

> ❝*The . . . cup which we bless, is it not a sharing of the blood of Christ; and the loaf of bread which we break, is it not a sharing in the body of Christ?*❞
> 1 CORINTHIANS 10:16

Thirty Pieces of Silver

Judas Iscariot, who looked after all the disciples' money, betrayed Jesus to the High Priests for 30 pieces of silver (Mark 14:10–11; 43–46), but it is not said why. Some take his name "Iscariot" from Sicarius, a dagger-carrying terrorist and campaigner against the Roman occupation. In that case, he may have been hoping to provoke Jesus into direct action against the Roman authorities. According to Matthew 27:3–5 and Acts 1:16–20, he committed suicide after returning the money given to him by the High Priests.

HONEST PARTICIPANTS

The disciples were largely ordinary people – among them fishermen and tax collectors. Taking the Eucharist, also called Communion, is open to all Christians, but the earliest tradition was that it must not be taken "unworthily," without examination of conscience for sin (1 Corinthians 2.28–32).

Damnation for Differing Beliefs

This 16th-century woodcut shows the embittered positions between Catholic and Protestant over the Eucharist: a preacher condemns to hell the priest saying "Mass" (see above) in Latin, in which only the bread was received. He praises the memorial service, held in the native tongue, in which the laity also received the wine.

THE CHANGING VIEW OF THE EUCHARIST

In the 16th century in Europe, changes took place in the Church (see pp.156–57), which meant that for many people the emphasis on the Eucharist moved from one of sacrifice (see top right) to one of remembrance. The commemorative bread and wine were often viewed more figuratively, rather than as literally "the body and blood of Christ" (a belief known as transubstantiation). People have tried to explain how Christ can be present in the bread and wine, but it is a matter of faith, well expressed in the words of Queen Elizabeth I of England: "'Twas God the Word that spake it, He took the bread and brake it, And what the Word doth make it, That I believe and take it." The Eucharist as a memorial meal may be celebrated once a month rather than each Sunday. At the Ecumenical Conference in 1982, it was agreed that "the Eucharist is . . . the effective sign of his sacrifice, accomplished once and for all on the cross and is still operative."

THIRTEEN PLACES SET

Thirteen places are set at the table for Jesus and the 12 disciples. He sent his disciples ahead to prepare for the meal (Matthew 26:17–18; Mark 14:13–16; and Luke 22:8–13). It is unclear whether it was a Passover meal (John 13:1).

WASHED FEET

Before the meal, Jesus washed his disciples' feet as a sign that those sharing the supper were to serve one another (John 13:1–15).

> **❝** *For the tradition I received from the Lord and also handed on to you is that on the night he was betrayed, the Lord Jesus took some bread, and after he had given thanks, he broke it and said, 'This is my body, which is for you; do this in remembrance of me.' And in the same way, with the cup after supper, saying, 'This cup is the new covenant in my blood. Whenever you drink it, do this as a memorial of me.'* **❞**

1 CORINTHIANS 2:23–5
EARLIEST ACCOUNT OF THE EUCHARIST

Bread and Wine

Bread and wine were an ordinary part of any meal. At the Passover (see pp.128–29) the bread must be unleavened. Because of the association between the Passover and the Last Supper, unleavened bread, in the form of wafers, has often been used in the West. But Eastern Christians (see pp.154–55) reject this because there is no New Testament requirement for unleavened bread.

Unleavened bread

Chalice

THE CRUCIFIXION

JESUS WAS CRUCIFIED OUTSIDE JERUSALEM, at the time of the
Passover, just before the Sabbath. He came into conflict with Temple
authorities who believed that the laws given to Moses by God
(see pp.116–17) must be kept before the Messiah (see p.118) could
come to bring God's kingdom on earth. Jesus' claim that he spoke with
God's authority, and his teaching that a covenant or true relationship
with God depends simply on the faith that it is possible, together
with a life expressing that faith, were far from their interpretation.
His refusal to submit to the High Priest, an offense punishable
by death (Deuteronomy 17:8), led to his being handed over to the
Roman authorities as a threat to the state and to his execution. Jesus
accepted his death and did not deny, despite coming close, all
that he had known and made known of God (Matthew 27:46).

THE CRUCIFIXION AS ATONEMENT

Christians believe that Jesus' death is a means of atonement,
or "at-onement," with God. There are at least five
interpretations of it, but central is the belief that
Jesus accepted the pain of death to show, in his
Resurrection (see pp.146–47), that God and his
love are not defeated by death. Christians
try to follow his example, uniting their
lives with God's purpose of rescuing
the world through love.

JESUS AS A KING

The death of Jesus as a criminal is often portrayed
as that of someone who did not cease to be a king,
hence the crown, since he is both God and man. Jesus
triumphs over death, and he has therefore been
seen as a young warrior leading his people to
victory; in this understanding of atonement he
is known in Latin as *Christus Victor*. In *The
Dream of the Rood* (*rood* is an Old English
word for cross), an Anglo-Saxon poet
wrote: "Then the young warrior, God
Almighty, Stripped himself, firm and
unflinching; He climbed Upon the cross,
brave before many, to redeem mankind.
A rood was I raised up; I bore aloft the
mighty King, the Lord of Heaven."

*Jesus' mother Mary holds her dead son,
shown here as Christus Victor*

> "And at the ninth hour Jesus cried out in a
> loud voice, 'Eloi, Eloi lama sabachthani?'
> which means, 'My God, my God, why have
> you forsaken me?'. . . Jesus gave a loud cry
> and breathed his last. And the veil of the
> Sanctuary was torn in two from top to bottom.
> The centurion, who was standing in front of
> him, had seen how he had died, and he said,
> 'In truth, this man was the Son of God.'"
>
> MARK 15:34–39

THE TREE OF THE CROSS

*This painting by the 14th-century artist Pacino da Bonaguida shows the
cross as a tree whose branches show different scenes from Jesus' life.
The lower four branches display his early life, especially his baptism;
the next four show the story of his Crucifixion; and the top four his
Resurrection and final glory. The wooden cross to which Jesus
was nailed has often been described as a family tree
tracing the ancestors of Jesus back through King
David (see pp.118–19) to Adam and Eve, where
fault and death began (see below). However,
in contrast to the tree from which
they ate forbidden fruit, this tree
begins new life.*

THE COMMUNION OF SAINTS

The cross not only bridges the gap between
the individual and God, it also bridges the
gap between individuals themselves, binding
them into new communities and creating,
through the sacraments, the Body of Christ
on earth (see p.150). This is the social
understanding of atonement, which sees
its fulfillment in the communion
of saints in heaven.

THE SACRIFICE

For Christians, Jesus' death can be
understood as the sacrifice of atonement,
paying the high price of sin in the world.
Evil (or sin) causes damage to the sinner
and the person sinned against. To repair
damage is costly and someone has to pay
the price. Christians believe that the damage
of evil and sin is so great that the price of
putting it right was sacrificially high.
Jesus performed that sacrifice
for everybody.

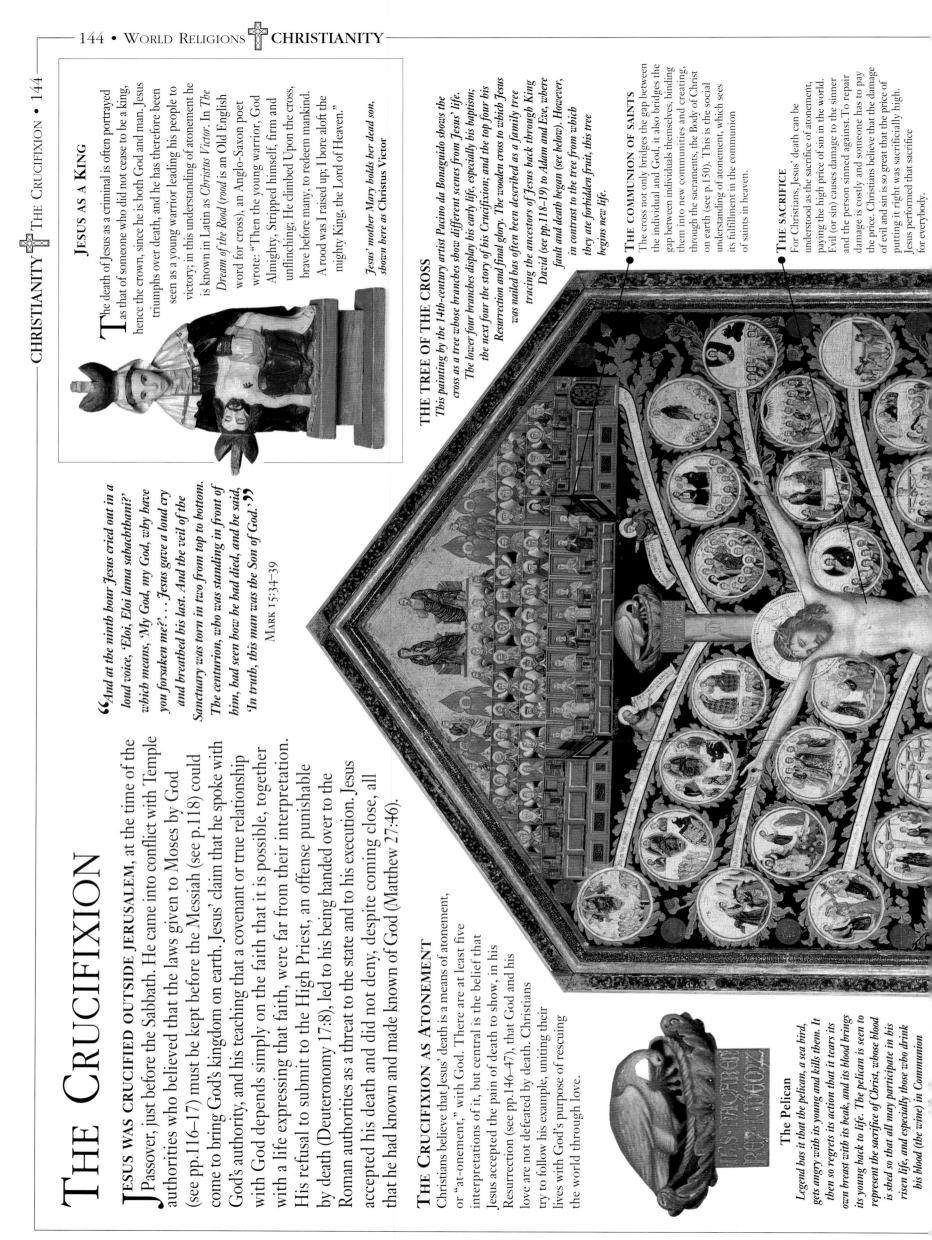

The Pelican

*Legend has it that the pelican, a sea bird,
gets angry with its young and kills them. It
then so regrets its action that it tears its
own breast with its beak, and its blood brings
its young back to life. The pelican is seen to
represent the sacrifice of Christ, whose blood
is shed so that all may participate in his
risen life, and especially those who drink
his blood (the wine) in Communion*

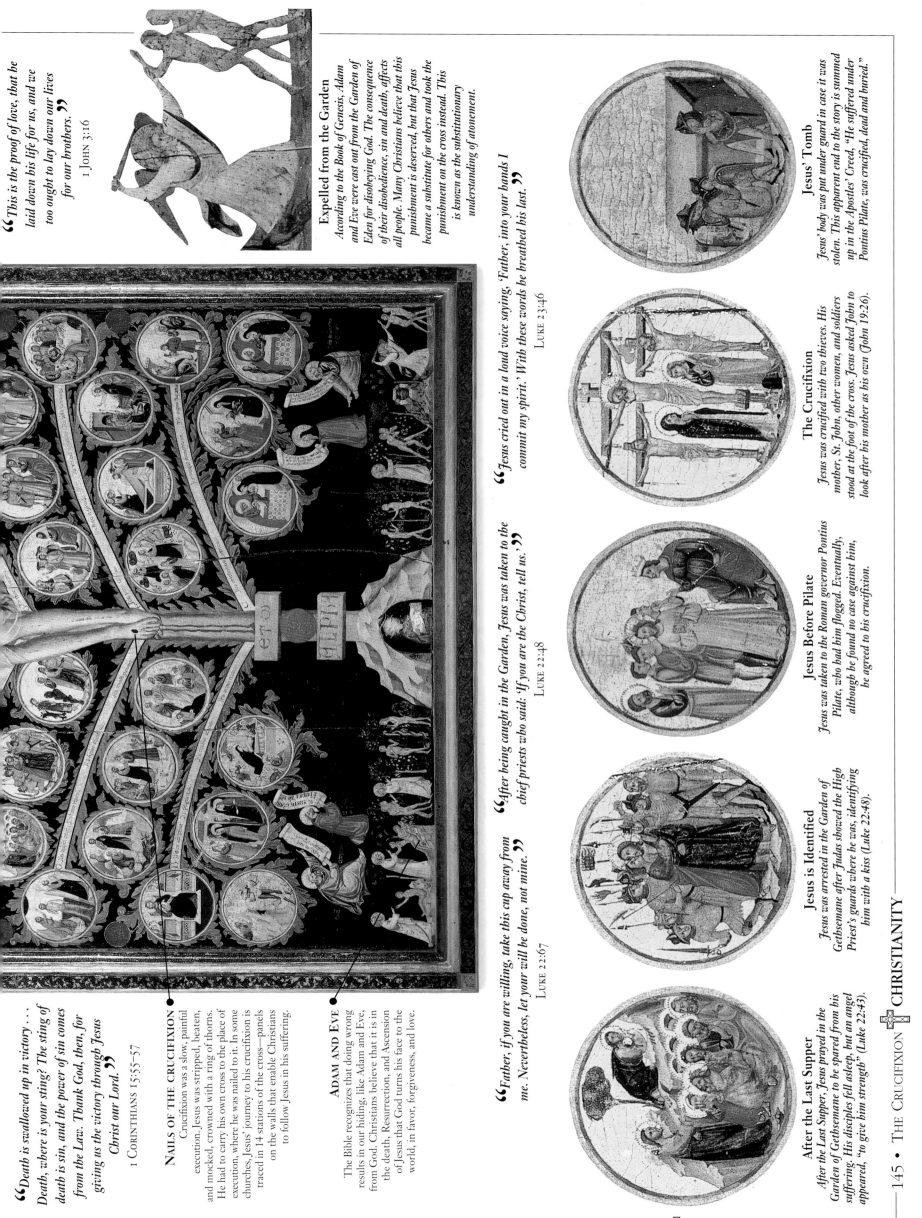

> *This is the proof of love, that he laid down his life for us, and we too ought to lay down our lives for our brothers.*
>
> 1 JOHN 3:16

Expelled from the Garden

According to the Book of Genesis, Adam and Eve were cast out from the Garden of Eden for disobeying God. The consequence of their disobedience, sin and death, affects all people. Many Christians believe that this punishment is deserved, but that Jesus became a substitute for others and took the punishment on the cross instead. This is known as the substitutionary understanding of atonement.

> *Death is swallowed up in victory.... Death, where is your sting? The sting of death is sin, and the power of sin comes from the Law. Thank God, then, for giving us the victory through Jesus Christ our Lord.*
>
> 1 CORINTHIANS 15:55–57

NAILS OF THE CRUCIFIXION

Crucifixion was a slow, painful execution. Jesus was stripped, beaten, and mocked, crowned with a ring of thorns. He had to carry his own cross to the place of execution, where he was nailed to it. In some churches, Jesus' journey to his crucifixion is traced in 14 stations of the cross—panels on the walls that enable Christians to follow Jesus in his suffering.

ADAM AND EVE

The Bible recognizes that doing wrong results in our hiding, like Adam and Eve, from God. Christians believe that it is in the death, Resurrection, and Ascension of Jesus that God turns his face to the world, in favor, forgiveness, and love.

> *Father, if you are willing, take this cup away from me. Nevertheless, let your will be done, not mine.*
>
> LUKE 22:67

> *After being caught in the Garden, Jesus was taken to the chief priests who said: 'If you are the Christ, tell us.'*
>
> LUKE 22:48

> *Jesus cried out in a loud voice saying, 'Father, into your hands I commit my spirit.' With these words he breathed his last.*
>
> LUKE 23:46

After the Last Supper

After the Last Supper, Jesus prayed in the Garden of Gethsemane to be spared from his suffering. His disciples fell asleep, but an angel appeared, "to give him strength" (Luke 22:43).

Jesus is Identified

Jesus was arrested in the Garden of Gethsemane after Judas showed the High Priest's guards where he was, identifying him with a kiss (Luke 22:48).

Jesus Before Pilate

Jesus was taken to the Roman governor Pontius Pilate, who had him flogged. Eventually, although he could be found no case against him, he agreed to his crucifixion.

The Crucifixion

Jesus was crucified with two thieves. His mother, St. John, other women, and soldiers stood at the foot of the cross. Jesus asked John to look after his mother as his own (John 19:26).

Jesus' Tomb

Jesus' body was put under guard in case it was stolen. This apparent end to the story is summed up in the Apostles' Creed, "He suffered under Pontius Pilate, was crucified, dead and buried."

THE RESURRECTION

THE FAMILY AND FRIENDS OF JESUS knew that he had died on the cross (see pp.144–45). Most of his disciples crept away, but the women stayed by the cross until he died. It was to them, amazed and unbelieving, that he first appeared alive beyond the annihilation of death. He was, recognizably and unmistakably, the Jesus they had known, but their surprise was so great that at first they failed to recognize him. Christians understand his Resurrection as the path-finding demonstration of what awaits us after death: it carries human life over the next step in its unfolding into God. Jesus remained for a time among his disciples; at his Ascension he left them as one who sets out on a journey and is separated from those he leaves behind. But he did not leave them comfortless: Christians believe that God, who sustained Jesus through his own life and teaching, entered the Church in the form of the Holy Spirit (see pp.138–39), 50 days after Jesus' Resurrection. The Holy Spirit has remained in the Church making evident the gifts of the Spirit (see opposite).

> **"For I am persuaded that neither death nor life, nor angels, nor principalities, nor powers, nor things present, nor things to come, nor height nor depth, nor any other creature shall be able to separate us from the love of God which is in Christ Jesus our Lord."**
> ST. PAUL TO ROMANS 8:38–39
> AUTHORIZED VERSION

The angel of the tomb, traditionally depicted with wings

The Angel at the Tomb
On arriving at the tomb, the women coming to visit Jesus were met by an angel who assured them that Jesus was not there. He said: "He is not here, for he has risen . . . Come and see the place where he lay" (Matthew 28:6). He asked them, "Why look among the dead for someone who is alive?" (Luke 24:5).

JESUS RISES FROM THE DEAD

These paintings, by the 15th-century Italian artist Mantegna, depict the stories of the Resurrection. Jesus was buried in a tomb and guards were put beside it, because Jesus had said he would rise from the dead. On Sunday morning, he rose, terrifying the guards. The women from Galilee then found the tomb empty, and Jesus appeared to Mary Magdalene in a garden. One of the signs Jesus used to show that he really was the man they had known and seen crucified was by showing his hands and feet and his wounded side.

SYMBOL OF THE RESURRECTION
Jesus is shown holding a banner with a red cross. It is the symbol of the Resurrection, and is often flown from a church on Sunday. It is also the flag of St. George.

SEALED TOMB
Jesus was laid in a tomb that was sealed by a large stone; this was said to be a new tomb hewn out of the rock and put at Jesus' disposal by Joseph of Arimathea (Matthew 27:57–60). To emphasize its security the artist has depicted both a rocky tomb and a Roman sarcophagus, a stone coffin.

"Like Dead Men"
Jesus' Resurrection frightened the guards, and they were "like dead men" (Matthew 28:4). The chief priests had asked Pilate for a guard "to have the sepulchre kept secure until the third day, for fear his disciples come and steal him away and tell the people" (Matthew 27:64).

DOWN TO HELL
St. Matthew's Gospel describes the Resurrection as an earthquake – hence the split rock. There was a traditional belief that between his death and his Resurrection, Jesus went down to hell, thereby extending his mission from God to those who could not have known him, because they had lived before him.

AWAITING THE EVENT
In exploring the significance of the Resurrection of Jesus, St. Paul stressed that the whole of creation was eagerly awaiting the event. This is symbolized by the inclusion of ducks and turtles, a dead tree with a new branch, and a variety of flora and fauna (Romans 8:22).

TONGUES OF FIRE

After his Resurrection and appearances to the women and to the disciples, Jesus was "taken up into heaven." He promised that the Holy Spirit would come upon those he left. The Acts of the Apostles tells the story of the disciples meeting together in an upper room, "when suddenly there came from heaven a sound as of a violent wind . . . and there appeared to them tongues as of fire; these separated and came to rest on the head of each of them" (Acts 2: 1–3). The descent of the Spirit on the disciples is believed to have taken place on the Jewish feast of Shavuot, called Pentecost in Greek. It is celebrated as a festival, some 50 days after that of the Resurrection, which is celebrated at Easter. The consequence of receiving the Spirit was that the disciples were able to preach to people of all languages – each understood them in his own tongue. They went on to baptize, to heal, and to preach the news that Jesus was risen from the dead. This was the beginning of the Christian era.

Jesus is taken up into heaven to join God the Father

The apostles speak in many different languages

● **SPREADING THE WORD**
After the angel rolled away the stone from the tomb to reveal it empty, the women ran to spread the word to the disciples.

> **"**Now if Christ is proclaimed as raised from the dead, how can some of you be saying that there is no resurrection of the dead?**"**
> 1 CORINTHIANS 15:12

● **JESUS APPEARS**
Jesus first appeared to Mary Magdalene in a garden, then went on to appear in the rooms where the apostles met, by the shore of the Sea of Tiberias, and with some of the disciples as they walked to Emmaus (1 Corinthians 15:1–8).

● **THE THIRD DAY**
The Resurrection probably occurred very early in the morning. Jesus was buried on Friday and rose on a Sunday. Counting in ancient style was inclusive: he rose on the third day, so it may have been only 36 hours after his burial.

● **THE SITE OF BURIAL**
There are doubts about the exact site where Jesus was buried. That it was in a garden is certain, and it is likely that it was outside the city. The embattled history of Jerusalem has obscured the evidence, and conflicting claims are made for the site.

The risen Christ

Mary Magdalene at the feet of Jesus

THE WOMEN AT THE TOMB
The women from Galilee, who may have included Mary Magdalene and Mary the mother of James the disciple, went to the tomb very early with spices and ointments to anoint Jesus' body. Instead of finding the guards and a sealed tomb, they found the tomb empty, and an angel showed them the place where the body had been.

RECOGNIZING JESUS ●
Mary Magdalene recognized Jesus and reached out to touch him. He told her not to, because he had not yet ascended to God, but to tell his disciples that he was going to his Father (John 20:11–18).

Looking for the Body of Jesus
The Gospel of St. John tells how Mary Magdalene stood near the tomb, weeping and looking for the body of Jesus. Jesus said to her, "Why are you weeping?" She turned to him, thinking he was the gardener, and said, "Sir, if you have taken him away, tell me where you have put him." Jesus then said, "Mary," and at once she realized she was talking to the risen Lord.

SAINTS AND MARTYRS

ALL CHRISTIANS ARE CALLED TO BE SAINTS, to show in their lives exceptional marks of love, loyalty, and devotion to Jesus, to his teaching, and to his Church. Saints are set apart by popular recognition and devotion or, in the Roman Catholic Church, by a formal process called canonization. There are, inevitably, some who have escaped notice. They are "saints" known only to God. In recent years the Roman Catholic Church has tried to remove from the list saints, such as St. Lucy and St. Christopher, whose historical authenticity is doubtful. They may not have existed, but they still represent some of the activities called for in saints. In the past, saints were thought to look after, or be patrons of, certain things, so St. Christopher watched over travelers. People also chose "personal saints." In the past, and in Roman Catholic churches today, saints are asked for their prayers. Protestants, while recognizing their special gifts, ask all believers to live in the communion of saints on earth. Martyrs are saints who died for their faith. A saint's remains may attract veneration, and their location may become a place of pilgrimage. Many saints are venerated on certain dates.

MODERN SAINTS AND MARTYRS

In the last two centuries many saints have concentrated on particular social ills – Mother Teresa of Calcutta, for example, has tended poor and dying children in India and is commonly believed to be a saint; Oscar Romero cared for the poor in El Salvador, where he alienated those who exploited them, and he was murdered. René Schutz, who founded the ecumenical community of Taizé in France, is recognized as fulfilling Christ's prayer "that all may be one" and that divisions among Christians should end. Martin Luther King Jr., champion of civil rights in the United States, was assassinated for a commitment born of his Christian faith. None have been canonized, either because they are still alive (canonization takes place after death) or because they are not Roman Catholics.

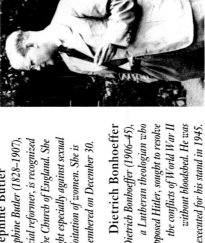

Josephine Butler
Josephine Butler (1828–1907), a social reformer, is recognized in the Church of England. She fought especially against sexual exploitation of women. She is remembered on December 30.

Dietrich Bonhoeffer
Dietrich Bonhoeffer (1906–45), a Lutheran theologian who opposed Hitler, sought to resolve the conflicts of World War II without bloodshed. He was executed for his stand in 1945.

Simeon the Stylite
Simeon the Stylite was an early 5th-century ascetic who served God by severe fasting and great prayer, and by living on a pillar at Telanissus, which was (eventually) 66ft (20m) high. People went to him for prayer and advice, and kind though he was, he sought to escape them and the world vertically.

THE LIFE OF ST. FRANCIS
These paintings from the back of the Sansepolcro Altarpiece by Sassetta show the life of St. Francis of Assisi (c.1181–1226), who followed Jesus so closely and so radically that he was declared a saint within two years of his death. He inspired many religious lives and has been seen as a model of sanctity. The back of this altarpiece faced the choir and might have been a reminder of saintly behavior.

SIGNS OF JESUS' PASSION
St. Francis went up a mountain to pray. The Bible fell open at the story of Jesus' Passion (see pp.144–45). Francis had long prayed to imitate Jesus in all that he did. A seraph appeared to him, and Francis received the stigmata, the marks of the nails of the Crucifixion of Jesus in his hands and feet and the mark of the spear in his side.

MONK'S HABIT
Francis wears the brown habit and knotted cord belt of the Franciscans, the religious order that he founded.

Seraph Messenger
Seraphs were traditionally the messengers of God and stood around his throne: "I saw the Lord . . . above him stood seraphs, each one with six wings: two to cover its face, two to cover its feet and two for flying" (Isaiah 6:1–2).

First set of wings

Second set of wings

Third set of wings

Marks of nails in hands are given to St. Francis

PRAYING TO IMITATE CHRIST
St. Francis was not the only saint who prayed that he might imitate Jesus. Other saints have also done so. One of the most famous was Mother Julian of Norwich (c.14th–15th C.) who had a series of visions of the Passion. After these, she became convinced of the loving nature of God and that "All shall be well, and all shall be well, and all manner of things shall be well."

FRANCIS LEAVES HIS FAMILY

St. Francis sought to be free of family ties in order to serve God more single-mindedly. He renounced his title to his father's lands and returned to his father all the clothes he was wearing. The bishop tried to cover his nakedness by covering him with his cloak.

FRANCIS'S FATHER

Francis's father tries to remonstrate with his decision. Many saints who followed Jesus renounced family life and earthly possessions: "No one who prefers father or mother to me is worthy of me" (Matthew 10:37).

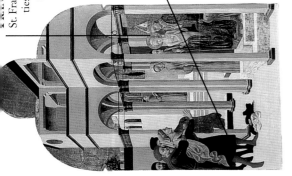

FRANCIS'S DREAM

St. Francis dreamed he was fighting under the flag of the risen Christ (see p.146) and realized he was to be part of a spiritual army. He set up a group of people to serve God. St. Ignatius Loyola (c.1491–1556 see p.157) also founded a community, the Jesuits, who were often seen as an army of Jesus.

CARE OF THE POOR

Care of the poor distinguishes many saints. Here, St. Francis gives his cloak to a poor knight. Other saints also did this, including St. Martin of Tours (c.315–97) who recognized Christ in a naked beggar and tore his cloak in two so that they could share it.

THE POPE

The pope is the head of the Catholic Church. Advised by his cardinals (in red hats), it is he who confers sainthood. Canonization requires proof of good works, miracles, and a life resembling Christ's own.

FRANCIS VISITS ROME

St. Francis went to Rome to ask the pope's approval for his new community of brothers (dressed in brown).

THE FRANCISCANS

St. Francis gathered a group of people who, like him, wished to live without possessions and to beg for food. It was only later that they even rented a house as they did not wish to make provision for the next day. Today, Franciscans are found all over the world among Roman Catholics and Anglicans.

DEATH OF FRANCIS

St. Francis died of natural causes. Other saints, like St. Peter who was crucified upside down, have been less fortunate and were killed for their beliefs. Many martyrs were victims of a political regime, such as the Roman Empire, rather than another faith. Until recently, Christians were victimized in Communist regimes, and it is possible that there have been more martyrs in the 20th century than in any other.

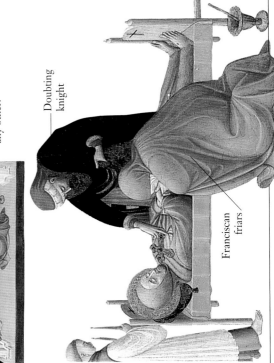

Doubting knight

Franciscan friars

FRANCIS AND THE WOLF

Legend tells how St. Francis, who loved animals and sought to restore the harmony of the Garden of Eden, persuaded a wolf that was devouring the people of Gubbio to stop doing so if it were fed at public expense. The Venerable Bede (d.735), also associated with animals, recognized that the Creator of all will be served by every creature.

FRANCIS BEARS WITNESS

Preaching to the Sultan when he went East to spread Christianity, St. Francis was asked to prove his faith (see below). Many saints, such as St. Francis Xavier (1506–52), were missionaries and have had to confront the claims of different faiths. Such missions were lonely and dangerous; many missionaries were killed and died abroad.

Proof of God's Favor

On St Francis' death, people came to see his body. But one, like the disciple Thomas who doubted Jesus had risen from the dead unless he could see the wounds on his hands and feet (John 20:25), would only believe in St. Francis's sanctity if he saw the stigmata himself. In modern times, many people, such as Padre Pio (d. 1968), are thought to have received the stigmata.

The Faith of St. Francis

In the East, St. Francis offered to prove his faith to the Sultan by walking through a great fire with several of the Sultan's own followers, one of whom fled at the suggestion.

THE CHURCH

THE CHURCH CONSISTS OF THOSE PEOPLE who have responded to Christ's invitation to continue his work on earth. They are referred to as the "Body of Christ" as they believe they are his living presence in the world. They follow his example by teaching, preaching, and serving others, notably those in need – but always as Christ's hands, feet, and body on earth. They are sustained in this by prayer and sacraments. Two sacraments, Baptism and Eucharist, come from the command of Christ. Baptism is the act by which people are accepted into the Church, receive the grace or power to do Christ's work, and although they must die, they enter a new life, which transcends death. Eucharist, also known as the Mass and the Last Supper, is when believers receive the bread and wine of the Last Supper (see pp.142–43), so being assured of his promise to be with them always.

OTHER SACRAMENTS

Some Christians believe there are five other sacraments – confirmation (a reaffirmation of baptismal vows); penance; marriage; anointing the sick; and ordination, the setting aside of bishops, priests, and deacons for Church work, such as administering these sacraments. Some Protestant Churches place less importance on these five sacraments and some are ignored altogether.

ALTARPIECE OF THE SACRAMENTS
This 15th-century altarpiece, painted by Roger van der Weyden (1399–1464) shows the crucifixion of Christ, surrounded by the seven sacraments, all within a church building. It is an ornate Catholic portrayal, before the great upheavals of the Reformation in the 16th century (see pp.156–57).

EUCHARIST ●
The priest celebrates the Eucharist (see pp.142–43) from an altar or table at the east end of the church. In recent years, some altars have been moved to the center of the church, so that the priest can face the people.

ROOD SCREEN ●
A rood (Old English for "cross") screen usually portrays St. John and Mary, Jesus' mother. This reminds the believer of the grief felt by his followers at his death.

PRAYER ●
All churches provide a place for people to praise God in prayer, ask for his help, and ponder his words in scripture. Many churches have a special area or chapel to preserve quiet while other activities are in progress.

CONFESSION AND PENANCE ●
In confession, believers acknowledge their sins – the ways in which they have failed God's commandments (see pp.116–17) – and promise to try to do better in the future. This acknowledgment, known as Confession, may be made privately, in a service congregationally, or individually before a priest. Priests are given power from Christ to declare God's forgiveness (John 20:23). Those forgiven may be asked to undertake reparation or some act of thanksgiving to show their penitence.

CONFIRMATION ●
At Confirmation believers reaffirm their vow, first promised at their baptism, to remain in the Church and follow its teaching. A bishop then lays hands upon them, as the apostles did to the early Christians, as an outward sign of the gifts of the Holy Spirit (Acts 8:14–17).

Some Christians are baptized as babies, and their vows taken for them by adults, who become known as their godparents

A special basin called a font is often used for baptism, but some denominations use a pool to immerse the whole body

Baptism
Baptism brings people into the Church, symbolically washing away their sins with water. It is the most important of the sacraments, showing the acceptance of believers into the Church and giving them the assurance of a new life in Christ, which overcomes death. Jesus himself was baptized by John the Baptist (Matthew 3:13–17). He also ordered his disciples to baptize all people (Matthew 28:19).

CONGREGATION ●
Most churches today have chairs or benches, called pews, for the congregation. In earlier times this was not the case and families and their pets would walk about, often causing a lot of noise.

CRUCIFIED CHRIST ●
In most churches, but not all Protestant ones, a cross or crucifix (a cross with Christ on it) is placed in a prominent position, often above the altar (see pp.144–45). The existence and work of the Church in the world are believed to be the result of the Crucifixion of Jesus.

THE CHURCH
The church is understood in Christianity in a number of ways: as a building, as the worshiping community using it, and as the whole body of believers—living and dead.

EVOLUTION OF CHURCH BUILDING

In early times churches were usually small rooms with an altar at the east end. Because they were vulnerable to attack, towers were often built close by as look-outs and defense points. Towers, which are square, and spires, which are round and pointed, became part of the building. They often have bells, which call people to services and announce events, such as marriage or death. There are many different styles of church buildings, from great cathedrals to plain New England churches, and from strikingly contemporary ones to simple one-room buildings.

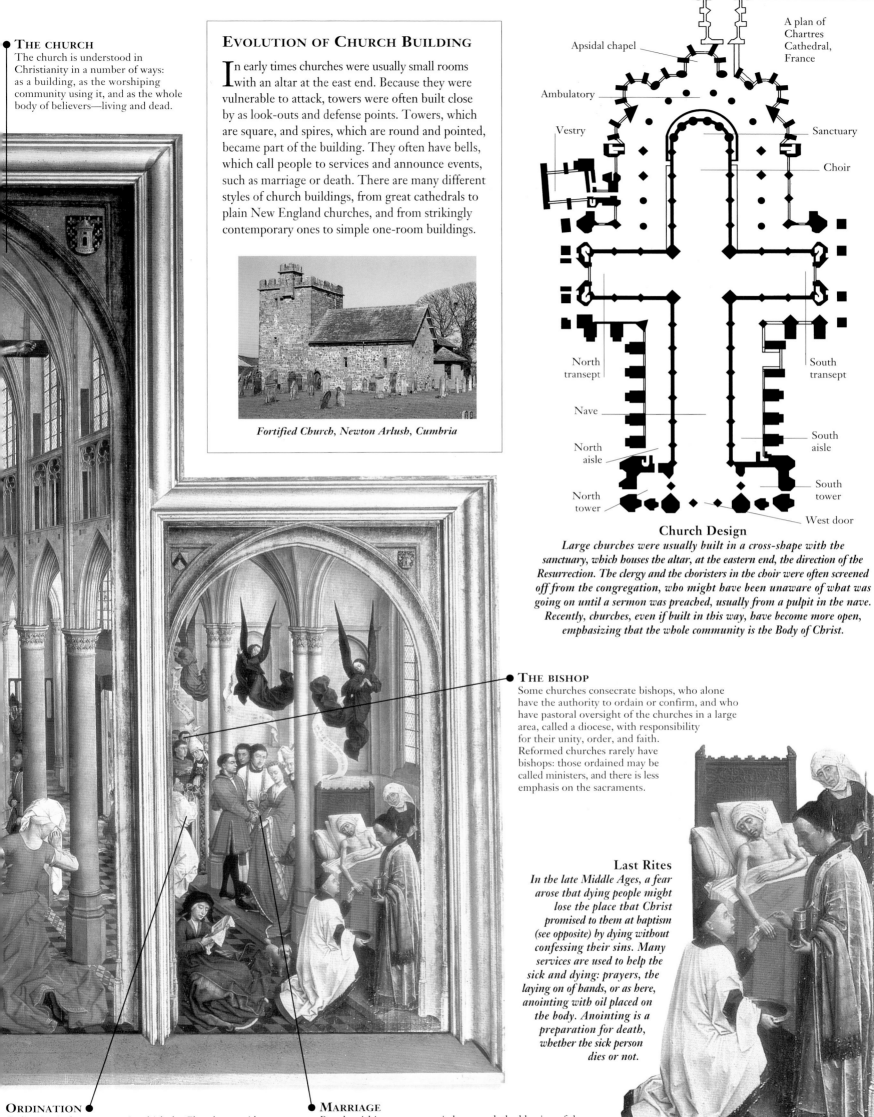

Fortified Church, Newton Arlush, Cumbria

A plan of Chartres Cathedral, France

Apsidal chapel
Ambulatory
Vestry
Sanctuary
Choir
North transept
South transept
Nave
South aisle
North aisle
South tower
North tower
West door

Church Design
Large churches were usually built in a cross-shape with the sanctuary, which houses the altar, at the eastern end, the direction of the Resurrection. The clergy and the choristers in the choir were often screened off from the congregation, who might have been unaware of what was going on until a sermon was preached, usually from a pulpit in the nave. Recently, churches, even if built in this way, have become more open, emphasizing that the whole community is the Body of Christ.

THE BISHOP
Some churches consecrate bishops, who alone have the authority to ordain or confirm, and who have pastoral oversight of the churches in a large area, called a diocese, with responsibility for their unity, order, and faith. Reformed churches rarely have bishops: those ordained may be called ministers, and there is less emphasis on the sacraments.

Last Rites
In the late Middle Ages, a fear arose that dying people might lose the place that Christ promised to them at baptism (see opposite) by dying without confessing their sins. Many services are used to help the sick and dying: prayers, the laying on of hands, or as here, anointing with oil placed on the body. Anointing is a preparation for death, whether the sick person dies or not.

ORDINATION
Ordination is the ceremony in which the Church sets aside particular people to become deacons, who assist in worship, in caring for the poor, the sick, and those in trouble, and who preach the Gospel (see p.140), or priests, who preside over the reenactment of the Last Supper (see pp.142–43), absolve sins, and teach.

MARRIAGE
People wishing to get married may seek the blessing of the Church on the promises they make to each other. In doing so, they become committed to a lifelong relationship, which the Church allows only to be broken and remade with someone else under particular conditions.

THE RELIGIOUS LIFE

IN THE BROADEST SENSE, PEOPLE CALLED "RELIGIOUS" are Christians who choose to live their lives apart from the world, such as monks, nuns, and friars. They all share a desire to follow Christ in his poverty, his obedience to his Father, and his single-minded commitment to all people which is believed to have been effected by remaining sexually chaste. The form that a religious life takes varies: men and women have sought it in the desert or as hermits; others have lived it in a closely knit community governed by a rule. Some are "contemplatives" who have devoted themselves to prayer; others have chosen a more active involvement by showing Christ's care for the world by serving the poor and the sick, and devoting themselves to missionary and educational work. Religious are therefore differentiated by the ways in which they live (contemplative or active), and by the rule that makes this possible. Some, like the Little Brothers of Jesus, wear ordinary clothes but do the most menial work available: this they combine with a life lived with others, interspersed with periods alone as hermits. In contrast, Trappists live in larger communities. They do not leave their houses, and they devote their time to prayer and to work that can be done within their own house. They preserve perpetual silence and live a life of extreme austerity.

The Offices
Much of a monk's day is devoted to saying, chanting, or singing the "office," or prayers at specific times of the day and night. In addition the Eucharist (see pp.142–3) is celebrated daily. Not all orders require all these offices; there has been an attempt to simplify the office for active communities. Many orders still sing their prayers in "plain chant." Gregorian and Ambrosian are the best-known of these chants.

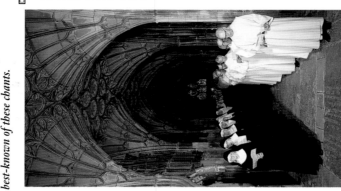

Mixed Orders
Monks and nuns (pictured in original habits with veils and long tunics) celebrate their calling to the religious life (above). A few orders in the Middle Ages, notably the Bridgettines, were mixed, as is the Anglican Benedictine house of Our Lady at Barford, England, today. More usually the sexes are separated in different houses even though they follow the same rule.

CLOISTERS AND ENCLOSURES
Benedictines and contemplative religious live in houses surrounded by a wall or "enclosure." Large communities have cloisters around the courtyard or church (as here), allowing religious to walk, read, or meditate in a partially covered area.

HEAD COVERINGS
Most religious have a head covering. This one has a cowl or hood attached to a cloak. Female religious always covered their heads with veils, which required the women to keep their hair short.

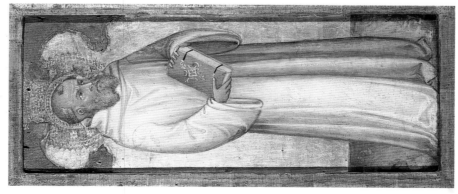

St. Benedict of Nursia
St. Benedict of Nursia (c.480–c.550) composed a rule for religious that became popular between c.550 and c.1150. The Benedictines follow his rule and spend their time in liturgical and private prayer, reading, and manual work. The rule is composed of unvarying routine, protection from the outside world, obedience to the abbot, and a respect for silence. Most religious "rules" are built on that of St. Benedict, or attempt to order the religious life in a different way.

COWLED RELIGIOUS
This fresco by Sodoma (1477–1549) can be found in Italy at the Abbey of Monteoliveto Maggiore in Siena.

RELIGIOUS HABITS
These religious are warmly clad; the "habit" or tunic was covered with a scapular, a sleeveless overall that protected the tunic; in hot climates these might be of thinner material. Women religious in the 20th century may wear ordinary clothes with a cross or brooch to signify their commitment. Until this century, nuns' habits were usually full-length and disguised heavy underskirts underneath: the very wearing of the habit in summer was recognized as an act of penitence.

TRAINING RELIGIOUS
Before finally commiting their lives to God, religious spend time testing whether God intends them to live in an order. The testing may be for about five years as postulants and novices. In the Middle Ages no one was allowed to make the solemn promises to God required by an order until the age of 15 for men and 13 for women. Today early professions (promises) are discouraged.

VOW OF POVERTY
In reaction to well-clothed and well-shod monks from wealthy orders, friars wore no shoes and sought a more austere form of the religious life. Certain monks and nuns made a point of begging to underline their total poverty, often founding new orders in an attempt to return to original ideals.

Securing a Tunic
Separate orders had different ways of vesting or securing the tunic, or vesting; St. Benedict suggested a belt. Later, it was not unusual for a discipline to be attached to it – a piece of either rope or leather – described in the Rule of St. Benedict as a scourge "to chastise the body." In austere orders such penitential instruments were kept in the monk's cell. Many religious wear a rope as a belt with knots in it that hang from the fastening. The knots are a symbol of the vows taken in the religious life, primarily those of poverty, chastity, and obedience.

Rosary beads
In the West, the rosary, often of 50 beads separated in groups of ten, is used by both religious and laity. It aids the repetition of certain prayers while contemplating. Christian monks in the desert counted prayers on beads or pebbles. In Greek Orthodox monasteries each brother is given a cord with knots instead of beads. They receive it to remind them to pray "Lord Jesus Christ, Son of God, have mercy on me a sinner."

These rosary beads, once used by an Anglican nun, are a way of helping prayer

> **It is clear to me that solitude is my vocation, not as flight from the world, but as my place in the world.**
> THOMAS MERTON (d.1968)
> TRAPPIST MONK

The abbey church, begun in 1088, was the largest church in Europe before St. Peter's, Rome, was begun in the 16th century

Chapter House

Cluny Monastery, France
Some religious houses, such as Monte Cassino or Cluny (left), were very large. Lay brothers (who were not priests) did most of the heavy work, especially where the house had extensive estates. The business of the community and the correction of its members took place in the chapter house. Not only did houses of this kind attract envy from grand nobles whose own houses were not as imposing, but they also detracted from the intended simplicity of religious life.

Benedictine monks were responsible for reproducing and guarding many of the manuscripts of the Ancient and early Christian world

The great infirmary hall could accommodate about 100 patients. It was flanked by the Lady Chapel

THE ORTHODOX CHURCH

THE ORTHODOX CHURCH is a group of self-governing churches who trace their history back to the apostles (see pp.142–43) and to the earliest missionary journeys in the Mediterranean world. The oldest are the Greek Orthodox Church and the Churches under the patriarchs of Alexandria, Antioch, and Jerusalem. The patriarch of Constantinople has primacy of honor, but no universal jurisdiction. The conversion of the Slavs was advanced by Saints Cyril and Methodius in the 9th century, and Russia became a Christian kingdom under St. Vladimir in 988. Other important Orthodox churches are those of Serbia, Romania, Bulgaria, former Czechoslovakia, Poland, Cyprus, and Albania. Although separated from other Christian churches, the Orthodox Church holds major beliefs in common with them but differs in emphasis and the style and practice of Christian life. Like the Protestant churches, the Orthodox Church does not recognize the Roman papacy (see p.136). The "Great Schism" between East and West came in 1054 when the patriarch of Constantinople and the patriarch of Rome could not resolve their differences.

Baptism and Confirmation

Baptism and the Eucharist are the two major sacraments for the Orthodox. Baptism and Confirmation (anointing with oils) are usually administered together.

THE IMPORTANCE OF ICONS

These four paintings are icons, a type of image that is very specific and of great importance to the Orthodox Church. Usually painted on wood (but sometimes on metal or ivory), their purpose is not to portray a scene like a photograph but to bring into reality to the subject-matter of the icon. They are windows into God and are used in devotion, because they bring the worshiper into the real presence of the subject.

ST. NICHOLAS
St. Nicholas is patron saint of Russia, sailors, and children. Churches named for him were often built on the coast as a landmark. He brought children gifts on his feast day, December 6th, later moved to the 25th, when as Santa Niclaus, he became Santa Claus.

ORTHODOX PRIESTS

Orthodox priests perform the Holy Thursday service, the commemoration of the Last Supper (see pp.142–43) and the washing of the disciples' feet. A hymn for this occasion says: "The Wisdom of God, who holds back the flooding surge, who tames the abyss, who restrains the sea, now pours water into a basin to wash the feet of his servants." Orthodox priests may be married (and priests usually are), but they may not marry after they are ordained, and bishops are always celibate and are therefore appointed from among monks (see pp.152–53). Priests have beards, in faithfulness to the Bible, (Leviticus 19:27). When priests in the West began to shave, they were severely criticized by Orthodox Christians.

Priests at the Holy Thursday Service

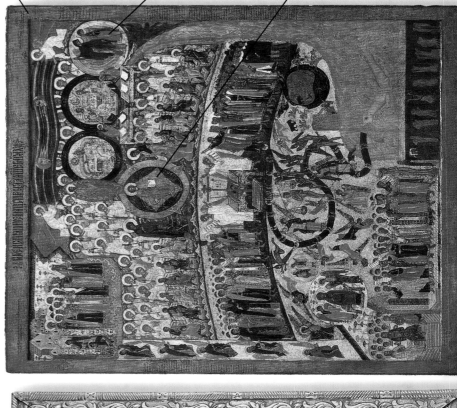

PLACING OF THE ICON
Icons are found in churches on the iconostasis, a wall with three doors separating the sanctuary and altar from the congregation. The central, or royal, door leads to the sanctuary and the altar, where a part of the service is conducted out of sight of the congregation.

THE LAST JUDGMENT
This icon depicts the story of the Last Judgment, Jesus' judgment of all souls before heaven and hell. The virtuous go to heaven and sinners go to hell. It appears both in Orthodox and other Christian traditions, although it is portrayed in very different styles (see pp.158–59).

DEPICTION OF CHRIST
Christ administers justice. Icons of Christ are most prominent on the iconostasis along with those depicting Mary and John the Baptist. The Annunciation (see p.138) would be on the royal door, with a row of icons above related to feast days and saints; above this are the apostles.

THREE SAINTS
Saints are deeply revered by the Orthodox. The saints in this icon are Mercurios, Tryphon, and Katherine. The process of designating a saint is not as formal as it is in the Roman Church; it is usually decided in a synod of bishops in any one of the self-governing parts of the Church, but sometimes devotion to a saint comes to be accepted through the popularity of that saint.

MERCURIOS AND KATHERINE
St. Mercurios (far left) was a Turkish martyr who, after converting to Christianity, refused to worship the Greek goddess Artemis and was consequently executed. St. Katherine of Alexandria was martyred for refusing to marry Emperor Maxentius because she believed she was married to Christ.

VENERATION OF AN ICON
Through the icon the worshiper enters into sacred space and time. Candles are burned before icons, which are venerated by kissing and prostration. They are often thought to have miraculous powers, and some are believed to have come into being miraculously: they are called *acheiropoietos*, "not made with hands."

PATRIARCH OF THE CITY
St. Tryphon was a monk who became patriarch of Constantinople from 928 to 931.

One of the monasteries at Mount Athos

THE HARROWING OF HELL
This icon depicts Christ "harrowing hell" – releasing the righteous, who died before his time. Although the subjects depicted in icons vary, they usually relate to scenes that are important in worship, rather than to historical events. They frequently present Christ, the saints, and the life-giving moments of the Church. Monasteries are likely to have icons relating the stories of their foundation.

CONCENTRATION ON CHRIST
An important form of prayer in Orthodoxy is hesychasm, or quiet concentration on Christ. Often it includes the Jesus prayer, or the prayer of the heart, which is repeated many times: "Lord Jesus Christ, Son of God, have mercy on me, a sinner." It is often accompanied by careful posture and attention to breathing in rhythm with the prayer, so that the whole person is drawn into God.

LEADING THE JUST
Christ leads the just, the patriarchs, and Adam and Eve into the light. The old man by Christ is probably Abraham.

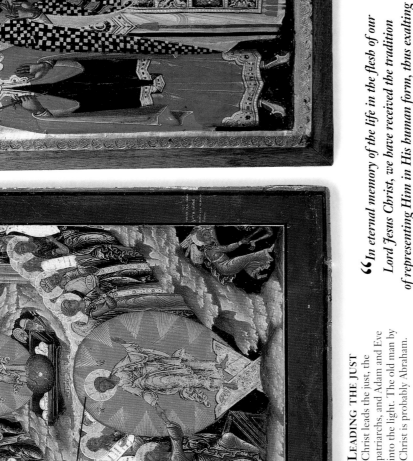

> ❝ In eternal memory of the life in the flesh of our Lord Jesus Christ, we have received the tradition of representing Him in His human form, thus exalting the self-humbling of God the Word. ❞
>
> GERMANUS (8TH CENTURY) DEFENDS THE USE OF ICONS

Mount Athos
Mount Athos is the Holy Mountain in northeastern Greece. It is the major center of Orthodox monasticism, and has been self-governing since 1927. The Great Lavra – the gathering of monks at a common place – was founded here in 962, and by the 11th century there were 180 monasteries. Today there are 20 senior monasteries and a number of houses, including the dwellings of hermits. Most are cenobitic – living a monastic, communal life. Women, even female animals, are forbidden. Icons on Mount Athos include famous miracle-working ones, such as those of Our Lady in the Great Lavra and the monastery of Iveron. Monasticism lies at the heart of Orthodoxy.

The Cathedral of Saint Basil
The Cathedral of Saint Basil is the most famous and familiar of the great churches of Russian Orthodoxy. It was built between 1555 and 1560 at the command of Ivan the Fourth ("the Terrible"), to commemorate and give thanks for his victory at Kazan in 1552, which greatly extended the territory of Russia and thus the sphere of the Russian Orthodox Church. It is the culmination of the Russian determination to outdo the Greek Orthodox in splendor and number of their churches. The more northern climate, especially the heavy snows and rains, made necessary the characteristic style of the roof, with domes rising from cylindrical drums.

Typically domed style of roof

THE REFORMATION

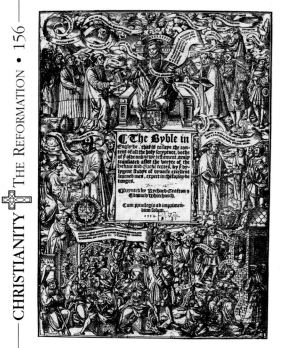

THE CHURCH is always in a process of reformation as it tries to live closer to Christ's teaching. However, Christians often disagree and occasionally movements break away (sometimes called "heresies") or different churches emerge (see pp.154–55). With the advent of the printing press in the 1450s, books, including the Bible, became increasingly available, and a call arose to reform the superstitious practices of the laity and introduce a closer following of Scripture. There was also a protest against corrupt Church practices and a move toward reforming the religious life. Then, a major break occurred in the 16th century. Out of these reform movements came new "Protestant" Churches. The Catholic Church stressed the papacy (see p.137), sacraments (see pp.142–43 and pp.150–51), and the controlled use of Scripture. The Protestant Churches stressed each individual's relationship with Christ without a priest or pope acting as intermediary, and the primacy of Scripture (now available in the vernacular, not just in Latin), as the foundation of preaching, teaching, and salvation.

The Great Bible
England was one of the last places to allow the Bible to be printed in the vernacular. The Great Bible, ordered by Henry VIII, was finally allowed into parish churches by 1539. Other unauthorized versions had preceded it, notably William Tyndale's New Testament. In Europe, biblical scholarship was advanced by Erasmus' Greek New Testament (1516), and by the Polyglot or "many tongues" Bible, with different languages side by side, from Ximenes in Spain (1522).

TWO KINDS OF PREACHING
This German woodcut highlights the differences between Catholic and Protestant preaching. In Germany, the Bible, crudely set in wood type, was available by the end of the 15th century. It is arguable that this breakthrough in information technology was responsible for making the 16th-century Reformation possible.

A PROTESTANT PREACHER
Protestant preaching was always from the Bible. Both preacher and congregation followed the passage that was read from the Scripture. Women, especially, found this helpful because it included them. Sermons were long – notice the hour-glass.

PLAIN AND SIMPLE
Protestant ministers dress simply in a black gown and their pulpits are plain; there is no ornament to distract the congregation from the uplifting Word of God.

TEACHING CHILDREN
All Christians saw the importance of teaching children. In the Protestant tradition, schools, and in the 18th century, Sunday schools, were seen as an invitation to teach children the basic truth of Scripture.

Wyliffe   Zwingli   Calvin   Knox   Luther   Melancthon

Hus

The Candle of Reformation is Lighted

We cannot   blow   it out

SEPARATE SIDES
A blind man points to the separated sides of the Church, so bitterly divided in the 16th century. Attempts to unite the divided Church are known as "ecumenical movements," but none of the major divisions, despite far greater understanding, has yet been healed.

Fathers of the Reformation
The founding fathers of the Protestant Reformation are seen lighting the candle of the Gospel, which will not be put out. Wycliffe of England and Hus of Bohemia predated the 16th-century reformers. The reformers shown here disagreed with each other on many things but were united in stressing the primacy of Scripture. Luther and Calvin were dominant figures, but Knox in Scotland and Zwingli in Zurich had an influence beyond their own areas. The problem for Protestant reformers was retaining unity against individual convictions.

Councils of the Church
General councils of the Church were thought to be the proper place to solve problems. The first is described in Acts 15; the next seven (325–787) are called Ecumenical Councils. "Ecumenical" means applying to the whole inhabited world, and the councils were so called because they were held before the Church divided. Later councils have been held but are not recognized by all parts of the Church. The Council of Constance (1414–18) was called to deal with the reformer John Hus and the division of the papacy, also known as the Great Schism. The Council of Trent (1545–63), shown here, was called to deal with the theological problems posed by Protestantism. It laid down guidelines for Catholics on contentious matters such as the liturgy or manner of worship, the nature of authority, and the relationship between the faith and the works of believers and their salvation.

● CATHOLIC PREACHING
Catholic preaching in the years before the Reformation took place only on certain days. It was moralistic and wide-ranging, and could therefore move far from the text of the Bible. The preacher here is shown without a Bible before him. Preaching was not the high point of the service.

● DECORATION IN DEVOTION TO GOD
The decorated pulpit and the robes of the Catholic priest are aspects of the visual nature of Catholic devotion. The rest of the church would also have been decorated, and stained-glass windows may have shown stories from the Bible. Devotion was made tangible by the prayer beads used by the congregation, who are not necessarily listening to the sermon. "Telling the beads" is the practice of saying the sequence of prayer known as the rosary. Each bead has its prayer, and each set of ten its focus of intention.

● EDUCATION
Catholics, especially in lands where they were persecuted, concerned themselves with education. Schools were set up in "safe areas," like Douai in France, for the education of English men and women. Catholics were barred from the universities in Protestant states like England.

● CATHOLIC CONGREGATION
The Catholic congregation had to be encouraged not to join the Protestant Church. As a result, a reformation arose from within the Catholic Church, producing its own leaders. One was Ignatius Loyola who founded the Society or Army of Jesus (the Jesuits) in 1534. Others were Teresa of Avila and John of the Cross, who tried to understand the ways in which the soul is embraced by the Holy Spirit in prayer.

> ❝*What gain, then, is it for anyone to win the whole world and forfeit his life?* ❞
> MARK 8:36
> A VERSE USED BY IGNATIUS LOYOLA

Persecution
Both Protestants and Catholics were persecuted and died, often by burning, for maintaining their beliefs. The formulation of cuius regio, eius religio ("to whom the region belongs, his shall be the religion") at the Peace of Augsburg in 1555, meant that each state or region had to adopt the faith of its ruler. For example, Mary I of England (1516–58), a Catholic, persecuted Protestants and her sister Elizabeth I (1533–1603), a Protestant, persecuted Catholics.

> ❝*Then you will be handed over to be tortured and put to death; and you will be hated by all nations on account of my name. And then many will fall away; people will betray one another and hate one another.* ❞
> MATTHEW 24: 9–11

THE LAST JUDGMENT

JESUS TAUGHT THAT there would be a Day of Judgment "when the Son of man comes in his glory" (Matthew 25:31), and all people would be judged. The judgment will turn on whether people have made plain the goodness and mercy of God: whether they have fed the hungry, given the thirsty something to drink, and clothed the naked. Those who have done these things, and those who have neglected to do them, will be separated as sheep from goats, the wicked "to eternal punishment, and the upright to eternal life" (Matthew 25:46). But Jesus knew that all people need the help and mercy of God. The Psalmist prayed, "Do not put your servant on trial, nor no one living can be found guiltless at your tribunal" (Psalm 143:2). Jesus is judge but also merciful redeemer. The Christian prays, "Look, Father, look on his anointed face, and only look on us as found in him." St. Paul therefore stressed that salvation cannot be by works alone: through the death of Christ (see pp.144–45) God freely forgives and cancels the charge at the tribunal. This is accepted by faith, and in the Spirit the works of mercy (see below) become possible.

THE LAST JUDGMENT
Michelangelo (1475–1564) painted the Last Judgment in the Sistine Chapel in Rome, referring to the Bible text that tells how the tribes of the earth "will see the Son of man coming on the clouds of heaven with power and great glory" (Matthew 24:30).

Jesus and Mary
Jesus stands with his mother. On his left are his disciples, with St. Peter carrying a key. Jesus told him: "I will give you the keys of the Kingdom of Heaven; whatever you bind on earth will be bound in heaven; whatever you loose on earth will be loosed in heaven" (Matthew 16:19).

INSTRUMENTS OF PAIN
The cross, crown of thorns, and pillar where Jesus was scourged before the Crucifixion, with other instruments of his Passion, are swept along by angels for the time when "there will be no more death, and no more mourning or sadness or pain" (Revelation 21:4).

THE SAVED
Those who have followed God's commandments or who have seen God in Jesus are saved; they are embracing one another and merge into groups of patriarchs, prophets, and disciples on either side of Christ.

CHRIST'S DISCIPLES
Christ's disciples are near him. St. Bartholomew, who was skinned alive before his execution, is shown with a knife and his skin. The painter is said to have put his own face on the skin.

Rosary beads

Faith Overcomes
The dead who have received their bodies are helped up to heaven. This couple holds on to a rosary that represents here a continuous chain of faith, rather than an aid to prayer.

ST. JOHN THE BAPTIST
Here, St. John the Baptist is close to the risen Christ. He baptized Jesus (see pp.140–41) at the start of Jesus's ministry. John was later beheaded at the request of Salome, Herod's daughter. St. John the Baptist is regarded as the forerunner of Jesus.

THE DAMNED
All who have chosen to live their lives in a way that denies God go into hell: the proud who think they are God; the greedy who use all that is in the world as though they own it, and all who use others for their own gain.

THE LAST TRUMPET
The judgment was said to be preceded by "angels with a loud trumpet" (Matthew 24:31) who stand at the four corners of the earth.

THE BOATMAN OF THE DEAD
A boatman, known in Graeco-Roman times as Charon, traditionally ferried the dead to their rest; here he is ferrying the damned to hell. He and the demons of hell are given grotesque features because Christians believe those who have chosen to reject virtue become less than human.

Spiked wheel or "Catherine wheel"

The Martyrs
The saints are shown with the instruments of their martyrdom. St. Catherine, said to have lived in the 4th century, is reputed to have been torn to death by spiked wheels for refusing to be the bride of any man except Christ.

LOVE, THE GREAT VIRTUE
Those ascending to heaven grasp and hug each other, symbolizing the greatest Christian virtue, which is love. It endures, and St. Paul says of it: "These remain: faith, hope and love, the three of them; and the greatest of them is love" (1 Corinthians 13:13).

A SYMBOL OF HOPE
Two monks with their eyes shut rise to eternal life and are a symbol of hope – the third of the three virtues. Hope is to desire and to expect something not yet fully accomplished.

ALL WHO HAVE LIVED
A scroll is being carried that holds the names and account of everyone who has lived.

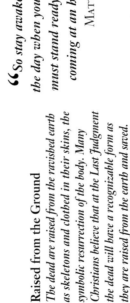

"I was thirsty and you gave me drink"

Raised from the Ground
The dead are raised from the ravished earth as skeletons and clothed in their skins, the symbolic resurrection of the body. Many Christians believe that at the Last Judgment the dead will have a recognizable form as they are raised from the earth and saved.

> *So stay awake, because you do not know the day when your master is coming . . . you must stand ready because the Son of man is coming at an hour you do not expect.*
> MATTHEW 24:42–44

THE WAY TO HEAVEN

Jesus was very clear about the Last Judgment: he said that those who have followed him will be known by their treatment of others, "For I was hungry and you gave me food, I was thirsty and you gave me drink, I was a stranger and you made me welcome, lacking clothes and you clothed me, sick and you visited me, in prison and you came to see me" (Matthew 25:35–36). In the Church these acts became known as the works of mercy, to which another was added, that of burying the dead. The seven works of mercy are seen as treating every person as though they are Jesus. More elaborate schemes of salvation were devised; in the Middle Ages it was thought that the way in which you died determined whether you went to heaven.

THE WAY TO HELL

To neglect the needs of others was in Jesus' words a certain way to go to hell: "In truth I tell you, in so far as you neglected to do this to one of the least of these, you neglected to do it to me" (Matthew 25:45). Jesus summarized the Ten Commandments for his followers: "You must love the Lord your God with all your heart, with all your soul, and with all your mind. This is the greatest and the first commandment. The second resembles it: You must love your neighbor as yourself" (Matthew 2:37–38). The church has traditionally summarized the deadly sins, or evils that deserve eternal punishment as pride, greed, lust, envy, gluttony, anger, and sloth. In every case the individual is placed above God or the needs of his neighbors. Jesus explained that he was not abolishing the Ten Commandments but giving them a new and more definitive form. Someone who speaks ill of another offends against God and his neighbor in the same way as murder or theft. Christians are told to love their enemies. The demands are high, but Jesus promised his help or grace to those who attempt them (see pp.150–51).

"I was sick and you visited me"

159 • THE LAST JUDGMENT ✠ CHRISTIANITY

159 • WORLD RELIGIONS ✠ CHRISTIANITY

ISLAM

THERE IS NO GOD BUT GOD

ISLAM IS THE RELIGION of allegiance to God that began historically with the prophet Muhammad, "peace be upon him" – a blessing repeated at each mention of his name, so greatly is he revered – in Arabia in the 7th century CE. However, according to its own teachings, Islam began as the way of life, or *din* (often translated as "religion"), which God intended for his creation from the start. Human rebellion and sin meant that God constantly sent prophets, including Moses, called Musa in Islam, and Jesus, the central figure in Christianity, called 'Isa by Muslims, to summon people back to the proper *din*. However, with the exception of Muhammad, all were rejected, persecuted, or killed.

Muhammad was told to warn his people in the town of Mecca, in what is now Saudi Arabia; although he too was rejected by the majority of people, some saw and heard the truth of God being spoken through him. These people made up the first small community of Muslims, who as a result of persecution moved with Muhammad to Yathrib in 622CE. This move to Yathrib, from then on called Medina, is known as the *hijra*, and the Islamic calendar, which is lunar and therefore slightly shorter than the solar one, begins from "after the *hijra*" (1417AH, for example, began on May 19, 1996). The Muslims who followed Muhammad are known as *Muhajirun* ("those who made the *hijra*"), and those who supported Muhammad in Medina are known as *Ansar* ("the helpers") – the descendants of both these groups are honored in Islam.

Islam is often translated as "submission." But the Arabic letters *slm* that appear in "Islam" are related to the Hebrew word *shalom*, the greeting of peace. Islam, therefore,

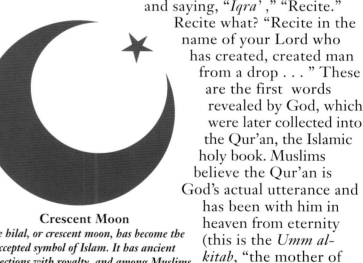

Crescent Moon
The hilal, or crescent moon, has become the accepted symbol of Islam. It has ancient connections with royalty, and among Muslims bears resonances of the lunar calendar, which orders their religious life.

The Angel Gabriel
This detail of Muhammad's ascent into heaven (see pp.164–65) shows the angel Gabriel, or Jibril in Arabic, who revealed God's word to Muhammad. Centuries earlier it was he who delivered the news to Mary (see p.138) of the imminent birth of Jesus, who, in Islam, is the prophet 'Isa.

means "entering into a condition of peace and security with God through allegiance and surrender to him." This is what Muhammad discovered when, as a young man, in the midst of rival claims about God from the Jews, Christians, and many polytheists in Arabia, he used to go to Mount Hira near Mecca to search for the truth about God. It was here, in a cave on the mountain, that he was overwhelmed with a tremendous sense of God (or his messenger Gabriel) pressing upon him and saying, "*Iqra'*," "Recite." Recite what? "Recite in the name of your Lord who has created, created man from a drop . . . " These are the first words revealed by God, which were later collected into the Qur'an, the Islamic holy book. Muslims believe the Qur'an is God's actual utterance and has been with him in heaven from eternity (this is the *Umm al-kitab*, "the mother of the book"). God has sent this utterance as guidance to humankind through successive messengers such as Musa and 'Isa, who each transmitted it to meet the needs of their own people. Finally, God sent the Qur'an in its complete form through the last messenger, Muhammad, who was only a man, exemplary though he was. He was the human channel of God's will.

From the first dramatic moment on Mount Hira, Muhammad was given the all-important understanding that if God *is* God, there cannot be rival accounts of "who God is," and there certainly cannot be rival gods or many gods. There can only be *God*, and for that reason he is called *Allah*, "the one who is God." Neither can there be rival religions or people divided against each other – all people come from God and return to him after death for exact judgment on their actions. All people should, therefore, become a single *umma*, or community, and every action and aspect of life should bear witness to the fact that "there is no god but God, and Muhammad is his messenger."

This witness is the *Shahada*, the first of the Five Pillars of Islam (*arkan al-din*), the foundations of Muslim life. The Five Pillars (see pp.168–69) give structure and unity to Muslims all over the world.

THE FOUNDATIONS OF LIFE

The Qur'an is the nonnegotiable authority in Muslim life and belief. But it does not cover all circumstances in detail, so the words and actions (and

The Astrolabe
The astrolabe was taken over from the Greeks and refined by Arab scientists. It was used to measure the angle of stars above the horizon, which enabled the latitude of the user to be worked out, and from that point the distance and time. One of its most important uses, apart from assisting travelers by land and sea, was to help find out the direction of Mecca, so that Muslims could perform their prayers in the right direction.

silences) of Muhammad and his companions are accepted as a living commentary on what the Qur'an means and how it should be applied. They were gathered in six revered collections, the *Sahih*, meaning "sound," and are known collectively as the *Hadith* or *Sunna*, the customary practice of the Prophet. Methods of exegesis or interpretation emerged, particularly that of consensus in the community and the use of analogy, *ijma'* and *qiyas*. Major traditions then developed that drew up law codes for life, known as *Shari'a* ("the well-worn path that camels take to the watering place"). There are four major schools of *Shari'a*, and most Muslims live their lives according to one of them (see pp.170–71).

DIVISIONS IN ISLAM

After the death of the Prophet Muhammad in 10 AH/632 CE, the Muslim community split. Those who thought that his successor or *caliph* should be the best qualified man chose Abu Bakr. They became the Sunni Muslims, those who follow the *Sunna* or custom of Muhammad. Others, the *shi'at 'Ali*, "the party of 'Ali," thought that his nearest relative, his cousin and son-in-law 'Ali, should succeed him, and they became the Shi'a Muslims. Not much

Prayer Mat
This sajjada, *or prayer mat, will be used by a Muslim who wishes to make sure he performs his prayers on a clean space. Woven into the mat is a picture of a mosque courtyard looking across at a dome and a minaret. In its center it has a compass set toward Mecca, so that the worshiper can always know the right direction in which to perform his prayers.*

separates the two groups in belief and practice, but Shi'as exalt their *Imams*, a succession of leaders, whom they regard as a line of inspired teachers. There have also been bitter political divisions.

THE INFLUENCE OF ISLAM

Within 100 years Islam had swept over the known world, reaching from the Atlantic to the borders of China. It has remained a rapidly expanding religion, with about a quarter of the world's population being Muslims. They form nearly total majorities in countries in the Middle East, northern Africa, parts of central Asia and Indonesia. There are also substantial minorities in the West, in countries such as France, Germany, the UK, and the United States. There is also a substantial population in China.

In its early centuries Islam led the world in the recovery of Greek science and philosophy (see pp.174–75) – words starting with *al-*, "the," such as "algebra" and "alchemy," the beginning of modern chemistry, are a trace of this. In later centuries, many Muslims turned against these studies as a distraction from the Qur'an, and Islam has not returned to that early celebration of God's creation in science and philosophy.

In another reaction, some drew closer to God, seeking to know his immediate presence. These were the Sufis, a name probably deriving from *suf*, the rough wool cloak that they wore (see pp.172–73). This mystical Islam became widespread in the 12th century and has remained influential ever since.

NO GOD BUT ALLAH

IN ARABIC "ALLAH" MEANS *"the* God." From his profound experience in the cave on Mount Hira (see p.164). Muhammad realized that if God does indeed exist, it is *God* who exists. There can only be what God is – there cannot be different or rival gods (for example, a god of the Jews, a god of the Christians, or the many gods of the polytheists). From this tremendous insight into the oneness of God, or *tawhid* (see below), the whole of Islam flows forth: all creation must be derived from God, including human life; all humans belong to a single *umma*, family or community; and all life returns to God from whom it comes. His is a way of life, or *din*, covering all spheres of human existence. All humans, therefore, will have to render on the Day of Judgment an account to God of how they have used the gift of life. God determines all things, but human beings are responsible for acquiring the possibilities that God creates for them. God is supreme but not remote – "He is closer than the vein in your neck" (*Sura* 50:16) – and Muslims live in the presence of God at all times, and are especially close in daily prayer (see p.168).

THE NATURE OF GOD

The Qur'an, the Islamic holy book, emphasizes repeatedly the might and majesty of God and his complete difference from other existent beings. This verse sums up what he is like fully and briefly, and asserts his power and omnipotence. It also lists four of the 99 Beautiful Names of God (Living, Eternal, Supreme, Tremendous). These are descriptive adjectives given throughout the Qur'an, which Muslims frequently repeat with the help of a *subha*, or rosary.

❝*Allah! There is no God save Him, the Living, the Eternal. Neither slumber nor sleep overtake Him; to Him belongs what is in the heavens and earth. Who will intercede with Him except by His leave? He knows what is before them and what is behind them, while they grasp nothing of His knowledge except what He wills. His throne encompasses the heavens and the earth, and He never wearies of keeping them. He is the Supreme, the Tremendous.* ❞

THE QUR'AN, *Sura* 2:255, THE VERSE OF THE THRONE

The Declaration of Faith
The Shahada, the Muslim declaration of faith, is painted on the tile above. It reads: "There is no god but God, and Muhammad is the messenger of God." The familiar blessing "God's mercy be upon him" is also inscribed. To Muslims, there is only One God, and he disclosed his last and complete guidance for humankind to Muhammad. Allah, Arabic for God, is made up of al and ilah, which mean "the God." Together they make Allah, emphasizing that he is the only divinity.

GOD THE GIVER OF MERCY
These words in gold ink are the opening words of this and all the chapters in the Qur'an, the Islamic holy book, with the exception of chapter nine. They read: "In the name of God the merciful the Giver of mercy." Muslims recite these words whenever they begin an activity.

THE LETTER DAL
These five curved characters are each the letter *Dal* in Arabic. They occur as rhymes at the end of each phrase and mark the stages through which the chapter builds to a climax.
The artist has portrayed this by placing the characters one above the other in steps to the top of the figure.

"SAY, HE IS GOD"
Among all the references to God in the Qur'an, these four verses that make up Chapter 112 and begin with this word *Qul* ("Say", the command from God to Muhammad), are probably the best known to Muslims. Muslims are taught them from childhood, and they are used in the five daily prayers (see pp.168–69). The Sura is known as *Surat al-Ikhlas*, the Chapter of Sincere Faith in God, and *Surat al-Tawhid*, the Chapter of God's Unity.

ONLY ONE GOD
This word, in Arabic *abad*, means "one", "single," or "alone." The artist has placed it at the apex of his composition to emphasize the Islamic teaching that there is only one god, and that he is an absolute unity rather than composed of many parts. That is why the last verse of the chapter asserts that there is no other like him. The emphasis on God's oneness in Islam is called *tawhid*, a word that is related to *ahad*, and means "maintaining God's unity."

AL-SAMAD
The word *samad* means a thing that remains undamaged. Among early Arabs it referred to men who were wise and dependable. In this *sura* it suggests that God is self-subsistent and unchanging and can be relied upon by his creatures.

COMPACTNESS AND CLARITY

In order to help readers follow the words and gradually understand their meaning, the artist has numbered each letter that makes up this shape. This is the first letter of the first word, numbered 11. In English the chapter reads: "In the name of God, the merciful, the Giver of mercy; Say, He is God, One; God the self-subsistent; He is not begotten, and does not beget; and like Him there is not one."

THE LAST WORD

This is the last word of the chapter. The importance of the teaching in the chapter is underlined by the Prophet Muhammad's words: "Reciting this chapter is equal to reciting a third of the Qur'an."

CHAPTER OF SINCERE FAITH IN GOD

This composition based on Surat al-Ikhlas by Ahmed Moustafa (1983) follows in the Islamic tradition in which calligraphy is used as decoration as well as for relaying information. It arises from the belief that the words of the Qur'an are God's eternal speech and so should be expressed as beautifully and with as much care as possible.

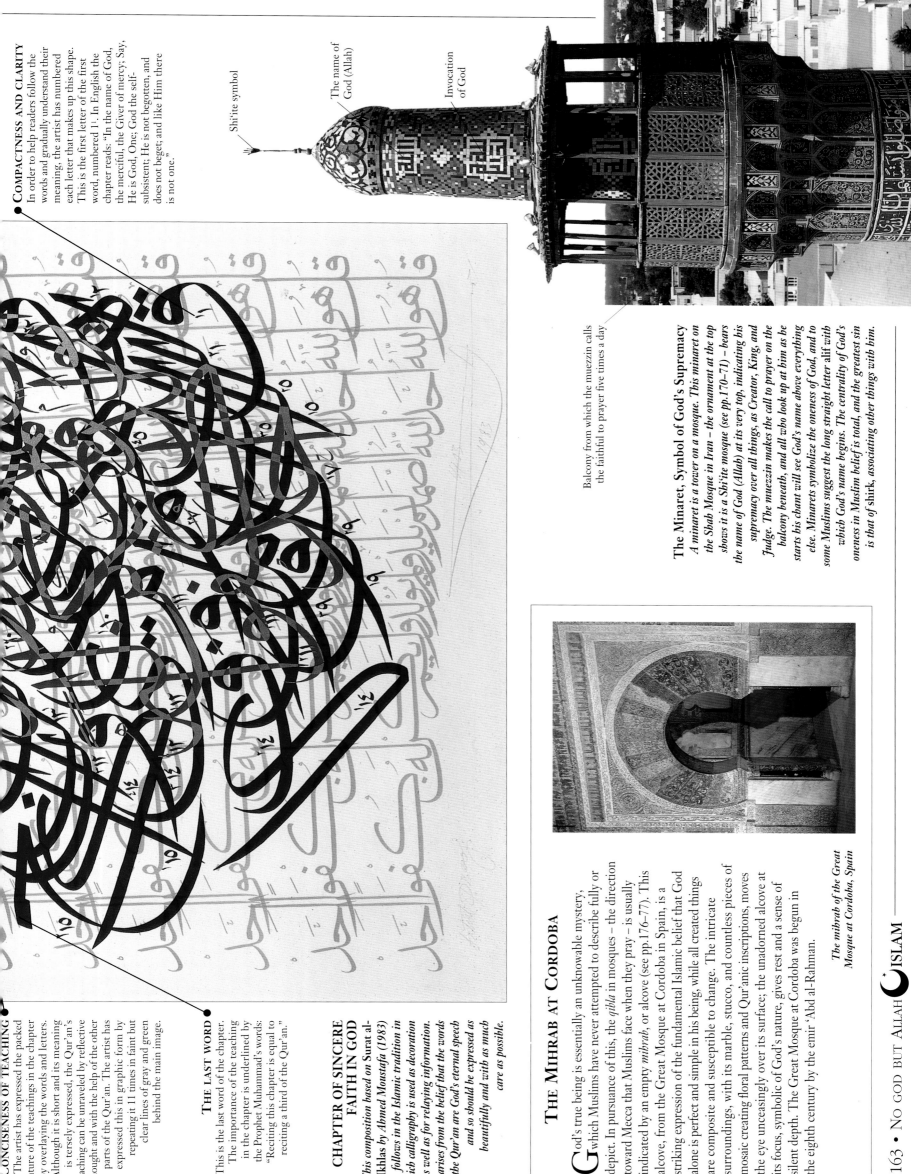

Shi'ite symbol

The name of God (Allah)

Invocation of God

The Minaret, Symbol of God's Supremacy
A minaret is a tower on a mosque. This minaret on the Shah Mosque in Iran – the ornament at the top shows it is a Shi'ite mosque (see pp.170–71) – bears the name of God (Allah) at its very top, indicating his supremacy over all things, as Creator, King, and Judge. The muezzin makes the call to prayer on the balcony beneath, and all who look up at him as he starts his chant will see God's name above everything else. Minarets symbolize the oneness of God, and to some Muslims suggest the long straight letter alif with which God's name begins. The centrality of God's oneness in Muslim belief is total, and the greatest sin is that of shirk, associating other things with him.

Balcony from which the muezzin calls the faithful to prayer five times a day

THE MIHRAB AT CORDOBA

God's true being is essentially an unknowable mystery, which Muslims have never attempted to describe fully or depict. In pursuance of this, the *qibla* in mosques – the direction toward Mecca that Muslims face when they pray – is usually indicated by an empty *mihrab*, or alcove (see pp.176–77). This alcove, from the Great Mosque at Cordoba in Spain, is a striking expression of the fundamental Islamic belief that God alone is perfect and simple in his being, while all created things are composite and susceptible to change. The intricate surroundings, with its marble, stucco, and countless pieces of mosaic creating floral patterns and Qur'anic inscriptions, moves the eye unceasingly over its surface; the unadorned alcove at its focus, symbolic of God's nature, gives rest and a sense of silent depth. The Great Mosque at Cordoba was begun in the eighth century by the emir 'Abd al-Rahman.

The mihrab of the Great Mosque at Cordoba, Spain

THE PROPHET MUHAMMAD

THE PROPHET MUHAMMAD was born in Mecca, now Saudia Arabia, in 570 CE. Orphaned as a child, he was brought up by his grandfather and later by his uncle. He worked as a trader and at the age of 25 married Khadija, a wealthy widow. As time went on, he took to reflecting and meditating on Mount Hira just outside Mecca, where in 610 he received the first of his revelations from God, brought by the angel Gabriel. From 613 he proclaimed these to the polytheistic people of Mecca but received a lukewarm welcome. His radical teachings of the oneness of God (see pp.162–63) angered them, and they persecuted him and his followers, some of whom fled to Ethiopia. In 622, still persecuted and now widowed, Muhammad accepted an offer of the people of Yathrib (later known as Medina) and went north. This migration, or *hijra*, marks the start of the Islamic era. Muhammad fought against the Meccans until 630, increasing his power and prestige as more and more tribes accepted Islam. When the Meccans accepted defeat, Muhammad declared an amnesty for all except a few of his former enemies, and began to think of spreading Islam beyond Arabia. However, in 632, at the age of 62, he died, having transmitted the revelations of God in their entirety.

A Perfect Example of Living

Although they insist upon his humanity, Muslims revere Muhammad, shown above, as the perfect example of living. The majority follow his Sunna, or customary practice, and thereby call themselves Sunni Muslims. They base their lives upon his sayings and actions, which were compiled into six authoritative collections by careful and pious experts, who separated the authentic Hadith, sayings of the Prophet, from others that have doubtful status. These collections rank second only to the Qur'an in importance for Muslims, and among them those of the two experts al-Bukhari and Muslim ibn Hajjaj are especially respected.

HALOS OF FIRE

The halos surrounding Muhammad and Gabriel denote their holiness. The Prophet's superior status is shown by his halo filling the whole space above his mount. The implied superiority of the human over the angel may derive from the Qur'an's account of the creation of humankind in which God commands the angels to acknowledge what he has made: "And when he said to the angels, Prostrate yourselves before Adam, they fell prostrate, all except Iblis" (*Sura 2:34*).

REVERENCE FOR THE PROPHET

The Prophet's face is hidden by a veil, not only to show his exalted status, but also because Islam conventionally prohibits depictions of him. No Muslim will hear criticism of Muhammad, and nearly all are accustomed to invoke God's blessing on him each time they mention or write his name. A minority of Muslims accord such great importance to the Prophet that they attribute to him

Accompanied by Angels

One of the greatest events in the Prophet's life was his Night Journey, when he was carried from Mecca to Jerusalem and from there made the Mi'raj, the ascent through the heavens to God's presence, before returning to Mecca in the morning.

ROBE OF HONOR

An angel and his companion bring Muhammad a robe and cap of honor, traditionally given by a great ruler to a subject with whom he is especially pleased. They are a way of showing Muhammad's special status with God. The green robe is always associated with the Prophet.

THE NIGHT JOURNEY

Muhammad's Night Journey into God's presence is commemorated in the Qur'an: "Glorified be He who carried His servant by night from the holy mosque to the far-distant mosque, the neighborhood of which We have blessed, so that We might show him our signs" (*Sura 17:1*). The "holy mosque" is understood to be the Ka'ba in Mecca (see pp.168–69), and the "far-distant mosque" to be the al-Aqsa mosque near the Dome of the Rock shrine in Jerusalem (see p.165).

ANGEL GABRIEL

Muhammad is guided by the angel Gabriel, the chief of God's angelic servants. Gabriel brought God's revelations to Muhammad and often listened to him reciting them. Here he conducts the Prophet on his journey.

THE BURAQ

Muhammad was carried through the heavens on a fabulous horselike beast with a female human head called *al-buraq*, meaning "Lightning." This was his mount for his journey from Mecca to Jerusalem where, before ascending, he led other prophets, including Abraham, Moses, and Jesus, in prayer.

> **"** *You certainly have in God's Messenger a beautiful pattern for anyone whose hope is in God and the Last Day and who often remembers God.* **"**
>
> THE QUR'AN, *Sura 33:21*

INTO THE HEAVENS

Muhammad ascended into the heavens on the 27th of the Islamic month of Rajab from the rock on the Temple Mount in Jerusalem, now marked by the sacred Dome of the Rock shrine. This rock is said to bear the Prophet's footprint, and even to hang in the air. On the Day of Judgment the angel Israfil will blow the trumpet from the rock, and according to some traditions the Ka'ba will come to it from Mecca like a bride.

MUHAMMAD'S ASCENT

This illustration of the Mi'raj, Muhammad's ascent, comes from the Khamseh of the poet Nizami, which was made in 1543 for the Persian Shah Tahmasp. It is considered to be the work of the court painter Sultan Muhammad.

MUHAMMAD ASCENDS

Accompanied by angels, Muhammad ascends toward the highest of the seven heavens.

According to some accounts, both Muhammad and Gabriel had to shield their eyes from the brilliance of God's presence. Gabriel then left, but the Prophet was eventually able to see God from whom he received directions about the daily prayers that all Muslims should perform (see pp.168–69). He was told to institute five times of prayer throughout each day.

Belief in Angels

Muslims believe that angels such as Gabriel, shown here, are God's servants in all matters. Particular angels have special responsibilities: Mika'il is the angel of providence, Azra'il is the angel of death, and Munkar and Nakir inquire of the dead in their tombs about their deeds.

The angel Iblis, also known as Shaytan, disobeyed God by refusing to prostrate himself before the newly created Adam. He thereby became the enemy of humankind.

> **"** *Recite in the name of your Lord who has created, created man from a drop of blood. Recite, for your Lord is most generous, Who taught by the pen, Who taught man what he did not know.* **"**
>
> THE FIRST WORDS OF THE REVELATION BROUGHT TO MUHAMMAD BY GABRIEL
>
> THE QUR'AN, *Sura 96:1–5*

EARLIER MESSENGERS

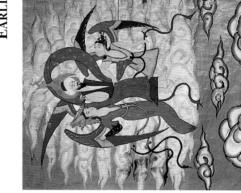

Muhammad was the last of God's many prophets sent to bring his guidance to humankind. Muslims believe that all these messengers, who include Noah, Abraham, Moses, David, and Jesus, brought revelations that, in essence, concurred with the Qur'an. "He has revealed to you (Muhammad) the Scripture with truth, confirming what was before it, just as he revealed the Torah and the Gospel" (*Sura 3:3*). According to Islam, all of the prophets, including Jesus, were human. In the Qur'an Jesus denies claiming divinity and looks forward to God's final messenger. Here, in accordance with the Qur'an, he is taken up to heaven, for: "They (the Jews) did not kill him or crucify him, but it appeared so to them ... but God raised him to himself"(*Sura 4:157-8*).

Jesus ascending to heaven, carried by angels

THE DEATH OF MUHAMMAD

Like all the prophets before him, Muhammad was human. He chose to be buried in his adopted town of Medina. His tomb lies in the mosque that the young Muslim community built when they arrived in Medina, where Muhammad and his wives, mostly widows whom he had married after the death of Khadija, lived. This mosque, the center for worship and the business of government during Muhammad's lifetime, has been expanded and embellished by Muslim rulers over the centuries. Muhammad died in the lap of his favorite wife 'A'isha, and was buried on the spot, in what was then her small apartment along one wall of the original mosque. His tomb is now flanked by those of Abu Bakr and 'Umar, two of his closest companions and the first two caliphs – leaders of the Muslim community – after his death.

THE QUR'AN

THE QUR'AN is the revelation from God of his speech (*kalam*) or Word, and is the foundation of Islam. The same message has been revealed through earlier prophets, such as Moses and Jesus, but earlier communities have corrupted the message entrusted to them. Thus only the Arabic Qur'an expresses without fault the Word of God. This is why the Qur'an cannot be translated into any other language – it can only be paraphrased or interpreted – and the reason why calligraphy is so important in Islam. To make beautiful the Word of God is an act of worship and thanksgiving. Although the Qur'an describes itself as a "clear book" (*Suras* 2:2 and 12:2), some of its passages are difficult to understand and need interpretation. The work of commentary, *tafsir* and *ta'wil*, has produced an enormous body of literature.

RECITATION OF GOD'S WORD

"Qur'an" means "recitation," and its words have habitually been chanted aloud. When Muhammad received the first verses in 610 CE, he was given the order by the angel Gabriel to "*Iqra*," "Recite!" These verses are usually held to be verses 1–5 of Chapter (*Sura*) 96: "Recite! in the name of your Lord who has created . . ." Divided into 114 *Suras*, the Qur'an covers many topics. It initially focuses on the unity of God (see pp.162–63), God's role in history, Muhammad's role as his prophet, the Last Judgment, and the need to help other people. Later *Suras* deal with communal matters relating to family, marriage, and legal, ethical, and social concerns relating to the growing *umma* in Medina.

THE QUR'AN
Muslims believe that the Qur'an has been kept on a preserved tablet in God's presence from eternity, until the time he willed to reveal it in its entirety: " This is indeed a noble Qur'an, in a book kept hidden." This Qur'an dates from the 17th or 18th century and comes from India.

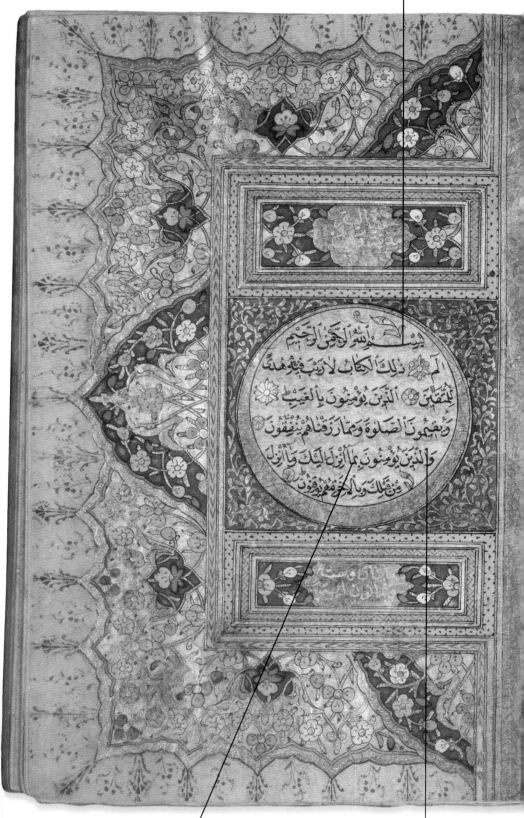

SECOND CHAPTER ●
Arabic is read from right to left. This is the beginning of the second chapter, *Surat al-Baqara*, "The Cow." The opposite page is the first chapter.

Eternal Utterance From God
God made his first revelation to Muhammad in 610 CE in the cave on Mount Hira, known as Jabal al-Nur, the "Mountain of Light." The revelations were brought by the angel Gabriel who continued to bring portions of God's utterance until Muhammad's death in 632 CE. Muhammad is shown here just after the first revelation.

EXACT WORDS ●
All the words in the Qur'an are believed by Muslims to be the exact utterance of God. Muhammad recited them to his companions, and they were then written down by scribes. Since being collected as a whole soon after Muhammad's death, they have remained unchanged.

READING ALOUD ●
The black markings above and below the letters denote the vowels. The Arabic alphabet does not include letters for the vowel sounds, and so they are written here as guides to pronunciation. The red marks indicate appropriate breathings at the end of each verse.

CHAPTER HEADING ●
The chapter heading gives the title, in this case *Surat al-Fatiha*, "The Opening", and indicates whether it was revealed to Muhammad in Mecca or Medina. This one was revealed in Mecca.

BEAUTY OF GOD'S WORDS
The first pages of most copies of the Qur'an are elaborately decorated. The most expensive copies, made for rulers or nobles, might be decorated throughout. In some periods geometrical designs would have been fashionable, in others curved patterns or, as here, floral compositions. They would take months or even years to complete, but such attention would be appropriate since what the artist was touching and the reader reciting is regarded by Muslims as God's actual utterance.

VERSE MARKERS ●
Each *aya*, or verse, is indicated by a gilded rosette at the end.

● **FIRST WORDS**
Both chapters (see also opposite) begin with the words, *bism illah al-rahman al-rahim*, "In the name of God, the merciful, the Giver of mercy." All 114 chapters, except Chapter 9, begin with these words.

THE QUR'AN IN ARCHITECTURE

This window in the Alhambra, the magnificent palace of the Nasrid emirs of Granada in Spain, represents a splendid example of the ways in which Arabic script, particularly verses from the Qur'an, was used for decorative purposes. The actual window is surrounded by relief work, which consists completely of Arabic script combined with abstract designs, forming a whole where the light fretwork quality creates the impression that the window is suspended from the arch above rather than supporting it. Above the colored tile dado, the outer band that frames the alcove is composed of the words "*Wa la ghalib illa Allah*," "There is no conqueror other than God," repeated throughout. This is particularly poignant given that the princes who built and expanded the palace were constantly on the defensive against the Christian forces who were gradually winning Spain from the Muslim rulers. The inner band framing the window itself and the medallion shapes above are all composed of Arabic script in differing calligraphic styles. Almost hidden in the surrounding tracery is a line along the window top in a style known as knotted Kufic. Kufic was a very early script, and remained popular in copying the Qur'an.

A window in the Alhambra, the palace of the Nasrid emirs of Granada in Spain.

Woven Words
This is part of the kiswa, *the cloth that covers the Ka'ba in Mecca, Islam's holiest shrine (see pp.168–69). The words of the* Shahada, *"There is no god but God . . ." are woven into its material and it is entirely decorated with text. The central cartouche relates to the Prophet's return to Mecca to cleanse the Ka'ba from polytheism and make it a Muslim shrine. It reads: "Truly God has fulfilled the vision of his messenger, You will enter the sacred mosque in security." (Sura 48:27).*

Chapter Heading
The Qur'an has 114 suras, or chapters. Here and in the same place on the opposite page of the Qur'an, the number of ayat or verses in each sura is given. "The Opening" has seven ayat and "The Cow," the longest sura, has 286. The shortest suras, suras 103, 108, and 110, have three ayat each.

THE FIVE PILLARS OF ISLAM

THE FIVE PILLARS support and give structure to Muslim life. The first pillar is the *Shahada*, the affirmation "There is no god but God, and Muhammad is the messenger of God." This declares that God is the only divinity, and that he has communicated his will through Muhammad. Its words are chanted daily in the *Adhan*, the call to prayer. The second pillar is *Salat*, the set prayers that Muslims must perform in the direction of the Ka'ba – the sacred shrine at the center of the mosque at Mecca – five times each day. The third pillar is *Sawm*, the daily fast that is performed throughout the month of Ramadan. Muslims refrain from food, drink, and sexual intimacy during daylight hours. In this way they practice discipline and experience the deprivations of the poor. Ramadan ends with 'Id al-Fitr, the Festival of Breaking the Fast, when congregational prayers are held, and Muslims exchange gifts. Many will observe the fourth pillar at this time, *Zakat*, almsgiving, which entails contributing wealth, usually one-fortieth of their annual income, for the poor and for charitable causes. The fifth pillar is *Hajj*, the pilgrimage to Mecca in the 12th Islamic month, which all healthy Muslims should try to make at least once in their lifetime.

A Woman Performing Prayer
Muslims are required to perform Salat, *the set prayers, each day near dawn, at midday, in the afternoon, at sunset, and in the evening. Each time they must prepare by performing ablutions, consciously stating their intention to pray, and finding a clean spot upon which they can face Mecca. Then they repeat a set ritual of bowing, kneeling, and prostrating, accompanied by calls to God and recitations of parts of the Qur'an in Arabic. Each group of postures and words is called a* rak'a. *Less formal requests to God are called* du'a. *This woman, with her hands raised, is engaged in* du'a.

THE SACRED MOSQUE AT MECCA
This Ottoman tile shows a plan of the Masjid al-Haram, the sacred mosque at Mecca with the Ka'ba, the cube-shaped building that is the focus of all Muslim prayer and the goal of the Hajj, the annual pilgrimage. Tiles such as this would inform prospective pilgrims of the layout of the mosque and help them prepare for the ceremonies to be performed.

THE KA'BA – FOUNDED BY ADAM, REBUILT BY ABRAHAM

Prayer at the Ka'ba

The Ka'ba is believed to have been built at God's command by Abraham and his son by Hagar, Ishmael. It stands on a site that many people believe to have been a sanctuary founded by Adam, the first man. In the pre-Islamic period it was a shrine to 360 Arabian deities, but it was not until 630 CE that Muhammad toppled these deities and rededicated the shrine to the one true God. Every year, two million pilgrims visit Mecca to perform *Hajj*. At the sight of the Ka'ba, they are often spiritually overwhelmed. As they enter the *haram*, the sacred area around Mecca, they exclaim the words *"Labbayka! Labbayka!,* "I am at your service!" From then on they focus only on God. *Hajj* can only be performed in the 12th month. When pilgrims visit at other times of the year they perform the *'umra*, the lesser pilgrimage, which imposes fewer requirements on them.

ALL WHO ARE ABLE
This Qur'anic inscription enjoins pilgrimage on all who are able: "Lo, the first sanctuary appointed for humankind was that at Mecca, a blessed place, a guidance to the peoples, wherein are plain memorials; the place where Abraham stood to pray; and whosoever enters it is safe. And pilgrimage to the House is a duty toward God upon humankind, for those who can find a way there. As for those who disbelieve, indeed God is independent of creatures" (*Sura 3:96–7*).

MINARETS
This minaret is at the northern corner of the sacred mosque and indicates that the four principal corners of the Ka'ba itself point in the four compass directions. It is not known whether this has any religious significance.

FOUR RITES OF ISLAM

This is the *maqam Hanafi*, the Station of the Hanafites, one of four positions around the Ka'ba, which symbolize the four rites of religious law in Islam (see pp.170–71). At main prayers, followers of each rite stand behind their leaders.

THE HOLY WALL

The *multazam*, the area of wall between the black stone and the door, is thought to be particularly holy. After performing the *tawaf*, pilgrims often try to press themselves against it.

THE MINBAR

A sermon is preached from the *minbar*, or pulpit, on the eighth day of the *hajj*. The pilgrims then go to the Mount of Mercy outside Mecca to stand before God in what is often thought of as an anticipation of the Last Judgment. This is the climax of the pilgrimage and without it the *hajj* is not complete.

THE GATE OF PEACE

Entering the Gate of Peace, men wear *ihram*, a white cloth wound around the waist and another draped over the left shoulder. Women show only their hands and faces. This form of dress must be worn during the *hajj*, and is often saved and used as a shroud on the pilgrim's death.

The *Hijr*, the enclosure in which Hagar and Ishmael, her son by Abraham, are said to be buried

The *Mataf*, the pavement surrounding the Ka'ba

The *Maqam Ibrahim* from which Abraham directed the rebuilding

The Place of Abraham

Muslims believe that the prophet Abraham and his son Ishmael rebuilt the Ka'ba at God's command. The Maqam Ibrahim, the place of Abraham, between the gateway and the minbar, is believed to be where he stood when he directed the builders. Abraham also has other links with Mecca. It was near Mecca, for example, that Muslims believe God told him to sacrifice Ishmael. The three pillars at Mina are said to represent the three times that Abraham rejected Satan's attempts to dissuade him.

CIRCUITS OF THE KA'BA

The *Hajj* involves many ceremonies in and around Mecca. As a preliminary observance, pilgrims first make the *tawaf*, the seven counter-clockwise circuits of the Ka'ba, performed on the *Mataf*, the pavement, around the shrine itself. On each circuit they should try to touch the black stone, or at least point in its direction.

SACRED BLACK STONE

A sacred black stone is built into the wall at the southeastern corner of the Ka'ba, near the door. Muslims believe that it was given by the angel Gabriel to Adam, and later Abraham put it in the rebuilt Ka'ba. Originally white, the stone has turned black because of the sins of humanity.

THE FESTIVAL CALENDAR

The Islamic calendar is made up of 12 lunar months, so a year in the Muslim calendar has 354 days.

Month 1: Muharram
The Islamic year starts on the day of the *hijra*, Muhammad's journey from Mecca to Medina in 622 CE.
'Ashura': The assassination of the Imam Husayn at Karbala' in 680 CE is commemorated on the 10th by Shi'ite Muslims.

Month 3: Rabi' I
Birth of the Prophet: Muhammad's birthday is celebrated on the 12th.

Month 9: Ramadan
Muslims do not eat or drink during daylight hours throughout the month.
Laylat al-Qadr: The commemoration of the first revelation to the Prophet is usually celebrated on the 27th.

Month 10: Shawwal
'Id al-Fitr: The Festival of Breaking the Fast at the beginning of Shawwal concludes the fasting period.

Month 12: Dhu al-Hijja
Month of pilgrimage (*Hajj*) to Mecca.
Yawm 'Arafat: On the 9th, fasting pilgrims perform the *wuquf*, standing before God on Mount Arafat.
'Id al-Adha: The Festival of Sacrifice on the 10th recalls the sacrificial ram God gave to Abraham in place of his son, and coincides with the end of *Hajj*.

BETWEEN TWO HILLS

After performing the seven circuits of the Ka'ba, pilgrims go through the Bab al-Safa, the gate of al-Safa, to perform the *sa'y*, the run between the two nearby low hills of al-Safa and al-Marwa. This recalls the story of Hagar's search for water for her baby son Ishmael. They move between the two hills seven times, and thus conclude the preliminary observances.

THE LADDER TO THE KA'BA

A ladder is pushed against the door of the Ka'ba when it is opened three times a year for the solemn cleaning. The door is about seven feet (two meters) off the ground to prevent the inside flooding.

NIGHT LIGHTS

Oil lamps in the archways around the Ka'ba were once used to light it up at night. Today, electric lights are used at night when pilgrims are praying, meditating, and performing rituals.

THE ISLAMIC STATE

AFTER MUHAMMAD'S DEATH IN 632, the Muslim community established government and laws in keeping with the Qur'an (see pp.166–67) and the *Sunna*, the Prophet's spoken and enacted response to revelation. The law, known as the *Shari'a*, was compiled by religious experts, and relates to all individual and communal activities. Methods and schools of interpretation developed, of which four have lasting influence on Sunni Muslims (see below). Their regulations provide individuals with the basic means of living a righteous life. The guardian of the *Shari'a* was originally the *khalifa* or caliph, successor and deputy to the Prophet. He was both the religious and political leader of the Islamic community. Although the caliphate was abolished in 1924, and there are now independent nation-states, Muslims look to the *Shari'a* for guidance on morality and faith. Shi'i Muslims differ in that they also follow the teachings of their Imams, descendants of the Prophet whom they believe to be inspired by God to give authoritative instruction. Since the late 9th century when the line of Imams ended, Shi'is have been guided by individual thinkers. The greatest experts, the *Ayatullahs* or "Signs of God," are both a source of wisdom and an example to imitate.

Muhammad gives his last sermon to his companions

SUCCESSORS TO THE PROPHET

The Prophet did not choose a successor before he died. Over the next 30 years, four men, Abu Bakr (632–34), 'Umar (634–44), 'Uthman (644–56), and 'Ali (656–61) led the Muslim community as caliphs. Sunni Muslims regard this as Islam's golden age. But Shi'is, members of the Shi'a or Party of 'Ali, hold that 'Ali, Muhammad's cousin and son-in-law, should have been the first caliph. This dispute continues, although both groups agree on fundamentals. On 'Ali's death, his rival, Mu'awiya, founder of the Umayyad dynasty (661–750), seized power. In 750 the 'Abbasid dynasty (750–1258) took over and moved the capital from Damascus to Baghdad. Here, Islam reached its height during the 8th century onward under the Sunni caliph Harun al-Rashid. In these years, Shi'is kept faith with their leaders, the Imams, descendants of the Prophet through 'Ali. Some Shi'is accept a line of 12 Imams; they believe that the last one went into hiding in the late 9th century and will return at the end of time as al-Mahdi, the Guided One.

The Law Schools

The Sultan Nasir al-Din mosque houses the four major Islamic legal schools, or rites, in quarters leading away from its four great alcoves. These rites, the Maliki, Hanafi, Shafi'i, and Hanbali, are four slightly different systems of legal methodology named after, and based on, the interpretations of the four leading legal experts in the early Islamic period (see above). Today most Muslims relate to one of these rites (Shi'is usually follow their own fifth rite) and can be identified, for example, by the way they perform actions in prayer, go about personal relations, or regard the treatment of criminals.

SULEYMAN VISITS A SHRINE

This picture of the Ottoman sultan Suleyman visiting Abu Ayyub's shrine, painted after his death, links him with the revered Companion of the Prophet and warrior of Islam, symbolically portraying him and his dynasty as pious Muslims in the Sunni tradition. It was later held that the Ottoman sultans had inherited the title of caliph, thus combining imperial power with religious authority. In the 19th century they were widely seen as the spiritual leaders of the Islamic world.

TOMB OF ABU AYYUB

The tomb of Abu Ayyub or Eyup Ansari is the holiest Islamic shrine in Constantinople. He was one of the *Ansar* who assisted the Muslims from Mecca when they arrived in Medina in 622 CE. He died in 672 in an attack on the Christian capital.

> ❝ . . . obey God and obey the Messenger, and those given authority among you. And if you have a dispute concerning any matter, refer it to God and the Messenger. . . ❞
>
> THE QUR'AN, *Sura* 4:59

MIRACULOUS TOMB

Soon after Constantinople was captured in 1453, Abu Ayyub's tomb was reportedly discovered outside the walls of the city.

THE LAW-GIVER

Suleyman al-Qanuni, "the Law-Giver," known in Europe as "the Magnificent," ruled from 1520 to 1566. He continued the expansion of Islam into Europe, which had begun in the 14th century when Ottoman armies crossed the Bosphorus. In his reign the Turks conquered most of southeastern Europe and laid siege to Vienna.

SUNNI SCHOLARS

Sunni scholars often expressed suspicion about devotion to saints and shrines as threats to the worship of God alone (although the majority of the population visit them regularly). Shi'i Muslims took a very different view and visited the tombs of their Imams as part of their religious observances.

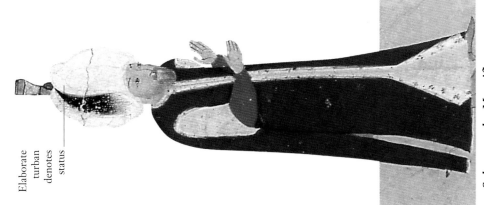

Elaborate turban denotes status

Suleyman the Magnificent

Suleyman the Magnificent was the greatest of the Ottoman sultans. Under him the empire challenged European powers on land and sea, while the capital Constantinople became the center of Islamic culture and thought. His chief architect Sinan constructed mosques that rank among the greatest buildings of the world, one of which (the Suleymaniye) is named after the sultan and houses his tomb in its enclosure.

VISITING THE SHRINE

After Suleyman's time, the link between the Ottoman sultans and this source of spiritual power was shown in a tangible way when the new sultan visited the shrine and was girded with the sword of Osman, the founder of the Ottoman or Osmanli dynasty. Turkish prime ministers are still known to visit the shrine on being appointed to office.

Sultan's weapons

Sultan's Attendants

The sultan's attendants were both his servants and signs of his prestige. His pages accompanied him to carry his weapons and look after his needs. One of the pages is carrying water for his ablutions before prayer. In the sultan's presence the whole court was silent, and Western visitors were often struck by the quiet that prevailed at great assemblies.

THE SULTAN IN PUBLIC

The sultan regularly attended Friday prayers at one of the mosques in Constantinople. He was accompanied by the officials of the empire, the court, and his soldiers. This ceremony, the *selamlik*, became the main occasion on which the sultan was seen in public and could be petitioned.

TURKIC ORIGINS

The saddle of the sultan's horse is the traditional Turkic kind. The Ottomans were descendants of Turkic peoples from central Asia who moved west in successive waves from early Islamic times. Their original spirituality was marked by devotion to holy places, and they preserved this when they became Muslim, as Suleyman's visit to this shrine shows.

SYMBOLS OF STATUS

Headdresses were clear signs of position and honor in a society where status was sharply distinguished.

> ❝ *'Ali is special to me and I am special to him; he is the supporting friend of every believer.'* ❞
> A SAYING OF THE PROPHET

ISLAMIC EXPANSION

The Islamic empire, from Spain to India, fragmented from the 9th century onward. Local rulers (sultans, *amirs*, kings, and caliphs) displaced the single Caliphs. The Mongols ended the Baghdad caliphate in 1258. In 1453, the Ottoman Turks took Constantinople and, with their Caliph, became the major Muslim power outside India, ruled by the Mughals. Shi'ites took power in Persia. European expansion in the 19th century threatened Muslim independence, now being vigorously reasserted. All able-bodied Muslims are required to defend Islam, whenever it is threatened in the lesser jihad ("Holy War"). The greater jihad is the war against sin and wrong-doing in oneself.

171 • THE ISLAMIC STATE ☾ ISLAM

ISLAM ☾ WORLD RELIGIONS • 171 • WORLD RELIGIONS ☾ ISLAM

SUFI ORDERS AND BELIEFS

SUFIS ARE MUSLIMS WHO SEEK a close and personal experience of God. The origin of the name is uncertain, but it may come from *suf*, referring to the humble woolen garment that early Sufis wore. Because Sufism is a complete commitment to God in absolute trust and obedience, it gave rise to intense experiences of God, and to the development of techniques and attitudes to make those experiences more likely. Some Sufis (for example, al-Hallaj, see below) went so far in emphasizing the union of the soul with God that they were thought to be claiming blasphemously that the soul and God are identical. Some have therefore seen a conflict between Sufis and those concerned with the proper ordering of life through *Shari'a*, the law of Islam (see p.170). But there was no real conflict: the Sufis emphasized both the observant life of Islam and the experience of love between the soul and God. One of the key figures in reconciling these conflicts was the Persian scholar al-Ghazali (1058–1111CE) who taught that all Muslims should follow the *Shari'a* and emphasized that Islam was monotheistic, having a belief in one God, not monistic, believing that all things (including God and the soul) are made of the same substance.

SUFI ORDERS

As Sufism spread through the Muslim world, most Muslims were attached to a Sufi order, in the sense that they looked to the leader of the order as a source of guidance and spiritual help. Most orders distinguish many spiritual stages in their teachings, and their members require the guidance of the *shaykh* or *pir*, the master, and other leaders to help them attain the higher levels of spiritual experience.

DANCING DERVISHES
This illumination of a Sufi saint or master dancing with his disciples comes from a Persian 16th-century manuscript of the Majalis al 'Ushshak. The whirling dance is part of the Dhikr ceremony of the Mawlawiyya order from Turkey, giving them the popular name of "whirling dervishes."

THE DHIKR CEREMONY
Dhikr, or remembrance, is the Sufi way of experiencing a direct sense of God's presence. Each Sufi order or *tariqa* employs its own practices to gain this state. Some use rhythmic beating or chanting; this order uses dance. The aim of *Dhikr* is to enable the dancers to intensify their awareness of God and forget the things around them. The repetition of this practice has led some to experience *fana*, or extinction, in which they lose all awareness of their sense of material self.

Splendid plumage, source of the Simurgh's fame

The Simurgh
The Simurgh is a symbol of the Sufi endeavor for unity with the divine. A Persian poem tells of how, when other birds hear of the Simurgh's splendor, they elect him king and set off to find him. Only 30 survive the journey, and when they reach his mountain they realize that he and they are really one, si murgh *meaning 30 birds in Persian.*

❝ *All in the created world will pass away, but the face of your Lord will remain.* ❞
THE QUR'AN, *Sura 55:26–27*

SPIRITUAL HOME
The ceremony takes place in a *khanaqa* or *zawiya*, a building designed and dedicated specifically for the purpose of ecstatic ritual.

VISION OF PARADISE
With this picture of flowers, the artist has symbolically imitated the purpose of *Dhikr* as a way of rising from the material to the heavenly. This picture may be interpreted as a vision of paradise, but it could equally be only a glimpse of the garden through the doorway, with beautiful stately blooms on long stems reaching out of earthen pots

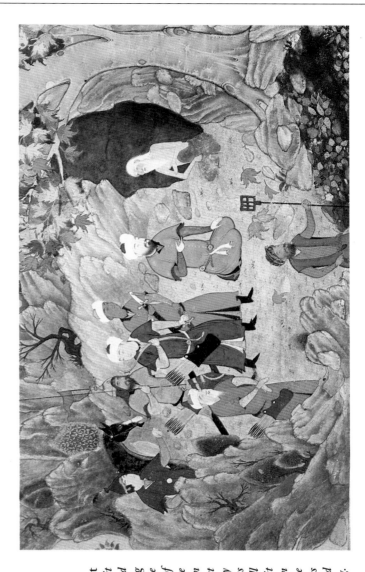

Eternal Spiritual Light
A prince visits a Sufi hermit in order to seek his advice and obtain his blessing. Their meeting symbolizes the contrast between the material world and the sphere of inner reality; the prince's entourage is armed against unknown dangers, while the hermit sits at ease. The contrast is symbolized by the prince's torchbearer who has lit the prince's way. His lamp will go out in time, but the hermit has eternal spiritual light from within. Hermits exemplify the Muslim mystical ideal: to pass beyond all that changes and decays to what is everlasting.

ECSTATIC STATE

The master has reached a trancelike, ecstatic state, in which he seems aware only of God. His body is swaying off balance as he turns with his mind fixed on the divine. His expression, with staring eyes and set mouth, shows that he is focused on the single activity, his physical movement being used to gain divine and psychic illumination. The master's three followers are known in Persian as *darwishes* or "poor men."

SHI'ITE LOYALTY

The religious loyalty of these Sufis as Shi'ites can be detected in the way they have folded their turbans 12 times across their foreheads. Each fold recalls one of the 12 Imams, the leaders of Shi'ite Islam (see pp.170–71).

THE MASTER

For many Sufis the master, known as the *shaykh* or in Persian *pir*, is himself the model on which their lives can be based and the source of their knowledge. He is revered as a teacher inspired by God, and he is treated as someone whose life is so blessed that he can pass on God's blessing to others. The *shaykh*'s arms are both raised, signifying that he has left behind earthly things and is entirely caught up in God's presence.

HEAVEN AND EARTH

Two young dancers have their hands in the pose characteristic of the Mawlawi order of Sufis, with one hand reaching up to heaven and the other pointing down to earth, in order to join the one with the other.

DANGEROUS DANCING

Attendants stand ready to assist anyone who may lose balance or be physically overcome by his trance. They watch the dancers carefully to make sure no one gets hurt.

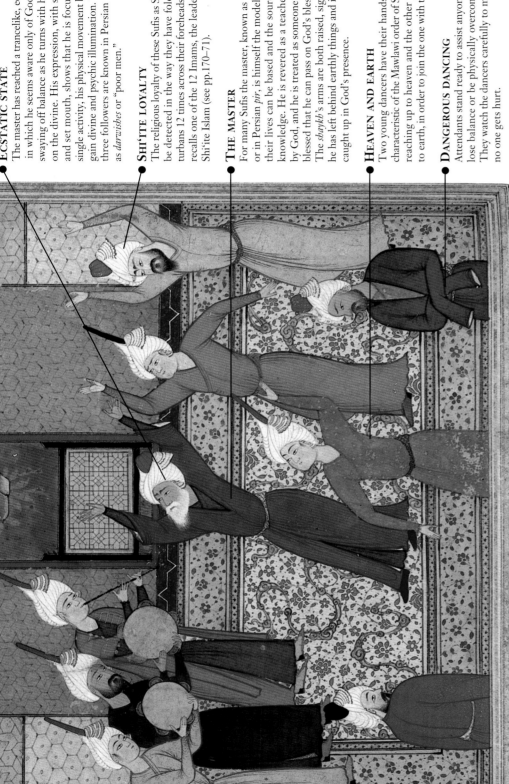

Style of turban indicates Shi'ite loyalty

Tambourine

Mystical Music
For many Muslims, music is avoided, because it excites the senses. But it has always held a revered place among the mystical Sufi brotherhoods. Sufis have habitually employed musical instruments, such as the tambourine and pipe shown here, as aids to their ceremonies, where repetitive chants and dances are involved. The musicians here play a steady rhythm in order to help the dancers keep up a pace.

f *O God, if I worship You for fear of hell, burn me in hell; If I worship You in hope of paradise, exclude me from paradise; But if I worship You for Your own sake Grudge me not Your everlasting beauty.* ™
RABI 'A AL-'ADAWIYYA (D.801), AN EARLY WOMAN SUFI

THE GREAT SUFI SAINTS AND SCHOOLS

Sufi schools or *tariqas* preserve the names of their successive masters back to the Prophet himself, whom they regard as their first *shaykh* or master. Important early Muslim mystics include al-Hallaj (d.922), who was executed for crying out, while in ecstatic union with God, "I am the Truth!"; Abu Hamid al-Ghazali (d.1111, see above); and Muhyi al-Din Ibn 'Arabi (d.1240), who taught that all beings exist in one unity. Sufi schools, dating mainly from the 12th century and after, include the Qadiriyya, which has spread through the Middle East, Africa, and the Caucasus; the Mawlawiyya, predominant in Turkey; and the Chishtiyya, based in Pakistan, India, and Southeast Asia. Over time, the Orders have broadened their activities; in medieval times, they could function as craft guilds, and up to the 19th century they were involved in education and community work. Even now, Sufi fraternities are involved in distributing resources to the poor; many members may not actually be mystics.

ISLAM AND SCIENCE

M USLIMS BELIEVE THAT GOD CREATED ALL THINGS and as a result, the
study and understanding of creation points to God and deepens insight and
understanding of his ways. For that reason, knowledge, *'ilm*, is given a high value in
Islam. Muhammad said, "He who leaves the home in search of knowledge is walking
in the way of God." The scholar Ibn Taymiyya said that the coming of knowledge to
the mind is like the coming of food to the body. Books and knowledge have always
been described by Muslims as spiritual food. Consequently, the contributions of
Muslims to philosophy, astronomy, chemistry, medicine, mathematics, and algebra
have been prodigious. But this does not mean that
'ilm equates with science in the modern sense.
Muslim science is always derived from God as the
source of all that is being investigated. All science
carries a worldview, even the science that purports
to be "objective" and therefore has no worldview.
Muslim understanding here unites with Christian—
that science without wisdom is a dangerous animal.
In the Latin in which this was first expressed,
scientia (knowledge) must be subordinate to
sapientia (wisdom).

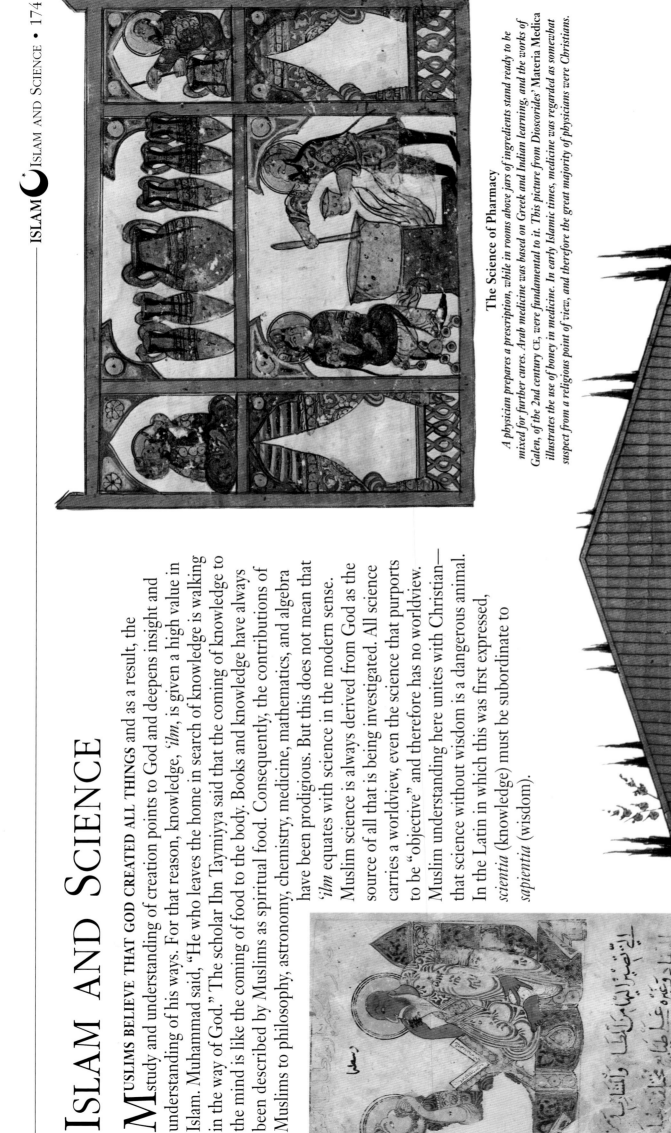

The Science of Pharmacy
*A physician prepares a prescription, while in rooms above jars of ingredients stand ready to be
mixed for further cures. Arab medicine was based on Greek and Indian learning, and the works of
Galen, of the 2nd century CE, were fundamental to it. This picture from Dioscorides' Materia Medica
illustrates the use of honey in medicine. In early Islamic times, medicine was regarded as somewhat
suspect from a religious point of view, and therefore the great majority of physicians were Christians.*

The Influence of Aristotle
*The works of Aristotle and Plato were translated
into Arabic by 800 CE. Greek philosophy influenced
early Islamic thought, and created tensions
between thinkers who favored reason and those
who preferred the guidance of revelation. Arabic
philosophy flourished, but interest in such ideas as
the eternity of the world earned condemnation from
conservative religious thinkers. The works
of Arabic masters of philosophy and medicine
such as Ibn Sina and Ibn Rushd exerted great
influence on European scholars.*

THE OBSERVATORY
*This is the observatory built in Istanbul in the
16th century for the astrologer Taqi al-Din.
By the 10th century, Islamic astronomy had
developed into a science in its own right, despite
continuous opposition from orthodox
Islamic theologians.*

● THE ASTROLABE
The master and a colleague are
examining an astrolabe, the instrument
invented by the Greeks for measuring
latitudes. Before them on the table are
two alidades, the rules which were fixed
to astrolabes for giving measurements.

THE OBSERVATORY CARETAKER

The figure standing meekly to one side may be the observatory caretaker. He appears mystified by the technical apparatus and keeps well away from touching anything. He is probably waiting to bring the books stored on the shelves behind him to the scholars when they are needed for consultation.

MATHEMATICAL SOPHISTICATION

The instruments on the table show how mathematically sophisticated Islamic science had become by the 16th century. Algebra, logarithms, and algorithms, which are named after the great scholar al-Khwarizmi of Khiva (d.846 CE), are all inventions of Arab mathematicians. Their use of the Indian number system made great advances possible.

EXAMINING A QUADRANT

Two kneeling scholars examine a quadrant, an instrument used for measuring the altitudes of stars. It consists of a graduated arc of 90° and a sighting mechanism attached to a movable arm. Many of the major stars are still known by their Arabic names.

THE QUEST FOR KNOWLEDGE

These two scholars discussing instruments exemplify the manner in which scientists responded to the Qur'anic challenge to seek out God's signs in the natural world. Some Muslims disapproved of the use in science and philosophy of reason and logic, which seemed to ignore the teachings of revelation, although these disciplines flourished under Islamic rulers.

MEASURING THE STARS

This scholar looks through a quadrant. In this period the positions of heavenly bodies were measured by apparatus of this kind as well as observation with the naked eye. Astronomers defended their work against critical theologians by claiming that they were revealing evidence of the wisdom of God.

HEAVENLY BODIES

These two crouching scholars are reading measurements off another instrument for plotting the movements of heavenly bodies, while near them a third scholar writes down their results.

INTERPRETING THE HEAVENS

Three scholars discuss an interpretation of heavenly movements. Arab astronomers were greatly influenced by Greek works, in particular Ptolemy's *Almagest*. Following the 10th-century translation of this work, Ptolemy's themes became orthodox Arabic explanations of planetary movements.

THE GLOBE

This globe has the most important place in the center of the foreground, as it probably embodies the fruits of the many measurements and calculations represented in this picture. It is appropriately turned to the point where Istanbul and the Ottoman domains (see p.170) are at the front. While the land masses are given correct proportions, they stretch too far south of the equator.

> *It is He who made the sun to be a shining glory, and the moon to be a light, and measured out its stages; that you might know the number of years and the count. God did not create this except in truth.*
>
> THE QUR'AN, *Sura* 10:6

The Importance of the Astrolabe

Muslims have to know the qibla, the direction of Mecca, so that they can perform their prayers. It was calculated in former times on the basis of star movements, so one of the most important instruments was the astrolabe. This consists of a graduated disk with a movable sighting device, by means of which the altitude of celestial bodies can be measured. Calculations based on the measurements give the time and the correct direction of Mecca.

The World According to Islam

From the 12th century on, Arab geographers produced maps of the world. One of the most famous cartographers was the Moroccan al-Idrisi (d.1166), whose great geographical compendium, based on his travels, plotted the shores of the Mediterranean and the Indian Ocean with considerable accuracy. This globe dates from a later time, when ships had circumnavigated the world.

Astrolabe

Quadrant

THE MOSQUE

THE WORD "MOSQUE" is derived, via French, from the Arabic word *masjid*, meaning "place of prostration." It is the place where Muslims gather to bow down in prayer, especially on Fridays, the Day of Assembly. While mosques are not essential for prayer, they are "houses which God has allowed to be built, that His name may be spoken in them" (*Sura* 24:36). The main officials of a mosque are the *Imam* who leads prayer, the *Mu'adhdhin* (muezzin) who calls to prayer (see p.163), and the *Khatib*, the preacher. Mosques became associated with education and also with the tombs of prominent Muslims, especially martyrs, caliphs, and Sufis (see pp.172–73). Mosques associated with Muhammad (see pp.164–65) are particularly venerated. In Medina, in addition to the Mosque of the Prophet (see below), is the Mosque of the Two Qiblas (where Muhammad first faced Mecca instead of Jerusalem in prayer); in Mecca is the most revered Masjid al-Haram; and in Jerusalem is Masjid al-Aqsa, where the scales will be set up on the Day of Judgment. Although the nearby Dome of the Rock is not a mosque (though it is sometimes called the Mosque of 'Umar), it is a revered site for it was from here that Muhammad made his ascension into heaven (see p.163).

> **❝** *O you who believe! When the call is heard for prayer on the day of congregation, hurry to remembrance of God and leave your trading. That is better for you if only you knew. And when the prayer is ended, then disperse in the land and seek God's bounty, and remember God much so that you may be successful.* **❞**
>
> THE QUR'AN, *Sura* 62:9–10

Teaching Religious Doctrine

From the 10th century on, special academies were established for the teaching of religious and legal doctrines. The University of al-Azhar in Cairo, shown here, was founded in 970 CE. It is the oldest functioning university in the world. Its teaching methods, in which a professor expounds a text to students who are literally gathered at his feet, remained unchanged in some colleges until recent times. Learning has always been central to Islamic culture. Within a century or so after the Prophet, Greek philosophical and medical works were being translated into Arabic (see pp.174–75), and the influence of the Qur'an stimulated sophisticated development in the religious sciences.

FACING MECCA

Worshipers always face Mecca when they pray. In the mosque Mecca is indicated by the position of the *mihrab*, which is usually in the form of an empty alcove. The mosque is arranged so that the maximum number of people can see the *mihrab*.

PREACHER

This preacher or *khatib*, who is engaged in a problem presented by the woman before him, carries the traditional preaching staff in his hand. At the start of his sermon, he asks God's blessing upon the Prophet and his family, and then upon the current political leader.

PULPIT

The pulpit is to the right of the *mihrab*, which marks the *qibla*, the direction of prayer. In essence a mosque comprises a clean space and an indication of the direction toward Mecca, enabling the worshipers to say their prayers according to the requirement to face towards the Ka'ba (see pp.168–69).

SERMONIZING IN THE MOSQUE

This illustration from a 13th-century edition of the Maqamat of al-Hariri (d.1122) was made in Baghdad and shows Abu Zayd, the old man who is the main character in each of the stories, preaching in the mosque when a woman appears among the male worshipers to remonstrate with him.

HEIGHT AND SPACE

The suggestion of high walls gives a sense of space ideal for worship. Uninterrupted space is created in many mosques by a lofty dome, which needs support only around the edges. For many Muslims the dome symbolizes the oneness of God (see pp.162–63).

FOCUS ON PRAYER

Mosque interiors are relatively bare, as the mosque exists solely for prayer. In most mosques there are few internal walls, since all that is required is a single space for worship. Some mosques are decorated with wall tiles; these are rarely representational but are usually painted with calligraphic designs based on verses from the Qur'an.

SERMON FROM THE MINBAR

The *minbar*, the stepped pulpit used on Fridays at the congregational prayer when the preacher gives his *khutba* or sermon, is often the most significant piece of furniture in the mosque. It is purely functional, enabling the preacher to be seen and heard by all.

RESPECT FOR THE PROPHET

The steps of the *minbar* lead to a platform at the top, but the preacher stands on a lower step out of respect for the Prophet and the early caliphs who occupied these highest positions.

"God is great (repeat four times)
I testify that there is no god
but God (repeat twice)
I testify that Muhammad is the
messenger of God (repeat twice)
Come to prayer (repeat twice)
Come to success (repeat twice)
There is no god but God."

THE ADHAN, THE CALL TO PRAYER MADE BY THE MUEZZIN BEFORE EACH PERIOD OF DAILY PRAYER

CLEANLINESS AND PRAYER

In order for prayer to be valid, a worshiper must follow certain procedures, including ablution, which entails washing the hands, face, nostrils, mouth, both arms up to the elbow, and feet up to the ankle. If water is unavailable, sand or earth may be used.

CORRECT DRESS

Correct dress is of vital importance when praying. A man must cover his body, at the very least, from the navel to the knees, and a woman may show only her face, hands, and feet. Clothing for both men and women should be modest.

ROOM FOR PRAYER

While the sermon is preached, the congregation squats on the floor. Since Muslim worship involves standing, kneeling, and prostrating, there are no chairs or benches. Rather, there is a clear space where the worshipers can form rows facing the *mihrab* in the *qibla* wall.

DOORWAY

There is a doorway at the bottom of the *minbar* steps. A curtain is frequently stretched across it to exclude everyone except the preacher.

WOMAN IN THE MOSQUE

The woman among the male worshipers is not typical. Traditionally men and women pray separately, and women often pray at home, although some mosques have special areas for them.

THE HISTORY OF THE MOSQUE

The first mosque, built by the Prophet and his followers in Medina, was probably very simple, consisting of a shelter made from palm-trunks and fiber roofing. Later mosques were more elaborate. The mosques here represent the two main styles: hypostyle, where the roof is supported on pillars (the Great Mosque at Cordoba), and domical, where the walls are surrounded by a dome (the Blue Mosque in Istanbul). Like the Prophet's mosque from which they are all derived, mosques provide space for worship, meeting, teaching, and study, whether they are converted terraced houses or architectural masterpieces.

Inside the Great Mosque in Cordoba

Carried Toward Prayer

One of the earliest surviving mosques is the Great Mosque in Cordoba, Spain. Begun in 785 CE, it was enlarged in the following centuries as the major mosque of the capital of Muslim Spain, in which space was required for large crowds on Fridays. The forest of arches supporting the roof is one of its most striking features, and creates a repetitive movement which carries the eye in the direction of prayer.

The Blue Mosque, Istanbul

This mosque, completed in 1617 under Sultan Ahmed I, is one of the last great achievements of Ottoman mosque building and a perfect space for worship. By supporting the weight of the central dome with semi-domes at the side rather than by solid vertical curtain walls, a vast inner space is created. The blue tiles and the stencil work inside the mosque create an other-worldly atmosphere for those at prayer.

Central dome

Minaret

Courtyard with fountain behind the trees

The Blue Mosque, Istanbul

177 • THE MOSQUE ☪ ISLAM

NATIVE RELIGIONS

REALM OF THE SPIRITS

ATIVE RELIGIONS ARE THOSE that are usually on a small scale and confined to particular families, tribes, and places. In the past, they were found everywhere, but now they have been displaced extensively or eroded by missionary religions such as Christianity and Islam, and even more by transistors and T-shirts—in other words, by the spread of global communications and multinational companies. In untouched form, native religions are today found only in some of the most inaccessible regions of the globe, for example, in the upper reaches of the Amazon or the hinterlands of a number of the Indonesian islands.

However, native religions have by no means entirely disappeared in other countries, such as central and southern Africa or India. They continue to exist although some have been influenced by the great religious traditions to which they have become exposed. Native religions have even retained a foothold in the heartlands of the modern world: Native American Indians in North America; the Aboriginal groups of Australia; the Maori of New Zealand.

THE SPIRITUAL REALM
Found from Assam to Mexico, native religions are by no means uniform in type, but some generalizations are in order. Perhaps the most widespread characteristic is that native religions teach that there are a great many, highly active spiritual beings. In contrast to religions such as Christianity and Islam (see pp.136–59 and pp.160–77), which emphasize a single God, the picture here is of spirits, gods, goddesses, and other powers

Ritual Mask
Rites of passage play a very important part in native religions. This mask from the Kuba people in Zaire is related to the ceremony that initiates young boys into manhood. The initiation period lasts over many months and is ended with celebrations and rituals, involving masked dances rich in symbolism.

influencing all of life: in nature (in such things as the spiritually significant animal, tree, or thunderstorm); in humans (the healer who can manipulate powers of good, while the witch has the power to harm others); and in other realms (where monsters may dwell in an underworld, or ancestral spirits who may live on some higher plane).

Native religions do not teach that the spiritual realm is the same as the realm of everyday life. Participants, therefore, have to make contact with the beings that surround them: to make requests; to obtain magical powers; to foretell the future; to obtain wisdom. Participants also have to find ways of fending off or placating beings that are intent on doing harm.

There are two frequently encountered ways of envisaging the relationship between the everyday world and that which exists beyond it. One is called spirit possession. Common in Africa, spirits are believed to have great power, initiative, and authority. They invade particular humans, especially women, and possess them—body and soul. Typically of evil bent, spirits make people ill, mad, or otherwise cause suffering. Those

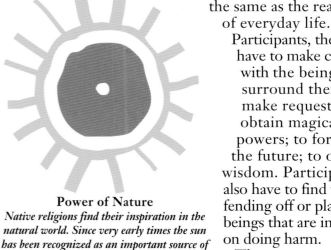

Power of Nature
Native religions find their inspiration in the natural world. Since very early times the sun has been recognized as an important source of life. Many myths describe the chaos that would ensue if the sun disappeared (see pp.102–3).

possessed must seek liberation, turning to ritual specialists who attempt to exorcise the malevolent.

In contrast to this dynamic, there is what is known as shamanism (see pp.180–81). Shamans – usually male – engage in rituals to control spirits in themselves and gain power to travel into the realms of the spirits. They do this to obtain what the spirits have to offer, to enable them – on their return – to combat various kinds of misfortune. Sometimes they go to these realms to find the erring soul of an ill person. These journeys are considered to be very dangerous, and it is possible, if the shaman is overcome by evil spirits, that he will not, himself, be able to return.

THE IMPORTANCE OF RITUAL

Spirit possession and shamanism both involve rituals, concerned, respectively, with exorcism and empowerment. As a whole, native religions are almost invariably strong on ritual and weak on abstract belief or theology. Pre-literate and relying on tradition, they are predominantly religions of practice and activity. This is well brought out in the importance attached to what are known as rites of passage (see pp.186–87). Often highly elaborate, these serve to symbolize transitions,

Fertility Dolls
These dolls from Cameroon, West Africa, on the left and Angola, southwest Africa, on the right, are carried by young women in the belief that they will make them fertile. Fertility of the earth and human fecundity are of vital importance in societies whose survival usually relies on successful crops and large families to look after the elders.

from one season to another, for example, or from one stage in life to another. They can also serve to bring about change, as when dying people are directed to their ancestors.

MYTH AND LEGEND

Native religions also give great importance to myth as well as to practice. Myths, frequently recounted while rituals are being performed, do not make much sense to those of us who take them literally and compare them with science. Strange, if not seemingly impossible, things happen. A myth told by the Huichol people of western Mexico (see pp.182–83), for example, recounts how animated water turns into a snake. However, such myths have a serious purpose. They enable people to make sense of their world, addressing questions that cannot be answered by science, such as the reasons for suffering or the meanings of life. That is why myth was so important to artists and musicians in the 19th century.

Native religions may appear strange, but in reality they provide their adherents with a sense of security: they are afforded the rituals to *do*

African Amulet
People who belong to native religions often carry objects that they believe will protect them from harm. This charm, or amulet, belonged to a healer in Africa and would probably have been used in healing rituals, in which the powers of the ancestors may have been invoked.

things to help their lives and the mythological knowledge to make *sense* of their circumstances.

GOOD AND EVIL

For this reason, native religions also dwell much on danger and evil. They enable humans to recognize and deal with the darker aspects of life. The frightening powers of the witch, for example, serve to highlight that which we know of as envy, spite, or jealousy; the equally threatening powers of the ancestral ghost articulate what we call "guilty conscience," the ghost serving to punish wrong-doers.

On the positive side, native religions serve to highlight what it is to live in harmony with the natural world. Participants learn that they live *within* nature; that it is crucially important to disturb nature as little as possible; that nature should be respected to the point of being worshiped; that the ancestors should be praised for what they are and what they have been. The harmonious view of many native religions helps explain why they are now undergoing something of a resurgence. Environmentalists, new agers, and pagans are among those now drawing upon and cultivating the wisdom that they consider native religions to possess.

SHAMANISM

SHAMANISM, ONE OF THE MOST arresting and widespread of religious practices, is especially associated with native peoples of northern Asia and the Americas. Shamans control spirits in the body and can leave everyday states of existence in order to travel, or fly, to what are taken to be other worlds. The shaman, usually male, may take hallucinatory substances or perform rituals in order to enter altered states of consciousness. The shaman thereby encounters entities belonging to spirit worlds. Spirits, if bad, have to be controlled or defeated; spirits, if good, have to be encouraged to provide help. On returning to the normal world, successful shamans are seen as providing essential services for their communities. The unsuccessful are believed to go mad, even to die. Using power and wisdom drawn from their encounters in other realms, they might heal, using song, massage, or herbal or magical remedies, predict the future, handle disputes, combat natural disasters, or attack enemies.

Mushroom-induced Visions
Some shamans, particularly in Siberia and North and South America, eat hallucinatory mushrooms to induce trances and visions. To shamans the plants are spirit teachers and by eating them, the shaman takes the properties of the spirit into himself.

YANOMAMO SHAMANS

Shamans belonging to the Yanomamo people of the South American Amazon must, like all shamans, be trained to communicate with spirits. The initiate is taught about the habits, attributes, songs, likes, and dislikes of the spirits or *hekura*, whom he wants to attract to live in his body. When the initiate becomes a shaman, the *hekura* then inhabit his body and are subject to his will. It is believed that his body houses a world much like this one, with hills, trees, and seas. The *hekura* help the shaman ward off and cure illness, which is often thought to be the result of enemy sorcery; they are often sent in revenge to eat enemy souls, particularly those of children, which are very vulnerable.

A South American Yanomamo shaman

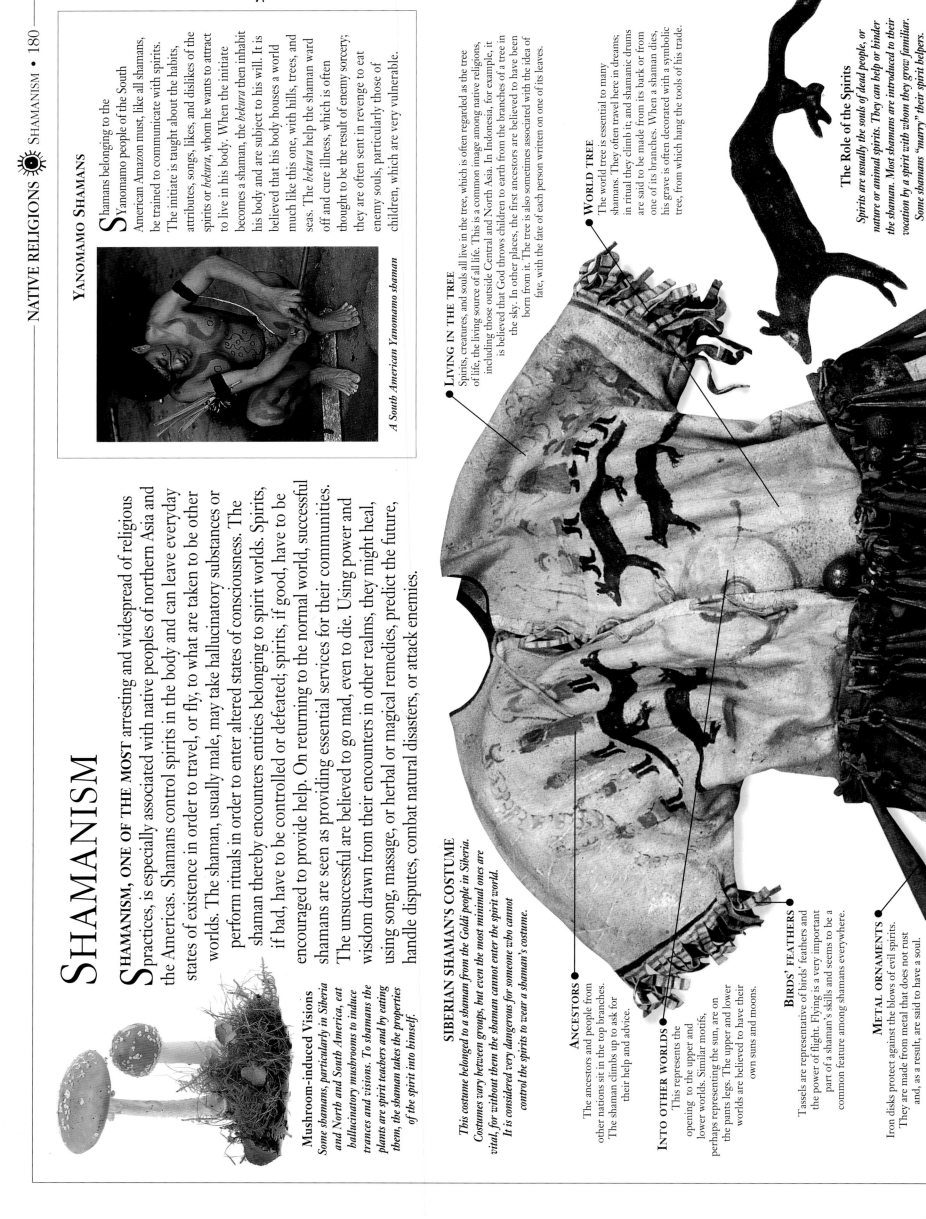

LIVING IN THE TREE
Spirits, creatures, and souls all live in the tree, which is often regarded as the tree of life, the living source of all life. This is a common image among native religions, including those outside Central and North Asia. In Indonesia, for example, it is believed that God throws children to earth from the branches of a tree in the sky. In other places, the first ancestors are believed to have been born from it. The tree is also sometimes associated with the idea of fate, with the fate of each person written on one of its leaves.

WORLD TREE
The world tree is essential to many shamans. They often travel here in dreams; in ritual they climb it; and shamanic drums are said to be made from its bark or from one of its branches. When a shaman dies, his grave is often decorated with a symbolic tree, from which hang the tools of his trade.

The Role of the Spirits
Spirits are usually the souls of dead people, or nature or animal spirits. They can help or binder the shaman. Most shamans are introduced to their vocation by a spirit with whom they grow familiar. Some shamans "marry" their spirit helpers.

SIBERIAN SHAMAN'S COSTUME
This costume belonged to a shaman from the Goldi people in Siberia. Costumes vary between groups, but even the most minimal ones are vital, for without them the shaman cannot enter the spirit world. It is considered very dangerous for someone who cannot control the spirits to wear a shaman's costume.

ANCESTORS
The ancestors and people from other nations sit in the top branches. The shaman climbs up to ask for their help and advice.

INTO OTHER WORLDS
This represents the opening to the upper and lower worlds. Similar motifs, perhaps representing the sun, are on the pants legs. The upper and lower worlds are believed to have their own suns and moons.

BIRDS' FEATHERS
Tassels are representative of birds' feathers and the power of flight. Flying is a very important part of a shaman's skills and seems to be a common feature among shamans everywhere.

METAL ORNAMENTS
Iron disks protect against the blows of evil spirits. They are made from metal that does not rust and, as a result, are said to have a soul.

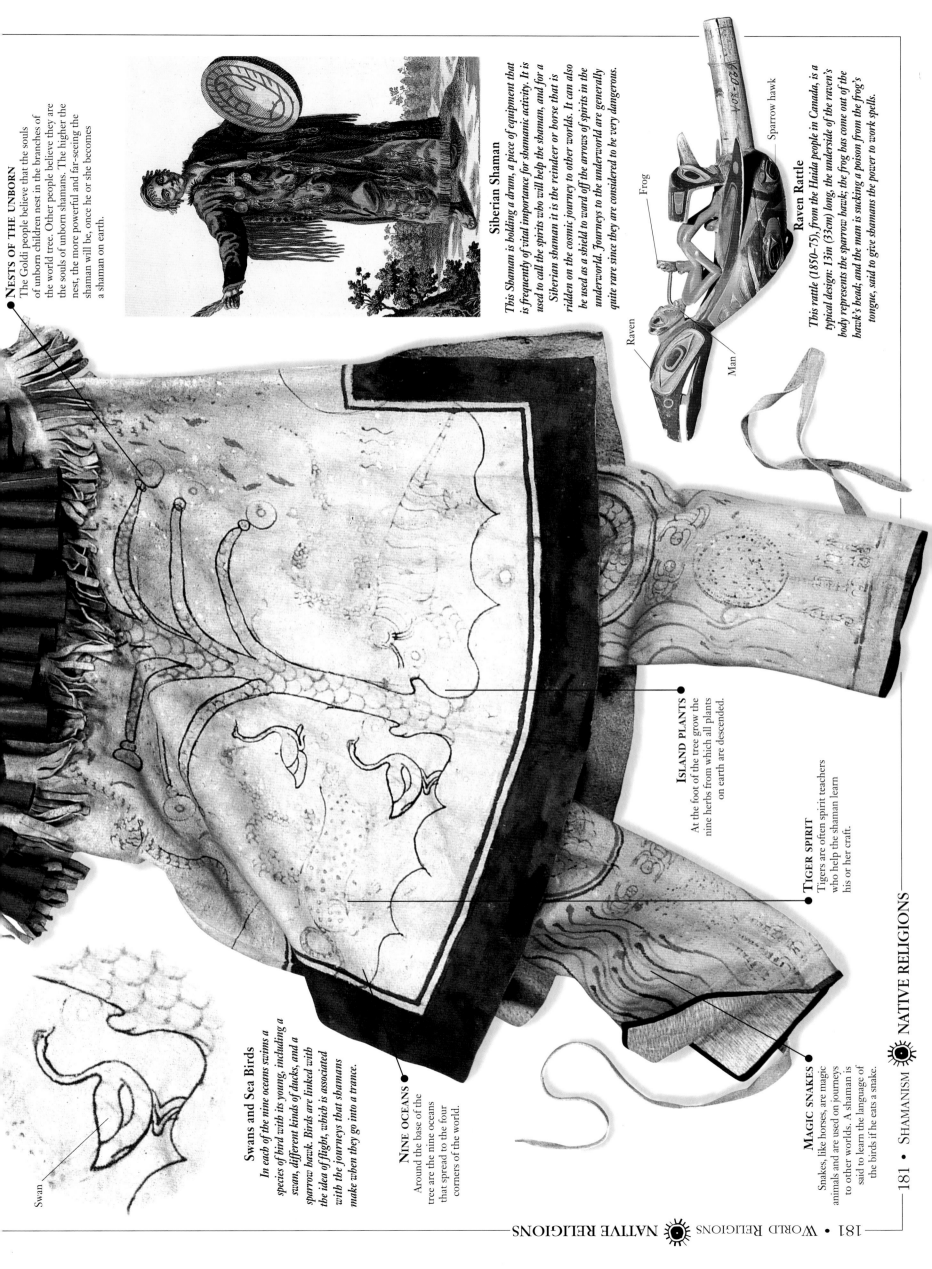

NESTS OF THE UNBORN

The Goldi people believe that the souls of unborn children nest in the branches of the world tree. Other people believe they are the souls of unborn shamans. The higher the nest, the more powerful and far-seeing the shaman will be, once he or she becomes a shaman on earth.

Siberian Shaman

This Shaman is holding a drum, a piece of equipment that is frequently of vital importance for shamanic activity. It is used to call the spirits who will help the shaman, and for a Siberian shaman it is the reindeer or horse that is ridden on the cosmic journey to other worlds. It can also be used as a shield to ward off the arrows of spirits in the underworld. Journeys to the underworld are generally quite rare since they are considered to be very dangerous.

Raven Rattle

This rattle (1850–75), from the Haida people in Canada, is a typical design: 13in (33cm) long, the underside of the raven's body represents the sparrow hawk; the frog has come out of the hawk's beak, and the man is sucking a poison from the frog's tongue, said to give shamans the power to work spells.

Sparrow hawk

Frog

Raven

Man

Swans and Sea Birds

In each of the nine oceans swims a species of bird with its young, including a swan, different kinds of ducks, and a sparrow hawk. Birds are linked with the idea of flight, which is associated with the journeys that shamans make when they go into a trance.

Swan

NINE OCEANS

Around the base of the tree are the nine oceans that spread to the four corners of the world.

ISLAND PLANTS

At the foot of the tree grow the nine herbs from which all plants on earth are descended.

TIGER SPIRIT

Tigers are often spirit teachers who help the shaman learn his or her craft.

MAGIC SNAKES

Snakes, like horses, are magic animals and are used on journeys to other worlds. A shaman is said to learn the language of the birds if he eats a snake.

MYTH AND COSMOS

Every culture has its myths. However, there is a stark contrast between the significance accorded to myths by contemporary Western and traditional native peoples. For the latter, myths express the meaning of life and of the world, and the ways in which humans are related to their environment. Even if it is shown that a myth cannot be literally true, it remains important to the culture it belongs to. Outsiders, such as psychologists and anthropologists, suggest that myths perform useful functions: perhaps the most obvious one is that myths serve as a kind of "science," explaining to people why the world is as it is—why there are both men and women, how fire was created, and so on. Another important function is that myths offer a form of morality, legitimating the order of things. For example, there are myths to justify the position of the chief. In these ways, myth creates the picture of a world in which people, in successive generations and through a shared tradition, can live with confidence.

CREATION MYTHS

Every religion has at least one story of creation, telling how the world, men, and women came into being. In some religions, the stories may be similar because of outside influence, or because the idea is obvious, or because stories travel. Stories of the world tree, or tree of life (see pp.180–81), are just one example. This painting shows an Australian Aboriginal creation myth. Painted by an artist known as Kneepad, from Arnhem Land, it shows the legend of a woman, (shown bottom right), who is not yet of this world and who is wandering with No. 2 star looking for a country where she can settle. But No. 2 star is not bright enough to find a place, so they both enlist the help of the morning star, who brings the daylight with him. Together they find Earth, shown at the top of the painting. The morning star then creates the sun and man, to whom he gives a spear for hunting. Woman then comes into being and finds Earth a good place and mates with man.

An Australian Aboriginal creation myth

Arrow

Mountain ancestor

Cauyumarie

ELDER BROTHER
Elder Brother Blue Deer, shown white, sacrificed himself on the mountain shown above. His selfless act enabled life to flourish in this world. The open flower behind him symbolizes life issuing from the earth.

The Outer Realm
Cauyumarie, the first man, shown with a deer head, sucks up all the power and words from the lower two worlds. The wavy yellow lines show that he is testing whether humans bear and respond to his words. To his right, is an ancestor who took on a mountain shape when leaving the underworld. The first arrow, which contains the wisdom of understanding, is placed here.

Haida Totem Pole
The mythology of Haida Indians of the Queen Charlotte Islands off the coast of northwest Canada, was based on the world of nature, which was conceived as the abode of spirit powers as well as of men. Many of the characters in the myths are totem creatures, neither entirely animal nor entirely human. As well as explaining the origins of such things as fire, the myths provide graphic accounts of how the totem creatures fought dangerous forces to help bring about an ordered and secure world.

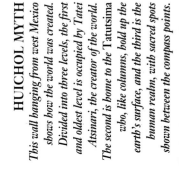

HUICHOL MYTH
This wall hanging from west Mexico shows how the world was created. Divided into three levels, the first and oldest level is occupied by Tatei Atsinari, the creator of the world. The second is home to the Tatutsima who, like columns, hold up the earth's surface, and the third is the human realm, with sacred spots shown between the compass points.

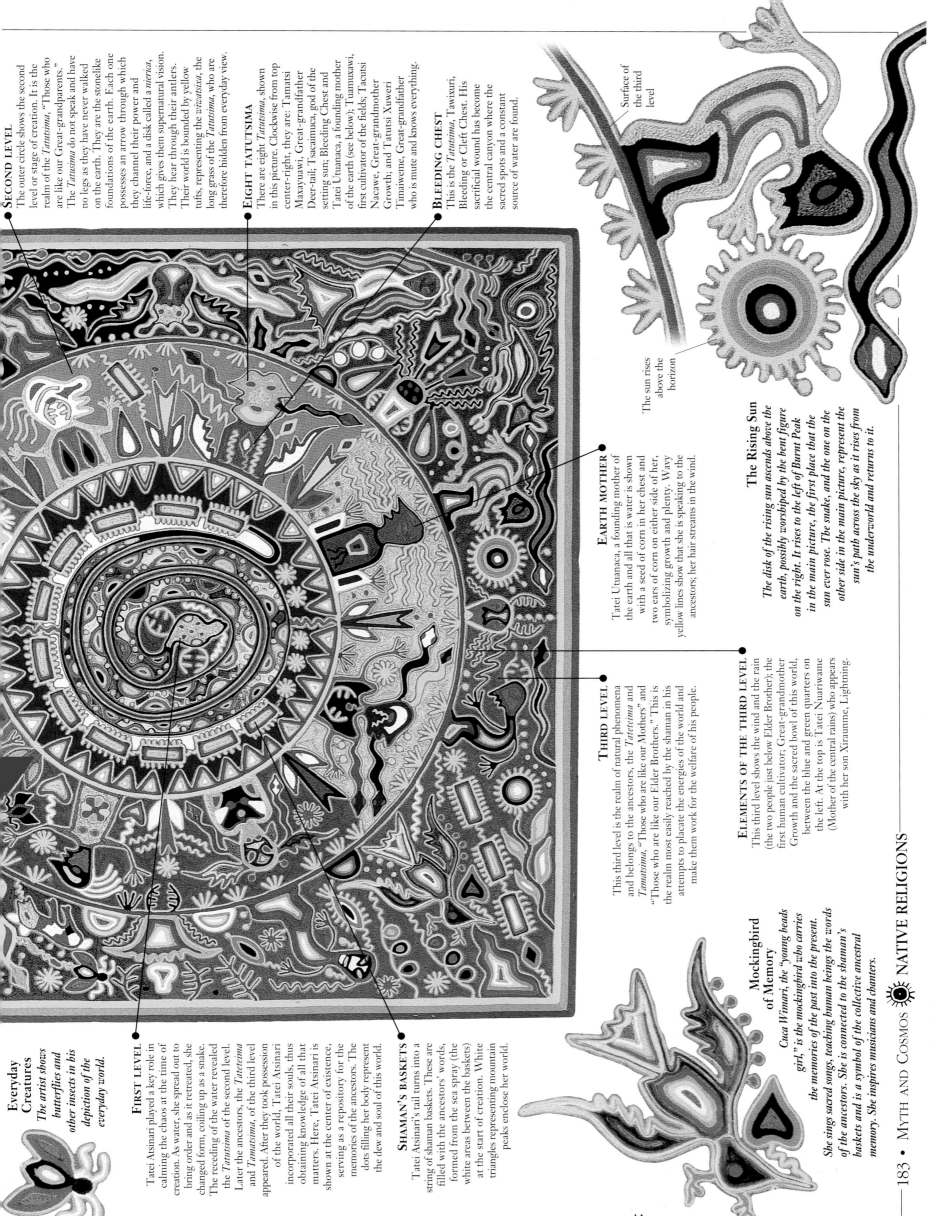

SECOND LEVEL

The outer circle shows the second level or stage of creation. It is the realm of the *Tatutsima*, "Those who are like our Great-grandparents." The *Tatutsima* do not speak and have no legs as they have never walked on the earth. They are the stonelike foundations of the earth. Each one possesses an arrow through which they channel their power and life-force, and a disk called a *muvieri*, which gives them supernatural vision. They hear through their antlers. Their world is bounded by yellow tufts, representing the *vixutsixa*, the long grass of the *Tatutsima*, who are therefore hidden from everyday view.

EIGHT TATUTSIMA

There are eight *Tatutsima*, shown in this picture. Clockwise from top center-right, they are: Tamatsi Maxayuawi, Great-grandfather Deer-tail; Tsacaimuca, god of the setting sun; Bleeding Chest and Tatei Utuanaca, a founding mother of the earth (see below); Tuamuxawi, first cultivator of the fields; Tacutsi Nacawe, Great-grandmother Growth; and Tatutsi Xuweri Timaweme, Great-grandfather who is mute and knows everything.

BLEEDING CHEST

This is the *Tatutsima*, Tawixuri, Bleeding or Cleft Chest. His sacrificial wound has become the central canyon where the sacred spots and a constant source of water are found.

Surface of the third level

The sun rises above the horizon

The Rising Sun

The disk of the rising sun ascends above the earth, possibly worshiped by the bent figure on the right. It rises to the left of Burnt Peak in the main picture, the first place that the sun ever rose. The snake, and the one on the other side in the main picture, represent the sun's path across the sky as it rises from the underworld and returns to it.

EARTH MOTHER

Tatei Utuanaca, a founding mother of the earth and all that is water is shown with a seed of corn in her chest and two ears of corn on either side of her, symbolizing growth and plenty. Wavy yellow lines show that she is speaking to the ancestors; her hair streams in the wind.

THIRD LEVEL

This third level is the realm of natural phenomena and belongs to the ancestors, the *Tateteima* and *Tamatsima*, "Those who are like our Elder Brothers." This is the realm most easily reached by the shaman in his attempts to placate the energies of the world and make them work for the welfare of his people.

ELEMENTS OF THE THIRD LEVEL

This third level shows the wind and the rain (the two people just below Elder Brother); the first human cultivator; Great-grandmother Growth and the sacred bowl of this world, between the blue and green quarters on the left. At the top is Tatei Nuariwame (Mother of the central rains) who appears with her son Xiraunme, Lightning.

Everyday Creatures

The artist shows butterflies and other insects in his depiction of the everyday world.

FIRST LEVEL

Tatei Atsinari played a key role in calming the chaos at the time of creation. As water, she spread out to bring order and as it retreated, she changed form, coiling up as a snake. The receding of the water revealed the *Tatutsima* of the second level. Later the ancestors, the *Tateteima* and *Tamatsima*, of the third level appeared. After they took possession of the world, Tatei Atsinari incorporated all their souls, thus obtaining knowledge of all that matters. Here, Tatei Atsinari is shown at the center of existence, serving as a repository for the memories of the ancestors. The dots filling her body represent the dew and soul of this world.

SHAMAN'S BASKETS

Tatei Atsinari's tail turns into a string of shaman baskets. These are filled with the ancestors' words, formed from the sea spray (the white areas between the baskets) at the start of creation. White triangles representing mountain peaks enclose her world.

Mockingbird of Memory

Caca Wimari, the "young beads girl," is the mockingbird who carries the memories of the past into the present. She sings sacred songs, teaching human beings the words of the past. She is connected to the shaman's baskets and is a symbol of the collective ancestral memory. She inspires musicians and chanters.

FORCES OF GOOD AND EVIL

LIKE ALL PEOPLE, those who follow native religions experience both good and evil things in their lives. They, too, know that there is often a conflict in themselves between what they know to be good and what they know to be wrong or evil. This conflict may seem abstract, in the realm of ideas and beliefs, but it often feels as if there is real combat going on – almost like a fight between two people. That is why the struggle between good and evil is often expressed in terms of personal agents at war – spirits, gods, witches, or demons. By translating the forces responsible for bad happenings, such as sickness, death, famine, pain, or injury, into personal terms, the means of fighting back are made personal as well. So instead of being powerless against the forces of nature, people in native religions have a code of symbols and actions through which they can do something about the evils in their world – not least by understanding that the causes for them lie outside their own responsibility.

Human head carved out of wood

Voice Disguiser
A voice disguiser, or imborivungu, *is a type of pipe made by the Tiv people of northern Nigeria. It represents the bone of Tiv, the ancestor from which the whole community believes itself to be descended. It emits a cry similar to that of the screech owl, a bird associated with occult powers. The* imborivungu *is used in rituals to ensure the fertility of the land and the prosperity of the people by creating a bond between the living and the dead. Although it brings prosperity, the pipe is also considered evil and dangerous because it is said that when it changes hands, human sacrifice, necessary but wicked in Tiv eyes, is required to ensure its continuing power.*

Pipe made from carved human bone

Voice hole and vibrating membrane (missing)

HOUSE MEMBERS
The figures at the back are members or followers of the trading house.

MIRRORS
These squares are usually thought to be mirrors, although some people see them as "windows." Mirrors often also decorate masquerade masks.

FISH-EAGLE FEATHER
The fish-eagle feather signifies membership of the Ekine society. The Ekine organized masquerades performed by masked members of the society. The society was so important that it was said a poor perfomance sometimes led a humiliated dancer to commit suicide.

ALAGBA HEADDRESS
This type of headdress was worn in the Alagba masquerade of the Ekine society, a group that was very important both socially and in business. Although not a spiritually powerful masquerade, it formed part of a test for members passing from junior to senior membership of the society. The headdress here shows that the ancestor passed this test.

Masquerade Masks
Masks, such as this one from the Yoruba people of Nigeria, play a very important part in ritual masquerades in which the dancers may be possessed by the spirits they are calling. In performance, masks are thought to be very powerful and are sometimes worn on top of the head, as this one is, to limit contact with onlookers.

KALABARI ANCESTRAL SCREEN
The Kalabari, a people in the eastern Niger Delta, produced this type of ancestral screen during the 19th century. They depict the chiefs of Kalabari trading houses that did business with European slave traders. These trading houses amounted to dynastic institutions and, in effect, the screens represent the Kalabari respect for wealth and success. The screens are important because they are the spiritual capital of the house, and it is through carved images alone that people can locate, control, and communicate with spirits.

ANCESTOR
The ancestor is larger than the other figures to show his importance. Ancestors are responsible for the well-being of their descendants.

FOREHEAD OF THE DEAD
Ancestral screens are called *duein fubara,* or "foreheads of the dead." The *teme,* the fixed spirit that resides in every person, plant, or object, resides in the forehead. The screens replace the actual bodies of the dead, especially the forehead, and act as a channel by which the *teme* may pass

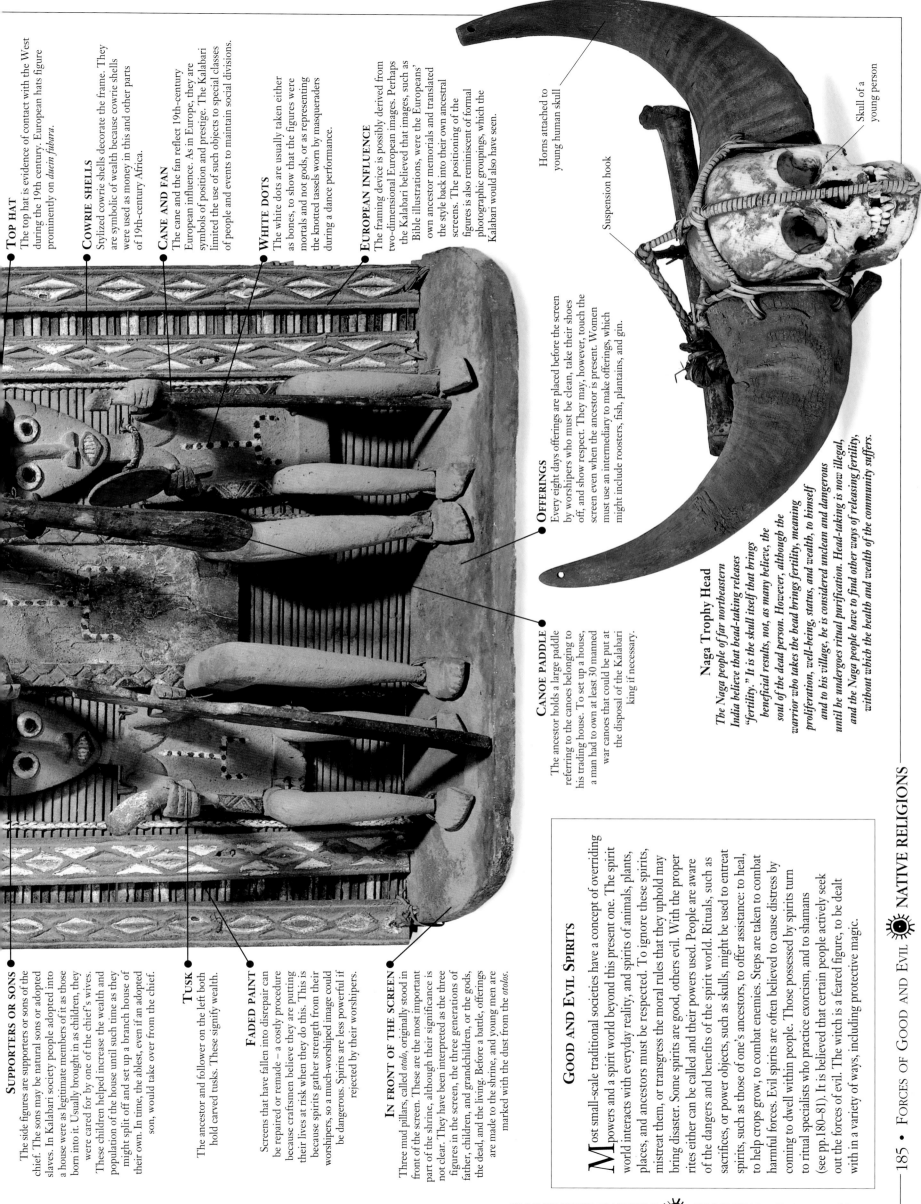

TOP HAT

The top hat is evidence of contact with the West during the 19th century. European hats figure prominently on *duein fubara*.

COWRIE SHELLS

Stylized cowrie shells decorate the frame. They are symbolic of wealth because cowrie shells were used as money in this and other parts of 19th-century Africa.

CANE AND FAN

The cane and the fan reflect 19th-century European influence. As in Europe, they are symbols of position and prestige. The Kalabari limited the use of such objects to special classes of people and events to maintain social divisions.

WHITE DOTS

The white dots are usually taken either as bones, to show that the figures were mortals and not gods, or as representing the knotted tassels worn by masqueraders during a dance performance.

EUROPEAN INFLUENCE

The framing device is possibly derived from two-dimensional European images. Perhaps the Kalabari believed that images, such as Bible illustrations, were the Europeans' own ancestor memorials and translated the style back into their own ancestral screens. The positioning of the figures is also reminiscent of formal photographic groupings, which the Kalabari would also have seen.

SUPPORTERS OR SONS

The side figures are supporters or sons of the chief. The sons may be natural sons or adopted slaves. In Kalabari society people adopted into a house were as legitimate members of it as those born into it. Usually brought in as children, they were cared for by one of the chief's wives. These children helped increase the wealth and population of the house until such time as they might split off and set up a branch house of their own. In time, the ablest, even if an adopted son, would take over from the chief.

TUSK

The ancestor and follower on the left both hold carved tusks. These signify wealth.

FADED PAINT

Screens that have fallen into disrepair can be repaired or remade – a costly procedure because craftsmen believe they are putting their lives at risk when they do this. This is because spirits gather strength from their worshipers, so a much-worshiped image could be dangerous. Spirits are less powerful if rejected by their worshipers.

IN FRONT OF THE SCREEN

Three mud pillars, called *otolo*, originally stood in front of the screen. These are the most important part of the shrine, although their significance is not clear. They have been interpreted as the three figures in the screen, the three generations of father, children, and grandchildren, or the gods, the dead, and the living. Before a battle, offerings are made to the shrine, and young men are marked with the dust from the *otolos*.

OFFERINGS

Every eight days offerings are placed before the screen by worshipers who must be clean, take their shoes off, and show respect. They may, however, touch the screen even when the ancestor is present. Women must use an intermediary to make offerings, which might include roosters, fish, plantains, and gin.

CANOE PADDLE

The ancestor holds a large paddle referring to the canoes belonging to his trading house. To set up a house, a man had to own at least 30 manned war canoes that could be put at the disposal of the Kalabari king if necessary.

Horns attached to young human skull

Suspension hook

Skull of a young person

Naga Trophy Head

The Naga people of far northeastern India believe that head-taking releases "fertility." It is the skull itself that brings beneficial results, not, as many believe, the soul of the dead person. However, although the warrior who takes the head brings fertility, meaning proliferation, well-being, status, and wealth, to himself and to his village, he is considered unclean and dangerous until he undergoes ritual purification. Head-taking is now illegal, and the Naga people have to find other ways of releasing fertility, without which the health and wealth of the community suffers.

GOOD AND EVIL SPIRITS

Most small-scale traditional societies have a concept of overriding powers and a spirit world beyond this present one. The spirit world interacts with everyday reality, and spirits of animals, plants, places, and ancestors must be respected. To ignore these spirits, mistreat them, or transgress the moral rules that they uphold may bring disaster. Some spirits are good, others evil. With the proper rites either can be called and their powers used. People are aware of the dangers and benefits of the spirit world. Rituals, such as sacrifices, or power objects, such as skulls, might be used to entreat spirits, such as those of one's ancestors, to offer assistance: to heal, to help crops grow, to combat enemies. Steps are taken to combat harmful forces. Evil spirits are often believed to cause distress by coming to dwell within people. Those possessed by spirits turn to ritual specialists who practice exorcism, and to shamans (see pp.180–81). It is believed that certain people actively seek out the forces of evil. The witch is a feared figure, to be dealt with in a variety of ways, including protective magic.

RITES OF PASSAGE

RITUALS ARE ACTIONS that are repeated in well-known ways. They help people give order and meaning to life because they are predictable and have been done in the same way for many generations. Rituals take place in all areas of the world and in all religions and may even be of a secular nature, such as celebrating birthdays or retiring from work. Rites of passage are rituals that mark the transition from one state in life to another. Obvious examples are being born, reaching adulthood, getting married, and dying. Most rites of passage concentrate on the transitional stage, which is known as "liminal," from the Latin *limen*, meaning "threshold," because it is full of uncertainty. Thus many death rituals concentrate on getting the person concerned from the state of being among the living to the state of being among the dead. In native religions, initiation into adulthood and death rites are considered to be the most important rituals, for without them the transitions cannot be made.

DREAM DESIGN

The design, dances, and rites related to a malanggan are often revealed in dreams. Each carving varies somewhat depending on the person it represents. The right to make a type of malanggan can be bought – the seller must teach the buyer the rites and may no longer make that style of malanggan himself.

MALANGGAN

Malanggans come from New Ireland in Melanesia and are made specifically for death rituals. They are symbolic of wealth and confer prestige. Not to have one made and proper rites performed for a dead relative would be socially demeaning. They are the most important ritual objects of the society and are taboo to women. Malanggans are also a vital part of initiation rites, when boys are circumcised and formally enter adult male society. Initiation takes place over eight months and involves circumcision, feasting, dancing, and sexual relations.

DEAD ANCESTOR

The carved figure, male or female, represents an ancestor for whom it has been made. The malanggan rites, even if performed during an initiation, are performed for the dead. Each malanggan belongs to a certain group with specific rituals attached to it. After the rites they are usually destroyed.

WOOD CARVING

A malanggan is carved by a specialist who follows the instructions of the man who owns the right to make it, passed down to him through his clan. During rituals, the way in which this right has come down through the clan, how much money the malanggans have cost, and for whom they are now being made is emphasized.

FEMALE INITIATION MASK

This mask is worn by the main officiant at the final initiation ceremony of young Mende girls in West Africa into the secret Sande society. It represents power, emotion, and womanly qualities and is the epitome of the Mende idea of female beauty. The Sande society prepares girls for adulthood, teaching them domestic, social, and sexual skills. Initiation takes place over six months and involves female circumcision, taking a new name, and living with the other initiates away from home to receive training.

A fat neck symbolizes wealth and beauty

By wearing the mask, the dancer is believed to become the spirit of Mende

Yellow pigment

MALE INITIATION MASK

This mask, from the Kuba people in Zaire, is used in the initiation rites of young boys. Separated from the women and uninitiated children, the boys pass between the legs of masked dancers, who represent the spirit ancestors. They emerge into the special initiation camp where other masked figures present the main aspects of Kuba religion.

Grasses flow over the dancer's shoulders

TRADITIONAL FISH ●

The fish is a traditional symbol on malanggan carvings, along with various birds and snakes. These animals do not seem to have any major symbolic meaning, only being significant insofar as they belong to the familiar environment. Fishing is a communal occupation for the men.

Ritual Ordeals

Circumcision, or imbalu, among the Gisu people of Uganda is a classic type of ordeal, which alone qualifies a boy as a man. Standing upright amid a crowd of assembled male relatives and neighbors, the boy must betray no signs of fear. Success is triumphantly celebrated as proof of the special quality of Gisu manhood and ethnic identity.

MANDAN INITIATION RITES

The Mandans were a North American Indian people, now extinct, who lived in the upper reaches of the Missouri River. By the 1830s, they had two communities, two miles (1.6 km) apart, which consisted of about 2,000 people, their numbers having been depleted over the years by continual strife with their neighbors. Known to traders as "the polite and friendly Mandans," they called themselves "people of the pheasants" and claimed to have been the first people on earth. They believed in good and evil spirits, presided over by the Great Spirit, and that on death they went to either a cold hell or warm, beautiful hunting grounds. Individuals could shuttle between the two depending on the worthiness of their deeds after death. In a four-day annual religious ceremony, young males underwent torturous initiation rites in order to appease the good and evil spirits and ensure, on death, their entry into the hunting grounds. They placed their trust in the Great Spirit to help them survive. Everyone watched, and the qualities of endurance were noted by the chiefs in their assessment of the boys as leaders and warriors.

The Bull Dance

While the initiates prepared for their ordeal, dances and other ceremonies took place outside the lodge. The Bull Dance, shown here, was one of the most prominent, danced many times in formations relating to the points of the compass. Eight men in buffalo hides danced, accompanied by chants asking the Great Spirit to continue its influence in sending buffaloes as food for the year.

Self-inflicted Torture

On the last day the initiates were cut on the chest, shoulders, arms, and legs, and splints were put through the wounds. They were then hung up, as shown. Weights hung from the arm and leg splints and the initiate spun around with a pole until he fainted. He was then cut down and left "entirely dead," in the keeping of the Great Spirit. He had to recover by himself before undertaking further challenges.

In the Medicine Lodge

The initiates entered the lodge following "the first or only man," who arrived in the village the day before. They carried weapons and a medicine bag, which they suspended above their heads before lying down. The "first and only man" smoked a pipe to their success and appointed a keeper of ceremonies, who cried out to the Great Spirit for strength, as shown here. He made sure the boys did not eat, drink, or sleep for four days and nights, in preparation for the rites.

THE GOLDEN RULE

CAN RELIGIONS WORK TOGETHER?

THE GOLDEN RULE EXISTS IN ALL RELIGIONS in some form. It is a statement, in summary, of the basic requirement for all human behavior. It appears sometimes in positive form: Jesus said, "Do to others whatever you would have them do to you" (Matthew 7:12). It also appears in negative form: Confucius said, "What you do not want done to you, do not do to others" (Analects 15.23). Since this is the fundamental obligation in all religions, why are religions involved in so many of the most bitter conflicts in the world? Why do religious people seem too often to be a living contradiction of love?

Part of the answer to those questions is that religions offer the resources, the programs, and the goals of worthwhile and successful lives (success being defined within the religions themselves). They cannot guarantee that people live their lives in those ways. All religions recognize that people, even with the best intentions, are pulled down by evil, sin, and ignorance. Religions offer ways of resisting what is wrong and dispelling ignorance, but they cannot compel people to live in those ways. Even worse, people use religions and use them as weapons to gain power for themselves and to do damage to others: think of the way men have used religious sanctions to keep control over women. In these days, when this is recognized within religions as wrong, there are still those who try to keep things the way they have always been: among those Christians who oppose the ordination of women, some accept that there is no serious argument against it except that it has never been done before.

> **None of you is a believer until you love for your neighbor what you love for yourself**
> MUHAMMAD

Looked at that way, religions are fertile ground where evil and the abuse of power flourish. But religions are also ground where lives of great beauty, holiness, and wisdom grow. Many millions of people around the world are quietly translating the Golden Rule and the other demands of their faith into life. Does this mean that all religions should therefore be working together on the basis of this common morality to bring new hope to the world? Given the huge problems of population, ecology, and poverty that the world faces, does this mean that we should try to draw religions together to work for the good of all? The meeting of religions in at Chicago in 1993

> **Do not hurt others with that which hurts yourself**
> THE BUDDHA

drew up a Global Ethic to do exactly that. Religious people could and should be a major resource in a resistance movement to the evils that threaten us all.

Why, then, are they not more obviously doing so? Part of the answer is that each religion has interests of its own. The accounts they give of the universe, of human nature, of the goals of life, of God or of a higher power, of the ways that lead to salvation, or to enlightenment, are deeply and irreconcilably different. Some have argued that the differences arise only because it is impossible to put these things into words: they claim that religions are accounts of the same things, but in different words; there may be many paths, but they all lead to the same goal. However, that claim cannot be true. Words are always inadequate. But it does not follow that they are therefore trying to describe the same things. There are indeed many paths, but they do not necessarily lead to the same place. Not all roads lead to New York, simply because they are roads. Religions will always defend the truths entrusted to them and remain different. If they are going to become allies against evil, they will only do so as equal but different partners. In what Winston Churchill, during World War II, called "the Grand Alliance," Americans, Canadians, British, Indians, Russians, Africans, Australians, and all the rest of the many Allies did not lose their own identities, interests, and characteristics just because they made common cause against an evil enemy.

> **This is the sum of all duty: do nothing to others which, if it were done to you, would cause you pain**
> FROM THE MAHABHARATA, THE GREAT HINDU EPIC

Could religious people then draw together on the basis of their experiences of being religious? Religions offer ways that people can enter into such profound experiences that they are often rightly described as being "out of this world." They are experiences of ecstasy, enlightenment, love, union with God, and many more. These experiences are described in different terms, but they are so brilliant and so far removed from everyday life that those who enter into them almost always say that they are "indescribable." In that case, can we say that there is one mystical experience, but that the descriptions of it are different? Again, we cannot be sure. Some of these experiences are of a relationship, others of absorption into whatever reality is. It is not possible to unite religions on the basis of experiences that may or may not be the same. In any case, some religions mistrust experience altogether and actively discourage people from seeking it.

If religions are to reinforce one another in the pursuit of truth and goodness, it must be on the basis of recognizing the fact that they are

> **What is hateful to you, do not do to others**
> HILLEL, A JEWISH TEACHER

different, and that they may be leading people to different final goals: nirvana is not the same as heaven; one is not made up of relationships, the other is, and both may be absolutely good in their own terms. There are choices to be made, and each person's final destiny depends on them. The Golden Rule is a common obligation for all. On this basis, religious people can encourage each other to achieve the best that their different traditions require of them and can join together in agreeing on the evils to be opposed. At the heart of each religion is the *Sengyo* or fish-run principle that Zen Buddhists derive from *Chuang-tzu* 31: "A fish-run is constructed to catch fish: we should keep the fish and forget the run. A snare is to catch a rabbit; we should keep the rabbit and forget the snare. Words are to transmit meaning; we should keep the meaning and forget the words."

The Golden Rule

The Golden Rule *by Norman Rockwell (1894–1978) illustrates the fundamental theme of all religions: to do to others whatever we would have done to us. The artist wished to stress the importance of aiming for a tolerance of the beliefs of others, and that every religion must respect the fact that other religions are different. Rockwell was an American illustrator noted mainly for his magazine covers depicting the idiosyncrasies of American life, but his later work, such as* The Golden Rule, *became increasingly concerned with moral issues.*

RELIGIOUS TIMELINES

THE TIMELINES are intended to give a rough comparison of events and developments in the major religions. Because the boxes cover 250 years, these can only be approximate, and some exact dates are in any case unknown or disputed, such as the life of the Buddha. The dates or periods are generally those mentioned in the text. Long-running periods, such as the Vedic period, are marked with a star*, and the names of important writings are italicized. More exact dates will be found in the text.

POPULATIONS OF WORLD RELIGIONS

Numbers are uncertain, and can only give a rough guide to proportional comparisons. Not all religions have been considered in this book, although some are important and numerous: e.g., the Bahais number about 5 million.

Religion	Followers	Religion	Followers
Christianity	1,900,174,000	Sikhism	20,204,000
Islam	1,033,453,000	Judaism	13,451,000
Hinduism	830,000,000	Confucianism	6,334,000
Buddhism	338,621,000	Jainism	3,987,000
Native	96,581,000	Shintoism	3,387,000

	ANCIENT RELIGIONS	INDIAN RELIGIONS	BUDDHISM	JAPANESE	CHINESE RELIGIONS	JUDAISM	CHRISTIANITY	ISLAM
2000–1750 BCE	Spread of Celts Egyptian Old, Middle, & *New Kingdoms	*Indus Valley Civilization			*Hsia Dynasty I Ching	Abraham, Isaac, and Jacob		*The Earlier Prophets *The Period of Ignorance
1750–1500 BCE	Scandinavian Bronze Age				*Shang Dynasty			
1500–1250 BCE	*18th Egyptian Dynasty Amenophis IV	Aryan invasion *Vedic Period			Oracle bones	Moses & the Exodus		
1250–1000 BCE	Zarathustra, founder of Zoroastrianism	*Brahmanas*			*Chou Dynasty	Settlement in Canaan		
1000–750 BCE		Mahabharata War Early *Upanishads* Parsva, 23rd Jain tirthankara			*T'ien-ming/the Heavenly Mandate	David & the capture of Jerusalem Solomon & the Temple Kings and Prophets		
750–500 BCE	*Archaic Age, Greece *Regal Period, Rome	Mahavira, 24th Jain tirthankara			*Spring-Autumn period K'ung Fu-tzu/ Confucius	Fall of Samaria Exile in Babylon		
500–250 BCE	Sassanians defeat Parthians: Zurvan *Classical Age, Greece *Early Roman Republic	*Epics* & early *Puranas* Digambara and Shvetambara division among Jains	The Buddha First Council at Rajagriha		Mo Tzu Lao Tzu Mencius Chuang Tzu	Second Temple built		
250 BCE–0 CE	*Hellenistic Age *Middle & Late Republic in Rome Emperor Augustus	*Bhagavad Gita* Emperor Ashoka *Manusmriti* *Ramayana*	Emperor Ashoka King Milinda/ Menander *Lotus Sutra*		*Ch'in Dynasty *Former Han Dynasty Confucianism as State Religion	Independence under Hasmoneans Temple extended Herod the Great		
0–250 CE	Height of Roman Empire	*Vishnu Purana* & early *Puranas* *Vaishnavism *Shaivism	*Mahayana Buddhism Nagarjuna & Madhyamaka Buddhism enters China		*Hsin Dynasty Collation of *Five Classics* *Latter Han Dynasty Buddhism in China	Temple destroyed Rabbis reconstruct Judaism *Mishnah*	Jesus Paul Completion of N. T. Council of Nicaea	
250–500 CE		Jain Council at Valabhi Gupta Dynasty	*Tibetan Buddhism Fa-Hsien in India Buddhism enters Korea Hui Yuan & Pure Land	Founding of Ise shrine	*Three Kingdoms *Chin Dynasty Spread of Buddhism & Taoism	Development of halakhah	Patrick & Ireland Desert saints Council of Chalcedon Fall of Rome	
500–750 CE	Parsis settle in India	*Vedanta age Hsuan-Tsang visits India *Bhakti movement	Buddhism enters Japan *Tantric Buddhism *Tien-T'ai	*Nara period Buddhism in Japan; declared state religion 17 Article Constitution	*Sui Dynasty State Buddhism *Tang Dynasty Empress Wu	Babylonian Talmud	Benedict & monasticism Augustine in England Synod of Whitby Venerable Bede	Muhammad The Hijra (622) First four Caliphs Sunni/Shi'a divide
750–1000 CE		Shankara *Bhagavata Purana* Bahubali image and shrine	Buddhism strong in Korea and China Borobodur in Java Atisa in Tibet	*Heian period *Kojiki* & *Nihongi* compiled Emperor Kammu	*The Five dynasties Repression of Buddhism	*Karaites	Cluny founded Beginnings of Mt. Athos Charlemagne Orthodoxy in Russia	*Abbasid Dynasty Cordoba mosque Schools of Shari'a *Sufism
1000–1250 CE		Ramanuja Madhva *Tantras* composed Jagannatha temple, Puri	Eisai & Zen Dogen Honen & Pure Land	Eisai & Zen *Kamakura period Dogen & Zen	*Sung Dynasty Confucian revival	Judah Halevi Maimonides Nahmanides	East/West Schism 1st Crusade Sts Francis and Clare Cisterians/Carmelites	Ibn Sina/Avicenna al-Ghazali, scholar Saladin Ibn Rushd/Averroes
1250–1500 CE		Mira Bai & Kabir, Bhakti poets	Nichiren Bayon Temple, Cambodia	Shinran No Drama Ippen & Ji *Ashikaga period	*Yuan Dynasty Tantric Buddhism *Ming Dynasty	Moses of Leon: *Zohar* Kabbalah Printed prayer book Expulsion from Spain	Dominicans Thomas Aquinas Julian of Norwich Spanish Inquisition	*Mamluke Dynasty *Ottoman empire Capture of Constantinople
1500–1750 CE		Guru Nanak Amritsar Guru Gobind Singh & *Guru Granth Sahib*	Buddhism restored to Sri Lanka Mongol invasion of Tibet	Original Shinto *Tokugawa period Motoori Noringa Hakuin & Koans	*Ch'ing Dynasty	Joseph Caro & *Shulchan Arukh* Ashkenazi & Sephardi communites develop	The Reformation Loyola & the Jesuits Council of Trent Missions to New World	Emperor Suleyman *Mughal Dynasty Islam in Java, Borneo Emperor Akbar
1750–2000 CE	Persecution of Zoroastrians under the *Qajar Dynasty, Iran	Brahmo, Arya, Samaj Mahatma Gandhi Independence & the partition of India	Rama IV in Thailand Chogye Buddhism in Korea Soka Gakkai	Nakayama & Tenrikyo Meiji Reform National Learning Soka Gakkai	T'ai Ping rebellion Sun Yat-sen Cultural Revolution	Hasidism Herzl & Zionism Shoah/Holocaust State of Israel	Missions Vatican Councils Josephine Butler Dietrich Bonhoeffer	Wahhabis capture Mecca Islamic Reform End of Caliphate Founding of Pakistan

RELIGIOUS MAPS

THESE MAPS SHOW THE HOMELAND or the extent of each religion in this book. All religions have extensive holy sites, often many in number. They may relate to myths or to historical events or to important people. In some cases, such as in China and Japan, they are considered to be the homes of spirits or deities. For a religion such as Judaism, historical sites are intrinsically bound up with national and religious identity. Although communities belonging to most of the religions in this book can be found in many parts of the world – there is a large Sikh community in North America – Buddhism, Christianity, and Islam spread beyond their land of origin. Islam is particularly strong in the Middle East and Africa; Christianity has spread worldwide. Indian religions are predominant in the East, particularly Hinduism and Buddhism, although Pakistan and Bangladesh are Muslim.

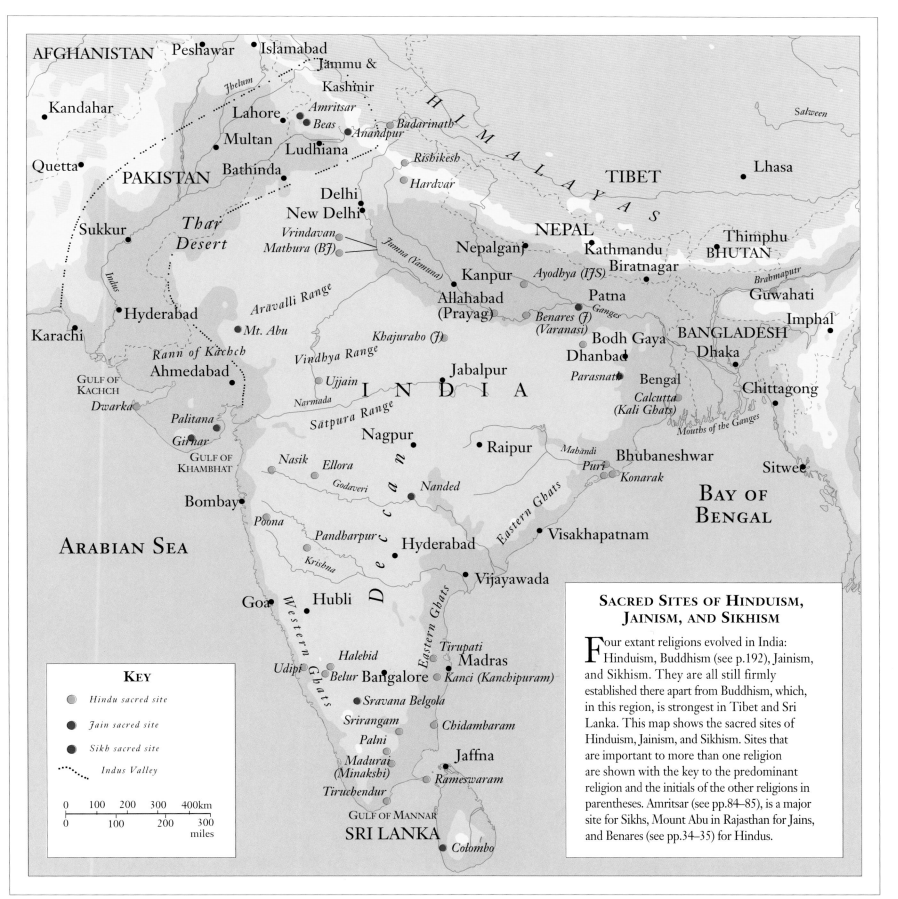

KEY

- ● Hindu sacred site
- ● Jain sacred site
- ● Sikh sacred site
- ⋯ Indus Valley

```
0   100  200  300  400km
0      100    200    300
                     miles
```

SACRED SITES OF HINDUISM, JAINISM, AND SIKHISM

Four extant religions evolved in India: Hinduism, Buddhism (see p.192), Jainism, and Sikhism. They are all still firmly established there apart from Buddhism, which, in this region, is strongest in Tibet and Sri Lanka. This map shows the sacred sites of Hinduism, Jainism, and Sikhism. Sites that are important to more than one religion are shown with the key to the predominant religion and the initials of the other religions in parentheses. Amritsar (see pp.84–85), is a major site for Sikhs, Mount Abu in Rajasthan for Jains, and Benares (see pp.34–35) for Hindus.

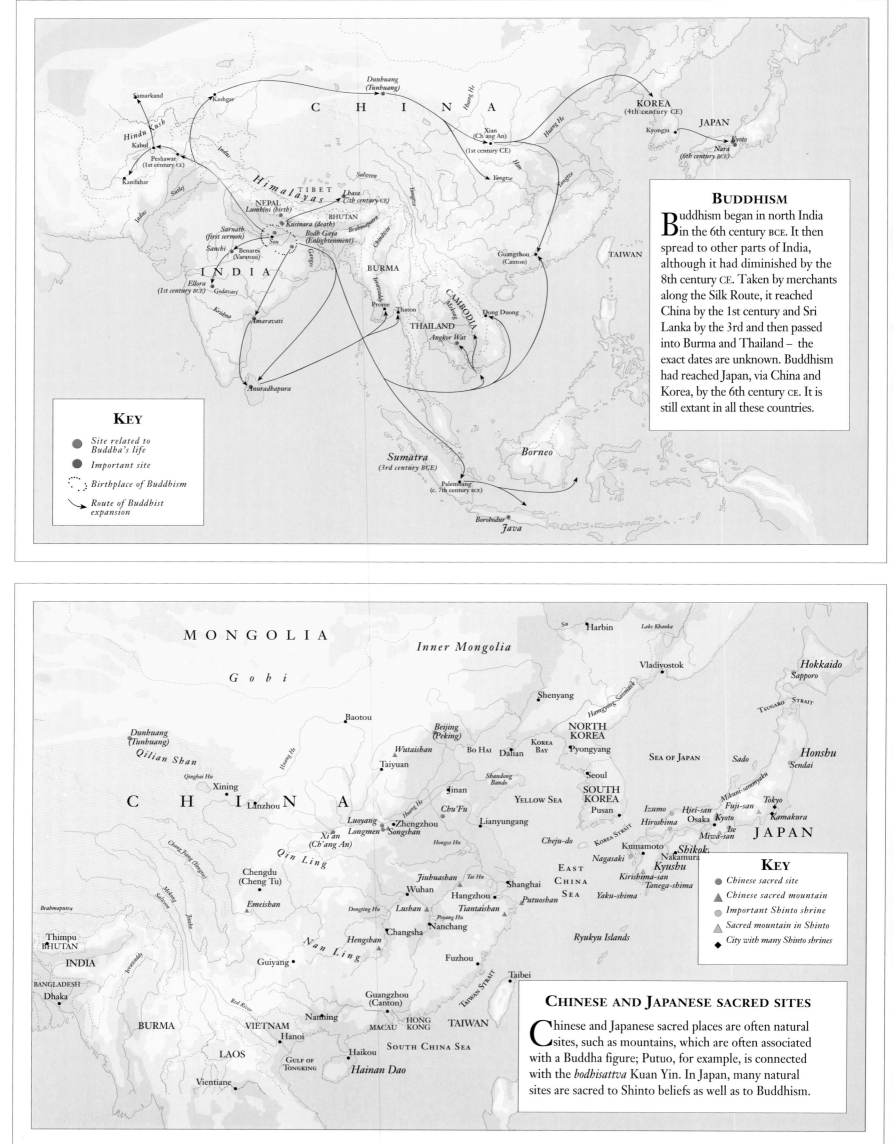

KEY

- Site related to Buddha's life
- Important site
- Birthplace of Buddhism
- Route of Buddhist expansion

BUDDHISM

Buddhism began in north India in the 6th century BCE. It then spread to other parts of India, although it had diminished by the 8th century CE. Taken by merchants along the Silk Route, it reached China by the 1st century and Sri Lanka by the 3rd and then passed into Burma and Thailand – the exact dates are unknown. Buddhism had reached Japan, via China and Korea, by the 6th century CE. It is still extant in all these countries.

KEY

- Chinese sacred site
- Chinese sacred mountain
- Important Shinto shrine
- Sacred mountain in Shinto
- City with many Shinto shrines

CHINESE AND JAPANESE SACRED SITES

Chinese and Japanese sacred places are often natural sites, such as mountains, which are often associated with a Buddha figure; Putuo, for example, is connected with the *bodhisattva* Kuan Yin. In Japan, many natural sites are sacred to Shinto beliefs as well as to Buddhism.

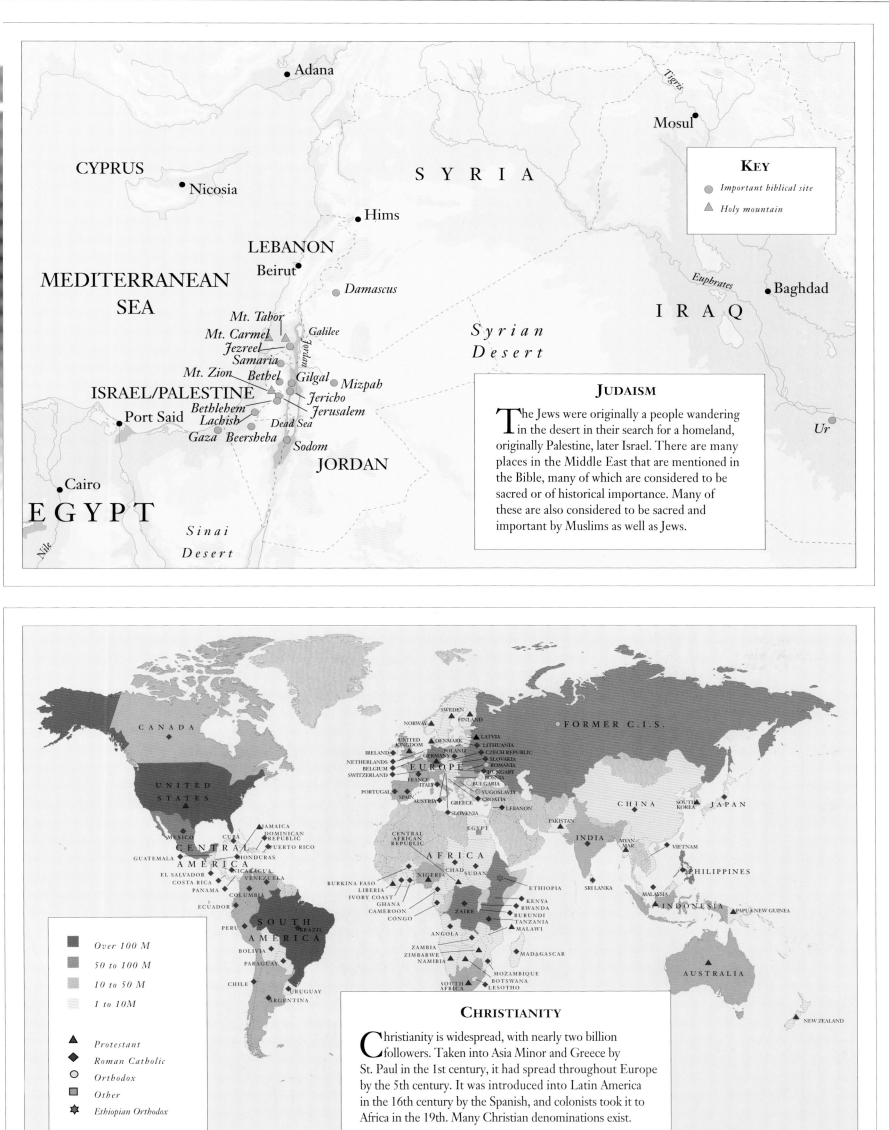

KEY

- ● *Important biblical site*
- ▲ *Holy mountain*

JUDAISM

The Jews were originally a people wandering in the desert in their search for a homeland, originally Palestine, later Israel. There are many places in the Middle East that are mentioned in the Bible, many of which are considered to be sacred or of historical importance. Many of these are also considered to be sacred and important by Muslims as well as Jews.

CYPRUS
Adana
Nicosia
SYRIA
Mosul
Hims
LEBANON
Beirut
MEDITERRANEAN SEA
Damascus
Euphrates
Baghdad
IRAQ
Mt. Tabor
Mt. Carmel
Galilee
Jezreel
Samaria
Syrian Desert
Mt. Zion
Bethel
Gilgal
Mizpah
ISRAEL/PALESTINE
Jericho
Jerusalem
Port Said
Bethlehem
Lachish
Dead Sea
Ur
Gaza
Beersheba
Sodom
JORDAN
Cairo
EGYPT
Sinai Desert
Nile

CHRISTIANITY

Christianity is widespread, with nearly two billion followers. Taken into Asia Minor and Greece by St. Paul in the 1st century, it had spread throughout Europe by the 5th century. It was introduced into Latin America in the 16th century by the Spanish, and colonists took it to Africa in the 19th. Many Christian denominations exist.

- ■ *Over 100 M*
- ▨ *50 to 100 M*
- ▨ *10 to 50 M*
- ▨ *1 to 10M*

- ▲ *Protestant*
- ◆ *Roman Catholic*
- ○ *Orthodox*
- ■ *Other*
- ✶ *Ethiopian Orthodox*

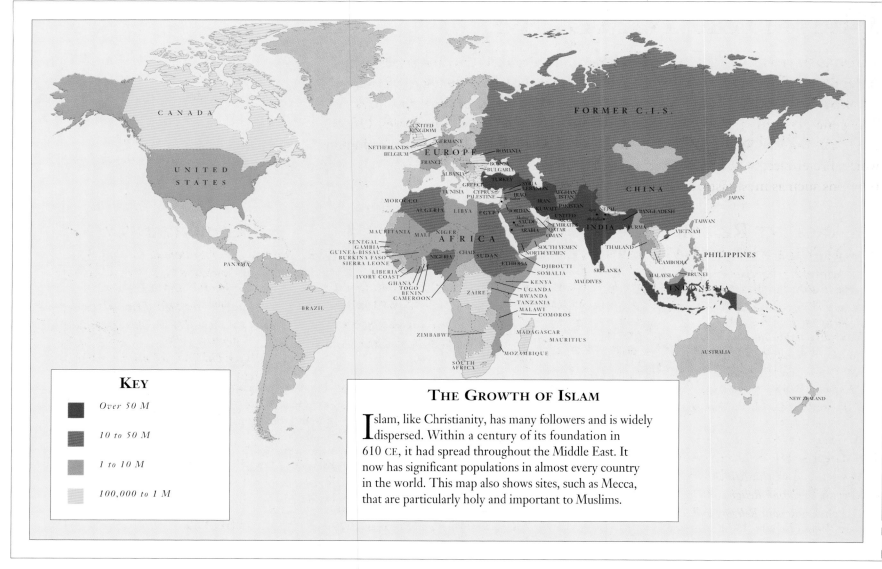

KEY

- Over 50 M
- 10 to 50 M
- 1 to 10 M
- 100,000 to 1 M

THE GROWTH OF ISLAM

Islam, like Christianity, has many followers and is widely dispersed. Within a century of its foundation in 610 CE, it had spread throughout the Middle East. It now has significant populations in almost every country in the world. This map also shows sites, such as Mecca, that are particularly holy and important to Muslims.

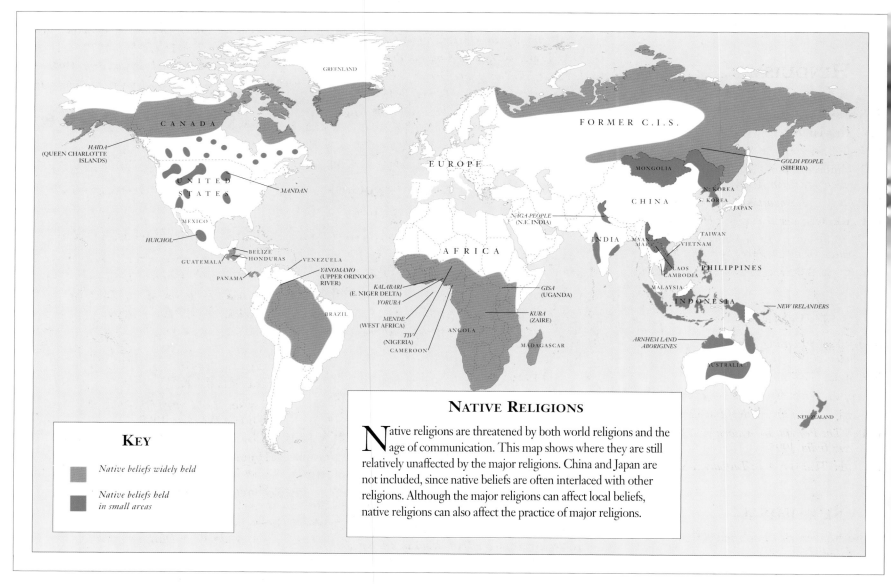

KEY

- Native beliefs widely held
- Native beliefs held in small areas

NATIVE RELIGIONS

Native religions are threatened by both world religions and the age of communication. This map shows where they are still relatively unaffected by the major religions. China and Japan are not included, since native beliefs are often interlaced with other religions. Although the major religions can affect local beliefs, native religions can also affect the practice of major religions.

FURTHER READING

BOOKS HAVE BEEN INCLUDED on each religion's history, beliefs and practices, and art and architecture. For some religions, introductory anthologies and atlases are also mentioned. The order of the bibliography follows the order of this book. The general section includes particularly useful introductory reference titles. Of these, *The Oxford Dictionary of World Religions* is the most comprehensive one-volume work of reference, with over 8,000 entries, and an index on major topics in religions such as mysticism, sexuality, death beliefs, and customs.

ANCIENT RELIGIONS

R. Armour *Gods and Myths of Ancient Egypt* 1986

A. H. Armstrong *Classical Mediterranean Spirituality: Egyptian, Greek, Roman* 1986

M. Boyce *Zoroastrians: Their Religious Beliefs and Practices* 1979; *Sources for the Study of Zoroastrianism* 1977

W. Burkert *Greek Religion* 1985

H. E. Davidson *Gods and Myths of Northern Europe* 1986

P. E. Easterling and J. V. Muir *Greek Religion and Society* 1985

M. J. Green *The Gods of the Celts* 1986

H. A. Greuber *The Myths of Greece and Rome* 1990

K. H. Jackson *A Celtic Miscellany* 1971

S. Morenz *Egyptian Religion* 1973

R. E. Palmer *Roman Religion and the Roman Empire* 1974

E. O. G. Turville-Petre *Myth and Religion of the North* 1964

A. Wardman *Religion and Statecraft Among the Romans* 1964

HINDUISM

A. L. Basham *A Cultural History of India* 1975

R. Blurton *Hindu Art* 1992

R. C. Craven *Indian Art* 1976

D. Eck *Banaras: City of Light* 1983;

A. T. Embree and S. Hay *Sources of Indian Tradition* 1988

C. Flood *An Introduction to Hinduism* 1996

K. K. Klostermaier *A Survey of Hinduism* 1989

W. D. O'Flaherty *Hindu Myths* 1975; *Textual Sources for the Study of Hinduism* 1988

J. A. B. van Buitenen *The Bhagavadgita* 1981

JAINISM

M. Banks *Organising Jainism in India and England* 1992

P. Dundas *The Jains* 1992

A. Ghosh *Jaina Art and Architecture* 1975

P. S. Jaini *The Jaina Path of Purification* 1979

P. Pal *The Peaceful Liberators: Jain Art from India* 1995

N. Tatia *That Which Is: Tattvartha Sutra* 1994

BUDDHISM

H. Bechert and R. Gombrich *The World of Buddhism* 1993

M. Carrithers *The Buddha* 1983

E. Conze *Buddhist Texts Through the Ages* 1954; *Buddhist Scriptures* 1959

R. E. Fisher *Buddhist Art and Architecture* 1993

R. Gombrich *Theravada Buddhism* 1987

P. Harvey *An Introduction to Buddhism* 1990

P. Williams *Mahayana Buddhism* 1983

SIKHISM

Khushwant Singh *A History of the Sikhs* 1977

N. K. Kaur-Singh *The Name of My Beloved: Verses of the Sikh Gurus* 1996

W. H. McLeod *Textual Sources for the Study of Sikhism* 1995; *Historical Dictionary of Sikhism* 1995; *Popular Sikh Art* 1991

W. Owen-Cole and P. S. Sambhi *The Sikhs: Their Religious Beliefs and Practices* 1995

CHINESE RELIGIONS

J. Ching *Chinese Religions* 1993

W. T. deBary *Sources of Chinese Tradition* 1964

D. S. Lopez *Religions of China in Practice* 1996

J. Paper *The Spirits are Drunk* 1995

M. Sullivan *The Arts of China* 1984

L. G. Thompson *The Chinese Way in Religion* 1974; *Chinese Religion* 1979

M. Tragear *Chinese Art* 1985

JAPANESE RELIGIONS

M. Collcutt *Cultural Atlas of Japan* 1988

H. B. Earhart *Religion in Japanese Experience* 1974

J. Kitagawa *Religion in Japanese History* 1966

S. Noma *The Arts of Japan* 1966/1978

I. Reader *Religion in Contemporary Japan* 1991

J. Stanley-Smith *Japanese Art* 1984

R. Tsunoda *Sources of Japanese Tradition* 1986

JUDAISM

L. and D. Cohn-Sherbok *A Short History of Judaism* 1994; *A Short Reader in Judaism* 1996; *A Short Introduction to Judaism* 1997

D. Cohn-Sherbok *Atlas of Jewish History* 1992

N. de Lange *Judaism* 1996

M. Gilbert *Atlas of the Holocaust* 1982; *The Illustrated Atlas of Jewish Civilisation* 1991

L. A. Mayer *Bibliography of Jewish Art* 1967

A. Unterman *Jews: Their Religious Beliefs and Practices* 1981; *Dictionary of Jewish Lore and Legends* 1991

CHRISTIANITY

Catechism of the Catholic Church 1994

H. Chadwick and G. R. Evans *Atlas of the Christian Church* 1987

N. Gumbel *Questions of Life* 1993

L. T. Johnson *The Writings of the New Testament* 1986

H. Kung *On Being a Christian* 1977

J. McManners *The Oxford Illustrated History of Christianity* 1990

E. Newton and W. Neil *2000 Years of Christian Art* 1966

J. Rogerson *Atlas of the Bible* 1985

T. Ware *The Orthodox Church* 1963

T. Wright *Who Was Jesus?* 1992

ISLAM

I. R. and L. L. Al Faruqi *The Cultural Atlas of Islam* 1986

J. Bowker *Voices of Islam* 1981

W. C. Brice *An Historical Atlas of Islam* 1981

C. J. Du Ray *The Art of Islam* 1970

J. Jomined *How to Understand Islam* 1989

B. Lewis *The World of Islam* 1976; *Islam* 1987

F. Rahman *Islam* 1979

J. Renard *In the Footsteps of Muhammad* 1992

D. T. Rice *Islamic Art* 1970

A. Rippin *Muslims: Their Religious Beliefs and Practices* 1990; *Textual Sources* 1986

A. Schimmel *Mystical Dimensions of Islam* 1975

NATIVE RELIGIONS

J. Campbell *The Way of the Animal Powers* 1984

W. A. Fairservis *Costumes of the East* 1971

L. Spence *North American Indians* 1996

P. Vitebsky *The Shaman* 1995

F. Willet *African Art* 1993

GENERAL

J. Bowker *The Oxford Dictionary of World Religions* 1997

E. Cousins (ed) *World Spirituality* series

J. Holm *Keyguide to Information Sources on World Religions* 1992

J. Holm and J. Bowker (ed) *Themes in Religious Studies* 1994

P. Weller *Religions in the UK: A Multi-Faith Dictionary* 1986

INDEX

Words in **CAPITALS** are chapter headings; those shown in **bold** are first defined in the text on the page numbers also shown in **bold**. Words in *italic* are foreign words or book titles.

ACKNOWLEDGMENTS

*M*y thanks go above all else to Margaret, my wife, with whom this book has, in every way, been written; to the consultants who rose to the challenge with imagination and wisdom; to Sarah Brunning for her patient care in illness; to David Bowker, who brought to the book a unique insight and whose suggestions were invariably right; to Jeremy Brooks for his steady commitment in the last stages; thanks go to the DK team for their patience and design brilliance; and to Sean Moore who refused to panic.

DK Publishing, Inc. would like to thank Antonia Cunningham, Will Hodgkinson, Michael Wise, and Phoebe Todd-Naylor for their expertise, patience, and affection; all their consultants; Hamish Todd at the Oriental and India Office Collections of The British Library; Jeremy Coote at the Pitt Rivers Museum, Oxford; Suzette Heald for photo and information on the Gisu people; Dr. Ian Reader for information and photos on Japanese religions; Dr. John Marr for the map of Varanasi; Margaret Bowker for woodcuts; Vena Gheerawo for modeling; the Sikh Missionary Society, London; Tenrikyo HQ, London; John Delnero at SGI UK; Yvonne and Juan Negrin for permission to use their Huichol wall hanging; Cafod HQ, London; Rosie Steel; and Steve Croucher for design assistance; Catherine Costelloe; Martine Jeffries; Kate Duncan and Helen Stallion for additional picture research; Simon Murrell and European Map Graphics for cartography, and Sandra Raphael for proof-reading and providing the index.

PICTURE CREDITS

Abbreviations: t=top; b=below; c= centre;
l=left; r=right

Agence Photographique de la Réunion des Musées Nationaux:/Musée Guimet 65 br; 74-75 c; b. American Museum of Natural History Courtesy Department Library Services 2733(2) Photo by Thomas Beiswenger: 180-181 c; 181 tl. Ancient Art and Architecture Collection: 27r; 124 tr; 133 br; 140 tl; 170 tl/J. Beecham 151 tc. Andes Press Agency: 63 bl. Arnamagnaean Institute, Copenhagen:/Stofnum Arna Magnussonar à Islandi 16l. Artéphot/A.F. Kersting: 52-53. © 1994, The Art Institute of Chicago, The White Crucifixion, Marc Chagall, © ADAGP, Paris and DACS, London 1997: 134-135 c. The Asia Society, Mr & Mrs John D. Rockefeller 3rd Collection (1979.52 White Tara). Asian Art Museum of San Francisco/The Average Brundage Collection '95 (B62D28) 88 l (detail); 96-7 c (whole & details). Photo AKG London: 148 tr; 155 tl;/ Stockholm, Statens Historiska Museum 16tr. Ashmoleon Museum, Oxford: 6-7 t.

Beth Tzedec Reuben and Helen Dennis Museum, Toronto Canada, Cecil Roth Collection: Megillah Scroll from Kaifeng Fu, China CR533/photography: Russ Jones: 126-127 tc. Bodleian Library: MS SANK.a. 7 (R): 67r. 172 (MS. Elliott 246.f25) tr; 172-173 (MS Ouseley Add 24 Fol 119R) c; bl. Boyd Collection: 6 b. Collection of the American Interfaith Institute, Philadelphia: 113 bl. Bridgeman Art Library: 138; 138-139c; 139 br; 163 bl;/Bibliothèque Municipale, Rouen 147 tl;/Bibliothèque Nationale, Paris 90 tl; 176-177 c;/British Library, London 5 tr; 31 b; 58 r; 66-67 c; tl; 116 tr; 117 t ; 132 l; 132-133 c; 137 tr; 160 l; 164; 165 c; bl; 173 br; Christie's, London 152 cl;/Fitzwilliam Museum, University of Cambridge 147 tr;/Jewish College Library 132 r;/Koninklijk Museum voor schone Kunsten, Antwerp/Giraudon 136 l; 150 bl; 150-151 c; br;/ Lutherhalle, Wittenberg 116-117 c; /Museo Correr, Venice 130-131 c;/Musée Condée, Chantilly 166-165 c; 167 bl;/National Gallery of Victoria, Melbourne 38-39;/National Museum of American Art, Smithsonian, Permlet Art Resource 187 bl; 187 br;/National Museum of Iceland, Reykjavik 16br;/National Museum of India, Calcutta 54l; 55bl; National Museum of India, New Delhi 20-21; 23 bl; 44 tl; 59 r; 60-61 cl; bl; Oriental Museum, Durham University 56-57; 64-65; 68 r; 69l; 89 l; 98 tr;/Pierpont Morgan Library, New York 118 bl; 118-119 c; 119 r;/Private Collection 187 b;/Richardson and Kailas Icons, London 155 tr;/Perugia 15 tr;/Staaliche Museen zu Berlin 14 bl; /Stroganoff School 154 tl; bl;/Victoria & Albert Museum, London 19b; 114 bl. Bridgestone Museum of Art: Ishibashi Kan'ichiro Collection 70-71. British Library, London: 17 t; 78 cl; bc; 84-5 bc; 106-107 c; bl; br; 124-125 c; 128 tl; 128-129 c; 129 br; 140-141; 156 tl; 174 tl. Trustees of the British Museum: 2; 4 c;12 tl; tr; bl; br; 18 l; 19 t; 28 t; 29; 32-33; 55 tr; 57 bl; 60 tc; 60-61 tc; 62 r; 62-63 c; r; 72 r; 162-163 c;/Peter Anderson 28b.

© Dean & Chapter of Canterbury/Sebastian Strobl: 139 bl. Jean Loup Charmet: b; /Bibliothèque des Arts Décoratifs 181 tr;/Bibliothèque Nationale, Paris 92; 92-93 c; 99 tl; 176 tl. Circa Photo Library: 3 tr; 5 tl; 7 br; 70 c; 82 tl; 94 r; 96; 97 tl; 98 tl; 144 tr. Reproduced by kind permission of the Trustees of the Chester Beatty Library, Dublin: 170-171 c; 171 l; r. © Cleveland Museum of

Art, 1995, Gift of Severance and Grita Millikin, 67.244 /Jain Ascetic Walking along a Riverbank color on paper, ca. 1600, 38.8 x 26.3 cm India, Basawan, Mughal School: 50-51 c. C.M. Dixon/Victoria & Albert Museum 44 tr; 52 tl.

e.t. Archive: 152 c; cl; Archaeological Museum, Ferrera 11 l; 14 br/British Museum 10 r; 36-37; 89 c; 95; /Freer Gallery of Art 98-99;/Museum der Stadt Wien, Vienna 121 bl; /Museum of Turkish & Islamic Arts 170 tr/National Palace Museum, Taiwan 90 c 90-9;/University Library, Istanbul 174-175 c; 175 bl; br;/Private Collection 93tr; /Victoria & Albert Museum 23bc; 24-25; 26-27; 72-73.

Dan Burn-Forti: 152tr.

Giraudon, Paris: 7 bl; 103 tl; 108 bl; 108-109 c; br; 124 tl. Glasgow Museum: 8 tr; 9 r; 82 cl; 82-3 c; 83 b; 161 l; The Burrell Collection 113 tr/The Saint Mungo Museum of Religions Life and Art 4 l; 137 cl; 178 l; 179 tr; 186 l; 186-187 c. Golders Green United Synagogue: 5c.

Sonia Halliday:/F.H. Birch 177 bl; /Laura Lushington: 112 l; 120-121 c; 121 tr; tl;/Barry Searle 128 tr; 130 tr. © S. Heald: 187 tl. John Hillelson Agency:/© Brian Brake 65 bl.Michael Holford:94l;/Louvre 154 br;/Musée Guimet: 22 tl; tr; 22-23 c; 58-59 c;59 br; 142 tr. © Jim Holmes: 34cl; 106 tr; 159 bc. Hutchison Library: 82 tr; 84 bl; 86 tr; l;/John Burbank 109 tl;/Carlos Freire 53 tl;/Felix Green 99 tr/Jeremy Horner 126 bl;/Macintyre 25 tl; 38 bl; 10 tr;/Edward Parker 25 tr; /Christine Pemberton 8 bl; 23 br; 36tr;/B Regent 62 l;/Liba Taylor 38 tl; 122 tr; br;/Isabella Tree 59 bc.

The Image Bank:/Toyofumi Mori 107 tl. Israel Museum: 118 t.

The Jewish Museum, London: 123 b. The Jewish National & University Library: 114-115.

©Rod Leach (SGI-UK): 110tr. Los Angeles County Museum of Art:/Collection Navin Kumar Gallery, New York City: 42; 44-45;/Linden-Museum Stuttgart (photo: U. Didoni): 48-49.

Magnum:/©Bruno Barbey 13 tr. Mary Evans Picture Library: 90 bl; 93 br; 148 tc; 126-7;/Explorer 30 cl; 157 tr. Mansell Collection: 26 r; 90 cl; 119 b. The Metropolitan Museum of Art, Bequest of Michael Friedsam, 1931. The Friedsam Collection. (32.100.143) © 1989 By The Metropolitan Museum of Art: 142 tl; 142-143. ©Roland & Sabrina Michaud: 165 br. Museum of Fine Arts, Boston, Courtesy of William Sturgis Bigelow Collection: 102 l.

Reproduced by Courtesy of the Trustees, The National Gallery, London: 146; 146-147 c;147c; br; 148-149. National Museum of Ireland: 17b. National Museums of Scotland: 161 r. © Yvonne & Juan Negrin: 182-183.Tatei Atsinari, 1980, by José Benitez Sanchez, 1.22 x 1.22 meters. Collection of The Newark Museum Purchase 1920 Albert L. Shelton Photo: John Bigelow Taylor, N.Y.C.: 66tl.

Panos Pictures:/Jean - Léo Dugast 32 tl. Ann & Bury Peerless: 20 cl; tr; 26 l; 33 bc; 46t; 47; 50 cr; 53 tr; 119 bl. Pictor International Ltd: 17 c; 154 tr. Pitt Rivers Museum University of Oxford: 182 tr; 184 tr; 184-185 c; 185 br; 186-187 r. Powell Cotton Museum: 101 r; 179 bl. Dr. Ian

Reader (Nordic Institute of Asian Studies, Copenhagen) 101 l; 104 tl; bl; 107 tr; 109 tr.

Robert Harding Picture Library: 14 c; 116 bl;/Robin Hanbury-Tennison 180 tr;/Simon Westcott 65 bc. Photo courtesy of The Norman Rockwell Museum at Stockbridge, Printed by permission of the Norman Rockwell Family Trust Copyright © 1061 the Norman Rockwell Family Trust: 189.

Peter Sanders: 167 br; 168 tr. Scala:/Academia, Firenze 144l; 144-145; /Museo Nazionale Reggio Calabria 14 tr;/Salla del Cambio, /Casa dei vettii, Pompei 15 c; / Cappella Sistina, Vatican 158; 158-159c; 159 l r;/Vaticano, museo Pio degli Animali 15b.

Staaliche Kunstsammlungen Dresden: 143 br. © Sean Sprague 1990: 159 bl.

Staatliche Museen zu Berlin - PreuBischer Kulturbesitz Museum fur Indische Kunst © BPK: 56tl.

Tenrikyo Church Headquarters: 111. The Board of Trinity College, Dublin: 140 tr.

Trip: J. Arnold 61 bc;/Dinodia 48 tr; 50 tl; A Gamiet 168 tl;/W Jacobs 66bl; R.K. Vaghela 50 tr/H. Rogers 77 r; 80-81; 84tl; c; 86-7 c; 127 tr; 177 br;/B Turner 155 bl;/M Turner 131 br.

By Courtesy of the Board of Trustees of the Victoria & Albert Museum: 30-31; 46-47; 48 tl; 58l; 100 l; 102-103 b; 102bl; 103 tr; 168-169 c; 169 br.

Viewfinder Colour Photo Library: 36 tl; 70 bl; 71 tr; 152 cr; 163 br.

Photo John Webb (The Art of Tantra by Philip Rawson, Thames & Hudson Ltd, London): 40-41. Weiner Library/ photo no. 2913/862768/ National Archives: 135 bl; /Auschwitz Museum no. 817 135 br. Werner Forman Archive: 32tr; 114 tl; 148 l; 167 r;/Archiv / Thjodminjasafh, Reykjavik, Iceland11r;/Metropolitan Museum, New York 174 tr; /Museum of Anthropology & Ethnography, St. Petersburg 181 br;/Philip Goldman Collection, London 25br; 74bl;75tr; /Private Collection 1c; 43tr; bl; 45br; 70tl;/Victoria and Albert Museum, London 162 tl. Westminster Cathedral: 137 bl.

Zefa:/Bob Croxford 63 br; 120 tl;/Konrad Helbig 155 br. © Zev Radovan: 122 tl; tr; bl; 122-123 c; 123 tl; cr; 131 bl; 133 bl. The Zoroastrian Association of Europe: 13 b.

Jacket: front,Bridgeman Art Library:/British Library tl;Bibliothèque Nationale, Paris cbl;By Courtesy of the Bord of Trustees of the Victoria and Albert Museum:cl; Werner Forman Archive:tr;br;Glasgow Museum:cbr. Inside front flap: Scala:/Accademia Firenze t. Back Jacket: Ashmolean Museum, Oxford: bl;Bridgeman Art Library: /British Library cl; Sonia Halliday and Laura Lushington: cr.

Every effort has been made to trace the copyright holders and we apologise in advance for any unintentional omissions. We would be pleased to insert the appropriate acknowledgement in any subsequent edition of this publication.